MCKNIGHT AND ZAKI
ON
THE LAW OF LOAN AGREEMENTS
AND SYNDICATED LENDING

MCKNIGHT AND ZAKRZEWSKI

ON

THE LAW OF LOAN AGREEMENTS AND SYNDICATED LENDING

RAFAL ZAKRZEWSKI

GEOFFREY FULLER

OXFORD
UNIVERSITY PRESS

Great Clarendon Street, Oxford, OX2 6DP,
United Kingdom

Oxford University Press is a department of the University of Oxford.
It furthers the University's objective of excellence in research, scholarship,
and education by publishing worldwide. Oxford is a registered trade mark of
Oxford University Press in the UK and in certain other countries

Published in the United States of America by Oxford University Press
198 Madison Avenue, New York, NY 10016, United States of America

British Library Cataloguing in Publication Data
Data available

Library of Congress Control Number: 2018957182

ISBN 978–0–19–879995–5(pbk.)
ISBN 978–0–19–879994–8(hbk.)

PREFACE

This book is based on the chapters of *McKnight, Paterson, & Zakrzewski on the Law of International Finance* concerned with introductory matters of contract law, loan agreements, syndicated lending, and transfers of loan participations.

It opens with an overview setting out the key concepts and principles of contract law that are important for understanding commercial lending transactions. There follows a chapter on loan facility agreements which explores the usual contents of such agreements, and the relevant law. The chapter on syndicated lending analyses the relationships between the lenders, the arrangers and the agent, and explores the problems that may arise. The final chapter examines the legal issues surrounding transfers of participations in loans.

Our aim in preparing this book has been to maintain the content and character of the relevant parts of the parent work whilst only updating the text for case law developments and legislative changes that have occurred since the parent work was published. The reader should appreciate that, except for the aforementioned updating and the renumbering of chapters and paragraphs, this work largely reproduces the relevant chapters of the parent work. Chapter 1 of this book correlates to chapter 1 of the parent work, Chapter 2 correlates to chapter 3 of the parent work, Chapter 3 correlates to chapter 9 of the parent work, and Chapter 4 correlates to chapter 12 of the parent work. Rafal has been responsible for updating Chapters 1, 2 and 3 and Geoffrey has updated Chapter 4.

We hope that, in this format, this core material will be more accessible to a wider audience and that, alongside the parent work, it will continue to be a useful resource for students, academics and practitioners who need to refer to the law of England and Wales relating to loan agreements and syndicated lending.

We would like to express our continuing gratitude to Andrew McKnight who wrote the first edition of the work on which this book is based. We also extend our thanks to Sarah Paterson who had previously updated the material in Chapter 1 for the purposes of the second edition of the parent work.

We thank the publishers for their assistance throughout the process of bringing this project to press.

We have attempted to state the law as it stood from sources available to us on 31 July 2018, although some updates may have been included at a later stage. We have not attempted to predict the outcome that the negotiations regarding the United Kingdom's exit from the European Union will have on the law as set out in this book.

Rafal Zakrzewski
Geoffrey Fuller
London
21 November 2018

TABLE OF CONTENTS

3 Syndicated Lending

TABLE OF CASES

UNITED STATES

TABLE OF LEGISLATION

LIST OF EDITORS

Dr Rafal Zakrzewski is a solicitor (admitted in Australia in 1999 and in England & Wales in 2003) specialising in corporate finance with an emphasis on complex lending transactions. He also possesses extensive corporate and commercial law experience. Rafal has practised with Clifford Chance since 2003 but recently worked at the European Bank for Reconstruction and Development as a Senior Counsel and Associate Director on financings in the CEE region. Rafal was the inaugural University Lecturer in Corporate Law and Transactions at the University of Cambridge, where he established a graduate course on corporate transactions on the Masters in Corporate Law programme and lectured on the Corporate Finance LLM course. He was also a Career Development Fellow at St Hugh's College at the University of Oxford. He holds a doctorate from that university and a bachelor of laws from the University of Queensland. Rafal has worked in Whitehall as an Assistant Parliamentary Counsel on, among other things, the Companies Act 2006. Rafal is an editor of *McKnight, Paterson, & Zakrzewski on the Law of International Finance*, author of *Remedies Reclassified* on English private law remedies, a co-author of *The Law of Rescission* and a contributor to *International Acquisition Finance* (all published by OUP). He is also a contributor to the *Encyclopaedia of Banking Law* and *Gore-Browne on Companies*.

Geoffrey Fuller is a consultant and former partner in the International Capital Markets department of Allen & Overy LLP, advising on debt capital markets issuance. His particular areas of expertise include public sector debt, structured finance, social housing finance, liability management, Islamic finance, and advising corporate trustees. He graduated with an MA from Oxford University, and was admitted as a solicitor in 1986. He is the author of *Corporate Borrowing—Law and Practice* and *The Law and Practice of International Capital Markets*, and of three chapters in *Gore-Browne on Companies*.

1

INTRODUCTORY MATTERS

1.1 Preliminary Points

This book is concerned with loan transactions governed by English law under **1.01** which finance is arranged for provision to those who require it, whether they be located in the United Kingdom or abroad. It will examine the legal issues that arise concerning such transactions, which it will do from the perspective of English law. This book does not purport to consider the multifarious local law matters which may be relevant to such a financing transaction where it involves foreign elements. The focus is solely on the laws applied by courts in England and Wales and arbitral tribunals applying English law.

There are a number of ways in which finance may be raised, ranging from fi- **1.02** nance provided under loan facilities of various different types, to capital markets issues of bonds and notes and structured finance in the form of a securitisation. Derivatives transactions may also be a relevant part of the way in which a financial package is structured. Finance may also be raised by a receivables or debt purchase transaction or through an equipment finance facility, in the latter case, by leasing, hire-purchase, and conditional sale. Sometimes a supplier (which may, in fact, be a financier) may be prepared to extend credit by giving time to pay, or a purchaser may be prepared to make an advance payment. In addition, finance may be raised by other methods such as through the issuance of share capital. Project finance utilises one or more methods of raising finance for the development of large-scale asset-based projects. A number of these various methods of raising finance in the London markets are addressed in this book's parent work *McKnight, Paterson, & Zakrzewski on the Law of International Finance*. But this book focuses on the most fundamental and most common of these financing methods: loan facilities. It examines the law surrounding loan transactions involving just one lender and one borrower (bilateral loans) and complex multilateral loan transactions involving groups of lenders (syndicated loans) and issues connected with transfers of participations in such loans.

1.03 There are number of important matters that may affect the structure, costs, and risk allocation of an English law-governed loan financing transaction and yet are beyond the scope of this book. The reader is referred to the parent work for their detailed analysis, however, these matters are flagged here at the outset to highlight their importance.

1.04 First, the transaction may be affected by regulatory matters which concern the bank or banks that provide the finance. This can have a significant impact on the structure and costs of the transaction. It is therefore relevant, in that connection, to consider banking regulation.[1]

1.05 Because of the cross-border nature of international finance and the associated issues that may arise under the laws of different jurisdictions, the subject of conflict of laws will be important in any consideration of such transactions. The conflict of laws position must be analysed as a preliminary matter, as the application of the relevant conflicts rules will indicate the domestic system or systems of law which should be applied in determining the structure and effect of a transaction, and, indeed, if it is possible for the transaction and its various constituent elements to be recognised and enforced in each relevant jurisdiction. This will concern the transactional and proprietary issues that may arise, the resolution of disputes and enforcement of judgments or awards, sovereign immunity, and the effect of the insolvency of a party which is a participant in the transaction. A word of caution must be sounded at this point. Whilst there has been some limited

---

[1] See Sarah Paterson and Rafal Zakrzewski (eds), *McKnight, Paterson, & Zakrzewski on the Law of International Finance* (2nd edn, OUP 2017) ch 2.

standardisation as between different jurisdictions of their conflicts rules (for instance, under EU law or by international treaties and conventions), the general position is that each jurisdiction has its own conflicts rules and so there can be no guarantee that the conflicts analysis under the rules of one jurisdiction will be the same as that which is applied in a different jurisdiction. A practical consequence of this is that it may be necessary to obtain legal advice in each jurisdiction that has a connection with a transaction, or with those who are involved in it or may be affected by it, so as to determine how the transaction will be viewed, and whether it will be acknowledged and enforced, in that jurisdiction. Due to their importance, the subject of conflict of laws, and the subjects that are associated with it, require careful analysis and management in any transaction involving a foreign element.[2]

A perennial problem that must be faced by those who provide credit is the possi- **1.06** bility of suffering a default in repayment of the indebtedness that has been incurred in utilising the credit. If it has not become apparent beforehand, the problem will do so when the entity that has obtained the credit becomes insolvent. To guard against this problem, or at least to mitigate against its effect, credit protection may be sought in various different ways. Once again, a conflict of laws analysis will be important in considering the methods of protection that may be available and, of course, the commercial adequacy of what is available will also have to be assessed. The possible methods to achieve credit protection will include taking security over assets of the debtor, use of the techniques of set-off or netting of claims, holding proprietary claims against assets that are used by the debtor or generated by its business or by obtaining the commitment of a third party to be answerable for the debtor's default by way of a suretyship obligation, which may itself be protected by taking security over the surety's assets, or using one of the other techniques that have just been mentioned. Equipment finance is a subject that is related to the techniques for holding proprietary protection in assets. These various matters are covered in detail in the parent work and will not be repeated here.

This book is laid out in the following way. This chapter deals with general matters **1.07** of contract law that are important to understanding English law-governed loan transactions. Chapter 2 concerns loan facilities. Chapter 3 deals with legal issues arising in respect of syndicated lending. Chapter 4 deals with loan transfers.

It is now relevant to turn to a consideration of various general issues of a legal **1.08** nature that might concern a lending transaction (particularly as to contractual matters), which will occupy the remainder of this introductory chapter.

---

[2] ibid chs 4 to 6.

1.2 Contractual Issues

1.09   From a legal perspective, the law of contract lies at the heart of all loan transactions. What follows explores contractual issues that may arise under English law and which are of particular relevance to finance transactions. Similar issues are likely to arise under any other system of law that may be connected with a transaction, although the analysis and outcome may be different. It is not possible to provide a treatise on the whole of the law of contract,[3] so the discussion will cover some of the particular contractual issues that may arise in the context of the provision of finance, in particular where the applicable principles may differ from those in continental legal systems.

1.2.1 Some contractual prerequisites

1.10   Generally speaking, English law does not prescribe any formal requirements that must be fulfilled in entering into contracts,[4] although it should always be remembered that a contract must be supported by consideration[5] (a simple contract) or be made by way of a deed.[6] Accordingly, a contract may be reduced to writing, be oral, be evidenced by conduct, or be a mixture of those things. In a limited number of instances, however, the law (principally statutory law) does prescribe certain formal requirements.[7]

---

   [3] For a detailed analysis see eg Hugh Beale (ed), *Chitty on Contracts* (32nd edn, Sweet & Maxwell 2015).

   [4] *Rock Advertising Limited v MWB Business Exchange Centres Limited* [2018] UKSC 24 [7].

   [5] Consideration is simply 'something of value', either a detriment to the recipient of a contractual promise or a benefit to the promisor. The most common form of consideration is a mutual promise (eg to pay a price for goods or services which are to be provided). However, almost anything of value, subject to a few exclusions based on judicial precedent, will suffice to constitute consideration if it confers a practical benefit: *Williams v Roffey Bros & Nicholls (Contractors) Ltd* [1991] 1 QB 1 (CA) and *MWB Business Exchange Centres Ltd v Rock Advertising Ltd* [2016] EWCA Civ 553.

   [6] As to the requirements for making a deed, see s 1 of the Law of Property (Miscellaneous Provisions) Act 1989 and *HSBC Trust Co (UK) Ltd v Quinn* [2007] EWHC 1543 (Ch). As to execution of a deed, see that section, ss 44 and 46 of the Companies Act 2006 (replacing ss 36 to 36AA of the Companies Act 1985), and ss 74, 74A, and 76 of the Law of Property Act 1925. As to execution of deeds by companies incorporated outside the UK see Overseas Companies (Execution of Documents and Registration of Charges) Regs 2009, SI 2009/1917. Where a deed does not satisfy the statutory requirements, it might still take effect as a simple contract: *Zurich Insurance plc v Nightscene Ltd* [2017] EW Misc 27 (CC), *Banque Cantonale de Genève v Sanomi* [2016] EWHC 3353 (Comm) [46]; see also *Bank of Scotland v Waugh* [2014] EWHC 2117 [60]–[61]; but contrast *R (on the application of Mercury Tax Group and another) v HMRC* [2008] EWHC 2721 (Admin) [40].

   [7] The view taken by the Law Commission in its paper *Electronic Commerce: Formal Requirements in Commercial Contracts* (2001) was that the requirements for writing and signatures that are required by statutory provisions in relation to commercial contracts can be satisfied by electronic means and that there was no need for English law to take any legislative steps by way of further implementation of the EC Directive on electronic commerce (EC 2000/31 OJ L178/1 17/7/2000) or the EC Directive on electronic signatures (EC 1999/93 OJ L13/12 19/1/2000). See also the Electronic Communications Act 2000 and the Signatures Regs 2002, SI 2002/318. The EC

By way of example, a guarantee must be in writing or evidenced by a note or **1.11** memorandum which is in writing and the guarantee or the note or memorandum must be signed by or on behalf of the guarantor.[8] A contract for the disposition of an interest in land must be in writing, signed by both parties.[9] A disposition of an equitable interest in an asset must be in writing and signed by the disponor or his agent.[10] A conveyance of land or an interest in land must be by way of deed if it is to convey or create a legal estate in the land.[11] A power of attorney must be in the form of a deed.[12] A dealing with a patent (including the grant of a security interest) must be in writing.[13] An absolute (or legal) assignment of a chose in action must be in writing under the hand of (signed by) the assignor and written notice must be given to the debtor.[14] The principal statutory enforcement remedies for security only apply if the security was made by deed.[15] A further requirement arises in relation to contracts which the law requires to be in writing or evidenced in writing. An amendment or variation of such a contract which requires a written form must also be in writing, otherwise it will be ineffective.[16] It is important to note that a loan agreement does not come within any of the aforementioned categories requiring some kind of formality. Accordingly it may be entered into in writing, orally, or by conduct.

Amendments to simple contracts such as loan agreements have also traditionally **1.12** been treated by English courts as requiring no particular form. This used to be the case even if the terms of the contract provided to the contrary such as by stipulating that to be effective amendments have to be in writing and signed by both parties.[17] However, recently the Supreme Court adopted a different position in *Rock Advertising Ltd v MWB Business Exchange Centres Ltd.*[18] It held that English law should give effect to a contractual provision requiring specified formalities to be observed for a variation.

Directive on electronic signatures was repealed by reg (EU) 910/2014 of the European Parliament and Council of 23 July 2014 on electronic identification (eID) and trust services for electronic transactions in the Internal Market which applies from 1 July 2016 and provides for the mutual recognition of electronic signatures and identities across the EU.

   [8] S 4 of the Statute of Frauds 1677. In *N Mehta v J Pereira Fernandes S.A.* [2006] EWHC 813 (Ch), it was held that an email can be a sufficient 'memorandum or note' of the guarantee for purposes of this section.
   [9] S 2 of the Law of Property (Miscellaneous Provisions) Act 1989.
   [10] S 53(1)(c) of the Law of Property Act 1925, but this is subject to reg 4(1)(2) of the Financial Collateral Arrangements (No 2) Regs 2003, SI 2003/3226.
   [11] S 52 of the Law of Property Act 1925.
   [12] S 1(1) of the Powers of Attorney Act 1971.
   [13] S 30(6)(a) of the Patents Act 1977.
   [14] S 136 of the Law of Property Act 1925, but this is subject to reg 4(1)(3) of the Financial Collateral Arrangements (No 2) Regs 2003, SI 2003/3226.
   [15] S 101 of the Law of Property Act 1925.
   [16] *McCausland v Duncan Lawrie Ltd* [1997] 1 WLR 38.
   [17] *Globe Motors Inc v TRW Lucas Varity Electric Steering Ltd* [2016] EWCA Civ 396.
   [18] [2018] UKSC 24.

1.13 It has become increasingly common for agreements, both simple contracts and deeds, to be executed by the exchange of scanned documents by email. Certain principles have been laid down by case law[19] and have given rise to recommended practices in respect of such virtual signings conducted by email. In the *Mercury case* the judge held that attaching a separately executed signature page to a deed document or using a signature page from a previous draft on a subsequent draft of the deed would not generate a validly executed deed. This led The Law Society Company Law Committee and The City of London Law Society Company Law and Financial Law Committees to prepare guidance on the execution through electronic signings of documents governed by English law.[20] In short, the recommended guidance provided that, in the case of deeds, the scanned signature page should be returned with the full final version of the deed being executed (which itself could be in electronic form), whereas simple contracts, such as loan agreements, could be executed through the authorised attachment of pre-executed signature pages to subsequent drafts. However, best practice, to avoid uncertainty and future disputes, is to require signature pages to be emailed with the final form of the document that they relate to.

1.2.2 Corporate entities and other legal persons

1.14 Where a legal person, that is, an entity other than a natural person, wishes to enter into a transaction, it must possess the constitutional power to do so under the law that governs it, and those who purport to make decisions for it and act on its behalf must be duly authorised to do so. There may be formal processes that must be undertaken internally before it can enter into the transaction. These matters raise conflict of laws questions that are outside the scope of this book.[21] As a matter of English law, a person who deals with an English company (strictly speaking, a company incorporated under one of the Companies Acts) enjoys various protections against the consequences if it transpires that the company lacked the constitutional capacity to enter into the transaction or if it was not properly sanctioned by the directors.[22]

1.2.3 Intention to contract and certainty of agreement

1.15 There must be an intention on the part of both parties to enter into a legally binding contractual relationship, and there must be certainty as to the essential terms of their agreement, before there can be a valid agreement between them.

---

[19] In particular *R (on the application of Mercury Tax Group and another) v HMRC* [2008] EWHC 2721 (the '*Mercury case*').

[20] See http://www.citysolicitors.org.uk/attachments/article/121/20100226-Advice-prepared-on-guidance-on-execution-of-documents-at-a-virtual-signing-or-closing.pdf.

[21] See Sarah Paterson and Rafal Zakrzewski (ed), *McKnight, Paterson, & Zakrzewski on the Law of International Finance* (2nd edn, OUP 2017) ch 4 for a discussion of these matters.

[22] Ss 39 and 40 of the Companies Act 2006 (ss 35 and 35A of the Companies Act 1985).

Thus, a document which makes it clear that a party does not intend to under- **1.16**
take a binding obligation or which simply sets out a non-binding statement of
intention will not give rise to a contract which is enforceable against that party,
as has been evident in various cases concerning so called 'comfort letters' issued
in lieu of giving a guarantee.[23] In similar vein, there have been cases where there
has been no evidence that an alleged guarantor ever agreed to give a guarantee or
any other type of commitment.[24] A document that has the appearance of being a
contract but which is expressed to be 'subject to contract' will mean that there is
no binding agreement until such later stage as the parties then agree that the contract is binding, or unless they subsequently conduct themselves so as to indicate
that they have entered into an agreement on the terms of the earlier document.[25]
On the other hand, the mere fact that it is envisaged that an earlier document or
understanding will be superseded or replaced by a later and more formal document does not, of itself, mean that the earlier arrangement might not constitute a
binding agreement.[26] As to the enforceability of a preliminary arrangement, it will
depend upon whether the parties had the necessary intention to contract at the
earlier stage and if there was sufficient certainty as to the essentials of what they
had agreed.[27] The question of intention will be judged objectively, by reference to
whether a reasonable man, versed in the business of the nature involved, would
have understood the exchanges between the parties as sufficient to indicate an intention on the part of both parties to enter into a binding contract.[28]

Another of the prerequisites to a valid contract is the requirement as to the cer- **1.17**
tainty of its essential terms.[29] 'There can be no contract without some terms,
express or implied. If the express terms that are pleaded are significant, but are
too uncertain and vague to be legally enforceable, there can be no concluded and
binding agreement.'[30] Thus, a supposed agreement between the parties that they

[23] See eg *Kleinwort Benson v Malaysia Mining* [1989] 1 All ER 785 (CA).
[24] For instance, *Carlton Communications plc v The Football League* [2002] EWHC 1650 (Comm)
and *Manches LLP v Freer* [2006] EWHC 991 (QB).
[25] *Rugby Group Ltd v Proforce Recruit Ltd* [2005] EWHC 70 (QB). The case was subject to an appeal, but not on this point: [2006] EWCA Civ 69. See also *Taylor v Burton* [2015] EWCA Civ 142
[35] and *Global Asset Capital Inc v Aabar Block Sarl* [2017] EWCA Civ 37. In *RTS Flexible Systems
v Molkerei Alois Müller GmbH* [2010] UKSC 14 an unsigned draft which contained a clause stipulating that it 'shall not become effective until each party has executed a counterpart and exchanged
it with the other' was waived by conduct which gave rise to a contract on the terms contained in
the draft.
[26] *Pagnan SpA v Feed Products Ltd* [1987] 2 Lloyd's Rep 601, 619; *Bear Stearns Bank plc v Forum
Global Equity plc* [2007] EWHC 1576 (Comm); *Immingham Storage Co Ltd v Clear plc* [2011]
EWCA Civ 89; *Air Studios (Lyndhurst) Ltd v Lombard North Central plc* [2012] EWHC 3162 (QB);
Bieber v Teathers Ltd (in Liquidation) [2014] EWHC 4205 (Ch).
[27] *Pagnan SpA v Feed Products Ltd* [1987] 2 Lloyd's Rep 601, 619.
[28] *Bear Stearns Bank plc v Forum Global Equity plc* [2007] EWHC 1576 (Comm) [171]. Thus
an agreement made at an informal meeting in a pub did not give rise to a binding contract: *Blue v
Ashley* [2017] EWHC 1928 (Comm).
[29] *May and Butcher Ltd v R* [1934] 2 KB 17; *Wells v Devani* [2016] EWCA Civ 1106.
[30] Per Mummery LJ in *Cayzer v Beddow* [2007] EWCA Civ 644 [57].

will negotiate so as to conclude a contract, even if expressed to be an agreement to negotiate in good faith, is unenforceable and will fail for uncertainty[31] because it will amount to nothing more than an unenforceable agreement to agree. On the other hand, a 'lock out' agreement, by which a person agrees not to enter into negotiations concerning a specified subject matter with third parties for a defined period, may be enforceable.[32] Certainty can be achieved where the contract refers to an external and independent criterion for fixing a matter (as, for instance, is often done in loan facilities where the interest rate is fixed by reference to a Libor rate) or by reference to an objective criterion, such as a standard of reasonableness,[33] provided the court can determine what that criterion should be.[34] Certainty can also be achieved by the use of a master agreement, by which the parties agree that future dealings between them should be subject to the terms as contained in the master agreement. Such a mechanism will only be effective, however, if it can be certain when the parties deal that they meant to do so by reference to the master agreement and not independently of it.

1.18 The courts generally work on the basis of seeking to uphold bargains rather than finding them to be of no effect, particularly where one or both of the parties have acted on the agreement, and so the courts will sometimes be prepared to uphold an agreement which omits certain matters or leaves them to be agreed at a later time by finding ways to fill in the gaps,[35] such as by reference to established customs of trade or usage,[36] or previous dealings between the parties, or by the implication of a term, such as not to act irrationally. In the words of Lord Goff, speaking extra-judicially:

> We are there to help businessmen, not to hinder them; we are there to give effect to their transactions, not to frustrate them; we are there to oil the wheels of commerce, not to put a spanner in the works, or even grit in the oil.[37]

---

[31] *Walford v Miles* [1992] AC 128; *Barbudev v Eurocom Cable Management Bulgaria Eood* [2011] EWHC 1560 (Comm). But see also *Emirates Trading Agency LLC v Prime Mineral Exports Limited* [2014] EWHC 2104 in which an obligation to undertake 'friendly discussion' prior to arbitration was an enforceable condition precedent.

[32] *Walford v Miles* [1992] AC 128 and *Pitt v PHH Asset Management Ltd* [1993] 1 WLR 327.

[33] *Hillas & Co Ltd v Arcos Ltd* (1932) 147 LT 503.

[34] *Baird Textile Holdings Ltd v Marks & Spencer plc* [2001] EWCA Civ 274, [2002] 1 All ER (Comm) 737.

[35] *Hillas & Co Ltd v Arcos Ltd* (1932) 147 LT 503; *Foley v Classique Coaches Ltd* [1934] 2 KB 1; *Scammell v Ouston* [1941] AC 251; *British Bank of Foreign Trade v Novimex Ltd* [1949] 1 KB 623; *F&G Sykes (Wessex) Ltd v Fine Fare Ltd* [1967] 1 Lloyd's Rep 53; *Sudbrook Trading Estate Ltd v Eggleton* [1983] 1 AC 444; *G Percy Trentham Ltd v Archital Luxfer Ltd* [1993] 1 Lloyd's Rep 25; *Mamidoil-Jetoil Greek Petroleum Co SA v Okta Crude Oil Refinery AD* [2001] EWCA Civ 406, [2001] 2 Lloyd's Rep 76.

[36] However, incorporation of terms by usage and custom can only take place if the usage or custom is notorious, certain, and reasonable, not just if there is a mere trade practice: *Bear Stearns Bank plc v Forum Global Equity plc* [2007] EWHC 1576 (Comm).

[37] *Commercial Contracts and the Commercial Court* [1984] LMCLQ 382, 391, quoted with approval by Lord Steyn in *Homburg Houtimport BV v Agrosin Private Ltd, The Starsin* [2003] UKHL 12, [2004] 1 AC 715 [57].

1.2.3.1 Implication of terms

Traditionally, a term may have been implied if it was not contrary to the express **1.19** terms of the contract[38] and was considered to be so obvious that it 'goes without saying',[39] the parties would have thought it unnecessary to state it if asked by an 'officious bystander',[40] or if the term should be implied so as to give business efficacy to the contract.[41] In *BP Refinery (Westernport Pty) Ltd* Lord Simon said that the following conditions needed to be met before a term could be implied: it had to be reasonable and equitable; it had to be necessary to give business efficacy to the contract, so that no term would be implied if the contract was effective without it; it had to be so obvious that 'it [went] without saying'; it had to be capable of clear expression; and it had not to contradict any express term of the contract.[42] The courts have been more willing to imply a term in cases where, typically, the express terms were brief, such as relating to the use of care and skill in a services contract, but have not been so ready to imply terms to deal with a matter that was not expressly covered in a complex written contract where it may not be clear what the parties might have intended.[43] Additionally, the courts have been reluctant to imply terms in financing contracts (such as syndicated loans or bonds) that are intended to be traded to third parties, through assignment or novation. In *Law Debenture Trust Corp Plc v Ukraine* Blair J observed that '[t]he reason that the room for the implication of terms is limited in the case of such financial instruments is that transferees or potential transferees have to be able to ascertain the nature of the obligation they are acquiring (or considering acquiring) from within the four corners of the relevant contracts. Otherwise, the scope of transferability would be severely limited, and the market thereby compromised.'[44]

There has been some uncertainty as to the test on the basis of which terms are to **1.20** be implied in fact. Lord Hoffman in the Privy Council in the *Attorney General of Belize* case suggested (obiter) that there was only one question to be posed and answered: what the instrument, read as a whole against the relevant background, would reasonably be understood to mean.[45] However, Lord Hoffman's seemingly

---

[38] *Duke of Westminster v Guild* [1985] QB 688, 700. In *Irish Bank Resolution Corp Ltd (In Special Liquidation) v Camden Market Holdings Corp* [2017] EWCA Civ 7 it was held that the implied term must not be substantially inconsistent with the express terms, not only linguistically inconsistent.

[39] *Luxor (Eastbourne) Ltd v Cooper* [1941] AC 108 [137].

[40] Per MacKinnon LJ in *Shirlaw v Southern Foundries (1926) Ltd* [1939] 2 KB 206, 227 (affd [1940] AC 701).

[41] *The Moorcock* (1889) LR 14 PD 64.

[42] *BP Refinery (Westernport) Pty Ltd v The President etc of the Shire of Hastings* (1978) 52 ALJR 20, 26.

[43] See Rix LJ in *Socimer International Bank Ltd v Standard Bank London Ltd* [2008] EWCA Civ 116 [105]–[106]; and *Torre Asset Funding v RBS* [2013] EWHC 2670 (Ch).

[44] [2017] EWHC 655 (Comm) [355], this point was upheld on appeal [2018] EWCA Civ 2026 [209]–[215].

[45] *Belize Bank Ltd v Attorney General of Belize* [2009] UKPC 10 [19].

simple formulation was not without controversy,[46] and in *Marks & Spencer plc v BNP Paribas Securities Services Trust Company (Jersey) Ltd* there was a retrenchment. The Supreme Court drew a clear distinction between implying terms into a contract and interpreting a contract, and emphasised that terms should only be implied into a contract if it is really necessary to do so.[47] Lord Neuberger noted that implied terms do not depend upon the parties' intention, but rather on whether it is necessary for business efficacy for the contract in question that the term be implied. The test is not absolute necessity but whether, absent the suggested implied term, the contract would lack commercial or practical coherence.[48] It is not sufficient that it would be fair or reasonable to imply the term.[49]

1.21 A distinction is traditionally drawn[50] between terms implied in fact, on the basis described above 'in the light of the express terms, commercial common sense, and the facts known to both parties at the time the contract was made',[51] and terms implied in law which are usually implied by the courts on the basis of the relationship between the parties for the protection of one of the parties.[52]

1.22 In the context of loan agreements, generally it has not been necessary for courts to imply terms in law. Disputes in this context usually concern the question whether a term should be implied in fact into a particular contract which contains a gap.

1.2.3.2 Filling gaps—summary of principles

1.23 Whilst it was not meant to be a definitive guide, the general position as to finding certainty and filling gaps was succinctly summarised by Rix LJ in *Mamidoil-Jetoil Greek Petroleum Co SA v Okta Crude Oil Refinery AD*[53] as follows:

---

[46] See eg Richard Hooley, 'Implied Terms After Belize Telecom' (2014) 73(2) Cambridge Law Journal 315 and *Mediterranean Salvage & Towage Ltd v Seamar Trading & Commerce Inc* [2009] EWCA Civ 531.

[47] [2015] UKSC 72.

[48] '[T]he fact that without the term the contract might potentially work to the disadvantage of one party in certain circumstances, in that it does not make a profit it might have made other times, does not necessarily render the contract as a whole incoherent': *J Toomey Motors Ltd v Chevrolet UK Ltd* [2017] EWHC 276 (Comm) [91]–[92]. As *Arnold v Britton* [2015] UKSC 36 demonstrates, business necessity can pose a high threshold.

[49] *Rosenblatt (A Firm) v Man Oil Group SA* [2016] EWHC 1382 (QB) [59].

[50] *Geys v Société Générale, London Branch* [2012] UKSC 63 [55].

[51] *Marks & Spencer plc v BNP Paribas Securities Services Trust Company (Jersey) Ltd* [2015] UKSC 72 [14].

[52] In addition, in other situations, statutory law may fill a gap by also providing for implied terms. In addition to the examples given by Rix LJ in the passage from the *Mamidoil-Jetoil* case that follows (see text to n 53), the following (which is not an exhaustive list) further statutory implied terms might be mentioned: ss 12–15 of the Sale of Goods Act 1979 (implied terms as to title, description, quality and fitness, and samples), together with several other provisions of that Act and provisions of the Supply of Goods (Implied Terms) Act 1973 and of the Supply of Goods and Services Act 1982 (including s 13 as to a duty of care and skill in a contract for the supply of services) and the implied covenants for title contained in the Law of Property (Miscellaneous Provisions) Act 1994.

[53] [2001] EWCA Civ 406, [2001] 2 Lloyd's Rep 76 [69].

In my judgment the following principles ... can be deduced from [the] authorities, but this is intended to be in no way an exhaustive list. (i) Each case must be decided on its own facts and on the construction of its own agreement. Subject to that, (ii) where no contract exists, the use of an expression such as 'to be agreed' in relation to an essential term is likely to prevent any contract coming into existence, on the ground of uncertainty. This may be summed up by the principle that you 'cannot agree to agree'. (iii) Similarly, where no contract exists, the absence of agreement on essential terms of the agreement may prevent any contract coming into existence, again on the ground of uncertainty. (iv) However, particularly in commercial dealings between parties who are familiar with the trade in question, and particularly where the parties have acted in the belief that they had a binding contract, the courts are willing to imply terms, where that is possible, to enable the contract to be carried out. (v) Where a contract has once come into existence, even the expression 'to be agreed' in relation to future executory obligations is not necessarily fatal to its continued existence. (vi) Particularly in the case of contracts for future performance over a period, where the parties may desire or need to leave matters to be adjusted in the working out of their contract, the courts will assist the parties to do so, so as to preserve rather than destroy bargains, on the basis that what can be made certain is itself certain. Certum est quod certum reddi potest. (vii) This is particularly the case where one party has either already had the advantage of some performance which reflects the parties' agreement on a long-term relationship, or has had to make an investment premised on that agreement. (viii) For these purposes, an express stipulation for a reasonable or fair measure or price will be a sufficient criterion for the courts to act on. But even in the absence of express language, the courts are prepared to imply an obligation in terms of what is reasonable. (ix) Such implications are reflected but not exhausted by the statutory provision for the implication of a reasonable price now to be found in S. 8(2) of the Sale of Goods Act 1979 (and, in the case of services, in S. 15(1) of the Supply of Goods and Services Act 1982). (x) The presence of an arbitration clause may assist the courts to hold a contract to be sufficiently certain or to be capable of being rendered so, presumably as indicating a commercial and contractual mechanism, which can be operated with the assistance of experts in the field, by which the parties, in the absence of agreement, may resolve their dispute.

In the later case of *BJ Aviation* Chadwick LJ referred to five propositions: **1.24**

First, each case must be decided on its own facts and on the construction of the words used in the particular agreement. Decisions on other words, in other agreements, construed against the background of other facts, are not determinative and may not be of any real assistance.

Secondly, if on the true construction of the words which they have used in the circumstances in which they have used them, the parties must be taken to have intended to leave some essential matter, such as price or rent, to be agreed between them in the future—on the basis that either will remain free to agree or disagree about that matter—there is no bargain which the courts can enforce.

Thirdly, in such a case, there is no obligation on the parties to negotiate in good faith about the matter which remains to be agreed between them—see *Walford v Miles* [1992] A.C. 128, at page 138G.

Fourthly, where the court is satisfied that the parties intended that their bargain should be enforceable, it will strive to give effect to that intention by construing the words which they have used in a way which does not leave the matter to be agreed in the future incapable of being determined in the absence of future agreement. In order to achieve that result the court may feel able to imply a term in the original bargain that the price or rent, or other matter to be agreed, shall be a 'fair' price, or a 'market' price, or a 'reasonable' price; or by quantifying whatever matter it is that has to be agreed by some equivalent epithet. In a contract for sale of goods such a term may be implied by section 8 of the Sale of Goods Act 1979. But the court cannot imply a term which is inconsistent with what the parties have actually agreed. So if, on the true construction of the words which they have used, the court is driven to the conclusion that they must be taken to have intended that the matter should be left to their future agreement on the basis that either is to remain free to agree or disagree about that matter as his own perceived interest dictates there is no place for an implied term that, in the absence of agreement, the matter shall be determined by some objective criteria of fairness or reasonableness.

Fifthly, if the court concludes that the true intention of the parties was that the matter to be agreed in the future is capable of being determined, in the absence of future agreement, by some objective criteria of fairness or reasonableness, then the bargain does not fail because the parties have provided no machinery for such determination, or because the machinery which they have provided breaks down. In those circumstances the court will provide its own machinery for determining what needs to be determined—where appropriate by ordering an inquiry (see *Sudbrook Trading Estate Ltd v. Eggleton* [1983] A.C. 444).[54]

1.25 Both cases were referred to in the Court of Appeal in *MRI Trading AG v Erdenet Mining Corporation LLC*,[55] and together they provide a useful guide to the approach of the courts in this area.

1.26 One area where the issue as to certainty arises is in relation to contracts where a party is given a discretion which affects its own rights and obligations or the rights and obligations of the other party. This is particularly relevant to loan documentation and is discussed further later in this chapter.

1.2.4 Good faith and fairness

1.27 There is no general doctrine in English law which imposes an obligation on a party to act in good faith when negotiating and entering into a contract, such as by disclosing facts that might be relevant to another party in deciding if it wishes to contract or by not breaking off negotiations without a good reason.[56]

1.28 Nonetheless, an underlying principle of good faith is addressed by English law albeit in a more piecemeal manner than through the imposition of a general duty.[57]

---

[54] *BJ Aviation Ltd v Pool Aviation Ltd* [2002] 2 P&CR 25.
[55] [2013] EWCA Civ 156.
[56] *Walford v Miles* [1992] AC 128. See also the review conducted by Morgan J in *Berkeley Community Villages Ltd v Pullen* [2007] EWHC 1330 (Ch) [91]–[97]. See also *Rosalina Investments Ltd v New Balance Athletic Shoes (UK) Ltd* [2018] EWHC 1014 (QB).
[57] *Interfoto Picture Library Ltd v Stiletto Visual Programmes Ltd* [1989] 1 QB 433 (CA) 439; *MSC Mediterranean Shipping Co SA v Cottonex Anstalt* [2016] EWCA Civ 789 [45].

A misrepresentation (as opposed to mere silence)[58] that is made by a party in the course of such negotiations may be actionable or render the contract voidable,[59] a unilateral mistake by one party may make a contract void where the other was aware of it,[60] and there are particular situations where there is an obligation of good faith as, for instance, the obligation of good faith and disclosure that is inherent in entering into an insurance contract and the equitable obligations that arise out of a fiduciary relationship and under the law as to the exertion of undue influence where the necessary relationship of influence exists. However, in the context of loan agreements, it has been held on a number of occasions that a bank contracting with another party owes no duty to explain the nature or effect of the transaction.[61]

Nor is there any general concept of striking down contracts or contract terms **1.29** that are unfair as, for instance, because of an inequality of bargaining power,[62] although there has been some very limited statutory amelioration of this by the Consumer Rights Act 2015 and, after the Consumer Rights Act only for regulation of business-to-business contracts, the Unfair Contract Terms Act 1977. In addition, the courts have imposed obligations of fair dealing in the context of a fiduciary relationship or where the situation involved a relationship of undue influence.[63] The courts have also imposed notice requirements in relation to particularly onerous terms that appear in a party's pre-printed terms and conditions of business, which are beyond what the other party (which is adversely affected by them) might reasonably expect.[64]

---

[58] *Hamilton v Allied Domecq plc* [2007] UKHL 33.

[59] Depending on the facts, in the tort of deceit as a fraudulent misrepresentation, in negligence for a negligent misrepresentation, or under s 2 of the Misrepresentation Act 1967. It may also be possible to bring a claim based upon a collateral contract and, if the recipient acts expeditiously (but subject to s 2(2) of the Misrepresentation Act 1967), it may be able to rescind the contract. For a detailed consideration of rescission for misrepresentation see Chapter 4 of Dominic O'Sullivan, Steven Elliott, and Rafal Zakrzewski, *The Law of Rescission* (2nd edn, OUP, 2014).

[60] See eg *Associated Japanese Bank (International) Ltd v Credit du Nord SA* [1989] 1 WLR 255, which also discusses the concept of a common mistake that will make a contract void at common law. In *Statoil ASA v Louis Dreyfus Energy Services LP (The Harriette N)* [2008] EWHC 2257 (Comm) Aikens J, relying on the Court of Appeal decision in *Great Peace Shipping Ltd v Tsavliris Salvage (International) Ltd* [2003] QB 679, rejected the existence of any equitable jurisdiction that would render a contract voidable for unilateral mistake rather than void.

[61] *Bankers Trust International plc v PT Dharmala Sakti Sejahtera (No. 2)* [1996] CLC 518; *Property Alliance Group Ltd v Royal Bank of Scotland plc* [2018] EWCA Civ 355.

[62] *Pao On v Lau Yiu Long* [1980] AC 614; *National Westminster Bank plc v Morgan* [1985] AC 686.

[63] For a detailed consideration of vitiation of contracts due to undue influence and breach of fiduciary duties see Chapters 6 and 8 of Dominic O'Sullivan, Steven Elliott, and Rafal Zakrzewski, *The Law of Rescission* (2nd edn, OUP 2014).

[64] See the review on this subject by the Court of Appeal in *Interfoto Picture Library Ltd v Stiletto Visual Programmes Ltd* [1989] 1 QB 433. But it must be borne in mind that the *Interfoto* principle focuses on incorporation of contractual terms by notice and has no, or extremely limited, application when the contractual documentation is signed: *Woodeson v Credit Suisse (UK) Ltd* [2018] EWCA Civ 1103 [46].

1.30 Similarly, there is no general duty of good faith or reasonableness that is owed by a party in exercising its rights under a contract,[65] as the party is entitled to consider its own interests but, again, this is qualified by restrictions that are placed by the law in relation to the enforcement of penalties, the duties of a fiduciary towards its beneficiaries and the obligation of good faith and clean hands that is imposed on a party seeking equitable relief. In addition, an obligation to act in good faith may arise under an express term of a contract[66] and it may also be implied where it is in accordance with the presumed intention of the parties.[67] However, both interpretation of an express duty of good faith and implication of a duty of good faith are heavily dependent on the context.

1.31 In *Greenclose Ltd v National Westminster Bank PLC* Andrews J said:

> So far as the 'Good Faith' condition is concerned, there is no general doctrine of good faith in English contract law and such term is unlikely to arise by way of necessary implication in a contract between two sophisticated commercial parties negotiating at arms' length.[68]

1.2.5 The parties to a contract: mistake

1.32 Something similar to the requirement for certainty raises its head in relation to the identification of the parties to a contract. The consequence of a mistake by one party as to the identity of the other, particularly if that other is a rogue who has misled the mistaken party, was finally settled by the House of Lords in *Shogun Finance Ltd v Hudson*.[69] The majority[70] followed the previous case law, which had

---

[65] *Allen v Flood* [1898] AC 1. This may be contrasted with the obligation of good faith and fair dealing which arises under New York law in relation to the performance of a contract and the exercise of disputes and remedial action: see § 1-203 of the New York Uniform Commercial Code and, in relation to the exercise of a right to accelerate a payment obligation, § 1-208 of that Code. For a general commentary, see Robert S. Summers, 'Good Faith in Contract Law and the Sales Provisions of the Uniform Commercial Code' (1968) 54(2) Virginia Law Review 195.

[66] Unusually a loan agreement contained such an obligation in *Horn v Commercial Acceptances Ltd* [2011] EWHC 1757. It provided that 'each party shall act in absolute faith towards the other'. The concept of 'good faith' in such clauses was relatively widely construed in *Berkeley Community Villages Ltd v Pullen* [2007] EWHC 1130 (Ch) and *CPC Group Ltd v Qatari Diar Real Estate Investment Co.* [2010] EWHC 1535 (Ch) [246]. However, in the interest of certainty, later cases have taken a more conservative and restrictive approach to express undertakings to act in good faith: *Compass Group UK and Ireland Ltd (t/a Medirest) v Mid Essex Hospital Services NHS Trust* [2013] EWCA Civ 200 and *Sainsbury's Supermarkets Ltd v Bristol Rovers* (1883) Ltd [2016] EWCA Civ 160.

[67] *Yam Seng Pte Ltd v International Trade Corporation* [2013] EWHC 111 (QB) and *Al Nehayan v Kent* [2018] EWHC 333 (Comm). See also *Myers v Kestrel Acquisitions Ltd* [2015] EWHC 916 (Ch) and *Globe Motors Inc v TRW Lucas Varity Electric Steering Ltd* [2016] EWCA Civ 396. But other authorities suggest that duties of good faith would only be implied very rarely, if at all: *Compass Group UK and Ireland Ltd (t/a Medirest) v Mid Essex Hospital Services NHS Trust* [2013] EWCA Civ 200 [105], *Greenclose Ltd v National Westminster Bank plc* [2014] EWHC 1156 (Ch), *Carewatch Care Services Ltd v Focus Caring Services Ltd* [2014] EWHC 2313 (Ch), and *Ilkerler Otomotiv v Perkins Engines Co. Ltd* [2017] EWCA Civ 183.

[68] [2014] EWHC 1156 (Ch) [150].

[69] [2003] UKHL 62, [2004] 1 AC 919.

[70] Lords Hobhouse, Phillips, and Walker.

tended to distinguish between oral contracts concluded face to face and contracts entered into in writing. In the former situation, the courts took the view that, prima facie, the parties meant to deal with the person physically before them.[71] In the second situation, however, the courts were prepared to take the view that the only contract that could have existed would have been between the named parties so that the fictitious identity of one of the parties would render it void from the outset[72] and no legal relationship will arise between the parties. The majority of the House of Lords declined to adopt the more general approach favoured by the minority,[73] that the contract should be considered as being only voidable and so valid and enforceable until such time as it was avoided.

1.2.6 Mistake as to the subject matter of a contract

In passing, it is also worth mentioning that a common mistake by the parties as to the existence or essential character of the subject matter of a supposed contract, where the contract does not expressly make provision for the consequences of the mistake, will mean that the contract does not exist and is void.[74] If only one of the parties made a mistake as to the subject matter of the contract, the contract may be void if the other party was aware of the mistake when the contract was made.[75] Whereas previously the courts only granted relief in cases involving a mistake of fact, the courts will now grant relief as well in cases involving a mistake of law.[76] **1.33**

1.2.7 Privity of contract

A similar issue to that concerning the identity of the contracting parties concerns the effect of a contract which purports to extend the benefit of the contract (such as a right to receive a payment, the benefit of warranties or covenants, or the benefit of an exclusion clause) to third parties, including unrelated parties and the **1.34**

---

[71] See eg *Phillips v Brooks* [1919] 2 KB 243 and *Lewis v Avery* [1972] 1 QB 198, although a different conclusion was reached in *Ingram v Little* [1961] 1 QB 31.

[72] See eg *Cundy v Lindsay* (1878) 3 App Cas 459 and *Hector v Lyons* (1988) 58 P&CR 156. In *King's Norton Metal Co Ltd v Edridge, Merrett & Co Ltd* (1897) 14 TLR 98, a different result was reached but that was because the relevant contracting party was using an alias and its identity was not a material concern to the other party.

[73] Lords Nicholls and Millett.

[74] *Bell v Lever Bros Ltd* [1932] AC 161. See also *Associated Japanese Bank (International) Ltd v Credit du Nord SA* [1989] 1 WLR 255 and *Kyle Bay Ltd v Underwriters* [2007] EWCA Civ 57. The Court of Appeal in *Great Peace Shipping Ltd v Tsavliris Salvage (International) Ltd, The Great Peace* [2002] EWCA Civ 1407, [2003] QB 679 said that there was no jurisdiction in equity to grant rescission of a contract on the ground that the contract was voidable for common mistake where the common law would not have regarded the contract as void, thereby overruling its previous decision in *Solle v Butcher* [1950] 1 KB 671, as having been given in error.

[75] *Smith v Hughes* (1871) LR 6 QB 597.

[76] *Kleinwort Benson Ltd v Lincoln City Council* [1999] 2 AC 349.

servants or agents of a contracting party. There was previously a real difficulty at general law in achieving this as the doctrine of privity of contract would intervene to prevent the third party, which was not a party to the contract, from relying upon the provision or being able to enforce it.[77] If a contracting party sought to recover damages for the benefit of the third party, because the other party had failed to perform in favour of the third party, the contracting party would be met by the defence that it had suffered no loss, so it could not recover anything further than nominal damages.

1.35 There were, however, certain circumstances in which the contract might be enforced for the benefit of a third party as, for instance, where an agent or trustee had contracted for the benefit of the third party (particularly in the case of enforcing an exclusion clause for the benefit of a third party),[78] where a party could obtain an order for specific performance of the contract on the basis that damages would be an inadequate remedy because only nominal damages were recoverable,[79] where a party assigned its rights under the contract to the third party,[80] where the benefit of the contract was novated in favour of the third party, or where the case fell within the circumstances of agency mentioned in the next paragraph. A contract may also contain a promise by a party not to sue the servants or agents of the other party and the latter should be able to prevent the promisor from breaching the contract by suing the servants or agents.[81]

1.36 It should be noted that at common law, two parties to a contract cannot impose the burden of a contract upon a third party that is a stranger to the contract, although an agent can bind its principal because the contract is really between the principal and the other contracting party.

---

[77] See eg *Scruttons Ltd v Midland Silicones Ltd* [1962] AC 446, *Cosgrove v Horsfall* (1945) 62 TLR 140, and *Genys v Matthews* [1966] 1 WLR 758.

[78] See *New Zealand Shipping Co Ltd v AM Satterthwaite & Co Ltd (The Eurymedon)* [1975] AC 154 and *Port Jackson Stevedoring Pty Ltd v Salmond and Spraggon (Australia) Pty Ltd (The New York Star)* [1981] 1 WLR 138. Clauses under which a party to a contract acts as an agent in obtaining protection for a third party, when used in a contract for the carriage of goods by sea, are often referred to as 'Himalaya clauses' after the name of the vessel that was involved in *Adler v Dickson* [1955] 1 QB 158.

[79] *Beswick v Beswick* [1968] AC 58. However, see the further discussion of this issue at para 2.54.

[80] But an assignment is subject to equities, including that the assignee should not recover from the debtor or obligor to any greater extent than the rights that were vested in the assignor and could have been recovered by it: *Dawson v Great Northern & City Ry Co* [1905] 1 KB 260 (but see also *Technotrade Ltd v Larkstore Ltd* [2006] EWCA Civ 1079, [2006] 1 WLR 2926). Hence, the purported assignment of all of the rights of a lender under a facility agreement will include the right to receive payment of principal and interest but not necessarily the benefit of clauses that are purely personal to the circumstances of the assignor, such as under an increased costs clause if it relates only to the personal position of the assignor. Having transferred its commitment, it will not be exposed to the risks against which such a clause is intended to protect. However, where the increased costs clause is construed so as to extend to permitted assigns, then it would also cover the transferee.

[81] *Snelling v John G Snelling Ltd* [1973] QB 87.

The courts have also fashioned a particular exception to the operation of the doc-   **1.37**
trine of privity of contract (and the associated concept that a claimant should only
recover for its own loss) in cases that involved a contract to do work or perform
services relating to property that was later transferred to a third party. The courts
have recognised principles allowing the previous owner of property to recover
substantial damages against a contractor that it had employed to do work relating
to the property even though it had sold the property and had suffered no loss.[82]

In similar vein, in *Technotrade Ltd v Larkstore Ltd*[83] the Court of Appeal allowed   **1.38**
an assignee of the benefit of a contract for the performance of services relating
to an asset to recover substantial damages for breach of the contract by the other
contracting party. The breach had occurred prior to the date of the assignment,
but the assignor had disposed of the asset to the assignee prior to the loss be-
coming apparent and consequent damage being suffered. It did not matter that
the assignor had itself suffered no loss in that it had disposed of the asset to the
assignee for full value and without any responsibility for the loss to the asset that
later became apparent. The court distinguished the position in this case from the
general rule that an assignment is subject to equities and that the assignee cannot
recover for a claim or loss that would not have been recoverable under the contract by the assignor.[84] This was done on the basis that it was the cause of action
(as opposed to the manifestation and suffering of the loss arising from the breach)
that was assigned, and that had accrued prior to the date of the assignment. As
a matter of law, the cause of action was complete when the breach occurred,
even though the consequences of the breach were not manifested, and the consequential loss was not suffered, until a later time. To have found otherwise would
have permitted a legal 'black hole' to arise into which the claim would have dis-
appeared, with the result that the defendant would have escaped liability for its
breach of the contract.

The position at general law regarding privity of contract was substantially modified   **1.39**
by the Contracts (Rights of Third Parties) Act 1999,[85] although the Act does not
detract from any right that a third party may have at general law.[86] Accordingly, if
the third party cannot avail itself of the Act, it might still be able to fall back on
one of the limited exceptions that applied at general law to the doctrine of privity
of contract.[87] The Act provides that a third party which is intended to benefit

---

[82] *St Martins Property Corp Ltd v Sir Robert McAlpine Ltd* [1994] 1 AC 85; *Alfred McAlpine
Construction Ltd v Panatown* [2001] 1 AC 518. See also *Pegasus Management Holdings SCA v Ernst
& Young* [2012] EWHC 738 (Ch).
[83] [2006] EWCA Civ 1079, [2006] 1 WLR 2926.
[84] *Dawson v Great Northern & City Railway Co* [1905] 1 KB 260.
[85] Which applies, generally speaking, to contracts made after 11 May 2000 (s 10(2) of the Act),
but see also s 10(3) of the Act.
[86] S 7(1).
[87] In addition, in *Nisshin Shipping Co Ltd v Cleaves & Co Ltd* [2003] EWHC 2602 (Comm),
[2004] 1 Lloyd's Rep 38 it was held that a third party could avail itself of the Act even though at

from a provision of a contract[88] will be able to enforce the contract in its own right, unless on a proper construction of the contract it is apparent that the third party was precluded by the contract from doing so.[89] The Act makes it clear that the third party has the right to enforce an exclusion or limitation clause that was intended for its benefit[90] but that right is itself subject to any restriction on the operation of such a clause that might arise by virtue of other legislation, such as the Unfair Contract Terms Act 1977.[91] However, if a third party wishes under the Act to enforce a positive obligation in its favour in the contract, its right to do so will be subject to any limitations on that right which are imposed by the contract, such as a limitation or exclusion of liability for breach of the contract that is contained in the contract for the benefit of the promisor.[92]

1.2.8 The interpretation of a contract

1.40 It is surprising how frequently what was thought to be a well-crafted contractual document turns out to be ambiguous and not to be as clear as previously imagined. Different interpretations can be put on the same words by those with opposing interests, particularly when something has gone wrong and it is necessary to determine which party should bear the responsibility or suffer the resulting loss. Agreements that have not been carefully prepared are even more susceptible to ambiguity. It is appropriate, therefore, to consider the approach that the courts take to the construction or interpretation of the express provisions of a contract.

---

general law the contract might have been enforceable for its benefit under a trust in its favour of the contractual benefit.

[88] Ie, it is expressly named as being entitled to enforce the provision, it is a member of an identified class of intended beneficiaries, or if it answers a particular description, even if it was not in existence at the time of the contract: s 1(3). See the discussion on this point in *Avraamides v Colwill* [2006] EWCA Civ 1533, [2007] BLR 76. See also *Prudential Assurance Co Ltd v Ayres* [2007] EWHC 775 (Ch), in which it was held that a third party will be treated as entitled to benefit from a contractual term even if the intention that it should do so was not the predominant purpose of the term or that the term was also intended to benefit a contracting party or another person. Although the actual decision in the *Prudential Assurance* case was overturned on appeal ([2008] EWCA Civ 52, [2008] 1 All ER 1266), the appeal was not concerned with this issue.

[89] S 1(2). In *Nisshin Shipping Co Ltd v Cleaves & Co Ltd* [2003] EWHC 2602 (Comm), [2004] 1 Lloyd's Rep 38 it was held that the third party will be entitled to enforce the term for its own benefit unless the right to do so was contrary to the intention of the parties in the contract. Thus, if the contract is neutral on the point, s 1(2) will not operate against the third party. In *Laemthong International Lines Co Ltd v Abdullah Mohammed Fahem & Co* [2005] EWCA Civ, [2005] 1 Lloyd's Rep 688 the Court of Appeal quoted with approval from the opinion of the Law Commission, *Privity of Contract* (Report No 242 of 31/7/1996) para 7.18, that the proper construction of a term for the purposes of s 1(2) of the Act would include taking account of the surrounding circumstances in making the contract, such as industry practice relating to that type of contract.

[90] S 1(6).

[91] S 3(6).

[92] Ss 3(1)–3(5). It would also appear that the provisions of the Unfair Contract Terms Act 1977 (except for s 2(1)) would not affect the rights of the promisor under s 3(1)–(5).

The modern principles by which the courts undertake the process of construc- **1.41**
tion of contractual documents were summarised by Lord Hoffmann in *Investors
Compensation Scheme Ltd v West Bromwich Building Society*[93] as follows:

(1) Interpretation is the ascertainment of the meaning which the document would
convey to a reasonable person having all the background knowledge which
would reasonably have been available to the parties in the situation in which
they were at the time of the contract.

(2) The background was famously described by Lord Wilberforce[94] as the 'matrix
of fact', but this phrase is, if anything, an understated description of what the
background may include. Subject to the requirement that it should have been
reasonably available to the parties and to the exception to be mentioned next,
it includes absolutely anything which would have affected the way in which the
language of the document would have been understood by a reasonable man.

(3) The law excludes from the admissible background the previous negotiations of
the parties and their declarations of subjective intent. They are admissible only
in an action for rectification. The law makes this distinction for reasons of practical policy and, in this respect only, legal interpretation differs from the way we
would interpret utterances in ordinary life. The boundaries of this exception are
in some respects unclear. But this is not the occasion on which to explore them.

(4) The meaning which a document (or any other utterance) would convey to a reasonable man is not the same thing as the meaning of its words. The meaning of
words is a matter of dictionaries and grammars; the meaning of the document is
what the parties using those words against the relevant background would reasonably have been understood to mean. The background may not merely enable
the reasonable man to choose between the possible meanings of words which are
ambiguous but even (as occasionally happens in ordinary life) to conclude that
the parties must, for whatever reason, have used the wrong words or syntax (see
Mannai Investment Co. Ltd v Eagle Star Life Assurance Co. Ltd[95]).

(5) The 'rule' that words should be given their 'natural and ordinary meaning' reflects the commonsense proposition that we do not easily accept that people
have made linguistic mistakes, particularly in formal documents. On the other
hand, if one would nevertheless conclude from the background that something
must have gone wrong with the language, the law does not require judges to at-
tribute to the parties an intention which they plainly could not have had. Lord
Diplock made this point more vigorously when he said in *Antaios Cia Naviera SA
v Salen Rederierna AB, The Antaios*,[96] 'if detailed semantic and syntactical analysis
of words in a commercial contract is going to lead to a conclusion that flouts
business common sense, it must be made to yield to business common sense'.

In his opinion in the later case of *Bank of Credit and Commerce International SA* **1.42**
v Ali,[97] Lord Hoffmann explained that the starting point of the analysis should

---

[93] [1998] 1 WLR 896, 912–13. His Lordship made it clear that he had drawn his summary from
the approach previously enunciated by Lord Wilberforce in *Prenn v Simmonds* [1971] 1 WLR 1381
and in *Reardon Smith Line Ltd v Hansen-Tangen* [1976] 1 WLR 989.
[94] In *Reardon Smith Line Ltd v Yngvar Hansen-Tangen* [1976] 1 WLR 989.
[95] [1997] AC 749.
[96] [1985] AC 191, 201.
[97] [2001] UKHL 8, [2002] 1 AC 251 [39].

always be the wording that has been used as interpreted in accordance with conventional usage and that it should not be too readily accepted that people will make linguistic mistakes, particularly in formal documents. Subject to that point, the relevant background that could be considered was that which a reasonable man would consider to be relevant, rather than material which such a person would not consider to be relevant. The relevant background might include not just the factual background but also the parties' understanding of the law or the facts, even if that understanding was mistakenly held.[98] The courts have stressed that in a multiparty transaction, it would be wrong to take account of background facts which were not known or knowable to all of the parties.[99] It has been held that where parties contracted on the basis of Loan Market Association (LMA) recommended form documentation, the templates and user guides published by the LMA could be used as an aid to interpretation as a background fact.[100]

1.43 The importance of giving a commercially sensible interpretation to the construction of contracts, rather than taking a strict and literalistic approach, was emphasised by Lord Steyn in *Mannai Investment Co Ltd v Eagle Star Life Assurance Co Ltd*[101] and in *Sirius International Insurance Co (Publ) v FAI General Insurance Ltd*.[102] In making this point, his Lordship was echoing what had been said by Lord Diplock in *Antaios Cia Naviera SA v Salen Rederierna AB, The Antaios*,[103] and in *HHY Luxembourg SARL* the Court of Appeal was prepared to adopt a highly commercial approach in construing an intercreditor agreement which arguably differed markedly from any interpretation of the precise language used.[104] In *Rainy Sky* the Supreme Court provided further guidance on the role of 'business common sense' in the interpretation of contracts. In carrying out the exercise of construction, the court had to have regard to all relevant surrounding circumstances. If there were two possible constructions, the court was entitled to prefer the approach which accorded with business common sense, and reject the other.[105] In appealing to business common sense, the courts have considered whether a term's interpretation accords with its commercial objective or purpose,[106] although this should be the purpose of all the parties in agreeing the term, not just one of them.[107]

---

[98] See also *Spencer v Secretary of State for Defence* [2012] EWHC 120 in which knowledge of clear and well-known legal principles may be attributed to the parties.

[99] *Re Sigma Finance Corporation* [2009] UKSC 2 [37].

[100] *GSO Credit v Barclays Bank plc* [2016] EWHC 146 (Comm) [62], [65], and [78].

[101] [1997] AC 749, 771.

[102] [2004] UKHL 54, [2004] 1 WLR 3251 [18]–[19].

[103] [1985] AC 191, 201.

[104] *HHY Luxembourg SARL v Barclays Bank* [2010] EWCA Civ 1248.

[105] *Rainy Sky SA and ors v Kookmin Bank* [2011] UKSC 50.

[106] *Procter & Gamble v Svenska Cellulosa Aktiebolaget* [2012] EWCA Civ 1413.

[107] *Strategic Value Master Fund Ltd v Ideal Standard International Acquisition* [2011] EWHC 171.

In *Arnold v Britton* the Supreme Court did not apply the principle of commercial **1.44**
common sense because the clause in question was unambiguous.[108] Following
this decision, it had seemed to some practitioners and commentators that the
Supreme Court had backed away from the seemingly contextual approach to interpretation adopted in the *Rainy Sky* case, which focused on the factual matrix
and commercial purpose, to a more literal or textual approach, at least in cases
where the wording of the clause in question lacked ambiguity. However, in *Wood
v Capita Insurance Services Ltd*,[109] the Supreme Court held that the *Arnold* case
did not involve a recalibration of the approach in the *Rainy Sky* case. Lord Hodge
stated:

> The court's task is to ascertain the objective meaning of the language which the par-
> ties have chosen to express their agreement. It has long been accepted that this is
> not a literalist exercise focused solely on a parsing of the wording of the particular
> clause but that the court must consider the contract as a whole and, depending on
> the nature, formality and quality of drafting of the contract, give more or less weight
> to elements of the wider context in reaching its view as to that objective meaning.…
> Interpretation is, as Lord Clarke JSC stated in the *Rainy Sky* case (para 21), a unitary
> exercise; where there are rival meanings, the court can give weight to the implica-
> tions of rival constructions by reaching a view as to which construction is more
> consistent with business common sense.…
>
> This unitary exercise involves an iterative process by which each suggested interpret-
> ation is checked against the provisions of the contract and its commercial conse-
> quences are investigated: the *Arnold* case, para 77 citing *In re Sigma Finance Corpn*
> [2010] 1 All ER 571, para 12, per Lord Mance JSC. To my mind once one has read
> the language in dispute and the relevant parts of the contract that provide its con-
> text, it does not matter whether the more detailed analysis commences with the fac-
> tual background and the implications of rival constructions or a close examination
> of the relevant language in the contract, so long as the court balances the indications
> given by each.
>
> Textualism and contextualism are not conflicting paradigms in a battle for exclu-
> sive occupation of the field of contractual interpretation. Rather, the lawyer and
> the judge, when interpreting any contract, can use them as tools to ascertain the
> objective meaning of the language which the parties have chosen to express their
> agreement. The extent to which each tool will assist the court in its task will vary
> according to the circumstances of the particular agreement or agreements. Some
> agreements may be successfully interpreted principally by textual analysis, for ex-
> ample because of their sophistication and complexity and because they have been
> negotiated and prepared with the assistance of skilled professionals. The correct in-
> terpretation of other contracts may be achieved by a greater emphasis on the factual
> matrix, for example because of their informality, brevity or the absence of skilled
> professional assistance. But negotiators of complex formal contracts may often not
> achieve a logical and coherent text because of, for example, the conflicting aims
> of the parties, failures of communication, differing drafting practices, or deadlines

---

[108] *Arnold v Britton* [2015] UKSC 36 (Lord Carnwath dissenting).
[109] [2017] UKSC 24.

which require the parties to compromise in order to reach agreement. There may often therefore be provisions in a detailed professionally drawn contract which lack clarity and the lawyer or judge in interpreting such provisions may be particularly helped by considering the factual matrix and the purpose of similar provisions in contracts of the same type. The iterative process, of which Lord Mance JSC spoke in *Sigma Finance Corpn* [2010] 1 All ER 571, para 12, assists the lawyer or judge to ascertain the objective meaning of disputed provisions.

On the approach to contractual interpretation, the *Rainy Sky* and *Arnold* cases were saying the same thing.[110]

1.45 In short, as Lord Bingham had noted a couple of decades earlier, contractual construction is an exercise which is 'neither uncompromisingly literal nor unswervingly purposive'.[111] It is a combination of both, with the relative weight to be given to the ordinary meaning of the text and to the context (including purpose) varying in accordance with the language used and the surrounding circumstances.

1.46 The third point in Lord Hoffmann's summary reflects what was said by Lord Wilberforce in *Prenn v Simmonds*[112] and is sometimes referred to as the 'exclusionary principle'. It also partly reflects the so-called parol evidence rule,[113] by which extrinsic evidence was inadmissible to add to or subtract from the contents or meaning of a written agreement or instrument. In *Chartbrook* in the House of Lords the court indicated, obiter dicta, that there was no clearly established case for revisiting the rule in *Prenn*.[114] The principle is subject to a number of exceptions and qualifications, such as where the written document was not intended to contain the whole agreement,[115] where another document is incorporated by reference into the agreement or where there is a collateral contract,[116] where there is a claim for misrepresentation, where evidence is admitted as to the validity of the agreement[117] or that it is a sham,[118] where a term may be implied in the agreement, and where there is a claim for rectification of the document because it does not represent the true agreement between the parties.

1.47 It has also been held that evidence of the prior negotiations between the parties will be admitted to prove the meaning of an unusual expression that was used in the contract and which was commonly understood between the parties in their negotiations to have a particular meaning,[119] that evidence of prior negotiations may be admitted to establish the intended contents of an obvious omission on the face

---

[110] ibid [10]–[14].
[111] *Arbuthnott v Fagan* [1995] CLC 1396, 1400.
[112] [1971] 1 WLR 1381, 1383–85.
[113] *Goss v Lord Nugent* (1833) 5 B&Ad 58.
[114] *Chartbrook Ltd v Persimmon Homes Ltd* [2009] 1 AC 1101 [40]–[41].
[115] *Allen v Pink* (1838) 4 M&W 140.
[116] *Mann v Nunn* (1874) 30 LT 526.
[117] *Clever v Kirkman* (1876) 33 LT 672.
[118] *AG Securities v Vaughan* [1990] 1 AC 469.
[119] *Proforce Recruit Ltd v The Rugby Group Ltd* [2006] EWCA Civ 69.

of the document,[120] and that evidence from prior negotiations can be admitted to prove that background facts were known by the parties.[121] Evidence of prior negotiations may be admitted to prove the subject matter of the contract.[122] Evidence of a prior agreement between the parties can also be admitted.[123] However, the general rule continues to be that evidence of prior negotiations, such as prior drafts of the loan documentation, is inadmissible for the purposes of construing the execution copies.

For similar reasons, but subject to much the same exceptions, evidence of the conduct of the parties after the making of a contract is not admissible in construing the contract.[124] Nonetheless, such conduct may be admissible to prove that the contract had been varied by subsequent agreement[125] or to raise an estoppel.[126] It may also now be relevant to take into account the subsequent conduct of the parties in determining the true nature or character of a transaction, so as to ascertain if the transaction (and its mechanics) as provided for in the contract was carried into effect, or if, in reality, it was something else because the transaction represented by the agreement was not operated in the manner provided for in the contract. Lord Millett, in giving the advice of the Privy Council in *Agnew v Commissioner of Inland Revenue*,[127] made that point in relation to determining whether a charge over book debts should be characterised as a fixed or floating charge. His approach was approved by the House of Lords in *National Westminster Bank plc v Spectrum Plus Ltd*.[128] **1.48**

To reinforce the effect of the exclusionary principle and the parol evidence rule and to prevent reference to other agreements (including collateral contracts and earlier agreements) and other matters, a contract may contain an 'entire agreement' clause along the following lines: **1.49**

---

[120] *Caterpillar Financial Services Ltd v Goldcrest Plant and Groundworks Ltd* [2007] EWCA Civ 272. As to the ability of the court to interpolate missing words into a written contract, see Lord Bingham in *Homburg Houtimport BV v Agrosin Private Ltd* [2003] UKHL 12, [2004] 1 AC 715 [23].

[121] *Oceanbulk Shipping & Trading SA v TMT Asia Ltd* [2010] UKSC 44.

[122] *Macdonald v Longbottom* (1859) 1 E&E 977.

[123] Rix LJ in *HIH Casualty and General Insurance Ltd v New Hampshire Insurance Co* [2001] 2 Lloyd's Rep 161 [81]–[84], although his Lordship doubted the value of such evidence. The Court of Appeal did find an earlier agreement useful in *KPMG LLP v Network Rail Infrastructure Ltd* [2007] EWCA Civ 363, as the earlier agreement provided for the form of the later agreement, which erroneously omitted a significant matter which the court was able to correct as a matter of construction of the later document.

[124] *James Miller & Partners v Whitworth Street Estates (Manchester) Ltd* [1970] AC 583, 603 (Viscount Dilhorne) and 606 (Lord Wilberforce); *L Schuler AG v Wickman Machine Tool Sales Ltd* [1974] AC 325.

[125] *McCausland v Duncan Lawrie Ltd* [1997] 1 WLR 38.

[126] *James Miller & Partners v Whitworth Street Estates (Manchester) Ltd* [1970] AC 583.

[127] [2001] UKPC 28, [2001] 2 AC 710 [48].

[128] [2005] UKHL 41, [2005] 2 AC 680. See, in particular, Lord Walker at [140].

> This Agreement constitutes the entire contract between the parties and supersedes all prior or collateral representations, agreements, negotiations or understandings, whether oral or in writing.

1.50 Depending upon the wording that is used, such a clause should be effective to exclude consideration of a collateral contract and an earlier agreement, as well as an attempt to include terms that were not expressly set out in the contract.[129] However, if such a clause does not refer to pre-contractual representations then it cannot exclude consideration of them.[130] It has also been held that wording along the lines quoted above would not prevent the court from considering the pre-contractual negotiations between the parties to ascertain the meaning of an uncommon expression that was used in the contract and which the parties had agreed between them in those negotiations.[131]

1.2.9 Contractual discretions

1.51 A lender or financier is often given a measure of discretion in a facility as to what may be required of the borrower and the extent of the rights and obligations of the borrower under the facility. Such a discretion may go to matters such as setting interest rates, determining if conditions precedent have been fulfilled before the facility will be available for drawing, the extent of performance or observance of restrictions by the borrower that is required under the covenants and undertaking provisions of the facility, and the basis on which the lender will give consents when requested by the borrower. Sometimes the discretion has the appearance of being unlimited, in the sense of it being entirely within the will of the lender.[132] The question that arises is whether any limitation should be implied in such a case as to the factors that the lender should take into account and the grounds upon

---

[129] *Inntrepreneur Pub Co v East Crown Ltd* [2000] 2 Lloyd's Rep 611. See also *Matchbet Ltd v Openbet Retail Ltd* [2013] EWHC 3067 (Ch) [130]–[132] where such a clause was said to act as a contractual estoppel. However, an entire agreement clause does not prevent the implication of terms: *JN Hipwell & Son v Szurek* [2018] EWCA Civ 674.

[130] *Thomas Witter Ltd v TBP Industries Ltd* [1996] 2 All ER 573, 595–96; *AXA Sun Life Services plc v Campbell Martin Ltd* [2011] EWCA Civ 133 and *Cassa di Risparmio della Repubblica di San Marino SpA v Barclays Bank Ltd* [2011] EWHC 484 (Comm) [531]; but contrast *NF Football Investments Ltd v NFCC Group Holdings Ltd* [2018] EWHC 1346 (Ch). In any event, as the *Thomas Witter* case explained, an attempt to exclude or restrict reference to (and thus liability for) a misrepresentation will be subject to s 3 of the Misrepresentation Act 1967. This should be distinguished from the effect of a 'non-reliance' clause, by which a party confirms that it did not rely upon any representation in deciding to enter into the contract: contrast the approach in *Thomas Witter Ltd v TBP Industries Ltd*, at 596–97 with that taken in *Watford Electronics Ltd v Sanderson CFL Ltd* [2001] EWCA Civ 317, [2001] 1 All ER (Comm) 696 [38]–[41]. The approach taken on this latter point in the *Thomas Witter* case may now also be seen as being inconsistent with that taken by the Court of Appeal in *IFE Fund SA v Goldman Sachs International* [2007] EWCA Civ 811. See the further discussion at section 3.5.5.

[131] *Proforce Recruit Ltd v The Rugby Group Ltd* [2006] EWCA Civ 69.

[132] The position where the discretion is qualified, for example, where the decision-maker is to act reasonably, is discussed at para 1.58 below.

which it would be entitled to make a determination or take other action within its discretion.

Whilst it may appear to be in the lender's interest that there should be no such **1.52** limitation, there is a risk that a limitless discretion which goes to a fundamental matter under the contract may mean that there has been a failure to agree on an essential element of the contract and, in consequence, the contract may be unenforceable and fail for uncertainty for the reasons previously discussed. For example, an entirely unfettered discretion that is vested in the lender as to charging and setting the interest rate in a term loan facility might have the result that there was lack of certainty and agreement concerning a matter going to the heart of the contract, namely, as to the price payable by the borrower for the use of the money borrowed under the facility.[133] In a different vein, some limitation may be thought desirable where the lender appears to be given in a facility agreement a completely unfettered discretion in determining whether the borrower had fulfilled the conditions precedent for it to draw down under the facility (particularly if some of the conditions were within the lender's own control) or where no parameters are prescribed expressly as to the grounds upon which the lender may determine that a material adverse change has arisen that would entitle it to determine that an event of default has occurred.[134]

There have been a number of Court of Appeal decisions and a recent Supreme **1.53** Court decision[135] that have concerned this issue in relation to a variety of different contracts. These decisions have addressed the issue by seeing if a term could be implied into the contract as to the extent of, and the manner in which, the

---

[133] The same conclusion would not arise under an overdraft facility as, from a legal perspective, it is considered to be a contract from day to day, with each party being able to terminate at any time. Thus, the lender theoretically is treated as proposing an interest rate each day, which the borrower accepts by maintaining its borrowing or rejects by repaying the outstanding amount. In a term loan, however, the legal mechanics are different as the contract is intended to endure for the term of the facility and thus the borrower is meant to be bound as to the payment of interest for the term. For further discussion of the exercise of contractual discretion in the context of conditions precedent see section 2.9.2.

[134] In *Watson v Watchfinder.co.uk Ltd* [2017] EWHC 1275 (Comm) a discretion to veto a contractual right (a share option) was held not to be unfettered because if it were it would render the underlying contract meaningless, as the contractual right would be entirely within the gift of the party having the veto.

[135] *Abu Dhabi National Tanker Co v Product Star Shipping Ltd, The Product Star (No 2)* [1993] 1 Lloyd's Rep 397; *Gan Insurance Co Ltd v Tai Ping Insurance Co Ltd* [2001] EWCA Civ 1047, [2001] 2 All ER (Comm) 299; *Paragon Finance plc v Nash & Staunton* [2001] EWCA Civ 1466, [2002] 1 WLR 685; *Paragon Finance plc v Pender* [2005] EWCA Civ 760, [2005] 1 WLR 3412; *Lymington Marina Ltd v Macnamara* [2007] EWCA Civ 151; *Socimer International Bank Ltd v Standard Bank London Ltd* [2008] EWCA Civ 116; *McKay v Centurion Credit Resources LLC* [2012] EWCA Civ 1941; *Westlb AG v Nomura Bank International plc* [2012] EWCA Civ 495; *Mid Essex Hospital Services NHS Trust v Compass Group UK and Ireland Ltd* [2013] EWCA Civ 200; *Barclays Bank plc v Unicredit Bank AG* [2014] EWCA Civ 302; *Braganza v BP Shipping Ltd* [2015] UKSC 17; *LBI EHF v Raiffeisen Bank International AG* [2018] EWCA Civ 719.

discretion should be exercised and, if so, what the term should be. In summary, the following propositions may be drawn from the cases.

1.54 First, it is a matter of interpretation of the contract and, to the extent permitted by ordinary contractual rules, the implication of a term to determine if there is a fetter placed on the scope of the discretion and how it should be exercised. This should be done in the context of the contract as a whole. Unless the parties have otherwise provided, the contract should be interpreted in accordance with current law and not by the law as it was understood at the time of contracting.[136] If the relevant provision in the contract is plain and the contract works perfectly well without the necessity for such an implied term, then the contract should be applied on its own, without implying anything further.[137] However, a court will usually be prepared to imply terms along the lines next mentioned, unless there is an express provision which clearly ousts the minimum implied restrictions on contractual discretions.[138]

1.55 Secondly, where a term is to be implied, it should be the minimum that is necessary to meet the tests for its implication. It would appear that, if a term is to be implied, the minimum that might be implied would include an obligation to act in good faith, on the basis of the facts or the available material, with perhaps some obligation to review the adequacy of that material and seek further information if the material was obviously deficient.[139] In addition, it might be implied that the discretion should not be exercised capriciously, arbitrarily, or for a collateral purpose which was outside the legitimate scope of the contract.[140] For a time it was uncertain whether such an implied obligation would also encompass an

---

[136] In general, the effect of a court decision on the common law is retrospective and not just prospective: see *National Westminster Bank v Spectrum Plus Ltd* [2005] UKHL 41, [2005] 2 AC 680. However, a change to the parties' understanding of the law that is brought about by a later court decision might render the contract void and give rise to a restitutionary claim based upon a mistake of law: see *Kleinwort Benson Ltd v Lincoln City Council* [1999] 2 AC 349 and, for the effects of common mistake, see section 1.2.6.

[137] *Lymington Marina Ltd v Macnamara* [2007] EWCA Civ 151; *Marks & Spencer plc v BNP Paribas Security Services Trust Company (Jersey) Ltd* [2015] UKSC 72.

[138] See Rix LJ in *Socimer International Bank Ltd v Standard Bank London Ltd* [2008] EWCA Civ 116 [66] and [106]. However, both in the *Socimer* case and in *Westlb AG v Nomura Bank International plc* [2012] EWCA Civ 495 a qualifier allowing a valuation to be made in a party's 'sole and absolute discretion' did not exclude the implied restrictions. See also *Mid Essex Hospital v Compass Group UK and Ireland Ltd* [2013] EWCA Civ 200 [83].

[139] Contrast the approach of Arden LJ in *Lymington Marina Ltd v Macnamara* [2007] EWCA Civ 151 [42] and [43] with that of Pill LJ in that case, at [71] and of Mance LJ in *Gan Insurance Co Ltd v Tai Ping Insurance Co Ltd* [2001] EWCA Civ 1047, [2001] 2 All ER (Comm) 299 [76].

[140] *Lymington Marina Ltd v Macnamara* [2007] EWCA Civ 151. An example provided by *Paragon Finance plc v Nash & Staunton* [2001] EWCA Civ 1466, [2002] 1 WLR 685 would be where a lender had a discretion in setting the interest rate payable by a borrower and set an unduly high rate beyond what the lender knew the borrower could afford simply to force the borrower to repay because the borrower was a nuisance and the lender wished to be rid of the borrower. It should be noted that in *Sterling Credit Ltd v Rahman* [2002] EWHC 3008 (Ch) it was held that a lender would not be obliged to exercise its discretion and reduce the rate it charged the borrower.

obligation to refrain from acting in a way in which no other person in a similar position, acting reasonably, would act (known as the *Wednesbury* unreasonableness test[141]) as there were conflicting judicial pronouncements on this point.[142] But the Supreme Court in *Braganza v BP Shipping Ltd* set out to clarify the law by adopting a two-stage approach. First, the court looked at the decision-making process to see whether the right matters had been taken into account in reaching the decision (and also that irrelevant matters had not been taken into account).[143] Secondly, the court considered the result arrived at to see whether the outcome is so outrageous that no reasonable decision-maker could have reached it.[144] The second stage, somewhat controversially, transposes the *Wednesbury* unreasonableness public law concept into the law of contract.

Thirdly, except in the unusual case where the court would imply an obligation **1.56** to act in an entirely objective and reasonable fashion, the discretion may still be exercised in the commercial interests of the person exercising the discretion and, where appropriate (eg in setting an interest rate), by taking into account matters more generally relating to its business and its customers than just the particular circumstances of the other party to the contract, even if that meant that the other party had to pay more under the contract than the remaining customers of the person exercising the discretion.[145]

It is not every situation, however, in which a lender's discretion will be fettered by **1.57** an implied term. As is clear from the first of the propositions stated earlier, a term will be implied only if it is necessary to do so. If the contract works perfectly well without implying a term then the contract will be left in its original state. One particular area where it is submitted that a lender's discretion would be left unfettered is in relation to the determination by a lender of whether it wishes to make demand for repayment and enforce its security. For a commercial facility that is expressed to be repayable on demand, assuming that such a stipulation has not

---

[141] After the test formulated by Lord Greene MR in *Associated Provincial Picture Houses Ltd v Wednesbury Corp* [1948] 1 KB 223, 233–34, that should be applied in administrative law.

[142] *Paragon Finance plc v Nash & Staunton* [2001] EWCA Civ 1466, [2002] 1 WLR 685 [38]; cf *Lymington Marina Ltd v Macnamara* [2007] EWCA Civ 151 [37].

[143] However, in *Lehman Brothers International (Europe)(in administration) v Exxonmobil Financial Services BV* [2016] EWHC 2699 (Comm) Blair J expressed the view that the *Braganza* case did not require the kind of analysis of the decision-making process that was required in the context of public law.

[144] *Braganza v BP Shipping Ltd* [2015] UKSC 17. The two-stage test was applied in *Watson and Others v Watchfinder.co.uk* [2017] EWHC 1275 (Comm) and *BHL v Leumi ABL Limited* [2017] EWHC 1871 (QB).

[145] *Paragon Finance plc v Nash & Staunton* [2001] EWCA Civ 1466, [2002] 1 WLR 685 and *Paragon Finance plc v Pender* [2005] EWCA Civ 760, [2005] 1 WLR 3412. In the first of those cases, Dyson LJ said that a lender was free to raise the interest rate payable by a borrower because of financial difficulties suffered by the lender or to set a rate which provided a subsidy to compensate for what it received from other customers. In *Barclays Bank plc v Unicredit Bank AG* [2014] EWCA Civ 302 the decision-maker was entitled to prefer its own commercial interests even where it had agreed to exercise its discretion in a 'commercially reasonable manner'.

been waived or abrogated by the lender, the authorities have consistently allowed the lender to decide if and when it wishes to make demand, without having to ascribe any reason for doing so.[146] However, the Court of Appeal has also made it clear that the lender must be acting within its right to make a demand under the terms of the facility; that is, that the facility is expressed to be repayable on demand[147] or the demand is made in accordance with a provision which permits the demand to be made following the occurrence of an event of default.[148] Subject to that particular point, the view that a lender's discretion in deciding if it wishes to make demand is unlimited is reinforced by the freedom of a creditor at general law[149] to decide entirely within its discretion whether and how it will enforce its security or a guarantee it holds, as exemplified by the decision of the Privy Council in *China & South Sea Bank Ltd v Tan*.[150] Similarly, a party's right to terminate a contact is unfettered by any implied term.[151]

1.58 Finally, it is necessary to consider the position where the parties have expressly imposed fetters on the exercise of a contractual discretion; for example, where an express restriction has been inserted that the relevant power must be exercised in a commercially reasonable manner or that the lender must act reasonably (or not unreasonably). There is an important distinction to be drawn here between the parties agreeing that the outcome must be reasonable and only agreeing that the decision-making process must be conducted reasonably. In *Lehman Bros Special Financing Inc v National Power Corp*[152] an express requirement to 'act in good faith and use commercially reasonable procedures in order to produce a commercially reasonable result' was held to impose an objective standard of reasonableness, and not only rationality.[153] The earlier case of *Fondazione Enasarco v Lehman Brothers Finance SA*[154] had held that the words 'reasonably determines in good

---

[146] See *Bank of Baroda v Panessar* [1987] Ch 335. The Court of Appeal has indicated that it might on some future occasion be prepared to consider if the borrower should be allowed time to find the funds to make repayment following the making of a demand upon it: see *Lloyds Bank plc v Lampert* [1999] 1 All ER (Comm) 161, but there is no sign that this will happen. In *Nicholson v HSBC Bank plc* [2001] EWCA Civ 748, Rix J reiterated that 'on demand' means 'on demand', and *Panessar* was followed in *Su-Ling v Goldman Sachs International* [2015] EWHC 759 (Comm).
[147] See *Cryne v Barclays Bank plc* [1978] BCLC 548.
[148] See *The Angelic Star* [1988] 1 Lloyd's Rep 122. If, within the particular terms of the wording of an event of default, the lender is given an apparently unfettered discretion to make a determination, as for instance in determining (without any express limitation) if an adverse change has occurred, then there may be scope for the implication of a term as to the manner in which the lender may make its determination.
[149] To which there are statutory exceptions, such as under the Consumer Credit Act 2006 and under provisions regulating possession proceedings concerning residential land.
[150] [1990] AC 536. Cf *Property Alliance Group Ltd v Royal Bank of Scotland* [2018] EWCA Civ 355, where a lender's power to call for annual valuations of security was found, contrary to the first instance decision, to be subject to an implied term.
[151] *Monde Petroleum SA v Westernzagros Ltd* [2016] EWHC 1472 (Comm) and *Monk v Largo Foods Ltd* [2016] EWHC 1837 (Comm) [64].
[152] [2018] EWHC 487 (Comm).
[153] *Fondazione Enasarco v Lehman Brothers Finance SA* [2015] EWHC 1307 (Ch).
[154] [2015] EWHC (Ch).

faith' imposed a standard of rationality, not objective reasonableness. Similarly, in *Barclays Bank PLC v Unicredit Bank AG*[155] where a matter had 'to be determined by [the Bank] in a commercially reasonable manner', the Bank was only required to act rationally (the outcome did not have to be commercially reasonable) and could have primary regard to its own commercial interests. In each case, the effect of an express fetter on a contractual discretion will be a matter of construction of the words used in the context of the relevant contract.

Crowther v Arbuthnot Latham & Co Ltd[156] concerned an express obligation 'not **1.59** to withhold consent unreasonably'. There the court held that the test was one of objective reasonableness, not merely of rationality (*Wednesbury* reasonableness) nor one of just subjectively balancing commercial interests in a commercially reasonable manner.[157] A bank was found to have acted objectively unreasonably in withholding its consent to the sale of property used as security for the borrower's indebtedness because it attempted to enhance its rights rather than protect them. An objective standard of reasonableness requires the court to identify what is a reasonable outcome (with the court supplanting the decision-maker), whereas rationality requires the court to assess whether the process followed by the decision-maker adhered to a minimum standard of rationality (with the decision remaining that of the decision-maker).[158] Nonetheless, it must be remembered that both rationality and wholly objective reasonableness allow for a result that falls within a range.[159] Even when applying the reasonableness standard there is not necessarily a single correct answer.

1.2.10 Best endeavours and reasonable endeavours

One of the key strengths of English law as a risk allocation tool is the doctrine of **1.60** strict liability. This doctrine provides that where a contractual promise has been made, the promisor will be bound to perform and will only be released from the obligation in very limited circumstances.[160] However, strict liability places the promisor in a difficult situation if circumstances change or if a third party's

---

[155] [2014] EWCA Civ 302.

[156] [2018] EWHC 504 (Comm).

[157] In *No. 1 West India Quay (Residential) Ltd v East Tower Apartments Ltd* [2018] EWCA Civ 250 it was held that where a such decision to refuse consent was based on multiple reasons, the fact that one of the reasons was unreasonable would not normally render the whole decision unreasonable, if the other reasons for refusal were reasonable:

[158] *Hayes v Willoughby*[2013] UKSC 17 [14]; *Socimer International bank Ltd v Standard Bank London Ltd (No 2)* [2008] EWCA Civ 116 [66].

[159] *Lehman Brothers Special Financing v National Power Corporation* [2018] EWHC 487.

[160] *Paradine v Jane* (1646) 82 ER 897 which provided that 'when the party by his own contract creates a duty or charge upon himself, he is bound to make it good, if he may, notwithstanding any accident by inevitable necessity, because he might have provided against it by his contract'. As the foregoing quotation illustrates, English contract law places the onus on the contracting parties to provide for supervening events in their contracts, for example by negotiating *force majeure* clauses.

agreement is required. Consequently the expressions 'best endeavours' and 'reasonable endeavours' are frequently used in contracts to soften obligations that would otherwise attract strict liability. These expressions are used to qualify what would otherwise be an absolute and unqualified contractual obligation that a party would have under the contract, so that the relevant party undertakes to use its best endeavours, or its reasonable endeavours,[161] to achieve a stated object, rather than undertaking an unqualified obligation to do so.[162] Given their frequent use, it is surprising that there has been only a modest amount of case law on the meaning of the two expressions and there is little precision as to their construction. It is apparent, however, that there is a distinction between an obligation to use best endeavours and an obligation to use reasonable endeavours and that the latter is less stringent than the former.[163]

1.61 In *Jet2.com* all three judges in the Court of Appeal focused on the need to identify whether the object of the best endeavours clause was sufficiently certain, and sufficient objective criteria had been supplied to determine whether it was met, in order for the clause to be enforceable.[164] It has been said that best endeavours does not mean second-best endeavours and, broadly speaking, that no stone should be left unturned in seeking to achieve the desired result: *Sheffield District Ry Co v Great Central Ry Co.*[165] Somewhat less stridently, the Court of Appeal said in *IBM United Kingdom Ltd v Rockware Glass Ltd*[166] that an obligation placed upon a party to use its best endeavours meant that the party should take all of the possible steps that a prudent and determined person would take, if he were acting in his own interests and wished to obtain or achieve the stated objective.

---

[161] It is important to note that an endeavours obligation is likely to be construed according to the resources and powers of the promisor: Hugh Beale (ed), *Chitty on Contracts* (32nd edn, Sweet & Maxwell, 2015) 13-064. Additionally it is usually construed by having regard to the circumstances pertaining at the time for performance: *Jet2.com Ltd v Blackpool Airport Ltd* [2012] EWCA Civ 417. Accordingly, the strength—and hence benefit of such an obligation to the promisee—may vary according to whether it is given by a resource-rich or resource-poor promisor and may fluctuate in line with the promisor's financial position. But contrast *Ampurius NU Home Holdings Ltd v Telford Homes (Creekside) Ltd* [2012] EWHC 1820 (Ch).

[162] An agreement to use best endeavours to achieve a stated result, which is an enforceable obligation, has been contrasted with an unenforceable agreement to negotiate: see Lord Ackner in *Walford v Miles* [1992] AC 128, 138.

[163] See Rougier J in *UBH (Mechanical Services) v Standard Life Assurance Co* (unreported, *The Times* 13 November 1986), Kim Lewison QC, sitting as a deputy High Court judge, in *Jolley v Carmel Ltd* [2000] 2 EGLR 154, and Julian Flaux QC, sitting as a Deputy High Court judge, in *Rhodia International Holdings Ltd v Huntsman International LLC* [2007] EWHC 292 (Comm).

[164] *Jet2.com Ltd v Blackpool Airport Ltd* [2012] EWCA Civ 417 (Lewison J dissenting from the result, but not the analysis). In the case of undertakings to use endeavours to enter into an agreement with a third party, there appears to be no problem with the certainty of object because it is easy to determine whether an agreement with a third party had been made: *Astor Management AG v Atalaya Mining plc* [2017] EWHC 425 (Comm) [67].

[165] (1911) 27 TLR 451.

[166] [1980] FSR 335.

This would include incurring reasonable expenditure. In *Terrell v Mabie Todd & Co*[167] it was said that the obligor could have regard to the likely commercial success of the steps to be taken as well as its own financial and commercial position. By way of further qualification, in another case it was held that an obligation on a company and its merchant bank advisers to use their best endeavours to obtain the approval of the company's shareholders to a transaction did not extend to recommending the transaction if there had been an intervening event which would make the transaction disadvantageous to the company and its shareholders, as to have given the recommendation in such circumstances would have amounted to giving bad advice to the shareholders and contrary to the obligors' duties to the shareholders.[168] Such an obligation cannot require the promisor to perform unlawful acts, including breaches of contracts with third parties by which the promisor is bound.

As with a best endeavours obligation, an obligation to use reasonable endeavours **1.62** must also stipulate an object which is sufficiently certain, and sufficient objective criteria to determine whether it is met.[169] An obligation to use reasonable endeavours does not require a party to sacrifice its commercial interests,[170] and the obligation must come to an end at the point when the party has exhausted the avenues available to it, although account had to be taken of events as they occurred, including extraordinary events. In deciding upon the available avenues, the obligor was entitled to consider the likelihood of success in achieving the desired result. However, if the contract actually specifies that certain steps must be taken as part of the endeavours then they must be taken, even if that would involve the party in sacrificing its commercial interests.[171] Subject to such a specific requirement as to the steps to be taken, it would appear that the party is entitled to have regard to its own financial interests in deciding upon what is required of it.[172]

It has been said that, as a matter of language and business common sense, an **1.63** obligation to use reasonable endeavours should only require a party to take one reasonable course of action, whereas an obligation to use best endeavours should require the party to take all reasonable courses that he can take.[173] Thus, an

---

[167] (1952) 69 RPC 234, affirmed by the Court of Appeal (1953) 70 RPC 97.
[168] *Rackham v Peek Foods Ltd* [1990] BCLC 895.
[169] *Astor Management AG v Atalaya Mining plc* [2017] EWHC 425 (Comm).
[170] *CPC Group Ltd v Qatari Diar Real Estate Investment Company* [2010] EWHC 1535.
[171] Lewison J in *Yewbelle v London Green Developments* [2006] EWHC 3166 (Ch) [122]–[123], which was approved on appeal by the Court of Appeal ([2007] EWCA Civ 475), although a different conclusion was reached on the application of the principle to the facts. See also *Rhodia International Holdings Ltd v Huntsman International LLC* [2007] EWHC 292 (Comm).
[172] *Phillips Petroleum Co UK Ltd v Enron Europe Ltd* [1997] CLC 329.
[173] *Rhodia International Holdings Ltd v Huntsman International LLC* [2007] EWHC 292 (Comm).

obligation to take 'all reasonable endeavours' probably equates to an obligation to use best endeavours.[174]

1.64 In *Astor Management AG v Atalaya Mining Plc*[175] the High Court recently considered an obligation to use all reasonable endeavours to obtain a senior debt facility by a specified date. It is worth noting that the specified date was construed as a target by which the object was to be achieved, and not as the date on which the endeavours obligation expired. If that is the intention, clear wording to that effect will be needed in the relevant clause.

1.3 Illegality

1.65 Illegality is a subject that might raise its head when considering the validity and enforceability of a finance transaction. This is particularly true in the current geopolitical climate where increasing regulation of markets, international sanctions, and trade wars seem to feature on the agenda of the world's major powers. The law as to the effect of illegality on a transaction is not terribly clear and what follows is an attempt to summarise a rather difficult area.[176] Illegality in this sense means unlawfulness under statute or at common law, the latter including contracts to commit a crime or a tort and contracts which offend against morals or public policy. Illegality may affect a transaction where the entry into or the performance of the transaction is unlawful in itself, where the intended purpose or use of the subject matter of the transaction is unlawful, or where some related transaction is unlawful so that it taints the principal transaction. The illegality is likely to be raised as an objection to reliance on the transaction or as a defence against a claim for non-performance of one or more putative obligations under it.

1.66 The discussion that follows will commence by examining the effect of illegality under statute and then turn to unlawfulness at common law. It will go on to examine the situations where title in property may pass notwithstanding an illegal contract and the right of a party to an illegal contract to bring a restitutionary claim to recover benefits it has conferred on the other party under the contract,

---

[174] See also Mustill J in *Overseas Buyers v Granadex SA* [1980] 2 Lloyd's Rep 608, 613, Buckley LJ in *IBM United Kingdom Ltd v Rockware Glass Ltd* [1980] FSR 335, 343, and *UBH (Mechanical Services) Ltd v Standard Life Assurance Co*, n 163.

[175] [2017] EWHC 425 (Comm).

[176] For a more detailed review, see Law Commission, *The Illegality Defence* (Law Com No 320). The Law Commission found the rules in the area to be complex and confused but concluded that, other than for a limited reform to trusts law, it was not possible to lay down strict rules about when the illegality defence should apply. In so far as the law of contract is concerned, the Law Commission left it to the courts to 'consider the policy rationales that underlie the defence and apply them to the facts of the case' (at p vi).

before concluding with the approach that the courts should take in considering pleadings or evidence which concern illegality.

1.3.1 Statutory illegality

As a preliminary matter, a distinction should be drawn between the effect of an **1.67** illegality that existed under statute at the time the contract was made and supervening illegality under legislation that came into force after that time. In the latter situation, it is likely that the contract will be frustrated[177] unless the illegality affects the contract in some minor way that is irrelevant to the main purpose or fulfilment of the contract[178] or if it arises in consequence of an earlier default of the relevant party.[179] It would appear that the effect of a supervening illegality is not a matter for which the parties can expressly provide in the contract so as to preclude the contract from being frustrated,[180] unlike the position in most other situations that would otherwise give rise to a frustration of a contract.

Where the unlawfulness is proscribed from the outset by statute then the legisla- **1.68** tion may itself provide for the consequences of the unlawfulness as, for instance, is the case in relation to transactions that are made in breach of the general prohibition contained in section 19 of the Financial Services and Markets Act 2000[181] and the fact that contracts and promises that were made in breach of section 18 of the Gaming Act 1845 or section 1 of the Gaming Act 1892 were void.[182] In such cases, the statute may provide that the transaction remains valid or that it is rendered unenforceable by both parties or only by the party that is in breach of the statutory requirement. The statute may also provide for restitutionary remedies that would be available to the parties. In other cases, the effect of the legislation will be less clear and will depend upon whether the transaction is rendered unenforceable by an implication to be drawn from the legislation and, if so, whether both parties are affected or only the party which is in breach of the statutory requirement. It follows that not every breach of a statutory requirement that relates to the entry into the transaction or its performance will lead to a transaction being unenforceable.[183]

---

[177] *Wynn v Shropshire Union Railways and Canal Co* (1850) 5 Exch 420.
[178] As eg in *Cricklewood Property and Investment Trust Ltd v Leighton's Investment Trust Ltd* [1945] AC 221.
[179] *Ocean Tramp Tankers Corp v V/O Sovfracht, The Eugenia* [1964] 2 QB 226.
[180] *Ertel Bieber & Co v Rio Tinto Co Ltd* [1918] AC 260.
[181] See ss 26–29 of the Act.
[182] Those two sections were repealed by s 334 of the Gambling Act 2005, as to contracts entered into after the date of the repeal (1 September 2007). Prior to that repeal, s 412 of the Financial Services and Markets Act 2000 provided that certain contracts (ie contracts relating to investments that met prescribed criteria) were not avoided or rendered unenforceable by those sections.
[183] As eg in *St John Shipping Corp v Joseph Rank Ltd* [1957] 1 QB 267; *Archbolds (Freightage) Ltd v Spanglett Ltd* [1961] 1 QB 374; *Yango Pastoral Co Pty Ltd v First Chicago Ltd* (1978) 139 CLR 410; and *Hughes v Asset Managers plc* [1995] 3 All ER 669.

1.69   Various considerations have been put forward in determining the intended effect
of a statute on transactions, although none of them provides a conclusive test that
can be applied in all situations and there is more than an element of contradiction
between them. The following things have been said. The intended effect should
be gauged by asking, first, if the statute intended any prohibition of transactions
at all and, if so, whether the particular transaction under consideration belonged
to the class of transactions that the statute was intended to prohibit.[184] The matter
should be tested against the mischief at which the statute is aimed, the language
it uses, the scope and purpose of the statute, the consequences to the parties
(particularly to an innocent party) should the transaction be found to be unenforceable, and any other relevant considerations.[185] A statute is unlikely to affect a
transaction whose purpose is lawful and which could therefore be performed and
carried out lawfully but where one of the parties chooses (without the encour-
agement of the other party) to perform in a manner which involves a breach of a
statute dealing with some peripheral or incidental matter.[186] It is now clear that
only acts which are criminal or 'quasi criminal' may make it unlawful to enter
into or perform a transaction. A quasi-criminal act is one that engages the public
interest in the same way as a crime.[187] As a result, breach of a statutory rule which
carries only a civil or regulatory sanction may render a transaction unlawful, but
only if the statutory rule is enacted to protect the public interest.[188]

1.70   If the transaction is affected by statutory illegality, the next question is to ascertain
if the illegality affects both parties, even if one of them is entirely innocent, or
only the party which is in breach of the statute. Where the latter applies, the transaction will remain enforceable by the innocent party which is not in breach and
was unaware of the other party's unlawful conduct.[189] Once again, the matter may
be addressed specifically by the statute but in other cases it will be necessary to
determine the issue by the implication that should be drawn from the statute. In
some cases, the courts have held that the illegality should only affect the party that
was in breach of the statute,[190] particularly if the innocent party was a member of

---

[184] *St John Shipping Corp v Joseph Rank Ltd* [1957] 1 QB 267, 287–288 (Devlin J).

[185] *Phoenix General Insurance Co of Greece SA v Halvanon Insurance Co Ltd* [1988] QB 216, 273
(Kerr LJ).

[186] *St John Shipping Corp v Joseph Rank Ltd* [1957] 1 QB 267; *Archbolds (Freightage) Ltd v
Spanglett Ltd* [1961] 1 QB 374.

[187] *Les Laboratoires Servier v Apotex Inc* [2014] UKSC 55.

[188] *Safeway Stores Ltd v Twigger* [2010] EWHC 11 (Comm), subsequently reversed on appeal but
not on these grounds.

[189] Even in cases where a party had knowledge of the other party's unlawful activity, it may still
be able to argue that it was unaffected by mere knowledge which did not amount to 'participation'
in the unlawfulness, along the same lines as are discussed later in connection with participation in
an unlawfulness that affects contracts at common law.

[190] See eg the explanations provided in the Court of Appeal in *Marles v Philip Trant & Sons Ltd*
[1954] 1 QB 29, 32 (Singleton LJ) and 36 (Denning LJ) as to its earlier decision in *Anderson Ltd v
Daniel* [1924] 1 KB 138.

a class which the statute was intended to protect, so that the transaction should remain enforceable by the innocent party.[191] However, that approach is not universal and there are other cases where the affected transaction has been held to be unenforceable by both parties to it, even though one of them was innocent, ignorant of the unlawfulness of the other's conduct, and might have fallen within the class of those whom the statute was intended to protect.[192]

The point was discussed by Kerr LJ in *Phoenix General Insurance Co of Greece* **1.71** *SA v Halvanon Insurance Co Ltd*,[193] in which his Lordship said that a contract of insurance entered into by an unauthorised insurer in breach of the Insurance Companies Act 1974 would be void and so unenforceable by both parties, even though the statutory obligation to be authorised was placed upon the insurer and was intended to protect the public, including the insured, against the activities of unauthorised insurers. This was because the statute prohibited the entry into and carrying out of contracts of insurance, rather than just entering into such contracts, although it is submitted that the distinction is not easy to follow.[194] All will not be entirely lost in such a situation, however, as the innocent party should be able to recover moneys that it has paid in purported pursuance of the contract (such as premiums under an insurance policy) under a restitutionary remedy based upon a mistake of fact by the innocent party (that the other party was duly authorised)[195] or of law[196] or that the innocent party was not the person primarily responsible for the mistake.[197]

---

[191] As eg in *Hughes v Asset Managers plc* [1995] 3 All ER 669. See also *Mistry Amar Singh v Kulubya* [1964] AC 142, in which the plaintiff was held by the Privy Council, relying upon *Browning v Morris* (1778) 2 Cowp 790 and *Kearley v Thomson* (1890) 24 QBD 742, to be a member of the class for whose benefit the statute had been introduced, so that his claim should not be defeated by the statute. In *Kasumu v Baba-Egbe* [1956] AC 539, a lender under an unlawful money lending transaction was precluded from enforcing its security but the borrower was held by the Privy Council to be entitled to plead the illegality of the transaction and recover his security without being obliged to repay the moneys that had been borrowed, as the borrower was a member of a class that the statute was intended to protect.

[192] *Re Mahmoud and Ispahani* [1921] 2 KB 716 and *Chai Sau Yin v Liew Kwee Sam* [1962] AC 304.

[193] [1988] QB 216, 267–77.

[194] The judgment on this point was obiter, as it was held that the insurer was authorised. However, the statement of principle enunciated by Kerr LJ was followed in *Re Cavalier Insurance Co Ltd* [1989] 2 Lloyd's Rep 430, *Overseas Union Insurance Ltd v Incorporated General Insurance Ltd* [1992] 1 Lloyd's Rep 439, and *DR Insurance Co v Seguros America Banamex* [1993] 1 Lloyd's Rep 120. The statutory provision (subsequently contained in s 2 of the Insurance Companies Act 1982) was replaced by s 132 of the Financial Services Act 1986, which gave the insured the right to enforce the policy against an unauthorised insurer. The Insurance Companies Act 1982 and the Financial Services Act 1986 were, in turn, repealed by art 3 of the Financial Services and Markets Act 2000 (Consequential Amendments and Repeals) Order 2001, SI 2001/3649. The matter is now governed by ss 26–28 of the Financial Services and Markets Act 2000.

[195] *Oom v Bruce* (1810) 12 East 225.

[196] In reliance upon the decision of the House of Lords in *Kleinwort Benson Ltd v Lincoln City Council* [1999] 2 AC 349.

[197] *Re Cavalier Insurance Co Ltd* [1989] 2 Lloyd's Rep 430.

1.3.2 Unlawfulness at common law

1.72 It is now convenient to consider the position at common law as to the effect of unlawfulness on a transaction.[198] This covers transactions which involve (in their formation, their performance, or in the use to which their subject matter will be put) the commission of a crime or, as discussed earlier, a quasi-criminal act which engages the public interest in the same way as a crime.[199] A related matter that will also be discussed concerns the enforceability of transactions that, taken in isolation, could be valid and enforceable but which are linked to or tainted by some other unlawful transaction.

1.73 With respect to the intended purpose or manner of performance of the immediate transaction between the parties, traditionally if both parties from the outset were fully aware and complicit in the facts giving rise to the illegality,[200] albeit ignorant of the legal consequences, the transaction would be unenforceable by either of them against the other.[201] However, where one party in entering into the transaction relied upon a representation or undertaking by the other that the transaction was lawful or that the other would obtain the necessary permissions so that the transaction could be carried out lawfully, the first of those parties might have a claim which it could assert against the other in deceit, or for fraudulent misrepresentation,[202] or for a breach of a collateral contract, or in negligent misrepresentation.[203] Where one of the parties (the 'innocent party') was unaware of the facts which made the transaction unlawful, or if the innocent party was unaware of the other party's intention to perform it in an unlawful manner, in a situation where the transaction could otherwise have been entered into and performed lawfully, the innocent party would be entitled to enforce the transaction

---

[198] To some extent, the analysis on this issue will overlap with that set out earlier concerning the effect of statutory illegality, as a contract which involves a breach of a statute could be seen as a contract to commit a crime and as being against public policy. There may also be an overlap, on the facts of a particular case, between this area and those concerning the tort of conspiracy to commit a crime or to injure a third party (see *Belmont Finance Corp v Williams Furniture Ltd (No 2)* [1980] 1 All ER 383), claims for dishonest assistance in a breach of trust (see *Agip (Africa) Ltd v Jackson* [1990] 1 Ch 265; *Royal Brunei Airlines v Tan* [1995] 2 AC 378; *Twinsectra Ltd v Yardley* [2002] UKHL 12, [2002] 2 AC 164; *Barlow Clowes International Ltd v Eurotrust International Ltd* [2005] UKPC 37, [2006] 1 WLR 1476; and *Abou-Rahmah v Abacha* [2006] EWCA Civ 1492, [2007] 1 Lloyd's Rep 115), and claims for knowing receipt of trust property (see *Agip (Africa) Ltd v Jackson* [1990] 1 Ch 265; *El Ajou v Dollar Land Holdings plc* [1994] 2 All ER 685; and *Heinl v Jyske Bank (Gibraltar) Ltd* [1999] Lloyd's Rep 511).

[199] *Les Laboratoires Servier v Apotex Inc* [2014] UKSC 55.

[200] For instance, because the very purpose of the contract binds them into carrying out an unlawful activity.

[201] *JM Allan (Merchandising) Ltd v Cloke* [1963] 2 QB 340; *Ashmore Benson Pease & Co Ltd v Dawson Ltd* [1973] 1 WLR 828.

[202] *Shelley v Paddock* [1980] QB 348; *Saunders v Edwards* [1987] 1 WLR 1116. Such a claim was refused in *Parkinson v College of Ambulance Ltd and Harrison* [1925] 2 KB 1 because of the claimant's own turpitude.

[203] *Strongman (1945) Ltd v Sincock* [1955] 2 QB 525.

with respect to rights that had accrued in its favour up to the time the unlawfulness was discovered,[204] but the party which intended to enter into the transaction for a purpose which was unlawful or which intended from the outset to perform it in a manner which was unlawful would be unable to enforce the transaction.[205] It might also be the case that a party which enters into a transaction whose purpose is lawful and with an intention to perform lawfully, but which breaches the law in performing the transaction, might still be entitled to enforce it, at least where the unlawful performance was merely incidental to the main purpose and intent of the transaction.[206]

The question then arose as to the extent or degree to which a party's awareness of   **1.74** the other party's intended unlawful behaviour (in entering into the transaction, in its manner of performance, in the intended use of the subject matter of the transaction, or in its connection with a related transaction that is tainted by illegality) would be taken to amount to a sufficient knowledge of that unlawfulness, so as to prevent the first of those parties from being able to rely upon and enforce the transaction. Where, on the facts, the essence of the transaction was to engage in an unlawful activity or there is an obvious shared intention to engage in such an activity,[207] the parties would be equally complicit and neither would be able to enforce the transaction. In one early case it was held that mere knowledge on its own would amount to a sufficient participation in the other party's unlawful activities so as to deny the right to enforce the contract,[208] but in another case (which was decided a few months later) the court came to the opposite conclusion.[209] The approach that developed over time had been to see the issue as a matter of the degree of a party's involvement or 'participation' in the unlawfulness, rather than judging it in absolute terms.[210] The question was whether the parties had a common design or a shared intention so that they each participated in the unlawfulness. However, it has not always been easy to draw the line, and the effect of the relevant unlawfulness has depended upon the facts of the particular case.

If a party actively participated and assisted in the other party's scheme, that   **1.75** would mean that it cannot enforce the transaction.[211] Similarly, if a party to what might be a lawful transaction knows of, or deliberately shuts its eyes to, the

---

204 *Clay v Yates* (1856) 1 H&N 73.
205 *Archbolds (Freightage) Ltd v Spanglett Ltd* [1961] 1 QB 374.
206 *Wetherell v Jones* (1832) 3 B&Ad 221; *St John Shipping Corp v Joseph Rank Ltd* [1957] 1 QB 267; *Coral Leisure Group Ltd v Barnett* [1981] ICR 503.
207 As there was in *JM Allan (Merchandising) Ltd v Cloke* [1963] 2 QB 340 and *Ashmore Benson Pease & Co Ltd v Dawson Ltd* [1973] 1 WLR 828.
208 *Langton v Hughes* (1813) 1 M&S 593.
209 *Hodgson v Temple* (1813) 5 Taunt 181.
210 See the review of this subject by Toulson LJ in *Anglo Petroleum Ltd v TFB (Mortgages) Ltd* [2007] EWCA Civ 456 [70]–[83].
211 *Biggs v Lawrence* (1789) 3 TR 454 and *Weymell v Reed* (1794) 5 TR 599, which were cases where goods were sold in a form made ready for smuggling by the other party.

unlawful purpose for which the other party had entered into the transaction or of the unlawful purpose for which that party intends to use the subject matter of the transaction, the first party would be unable to enforce the transaction.[212] On the other hand, if a party to what could be a lawful transaction innocently assisted the other party in pursuing some unlawful purpose but without realising the unlawful intention of the other party, the first party should be entitled to enforce the transaction.[213] A further difficult question arose as to whether the extent to which a party to a claim needed to rely on an illegal act was relevant in establishing whether the other party had a defence based on illegality. In *Hounga v Allen* the court suggested that the illegality defence rested on public policy and depended on the particular context.[214] But other decisions seemed to prefer a rule-based approach, with a strict test of whether or not the party to the claim needed to rely on the illegal act.[215]

1.76 These cases led to an increasingly clear division between members of the judiciary as to the correct approach in this area.[216] Whilst some judges favoured the application of rigid rules, others preferred a more flexible approach which took account of what Andrew Burrows has called 'a range of factors'.[217] In *Chandrakant Patel v Salman Mirza*, a majority decision of a nine-strong Supreme Court resolved the issue in favour of a public policy approach.[218] Lord Toulson (with whom Lady Hale and Lords Kerr, Hodge, and Wilson agreed) concluded that:

> [The effect of illegality] is not a matter which can be determined mechanistically. So how is the court to determine the matter if not by some mechanistic process? In answer to that question, I would say that one cannot judge whether allowing a claim which is in some way tainted by illegality would be contrary to the public interest, because it would be harmful to the integrity of the legal system, without a) considering the underlying purpose of the prohibition which has been transgressed,

---

[212] *Pearce v Brooks* (1866) LR 1 Exch 213 (the case concerned the sale of an 'ornamental' brougham to a known prostitute, who plied her trade in it. The seller was denied its claim for the price of the goods.) By contrast, in *Appleton v Campbell* (1826) 2 C&P 347 a contract to let a room to a prostitute who practised her occupation elsewhere was held to be valid. Similarly, in *Lloyd v Johnson* (1798) 1 B&P 340 a washerwoman who washed the clothes of a prostitute at normal rates was entitled to recover payment. Lord Denning MR suggested in *JM Allan (Merchandising) Ltd v Cloke* [1963] 2 QB 340, 348, that tradesmen who supplied ordinary goods at normal commercial rates to such a person would not usually be taken to be assisting them in an unlawful or immoral purpose. On the other hand, if the price was inflated, that would be evidence of participation in the unlawful or immoral purpose. His Lordship also distinguished *Waugh v Morris* (1873) LR 8 QB 202 on the grounds that in *Waugh v Morris* there was no common design nor any participation in an unlawful activity.
[213] *Fielding & Platt Ltd v Najjar* [1969] 1 WLR 357; *Anglo Petroleum Ltd v TFB (Mortgages) Ltd* [2007] EWCA Civ 456.
[214] *Hounga v Allen* [2014] WLR 2889.
[215] *Tinsley v Milligan* [1994] AC 340 and Lord Sumption's obiter remarks in *Les Laboratoires Servier v Apotex* [2014] 3 WLR 1257.
[216] See also *Jetivia SA v Bilta (UK) Limited (in liquidation)* [2015] UKSC 23 [15].
[217] Andrew Burrows, *A Restatement of the English Law of Contract* (OUP 2016) 229.
[218] *Chandrakant Patel v Salman Mirza* [2016] UKSC 42.

b) considering conversely any other relevant public policies which may be rendered ineffective or less effective by denial of the claim, and c) keeping in mind the possibility of overkill unless the law is applied with a due sense of proportionality.[219]

Thus the majority endorsed the range of factors approach.[220] The minority, Lord **1.77** Sumption (with whom Lord Clarke and Lord Mance agreed), considered that the range of factors test was 'far too vague and potentially far too wide to serve as the basis on which a person may be denied his legal rights'.[221]

A transaction which may appear to be valid in itself may, nonetheless, be unen- **1.78** forceable if it is tainted by an illegality or impropriety that affects a connected transaction.[222] Before the illegality or impropriety will affect the transaction, there must be a relevance in the connection between it and the other transaction that is sufficiently substantial to taint it,[223] rather than a more distant connection which is merely collateral or peripheral to the transaction and the claim that is made to enforce it.[224]

1.3.3 Passing of title under an unlawful transaction

Notwithstanding the unlawfulness of a transaction which affects a party to it, **1.79** title[225] in an asset may pass under the transaction and be recognised in favour of such a party where the tainted obligation to effect the conveyance has been fulfilled so that it is no longer executory and in need of assistance by the court.[226] This will not be the case, however, if the illegality arises under a statute and the statute (either expressly or by implication) prevents the passing of title under the impugned transaction.[227] It has held that the grant of a limited interest in property under an unlawful transaction that affects the grantor will not prevent the

---

[219] At [110].
[220] At [113].
[221] At [265].
[222] *Fisher v Bridges* (1854) 3 El & Bl 643 (a separate deed of covenant was held to be unenforceable as it constituted an undertaking by a purchaser to pay part of the purchase price of land that remained outstanding under an earlier illegal contract of sale). See also *Spector v Ageda* [1973] Ch 30 (the borrower's obligation to repay a loan was held to be unenforceable as the loan had been advanced to provide the funds to pay off an earlier unlawful loan that had been made to the borrower by a third party) and *Mansouri v Singh* [1986] 1 WLR 1393 (which discussed the enforceability of a cheque or other negotiable instrument given in pursuance of a transaction which is made unenforceable by the Bretton Woods Agreement).
[223] *Tinsley v Milligan* [1994] 1 AC 340 and *Standard Chartered Bank v Pakistan National Shipping Corp* [2000] 1 Lloyd's Rep 218.
[224] *Sweetman v Nathan* [2003] EWCA Civ 115, [2004] PNLR 89; *Hewison v Meridian Shipping Services Pte Ltd* [2002] EWCA Civ 1821; *Donegal International Ltd v Republic of Zambia* [2007] EWHC 197 (Comm).
[225] Including equitable title: *Tinsley v Milligan* [1994] 1 AC 340.
[226] *Singh v Ali* [1960] AC 167; *Belvoir Finance Co Ltd v Stapleton* [1971] 1 QB 210.
[227] In *Mistry Amar Singh v Kulubya* [1964] AC 142 the Privy Council held that a leasehold interest in land could not have been created in contravention of the relevant statute.

recovery of the property by the grantor upon the determination of that interest.[228] It has also been held in the case of statutory illegality that the grantor of a limited interest in property (for instance, a grant by way of security or by way of a tenancy) may recover the full ownership of the property if it was in a class of persons that the statute was intended to protect.[229]

1.3.4 Restitutionary claims

1.80 A party to a transaction that is unenforceable because of illegality may also have a restitutionary claim to recover benefits it has conferred on the other party in pursuance of the transaction, such as for money it has paid. The claim may be based upon a mistake of fact[230] or of law[231] giving rise to the illegality or, more generally, that the claimant was misled by the other party in entering into the transaction,[232] was compelled by the duress of the other party in entering into it[233] or was not the person primarily responsible for the mistake.[234] However, if the claimant was the instigator of the illegality or was otherwise at fault then it will not be permitted to recover the benefits it has conferred under the transaction, at least in relation to restitutionary claims based on a total failure of consideration.[235] The court may award simple interest on the amount of a restitutionary award.[236]

1.3.5 Pleadings and evidence concerning illegality

1.81 The approach that the courts should take in considering pleadings or evidence which concern illegality was addressed in *North Western Salt Co Ltd v Electrolytic Alkali Co*,[237] *Edler v Auerbach*,[238] and *Snell v Unity Finance Co Ltd*.[239] They were

---

[228] *Bowmakers Ltd v Barnet Instruments Ltd* [1945] KB 65; *Mistry Amar Singh v Kulubya* [1964] AC 142, although note the overruling of the reliance test in *Chandrakant Patel v Salman Mirza* [2016] UKSC 42.

[229] *Kasumu v Baba-Egbe* [1956] AC 539; *Mistry Amar Singh v Kulubya* [1964] AC 142.

[230] *Oom v Bruce* (1810) 12 East 225.

[231] *Kleinwort Benson Ltd v Lincoln City Council* [1999] 2 AC 349.

[232] *Hughes v Liverpool Victoria Friendly Society* [1916] 2 KB 482.

[233] *Smith v Cuff* (1817) 6 M&S 160; *Davies v London and Provincial Marine Insurance Co* (1878) 8 ChD 469.

[234] *Kiriri Cotton Co Ltd v Dewani* [1960] AC 192; *Re Cavalier Insurance Co Ltd* [1989] 2 Lloyd's Rep 430.

[235] *Parkinson v College of Ambulance Ltd and Harrison* [1925] 2 KB 1; *Berg v Sadler and Moore* [1937] 2 KB 158. Contrast the position in those cases with *Mohamed v Alaga & Co* [2000] 1 WLR 1815, in which the Court of Appeal allowed a *quantum meruit* claim for services provided under an unlawful contract because the claimant was less blameworthy than the defendants, who were in a much better position to realise the unlawfulness of the transaction and who had, nonetheless, knowingly entered into the contract in disregard of the unlawfulness.

[236] *Prudential Assurance Co Ltd v Revenue and Customs Commissioners* [2018] UKSC 39.

[237] [1914] AC 461.

[238] [1950] 1 KB 359.

[239] [1964] 2 QB 203.

summarised as a set of propositions by Lord Mance in giving the advice of the Privy Council in *Morrell v Workers Savings & Loan Bank*[240] as follows:

> First, where a contract is ex facie illegal, the court will not enforce it, whether the illegality is pleaded or not; secondly, where the contract is not ex facie illegal, evidence of surrounding circumstances tending to show that it has an illegal object should not be admitted unless the circumstances are pleaded; thirdly, where unpleaded facts, which taken by themselves show an illegal object, have been revealed in evidence (because, perhaps, no objection was raised or because they were adduced for some other purpose), the court should not act on them unless it is satisfied that the whole of the surrounding circumstances are before it; but, fourthly, where the court is satisfied that all the relevant facts are before it and it can see clearly from them that the contract had an illegal object, it may not enforce the contract, whether the facts were pleaded or not.

1.4 Frustration of Contract and *Force Majeure* Clauses

English law does not recognise the civil law concept of *force majeure*, by which a party's obligations may be adjusted or terminated as a matter of law (and without the need to make express provision in the contract) in consequence of an adverse change in circumstances which makes it uneconomic or more difficult or onerous to perform the contract. The precise parameters of the doctrine of *force majeure* will depend upon the laws of the particular civil law jurisdiction which governs the contract. **1.82**

By contrast, the English law doctrine of frustration of contract is much stricter in its application and narrower in the circumstances in which it will operate. Under it, the whole contract is automatically terminated and each of the parties to it is discharged from having to make further performance. A contract will be frustrated if the relevant event is external (ie outside the control of one of the parties) and it is so fundamental as to affect the very basis of the contract, provided that the contract did not provide for one of the parties to bear the consequences thereof and the possibility of the relevant event was not foreseen by the parties. Unless those requirements are met, the contract will continue under English law despite the fact that its performance might have become more burdensome to one or other of the contracting parties.[241] If the contract is frustrated then a restitutionary remedy **1.83**

---

[240] [2007] UKPC 3 [35].

[241] The foregoing statement as to frustration is a summary of a large body of case law, including *Wynn v Shropshire Union Railways and Canal Co* (1850) 5 Exch 420 (supervening illegality, see also section 1.3); *Taylor v Caldwell* (1863) 3 B&S 826 (destruction of the subject matter of the contract); *Krell v Henry* [1903] 2 KB 740 (change in the fundamental basis of the contract); *Bank Line Ltd v Arthur Capel & Co* [1919] AC 433 (government requisition of the subject matter of the contract); *Hirji Mulji v Cheong Yue SS Co* [1926] AC 497 (the self-executing effect of frustration); *Davis Contractors Ltd v Fareham UDC* [1956] AC 696 (the requisite nature of a fundamental change in the basis of the contract, as opposed to a contract where performance has been delayed or become more onerous); *Peter Cassidy Steel Co Ltd v Osuustukkukauppa* [1957] 1 Lloyd's Rep 25 (a party

may lie to enable a party to recover moneys paid before it was frustrated, and to obtain compensation for benefits conferred under the contract, pursuant to the Law Reform (Frustrated Contracts) Act 1943.[242]

1.84 Nonetheless, English law does permit the parties in their contract to provide for the consequences of events which the contract stipulates will have the effect of modifying or discharging their responsibilities. Such clauses are often referred to, if somewhat confusingly, as '*force majeure* clauses'. They may comprehend matters that might fall within the civil law concept of *force majeure* or the more fundamental matters required before the common law doctrine of frustration could be invoked. Typically, such a clause will provide a list of possible events and then define the consequences thereof, which may include some or all of a temporary suspension of a party's obligations, an adjustment in the contract price, an extension of time to perform, restitution of moneys paid and compensation for work or services already performed, or a complete discharge from the obligation to make further performance of the contract. The list of events may include matters such as labour strikes and similar industrial action, external blockades and embargoes, war, terrorist attacks, civil commotion, and acts of God.[243] Another typical event is political risk and other governmental intervention which prevents or impedes performance.

1.85 Such provisions are often to be found in project, construction, development, and supply contracts, which contracts themselves will sometimes provide the basis for a financing. In such a case, it is essential for the financier to understand the circumstances in which the clause may operate in the underlying commercial contract and its consequences, both in relation to that contract and the financing arrangements.

1.86 In *Mamidoil-Jetoil Greek Petroleum Company SA v Okta Crude Oil Refinery AD*[244] Aikens J made a number of observations concerning the operation of such a clause,

---

could not plead frustration where it had assumed responsibility under the contract for the risk of the occurrence of the relevant events, in that case for obtaining an export licence); *Tsakiroglou & Co Ltd v Noblee Thorl GmbH* [1962] AC 93 (contract made more onerous and performance delayed but contract not frustrated); *National Carriers Ltd v Panalpina (Northern) Ltd* [1981] AC 675 (similar in its analysis to the *Davis Contractors* case); *J Lauritzen AS v Wijsmuller BV, The Super Servant Two* [1990] 1 Lloyd's Rep 1 (a party could not plead frustration where it was 'self-induced' or the party could have prevented the event from occurring).

[242] The Act was reviewed by Goff J in *BP Exploration Co (Libya) Ltd v Hunt* [1979] 1 WLR 783 (upheld at [1983] 2 AC 352). Recovery was possible at common law if there had been a total failure of consideration but not if there had only been a partial failure: *Fibrosa Spolka Akcyjna v Fairbairn Lawson Combe Barbour Ltd* [1943] AC 32.

[243] The original author of this chapter always said that he felt that if one believes in a benevolent God (whichever version of the deity that might be) then He receives a rather bad press in this regard. Surely, it would be more correct to refer to 'acts of the Devil'. In polytheistic systems, the expression might be 'acts of the gods'.

[244] [2002] EWHC 2210 (Comm), [2003] 1 Lloyd's Rep 1 (upheld on appeal at [2003] EWCA Civ 1031, [2003] 2 Lloyd's Rep 635).

as follows. In general and unless they provide otherwise, *force majeure* clauses are concerned to excuse performance of contracts where the relevant events are outside the control of the party claiming to be excused and their effect could not have been avoided or mitigated by reasonable steps taken by that party.[245] The evidential burden was upon the party relying upon the clause to establish that the facts fell within the terms of the clause. The alleged *force majeure* event had to be the effective cause of the failure to perform, rather than the real cause for such failure arising for some other reason.

Although *force majeure* clauses do not appear under that label in loan agreements, **1.87** it is arguable that they do appear in another guise. MAC or 'material adverse change' clauses, in so far as they suspend or release parties from obligations, may be considered to be a sub-species of *force majeure* clauses and consequently should be interpreted and applied in an analogous way.[246]

1.5 Enforcement and Recovery upon Breach of Contract

This matter concerns the remedies that are available to a party to a contract (the **1.88** 'innocent party') where the other party (the 'defendant') has breached the contract, always assuming that the contract is (and remains) valid and enforceable.[247] Needless to say, it is a complex area of law upon which there is a vast amount of case law. All that can be provided here is a summary. In particular cases, questions of waiver, estoppel, and acquiescence may arise as a defence to an innocent party's claim, which are beyond the scope of this book. The reader is referred to the standard texts on contract law for a fuller analysis. The discussion that follows will deal with breaches of contract in general, before examining the separate position concerning liquidated claims in debt.

1.5.1 The general position

Breaches of contract, and their consequences, come in all shapes and sizes and **1.89** this is recognised by English law. Some breaches are of such significance that they obviously go to the heart or root of the contract. Other breaches are comparatively minor. In between, there are breaches which initially may be regarded as minor but which, by continuance or repetition, build up to such a stage that they

---

[245] See *Channel Island Ferries Ltd v Sealink UK Ltd* [1988] 1 Lloyd's Rep 323.

[246] This argument is further developed in Rafal Zakrzewski, 'When is a Material Adverse Change Clause a Force Majeure Clause?' (2012) 9 Journal of International Banking and Financial Law 547. For detailed discussion of MAC clauses see para 2.195ff.

[247] The ambiguous legal concept of a 'remedy' is examined in detail in the editor's doctoral thesis published as Rafal Zakrzewski, *Remedies Reclassified* (OUP 2005). That book also considers English law remedies such as awards of agreed sums, awards of damages, injunctions and specific performance, and the methods for their enforcement.

become significant as indicating an unwillingness on the part of the defendant to perform the contract. In addition, some terms of the contract (called 'conditions', as opposed to the other terms of the contract, which are called 'warranties') may be considered as being of such significance that a breach of such a term will automatically be considered as going to the heart of the contract.[248] On the other hand, a term of the contract may initially appear to be of neutral significance but a breach of it may, in fact, be of considerable significance. The parties may expressly provide that a particular term should be regarded as a condition as, for instance, by declaring that the term is of the essence of the contract,[249] but it may be necessary to show that the parties really meant to ascribe such a status to the term, especially where it would lead to an unreasonable result.[250] Otherwise, the status of the term must be determined by the language that the parties have used in the contract and the surrounding circumstances. [251]

1.90   The consequence of these distinctions goes to the remedial rights that will be available to an innocent party upon the occurrence of a breach of contract. A breach of contract by the defendant which goes to the heart of the contract, or which shows that the defendant no longer wishes to be bound by the contract, is called a repudiatory breach. The innocent party may treat such a breach as entitling it to terminate the contract and sue for damages for general loss of its bargain. In addition, if it becomes apparent to the innocent party before the time for performance by the defendant of an essential obligation that the defendant will be unable or unwilling to perform the obligation, the innocent party may anticipate the breach (thus called an 'anticipatory breach'), terminate the contract, and sue for damages.[252] A termination of the contract for (or in anticipation of) a repudiatory breach is only prospective; it does not effect a rescission of the contract *ab initio*.[253] The consequences of termination in such circumstances are discussed elsewhere in this book.[254]

---

[248] Terms requiring something to be done by a particular date are usually not considered to be conditions, that is, time is not usually 'of the essence'. However, it can be made of the essence where the innocent party gives notice requiring the relevant obligation to be performed within a reasonable time: *Multi Veste 226 BV v NI Summer Row Unitholder BV* [2011] EWHC 2026 (Ch). Cf *Dalkia Utilities Services plc v Celtech International Ltd* [2006] 1 Lloyd's Rep 599.

[249] *Lombard North Central plc v Butterworth* [1987] QB 527. But a mere right that is expressly given to an innocent party in a contract to terminate the contract for a breach does not mean that the provision that has been breached should always be treated as a condition of the contract or that the breach is so serious as otherwise to amount to a repudiatory breach of the contract: see *Financings Ltd v Baldock* [1963] QB 104 and *Capital Finance Co Ltd v Donati* (1977) 121 SJ 270.

[250] See Lord Reid in *L Schuler AG v Wickman Machine Tool Sales Ltd* [1974] AC 235, 251–52.

[251] *BNP Paribas v Wockhardt EU Operations (Swiss) AG* [2009] EWHC 3116 (Comm).

[252] This may be a dangerous strategy because if an incorrect assessment of the situation was made and the other party was, in fact, ready and willing to perform, then the party which wrongly purported to terminate will, by doing so, have committed a repudiatory breach of the contract and the tables will be turned upon it.

[253] For the effect of a termination in these circumstances, see Lord Diplock in *Moschi v Lep Air Services Ltd* [1973] AC 331, 350.

[254] See section 2.8.2.

As an alternative to terminating the contract in consequence of a repudiatory **1.91** breach, the innocent party may elect to continue with the contract by holding the defendant to it.[255] However, where a repudiatory breach has occurred (or is anticipated), the innocent party may find its hands tied if it is apparent that the defendant is no longer able or otherwise completely unwilling to perform the contract and may have no option but to accept the repudiation and terminate the contract. In this case, where the breach is an anticipatory breach, the innocent party's duty to mitigate will arise from the date on which it opts to terminate. Where there has been an actual breach the duty to mitigate arises immediately, and so the innocent party must not unreasonably delay in terminating the contract and seeking to mitigate its loss once it realises that the contract is lost, as, otherwise, it will suffer a reduction in its claim for damages arising from the breach and termination of the contract.[256] If it is reasonable for the innocent party to try and persuade the defendant to resile from its unwillingness to perform, the innocent party is entitled to defer terminating the contract and taking action to mitigate whilst so attempting to continue with the contract, until such time as it should realise that the contract is lost.[257]

In cases of a breach which do not amount to a repudiatory breach of the contract, **1.92** the innocent party will have a claim for damages for the loss that arises specifically from the breach, but it may not terminate the contract in consequence of the breach, nor will it have a claim in damages for loss of the benefit of the whole contract, as it would have been able to advance in a case where the contract had been terminated following a repudiatory breach. There is, however, a qualification to that statement. The contract may expressly provide the innocent party with a right to terminate the contract upon the occurrence of a non-repudiatory breach by the defendant. If such a breach occurs, the innocent party may terminate the contract in pursuance of its express right to do so but it will not have a claim in damages for general loss of bargain, although it will be able to claim damages that relate specifically to the breach that occurred.[258]

Generally speaking, a breach of the contract by the defendant does not entitle **1.93** the innocent party to withhold its own performance, unless the contract has been terminated in consequence of the breach.[259] However, the innocent party may be

---

[255] *Société Générale v Geys* [2012] UKSC 63.

[256] See Lord Wilberforce in *Johnson v Agnew* [1980] AC 367, 400, such question of reasonableness being relevant in assessing the time at which the buyer's duty to mitigate had arisen, as explained by Oliver J in *Radford v De Froberville* [1977] 1 WLR 1262, 1285. See also *Bear Stearns Bank plc v Forum Global Equity plc* [2007] EWHC 1576.

[257] *Bear Stearns Bank plc v Forum Global Equity plc* [2007] EWHC 1576.

[258] *Financings Ltd v Baldock* [1963] QB 104 and *Capital Finance Co Ltd v Donati* (1977) 121 SJ 270.

[259] See Lord Ackner in *Fercometal SARL v Mediterranean Shipping Co SA, The Simona* [1989] AC 788, 805. See also *DRC Distribution Ltd v Ulva Ltd* [2007] EWHC 1716 (QB).

relieved of its own obligation to perform by the express terms of the contract or by the fact that the defendant has impeded it from performing, such as where the innocent party's performance was dependent upon the prior performance by the defendant.[260]

1.94 Subject to the rules of remoteness, as referred to below, the general principle[261] governing the assessment of the quantum of damages in a claim for breach of contract is that the damages should compensate the innocent party, as the victim of the breach, for the loss it has suffered,[262] but it is up to the innocent party to prove its loss[263] and it has a duty to take reasonable steps to mitigate its loss (for instance, by finding an alternate source of performance).[264] In assessing damages, the innocent party is entitled to be placed, so far as money can do it, in the position it would have been in had the contract been performed.[265] Whilst these basic principles appear comparatively straightforward, they are subject to a number of controversies in their application and interaction in practice,[266] for example, as to the date at which damage is assessed and the consideration given to events arising after breach but before assessment of damage. No more detailed review is attempted here, and the reader is once again referred to the standard contract texts.

1.95 The recoverable loss for which damages are sought must also fall within the rules as to remoteness, classically, that the loss which is claimed must be of a type that could naturally be expected to arise or was foreseeable within the knowledge of the parties at the time of contracting.[267] The House of Lords' decision in *The*

---

[260] *Bulk Oil (Zug) AG v Sun International Ltd* [1984] 1 Lloyd's Rep 531.

[261] The House of Lords indicated in *Attorney General v Blake* [2001] 1 AC 268 that, in exceptional circumstances where normal remedies were inadequate to compensate for a breach of contract, the court may be prepared to order the defendant to account for the profits it had received or to which it was entitled. The difficulties that ensue from this are demonstrated by the subsequent decisions of the Court of Appeal in *Experience Hendrix LLC v PPX Enterprises Inc* [2003] EWCA Civ 323, [2003] 1 All ER (Comm) 830 and *World Wide Fund for Nature v World Wrestling Federation Entertainment Inc* [2007] EWCA Civ 286. In the first of those two cases, the Court of Appeal did not grant an account of profits but it did order the payment of a reasonable sum to compensate for an unauthorised breach of contract, even though no actual loss could be demonstrated. In the second case, the court refused (on a procedural issue concerning the case) to grant a remedy on those lines but acknowledged that an award could be made where it was not possible to demonstrate identifiable financial loss.

[262] See Parke B in *Robinson v Harman* (1848) 1 Exch 850, at 855 and the review conducted by Lord Scott in *Golden Strait Corp v Nippon Yusen Kubishika Kaisha* [2007] UKHL 12 [29]–[36].

[263] See Lord Nicholls in *Sempra Metals Ltd v HM Commissioners of Inland Revenue* [2007] UKHL 34 [95]–[96].

[264] The difficult question of when financial benefits brought about by mitigation must be taken into account was recently considered in *Globalia Business Travel SAU v Fulton Shipping Inc of Panama (the New Flamenco)* [2017] UKSC 43.

[265] See Lord Atkinson in *Wertheim v Chicoutimi Pulp Co* [1911] AC 301, 307.

[266] See eg Andrew Dyson and Adam Kramer, 'There is No Breach Date Rule: Mitigation, Difference in Value and Date of Assessment' (2014) 130 Law Quarterly Review 259, cf Michael G. Bridge, 'Markets and Damages in Sale of Goods Cases' (2016) 132 Law Quarterly Review 404.

[267] *Hadley v Baxendale* (1854) 9 Exch 341. The orthodox view has been that loss falling within the second limb of the rule in *Hadley v Baxendale* was 'consequential loss' for the purposes of

Achilleas appears to add a further condition: that even if the loss is forseeable it will only be recoverable if it is within the scope of an implied assumption of responsibility by the defendant in the contract.[268] This approach has now been endorsed in more than one Court of Appeal decision,[269] although its real effect may be limited to specialist markets such as shipping and banking. This matter is explored more fully in the chapter on loan facilities.[270]

Under the rules that used to apply relating to privity of contract (as described **1.96** earlier in this chapter), only a party to the contract (or its agent, trustee, or assignee) may enforce the contract, so that in general a third party could not enforce the contract for its own benefit. If the contracting party sought to enforce the contract for the benefit of a third party, the contracting party (unless it was the agent or trustee of the other person) was likely to be met by a defence that it had suffered no loss and so was only entitled to receive nominal damages. The Contracts (Rights of Third Parties) Act 1999 has overcome many of the problems associated with the privity rule, but the operation of the Act may be excluded or restricted and, in such cases, the rule will continue to be relevant.

1.5.2 Enforcement remedies

An innocent party may not be happy to be confined to a claim for damages. It **1.97** may want the contract to be performed by the defendant and so it may wish to obtain a mandatory order from the court to compel the defendant to perform its bargain.[271] Such orders are not readily available. Exceptionally, however, the court may make an equitable order requiring performance of the contract, by way of an order for specific performance or the grant of a mandatory injunction, but such a remedy is discretionary, the applicant for equitable relief must come to the court with clean hands (ie its own conduct in relation to the contract and its relationship with the defendant must be of a high standard),[272] the court will not (save in exceptional circumstances) order performance of a contract for the performance of personal services,[273] and there must be something exceptional or unique in

---

interpreting that phrase in contractual provisions: *Hotel Services Ltd v Hilton International Hotels (UK) Ltd* [2000] EWCA Civ 74. However, the courts are starting to move away from that view: *Star Polaris LLC v HHIC-PHIL Inc* [2016] EWHC 2941.

[268] *Transfield Shipping Inc v Mercator Shipping Inc (The Achilleas)* [2008] UKHL 48.
[269] *Supershield Ltd v Siemens Building Technologies FE Ltd* [2010] EWCA Civ 7; *Rubenstein v HSBC Bank plc* [2012] EWCA Civ 1184.
[270] See the discussion at para 2.69.
[271] Subject to the rules as to laches, there may be a benefit in seeking equitable relief by way of an order for specific performance, as the limitation period that applies to an ordinary claim at common law may not apply to such an equitable claim: *P&O Nedlloyd BV v Arab Metals Co, The UB Tiger* [2006] EWCA Civ 1717, [2007] 2 All ER (Comm) 401.
[272] *Fiona Trust Holding Corporation and ors v Privalov and ors* [2008] EWHC 1748 (Comm).
[273] *Johnson v Shrewsbury and Birmingham Ry Co* (1853) 3 De GM&G 358, *The Scraptrade* [1983] 2 AC 694, at 700–01, *LauritzenCool AB v Lady Navigation Inc* [2005] EWCA Civ 579, [2005] 1 WLR 3686.

the subject matter of the contract to warrant the intervention of the court in this manner, so that damages would not be an adequate remedy. Subject again to the exercise of its discretion, a court may be prepared to grant a prohibitory injunction to restrain a threatened breach or the continuance of a breach of a negative stipulation in a contract.[274]

1.5.3 Liquidated claims

1.98 The situation that has been described so far concerns contracts where the innocent party's claim for damages is an unliquidated claim where the loss has to be assessed by the court. The position is different where the innocent party as claimant sues for non-payment by the defendant of a monetary sum, a liquidated sum, that has fallen due for payment under the contract, as for instance for the repayment of a debt (including where the obligation for repayment has been accelerated in pursuance of a contractual right[275]), for the price of goods or services that have been sold or supplied,[276] or for recovery under some classes of indemnity.[277] In such a case, the claimant sues for that sum and does not have to prove its loss, is not subject to any rule as to remoteness,[278] nor (in the case of recovery of a debt) has it any obligation to mitigate its loss. However, if the claimant also sues for other damage or loss that it has suffered (for instance, for interest on the unpaid sum[279]) then it will have to meet the usual rules before it can recover that loss. Care must also be taken to distinguish between a genuine liquidated damages clause and a clause which amounts to a penalty. Whilst the former is enforceable, the latter is not and will be struck down.[280]

1.5.4 Part payment

1.99 In accordance with the rule in *Pinnel's* case,[281] part payment of a debt that has accrued due for payment will not amount to a discharge of the debtor and a promise by the debtor to pay part of the debt provides no consideration for the release of the debt; nor does either thing provide consideration for the creditor to give up

---

[274] *Lumley v Wagner* (1852) 1 De GM&G 604; *Doherty v Allman* (1878) 3 App Cas 709; *LauritzenCool AB v Lady Navigation Inc* [2005] EWCA Civ 579, [2005] 1 WLR 3686. See also the discussion of Briggs J on this point and on the point concerning the enforcement of contracts for personal services in *Akai Holdings Ltd v RSM Robson Rhodes LLP* [2007] EWHC 1641 (Ch).

[275] See section 2.18.

[276] This should, however, be distinguished from contracts, such as hire-purchase and lease contracts, where the claim relates to loss of the bargain to receive future contractual payments, as the claim in those situations will be an unliquidated claim for damages for the loss of the bargain.

[277] Rafal Zakrzewski, 'The Nature of a Claim on an Indemnity' (2006) 22 *Journal of Contract Law* 54; cf *Agarwal v ABN AMRO Bank NV* [2017] BPIR 816.

[278] *Jervis v Harris* [1996] Ch 195.

[279] See *Sempra Metals Ltd v HM Commissioners of Inland Revenue* [2007] UKHL 34. Departed from in part in *Prudential Assurance Co Ltd v Revenue and Customs Commissioners* [2018] UKSC 39.

[280] See the discussion at section 2.12.

[281] (1602) 5 Co Rep 117a.

its other remedies for non-payment or later payment, such as foregoing interest on a judgment debt. All the debtor has done is to perform or promise to perform part of an existing obligation, and that can provide no consideration in itself that can bind the creditor.[282]

However, the debtor may be able to raise promissory estoppel (discussed at para 1.102) as a defence, if it acted in reliance on the creditor's assurance that the debt had been discharged. Furthermore, there are various ways in which an agreement to compromise the debt can be made binding on the creditor. The agreement may be made by deed or the debtor may provide fresh consideration, such as by agreeing to pay early,[283] by agreeing to pay in a different currency to the currency in which the debt was originally payable, by agreeing to make payment together with the delivery of some other asset or benefit,[284] or by agreeing to forbear in the enforcement of a cross-claim. It has also been held that part payment of a debt by a third party, if accepted by the creditor, will release the debtor, and that this does not depend upon an agreement to which the debtor is a party.[285] In that regard, it is easy to see that the third party may enter into an agreement which it could enforce against the creditor, by preventing the creditor from suing the debtor, but, prior to the Contracts (Rights of Third Parties) Act 1999, it is difficult to understand how the debtor might have benefited directly from such an agreement. **1.100**

In similar vein, a debtor can enter into an enforceable agreement with its creditors, by which they all agree with the debtor to accept a compromise of their respective claims.[286] This has been extended by the provisions of the Insolvency Act 1986 concerning voluntary arrangements. In addition, under section 62 of the Bills of Exchange Act 1882, an unconditional renunciation in writing by the holder of a bill, at or after maturity of the bill, of the liability of the acceptor under the bill will amount to a discharge of the acceptor[287] and (if specified) other parties to the bill, and an earlier written renunciation by the then holder of the bill will bind the holder but not a subsequent holder in due course who took without notice. **1.101**

1.5.5 Promissory estoppel

There is also the difficult concept of promissory estoppel, whose parameters are not certain. In *Hughes v Metropolitan Ry Co*[288] it was held that it would be inequitable to allow a contracting party to enforce its strict contractual rights when **1.102**

---

[282] *Foakes v Beer* (1884) 9 App Cas 605; *D&C Builders Ltd v Rees* [1966] 2 QB 617.
[283] *Pinnel's* case (1602) 5 Co Rep 117a.
[284] ibid.
[285] *Welby v Drake* (1825) 1 C&P 557; *Cook v Lister* (1863) 13 CB (NS) 543.
[286] *Good v Cheesman* (1831) 2 B&Ad 328; *Boyd v Hind* (1857) 1 H&N 938.
[287] As against the acceptor, the renunciation can also be achieved by delivering the bill to the acceptor.
[288] (1877) 2 App Cas 439. See also *Birmingham and District Land Co v London and North Western Ry Co* (1888) 40 ChD 268 and *Ajayi v RT Briscoe (Nigeria) Ltd* [1964] 1 WLR 1326.

by its conduct it could be taken clearly and unequivocally to have agreed (albeit voluntarily) not to do so, where the other party had acted in reliance on that promise and altered its position. Generally speaking, it has been taken that the effect of this is that the rights are suspended and can be revived upon giving reasonable notice,[289] although there have been cases where, because of the passage of time, the occurrence of subsequent events, or the debtor incurring other liabilities in reliance on the promise, it has been held that it would also be impossible or inequitable to require any further performance of the original obligation.[290] It is respectfully submitted, however, that, contrary to the view expressed by Denning J in *Central London Property Trust Ltd v High Trees House Ltd*,[291] the application of the principle does not generally mean that the creditor will be taken to have given up its rights altogether and cannot sue for payment of an accrued debt after giving reasonable notice.

---

[289] *Tool Metal Manufacturing Co Ltd v Tungsten Electric Co Ltd* [1955] 1 WLR 761.

[290] See the third point mentioned by Lord Hodson in *Ajayi v RT Briscoe (Nigeria) Ltd* [1964] 1 WLR 1326, 1330 and eg *Ogilvy v Hope-Davies* [1976] 1 All ER 683 and *Maharaj v Chand* [1986] AC 898.

[291] [1947] KB 130, 134.

2

LOAN FACILITIES

2.1 Introduction

2.01 There are various types of loan facility that might be offered to a borrower, ranging from a bilateral facility between a single lender and a single borrower, to a facility offered by a single lender to a group of borrowers, and finally a syndicated facility between a group of lenders and one or more borrowers. Any of those facilities might be a committed facility, under which the lenders are obliged to advance up to a particular sum if certain conditions are met, or it might be an uncommitted facility (such as an overdraft facility) which could be revoked or terminated at any time. The facility might be a term facility, under which the moneys that have been borrowed remain outstanding until they are repaid on particular dates, and any repayments are final in the sense that what has been repaid cannot be re-borrowed under the facility. Alternatively, the facility may be a revolving facility under which a facility limit or ceiling is set with the borrower having the right from time to time to borrow and repay all or part of what has been borrowed but so that the aggregate outstanding amount at any one time may not exceed the limit. The classic example of a revolving facility is the overdraft facility, by which a bank permits its customer to make withdrawals that are debited to its current account (such as by drawing a cheque or by another payment instruction that the customer gives to its bank) and to which are credited any payments into the account that are made by the customer or collected on its behalf. A facility may be extended in one currency only, as a single currency facility, or it may be a multi-currency facility, under which the borrower is given a choice of the currencies in which it may borrow, with the possibility that borrowings may be outstanding at any one time in more than one currency and with the right to change between one currency and another during the period of the facility. For the purpose of setting the facility limit and for making other calculations, one currency will be specified as the base currency in a multi-currency facility. A senior facility is one which ranks in priority in terms of repayment over other payment obligations of the borrower in the event of insolvency.[1]

2.02 This chapter concentrates on loan facilities but there are many ways of raising finance other than simply under a loan facility. In terms of banking facilities,

---

[1] *Astor Management AG v Atalaya Mining plc* [2017] EWHC 425 (Comm) [56]–[58] turned on the meaning of a 'senior debt facility'. The court defined it as set out above. Furthermore, 'senior debt facility' was found to refer to a facility provided by one or more third party lenders and not an intra-group loan.

a customer may raise finance by an acceptance credit facility, under which the bank permits the customer to draw bills of exchange (each with a fixed period to its maturity) on the bank, which the bank will accept and then discount on the customer's behalf.[2] The proceeds that are received will be passed to the customer, which has the obligation under the facility to put the bank in funds on the maturity of a bill (to the amount of the face value of the bill), so that the bank can meet its own obligations as the acceptor of the bill. The customer will often meet the obligation by drawing another bill on the bank, with the proceeds of the discounting of the new bill being used to provide the funds for payment of the old bill. In that sense, it can be seen that this is another type of revolving facility. Other banking facilities include letters of credit and bonding and guarantee issuance facilities. A customer may be offered more than one type of facility within the framework of an overall facility arrangement, which is sometimes referred to as a multi-option facility. Leveraged acquisition finance facilities usually provide for revolving facilities (which may include letter of credit and other ancillary facilities) in addition to term facilities.

Outside the compass of banking facilities, funds can also be raised in various other **2.03** ways, such as through the capital markets, by a bond issue,[3] or by raising capital via an issue of shares or simply by borrowing from non-bank lenders. Finance can also be raised by receivables or debt purchase facilities and through equipment finance facilities, by leasing, hire-purchase, and conditional sale. Sometimes a supplier may be prepared to extend credit by giving time to pay or, at the opposite end of the scale, a purchaser may provide credit by making an advance payment before the time at which delivery of the relevant goods or services is to be made.

This chapter discusses the structure and content of loan facility agreements. **2.04** The chapter will proceed in the main by reference to bilateral loan facilities. Nonetheless, the discussion will be equally relevant to matters that are material to other types of transaction, including syndicated facilities.

2.2 Term Sheets

Before turning to the structure and content of loan facility agreements, it is rele- **2.05** vant to examine the nature and legal effect, if any, of documents that might be described as 'heads of terms', 'term sheets', or 'heads of agreement'. It is not unusual

---

[2] In the UK, if the bank is an 'eligible bank' then bills that it accepts ('eligible bills') are eligible for re-discount at the Bank of England, which means that the Bank of England will be prepared to purchase its bills, thereby giving the discount market a form of quasi-guarantee that if the bank fails before the maturity of a bill, a holder of the bill will be able to sell it to the Bank of England. There are various conditions that are imposed as to the types of bill that will qualify as eligible bills.

[3] See Sarah Paterson and Rafal Zakrzewski (eds), *McKnight, Paterson, & Zakrzewski on the Law of International Finance* (2nd edn, OUP 2017) ch 10.

in the discussions between a lender and a potential borrower that precede the granting of a facility for the lender to produce an initial document that bears one of those labels (which mean much the same thing). The lender is likely to do this once the commercial basis of the transaction has been discussed and settled. Such a document is intended to provide, in summary form, an outline of what should be covered by the proposed facility, with the intention that a more detailed and formal document will be entered into by the parties, perhaps after further negotiation of its detailed terms. The initial document will summarise matters such as the purpose, term, nature, currency and amount of the facility, the interest rate, fees, and similar financial or commercial matters, and a summary of other provisions, such as the conditions precedent to the right to borrow, the representations and warranties to be given by the borrower, the covenants that will be undertaken by the borrower, and the events of default upon the occurrence of which the lender will have the right to call in early repayment of the facility. Particular terms may be set out in great detail in schedules to the term sheet, especially where the financing is to be provided for a leveraged acquisition or a large infrastructure project.

2.06   The question may arise as to whether such a document might constitute a binding agreement in its own right.[4] If the document clearly states that it is not intended to have any binding effect then, in itself, it will not be binding, but it should be remembered that a later binding agreement, based on the provisions of the document, may be found to have come into effect if the parties have conducted themselves as if they were bound by what was contained in the document.[5] Without the expressed caveat that the document was not meant to constitute a binding agreement, the question would come down to whether the contents of the document evidenced a sufficient consensus and certainty as to the essential matters agreed between the parties as to be sufficient to constitute a binding agreement,[6] bearing in mind that the mere fact that the parties contemplated that an initial document might subsequently be superseded by a more formal and detailed agreement will not necessarily deprive the earlier document of contractual effect and the court may be prepared to fill in the gaps by implying terms.[7] However where solicitors

---

[4] In this regard, see further the discussion at ch 1.

[5] As eg in *The Rugby Group Ltd v ProForce Recruit Ltd* [2005] EWHC 70 (QB) (reversed, but not on this point, at [2006] EWCA Civ 69). See also the Supreme Court's decision in *RTS Flexible Systems Ltd v Mölkerei Alois Müller GmbH & Co KG* [2010] 1 WLR 753.

[6] In *Barbudev v Eurocom Cable Management Bulgaria Eood* [2012] 2 All ER (Comm) 963 a side letter concerning an investment was an unenforceable agreement to agree. See also *Dhanani v Crasnianski* [2011] 2 All ER (Comm) 799. In *Sax v Tchernoy* [2014] EWHC 795 (Comm) a memorandum of understanding relating to, among other things, a loan was found not to be intended to create legal relations.

[7] It is worth noting that Lloyd LJ in *Pagnan SpA v Feed Products Ltd* [1987] 2 Lloyd's Rep 601, at 619 expressly referred to 'heads of agreement' as being capable of constituting a binding contract. Cf *JAS Financial Products LLP v ICAP plc and anor* [2016] EWHC 591 (Comm) where non-binding

are acting for the parties and written agreements are to be produced and arrangements made for their execution, the normal inference will be that the parties are
not bound unless and until they sign the formal written agreements.[8] Whether
the parties intended to create legal relations will depend on 'how a reasonable man
versed in business would have understood the exchanges between the parties'.[9]
Care must be taken by lenders not to commit carelessly to making a loan. In some
circumstances, even an oral assurance can give rise to an obligation to lend prior
to formal documentation being signed by the parties.[10]

A term sheet which states that it is intended to create a binding obligation will **2.07**
give rise to a contract if all the other common law requirements for a binding
contract are met.[11] In *Maple Leaf Macro Volatility Master Fund v Rouvroy*[12] a term
sheet contained a 'footer' stating in small print that '[t]he terms included are intended to create a binding obligation on the part of the Borrowers'. The borrowers
unsuccessfully argued that in their experience of business term sheets were not intended to be legally binding, that they expected lawyers to be instructed to draw
up a legally binding document based on the term sheet, and that by signing the
term sheet they were giving a non-contractual commitment to continue negotiations. In *New Media Holding Company LLC v Kuznetsov*[13] a signed term sheet
was silent as to whether or not it was to be legally binding. It was held that it gave
rise to a binding contract as it was a document prepared by lawyers, framed in
language of legal obligation, and contained detailed notice provisions and a jurisdiction clause.

Even where such a document states that it is not intended to create a binding ob- **2.08**
ligation on the part of the lender to provide the facility, it may seek to impose certain subsidiary obligations that it states are to be binding.[14] In particular, it may

---

heads of terms had been agreed, but the parties were found not to have entered into a binding legal
agreement.

   [8] *Whitehead Mann Ltd v Cheverny Consulting Limited* [2006] EWCA Civ 1303 [45]. However, a
requirement to sign can be waived by conduct: see *Reveille Independent LLC v Anotech International
(UK) Ltd* [2016] EWCA Civ 443 and, in particular, *Novus Aviation Ltd v Alubaf Arab International
Bank BSC* [2016] EWHC 1575 (Comm) where the terms of a commitment letter issued by a bank
showed that it was intended to create legal relations and so it was held to be legally binding even
though it had not been countersigned by the borrower. It was accepted by conduct.
   [9] *Maple Leaf Macro Volatility Master Fund v Rouvroy* [2009] 1 Lloyd's Reports 47 [223] (upheld on appeal [2010] 2 All ER (Comm) 788); applied in *Dhanani v Crasnianski* [2011] 2 All ER
(Comm) 799 [80]–[81]. See also *RTS Flexible Systems Ltd v Mölkerei Alois Müller GmbH & Co KG*
[2010] 1 WLR 753 and *Proton Energy Group SA v Orlen Lietuva* [2014] 1 All ER (Comm) 972.
   [10] A statement made by a bank employee over the telephone that '[y]ou'll be pleased to know it's
all approved. Edinburgh [ie bank's head office] are going for it on both [financing projects]' gave
rise to an obligation to lend: *Carlyle v Royal Bank of Scotland plc* [2015] UKSC 13 (an appeal on
Scots law).
   [11] As to which see section 1.2.
   [12] [2009] 1 Lloyd's Reports 475, upheld on appeal [2010] 2 All ER (Comm) 788.
   [13] [2016] EWHC 360 (QB).
   [14] See eg *Charles Shaker v Vistajet Group Holding SA* [2012] 2 All ER (Comm) 1010.

state that the borrower will be obliged to meet the lender's legal costs and other expenses in entering into negotiations with the borrower, in proceeding to arrange the facility, and in preparing the facility documentation, even if a facility agreement is not concluded. It may also seek to impose a confidentiality undertaking on the lender with respect to any information that was provided by the borrower to the lender. If a lender is to enforce the first of those purported obligations, it will need to show that it provided consideration in support of the borrower's agreement and some element of certainty as to what was to be done; a nebulous statement of purpose on the part of the lender would not be sufficient. As to the confidentiality undertaking, the borrower should be able to argue that it reflects the position at general law[15] and thus it should be enforceable against the lender, at least to the extent that it reflects the position at general law.

2.3 The Overall Structure and Contents of a Loan Facility Agreement

2.09   On some occasions, the terms of the agreement may be set out in a facility letter, which is a letter from the lender addressed to the borrower, that is accepted by the borrower by its counter-signature on a copy of the letter, which it then returns to the lender. A facility letter may be used where there is only a single lender that is providing the facility (eg a term loan facility, an overdraft facility, or an acceptance credit facility), but it is very unlikely that such a document would be used for any other type of facility. Even in the case of a single lender facility a more formal form of agreement may be used.[16] Save in cases where a facility letter is used (or in the very unlikely event that the agreement will be oral or founded upon a term sheet), the agreement will be encapsulated in a formal agreement between the parties, with each party retaining a signed copy for its own purposes. There is no particular requirement as to the structure of such an agreement but, generally speaking, the pattern that is used and the order of the provisions are as follows.

---

[15] Either as a matter of the equitable principles relating to the receipt of confidential information (see *Attorney-General v Guardian Newspapers Ltd (No 2)* [1990] 1 AC 109, 281–82 (Lord Goff)) or as a part of the banker's duty of confidence to its customer (*Tournier v National Provincial and Union Bank of England* [1924] 1 KB 461) but, with respect to the latter, there may be an issue as to whether the relationship of banker and customer had come into existence sufficiently for the duty to arise.

[16] If the form used is held to be the bank's 'standard form' rather than a negotiated agreement this may potentially engage provisions of the Unfair Contract Terms Act 1977 subjecting certain provisions which protect the lender (such as exclusions of liability and set-off) to a reasonableness test. Such an argument failed on the facts in *African Export-Import Bank v Shebah Exploration & Production Company and ors* [2017] EWCA Civ 845. Note that the Unfair Contract Terms Act is now restricted to non-consumer cases, with Part 2 of the Consumer Rights Act 2015 covering unfair terms in consumer contracts.

In its overall structure and layout, the agreement will commence with a descrip- **2.10** tion of the parties, which may be followed by recitals setting out background information and that the parties have agreed to enter into the agreement so that the lender will provide the facility to the borrower, subject to the provisions contained in the agreement.[17] Those provisions (which are described further later) will then follow. After they have been set out, the agreement may contain schedules which address various mechanical and technical matters, a list of the conditions precedent, the documentary procedures for transfer of the facility and for the addition and removal of borrowers (if that is contemplated), the forms of notices and statements that might be required of the borrower and its officers during the life of the facility, and similar matters. Finally, there will be the signature page or pages, which will be signed by the representatives of the parties to evidence their acceptance of the agreement as contained in the document.[18]

The list of conditions precedent will contain references to various other docu- **2.11** ments that have to be provided or entered into as part and parcel of the overall transaction. Such documentation may include, for instance, security documents and guarantees that are to be given in support of the borrower's obligations under the facility. In that sense, the conditions precedent have a structural role, as they are the means by which that additional documentation is brought into the overall compass of the transaction. Further reference will be made to conditions precedent later in this chapter.

By way of overview and for the purposes of explanation, the provisions within the **2.12** body of the loan agreement may conveniently be described within the following broad categories, although the categories should not be seen as having any formal recognition. Many of them will be explored in further detail later in this chapter.

The first category, in terms of the usual layout of a loan agreement, contains the **2.13** interpretative provisions of the agreement, relating to the definitions of expressions that are used in the agreement and matters going to its interpretation.[19]

The next set of provisions will describe the facility and set out its purpose. In a **2.14** syndicated facility, these provisions will also set out matters relating to the contractual relationship of the syndicate members as between themselves and as between themselves and the borrower, to emphasise the several nature of their rights and obligations.[20]

---

[17] Recitals may bind the parties by giving rise to an estoppel. It may not be open to a party to argue otherwise if a fact is set out in a recital: *Prime Sight Limited v Lavarello (Official Trustee)* [2014] AC 436. Contrast *Chen v Ng* [2017] UKPC 27 [28]–[29].

[18] The signature blocks that are set out on the signature pages of a loan agreement do not necessarily prescribe the manner in which the loan agreement must be executed for it to be effectively concluded: *Maple Leaf Macro Facility Master Fund v Rouvroy* [2010] 2 All ER (Comm) 788 and *Kotak v Kotak* [2017] EWHC 1821 (Ch).

[19] See section 2.4.1.

[20] See paras 3.33 and 3.34.

2.15 The financial and operative provisions of a loan agreement include the clauses that cover the mechanics and procedures for drawing and utilisation of the facility, repayment, and interest.

2.16 Allied to those last mentioned provisions are the clauses that are designed to protect the lender's financial position and its rate of return on its financial commitment in the facility, the funds it has employed in granting the facility, and the amounts it is to receive under the facility. These 'margin protection' provisions allow the lender to make relevant assumptions for the purpose of making its decision to extend credit to the borrower at the particular price set out in the facility documentation and to quantify the risk that it will be assuming under the loan.

2.17 The monitoring and minding provisions cover the representations and warranties that are given by the borrower to the lender to induce it to enter into and maintain the facility, as well as the covenants and undertakings by which the borrower agrees to the things it will do and those it will not do, with respect to itself, its business, assets, and affairs, during the life of the facility.

2.18 The enforcement provisions cover, principally, the events of default and the circumstances in which the lender can accelerate the borrower's obligation for repayment. These protect the lender if the assumptions that it made on the basis of the borrower's representations, warranties, and undertakings turn out to be false. In such a case, it can demand early repayment or threaten to do so if the terms of the loan agreement are not amended appropriately.

2.19 If the facility is guaranteed then the guarantee may be contained within the loan agreement (in which case the guarantor will have to be a party to the agreement) or it may be contained in a separate document.[21]

2.20 Transfer provisions may occasionally be found in a straightforward bilateral facility, but they are much more common in syndicated facilities.[22] Both a bilateral facility and a syndicated facility may contain provisions that deal with the addition and subtraction of borrowers.

2.21 The so-called 'boilerplate' provisions deal with matters such as the giving of notices, the effect of waivers, the effect on the remainder of the agreement if one of its provisions is found to be unenforceable, the intention not to have a partnership, and so on. They are given that name because they appear in most types of formal agreements and cover fairly standard matters which might otherwise burst forth and cause a difficulty, particularly to the lender.

---

[21] Guarantees are considered in detail in See Sarah Paterson and Rafal Zakrzewski (eds), *McKnight, Paterson, & Zakrzewski on the Law of International Finance* (2nd edn, OUP 2017) ch 16.
[22] See ch 4.

Finally, the law and jurisdiction clauses provide for the choice of the law which is **2.22** to govern the agreement, and usually any non-contractual obligations arising out of or in connection with it, and the courts (or arbitral tribunal) which may hear disputes that arise in connection with the agreement.

2.4 The Interpretative Provisions

These provisions relate to the definitions of terms that are used in the agreement **2.23** and to matters going to its interpretation. There is a certain correlation between the matters of interpretation and construction that are dealt with in these provisions and some of the boilerplate provisions that are contained later in the agreement.

2.4.1 Definitions

The definitions clause contains those expressions which are used frequently in **2.24** the remainder of the agreement. They tend to have a technical meaning that is ascribed in view of the purpose and commercial context of the facility and its mechanics of operation. Using a single defined word or phrase avoids the necessity of setting out the whole meaning each time it is needed in the remainder of the agreement.[23] By way of example, an expression that is frequently used in a loan facility agreement is 'Benchmark Rate' (or formerly 'Libor', which is an abbreviation of the phrase 'London interbank offered rate'). There is no single or universal benchmark rate as such, so the means of ascertaining the rate for the purposes of the facility will be set out more fully in the definition of that expression as contained in the definitions clause. Sometimes the definitions can be extremely technical and laborious, and care needs to be taken in ensuring that the meaning is properly understood. There is an unfortunate practice that sometimes occurs in a document, by which one or more of the definitions goes further than simply defining a technical meaning, so that it becomes of dispositive effect. This should be avoided, as the substance of what is agreed should be dealt with in the main body of the agreement and not in the definitions clause.

2.4.2 Interpretation

The clause concerning interpretation deals with words and phrases that are used in **2.25** general speech and which are given a meaning for the purposes of the agreement, so as to avoid possible uncertainty or confusion. The clause also gives a guide to matters going to the construction and interpretation of the agreement. In relation

---

[23] But where such a defined term is used inconsistently throughout the agreement the court may give it an alternative meaning that makes commercial common sense: *Europa Plus Sca SIF v Anthracite Investments (Ireland) plc* [2016] EWHC 437 (Comm).

to fixing upon a meaning for an expression, the clause may adopt one of several possible meanings, it may choose a meaning that is set out in legislation, or it may expand upon a more restricted meaning than that which is used generally.

2.26 An example of the first type of usage concerns the concept of a month, which is usually given a precise meaning when used in a facility agreement. An example of the second of those usages would be the meanings ascribed to the words 'subsidiary', 'holding company', 'subsidiary undertaking', and 'parent undertaking', each of which is given a specific meaning in the Companies Act 2006. Those meanings are commonly adopted by facility agreements. An example of the latter usage would be the meaning given to the word 'person' which is usually defined in a facility agreement to mean not just a natural person but also a legal or other incorporated entity, a partnership and other collection of persons, or entities and states and administrative bodies. Another example will be the word 'bank', 'lender', or 'party' which will be defined to include the bank's, lender's, or party's successors and permitted assigns.[24]

2.27 For the purpose of construing the agreement, the interpretation clause should state that clause headings that are used in the text of the document, and the index to the document, are not to be taken into account in determining the meaning of any of the provisions in the agreement.

2.5 The Description and Purpose of the Facility

2.28 The provisions in this section of the agreement provide an overall description of the facility and set out the purpose for which it is to be provided. The description will include the type and the amount or the limit of the facility. In a syndicated facility, these provisions will also set out matters relating to the contractual relationship of the syndicate members as between themselves and as between themselves and the borrower, to emphasise the several nature of their rights and obligations.[25]

2.29 In most cases, the purpose of the facility is likely to be described in general terms, such as for the provision of working capital, or for the general corporate purposes of the borrower. Sometimes the purpose may be more specific. If the purpose is described with sufficient particularity and, following disbursement but prior to their use for the agreed purpose, the funds remain identifiable, the lender may be able to argue (within the applicable confines of English law) that, pending their use for the relevant purpose, the lender has the benefit of a resulting trust over the funds so that if they are not so used the lender has a proprietary claim for their return. This argument would be based upon the decision of the House of Lords

---

[24] For the practical significance of this extension of meaning, see para [2.135]ff.
[25] See further paras 3.33 and 3.34.

in *Barclays Bank Ltd v Quistclose Investments Ltd*[26] and the line of authority which has come after it.[27] However, a mere stipulation of a particular purpose for the loan is in itself insufficient to give rise to such a trust if neither the facility documentation nor the surrounding circumstances reflect any mutual intention that the funds should not be at the free disposal of the borrower.[28]

2.6 The Financial and Operative Provisions

The financial and operative provisions of a loan agreement include the clauses that **2.30** cover the mechanics and procedures for drawing and utilisation of the facility, repayment, cancellation and termination of the facility, the charging and payment of interest and fees, and the making of payments. Each of those matters will be examined. Before doing so, however, it is important to describe the sources of funding that may be available to a lender, as a great deal of the arrangements in a facility depend upon the relevant source of funds and the procedures or conventions that govern it. It is also important to understand the conventions that apply. Underlying this, of course, is the principle that lenders borrow the funds that they then lend on to their own borrowers. Thus, a lender will be a borrower in one capacity and a lender or creditor in the other capacity. The lender makes its profit by the difference between the cost to it of borrowing funds and the return that it receives in lending the funds, always assuming that the latter is higher than the former and that the lender does not suffer excessively from defaults by its own borrowers.

2.6.1 Sources of funding for bank lenders

Traditionally, the two principal sources of funds for a bank lender have been retail **2.31** deposits that are placed with it by its customers (in other words, which it borrows from its customers[29]) and wholesale funds that it borrows from other banks in the interbank market.[30] The crisis in the financial markets in the second part of 2007 served to question the viability of the interbank market. Banks showed an unwillingness to lend to other banks for periods that previously were normal for interbank lending. Where funds were provided during the crisis, the funding tended to be only for very short periods, such as overnight lending. This reflected

---

[26] [1970] AC 567.
[27] Particularly the decision of Lord Millett in *Twinsectra Ltd v Yardley* [2002] UKHL 12, [2002] 2 AC 164. See also *Cooper v PRG Powerhouse Ltd* [2008] 2 All ER (Comm) 964.
[28] *Gabriel v Little* [2013] EWCA Civ 1513. See Sarah Paterson and Rafal Zakrzewski (eds), *McKnight, Paterson, & Zakrzewski on the Law of International Finance* (2nd edn, OUP 2017) ch 14.
[29] *Foley v Hill* (1848) 2 HLC 28.
[30] Less significant sources of funding (in most cases) would be through the issuance of certificates of deposit and capital markets issues in the bond markets.

widespread fears about the financial soundness, liquidity, and solvency of banks, and the uncertainty and mistrust that resulted from those fears. This proved to be only a temporary problem. The situation was remedied through the actions of central banks and regulators. However some more long-term changes in the pattern of the debt markets and of dealings between borrowers and their creditors did result. Increased regulation placed banks under pressure to reduce their loan books and restricted bank lending. This had a number of follow-on effects. Other lenders such as insurance companies, pension funds, and specialised loan funds became more active on the primary and secondary loan markets. A private placement market for non-bank business lending has emerged.[31] The volume of bond issuance, particularly high yield bonds governed by New York law, increased as the volume of bank lending retracted in the years immediately following the financial crisis. However banks continue to play a major role in the financial markets.

2.32 Retail deposits are mainly denominated in the local currency of the place where they are held.[32] They tend to be held on a relatively short-term basis, often being repayable without prior notice at the customer's request. They normally bear interest at a rate that is referable to a domestic benchmark floating rate that is set from time to time by the bank. In the UK, such a benchmark rate for sterling is called a bank's 'base rate'. In the USA, for dollars, it is called the bank's 'prime rate'. Whilst in theory each bank sets its own base rate, in practice all the major banks in the UK set a similar rate which follows the rate set by the Bank of England. Banks tend to use such deposits to fund lending to domestic customers on a relatively short-term or immediately cancellable basis (such as under an overdraft), so that the bank may require repayment at any time. In the UK, base rate is calculated on the number of days that have elapsed in a relevant period and on a per annum basis by reference to a year of 365 or 366 days.

2.33 For other types of loan facility, it is likely that the facility will be predicated on wholesale funding by the bank through the interbank market. Such wholesale funding involves a bank borrowing the funds from one or more other banks in that market. The market in London is called the London interbank market and (with the exception of the European interbank market in relation to funding in euros) it is that market to which further market-based concepts of funding will refer in this chapter. The types of funds that are available in the London interbank market are not restricted to sterling but include most major currencies that are freely available and transferable, including US and Canadian dollars, Swiss francs, and Japanese yen. In theory, the interest rate (currently 'Libor') that is charged to a bank when it borrows funds in the market will reflect its own credit standing.

---

[31] This is a growing market in Europe and the Loan Market Association has published recommended form documents for private placements structured as loans.
[32] This is not a universal rule, as deposits in foreign currencies may be held by a bank in London, as was discussed in *Libyan Arab Foreign Bank v Bankers Trust Co* [1989] QB 728.

In practice, there are published composite rates or benchmark rates (called screen rates, as they are available electronically) which reflect an average of the rates that apply for the time being in the interbank market, from which the calculation of Libor is usually derived for the purposes of charging interest under a loan facility. By way of exception, the interest rate that is charged for borrowing in euros, as reflected in facility documents, refers to the Euribor rate that applies in the European interbank market. Finally, it should be noted that although banks are content to assume for the purposes of loan documentation that loans are funded in the interbank market, the reality is that banks now fund themselves from multiple sources of which the interbank market is just one example.

2.6.2 Libor reform and replacement

When the syndicated loan market first emerged, Libor was set by a handful of banks ('reference banks') providing a rate at which they thought they would be able to borrow funds in the interbank market and the numbers would be averaged.[33] Libor later became a screen rate produced by the British Bankers Association (BBA) on the basis of submissions from a panel of banks and shown on the Reuters information service. Approaching reference banks directly for a rate was seen as suitable fallback if the screen rate was not published for some reason. However during the financial crisis concerns emerged that the manner in which Libor was determined was open to manipulation, either to make the bank submitting a rate appear to be in better financial health or to favour its traders' positions.[34] The system was overhauled following the Wheatley Review published in 2012.

2.34

The Wheatley Review concluded that it would be better to reform, rather than replace, Libor for core maturities and currencies to prevent a large number of existing loan contracts based on such benchmark rates needing to be renegotiated and amended. The reforms included discontinuing benchmark rates for uncommon currencies and maturities (currently only thirty-five rates are published (five currencies for seven tenors or periods) as opposed to 150 before the reforms) as those less common could be more easily manipulated. Banks' submissions would only be published after a lapse of three months, so that there would be no incentive to underestimate a bank's cost of borrowing to make the bank

2.35

---

[33] Libor was thus an *estimate* made by leading banks of what interest rate they would be charged if borrowing from other banks. Euribor is slightly different. It is not an estimate of what the submitting bank would itself have to pay to borrow but what it believes one prime bank is quoting to another prime bank for interbank term deposits within the eurozone.

[34] Billions have been paid in fines by leading banks in respect of Libor manipulation. The first successful criminal prosecution of a trader for manipulating Libor resulted in a 14-year prison sentence. Borrowers have also sought to raise defences based on Libor manipulation to claims to recover loan repayments: eg see *Graiseley Properties Ltd and ors v Barclays Bank plc* [2013] EWCA Civ 1372 and *Deutsche Bank AG and Ors v Unitech Global Ltd and ors* [2016] EWCA Civ 119.

look stronger. Submissions had to be supported by evidence of real transactions which had to be kept for audit purposes. Finally, the setting of the rates was put on statutory footing with a change of administrator from the BBA (a trade body) to ICE Benchmark Administration Limited, a company owned and operated by Intercontinental Exchange, Inc, a listed American stock exchange and clearing house operator.

2.36   The reforms to Libor that followed the Wheatley Review had an impact on the market and recommended form documentation. Provisions were introduced to make it easier to change the screen rate with only a majority lenders decision (traditionally anything that affected a lender's return on the loan required unanimous consent). It also became apparent that banks were reluctant to act as 'reference banks' and to provide rate quotations for syndicates. This was due to a perceived risk of liability without any return for taking on that risk. Additionally, prospective reference banks feared that they would be breaching their regulatory obligations to keep their Libor submissions confidential.[35] Consequently appropriate disclaimers of a reference bank's liability were added to recommended form documentation and the confidentiality concern was cleared with regulators.

2.37   Yet ultimately it was decided by regulators that Libor should be replaced by a new benchmark rate. In the United States, the Alternative Reference Rate Committee (ARRC) was put in charge of finding a replacement for the dollar Libor. It decided that the SOFR (Secured Overnight Financing Rate) would be its replacement. SOFR is a measure of the cost of borrowing cash overnight collateralized by Treasury securities. It is calculated on the basis of transactions cleared through the Delivery-versus-Payment (DVP) service offered by the Fixed Income Clearing Corporation (FICC). SOFR is published by the New York Fed, in cooperation with the US Office of Financial Research. However, such an overnight benchmark rate is considered to be backward-looking, and in this regard it differs from Libor term rates which were forward-looking as they existed in different tenors (eg three or six months) and included an element of credit risk.

2.38   In the United Kingdom, Libor is to be phased out in 2021 when the Financial Conduct Authority will no longer compel banks to provide Libor submissions. A possible replacement is the sterling overnight index average (SONIA), a benchmark administered by the Bank of England since April 2016. SONIA is the weighted average rate of unsecured overnight sterling transactions reported to the Bank's sterling money market daily data collection within a particular time frame and a minimum transaction size of GBP 25 million. Work to settle a substitute London term benchmark rate for loans is continuing. The Loan Market

---

[35] Under the Libor Code of Conduct, contributing banks must not 'disclose rates which will be submitted in the future or have been submitted to the Libor Administrator but not yet published to any external individual or internal individual'.

Association (LMA) has attempted to address the uncertainty by publishing a revised 'replacement of screen rate' clause which provides for the eventuality that Libor may yet survive but not in the same form and a longstop period whereby if the replacement benchmark rate is calculated on an agreed temporary basis for a certain length of time, a process to permanently amend the loan's benchmark rate will be triggered.

In the European Union, Euribor is planned to be replaced by Ester (Euro short- **2.39** term rate). Ester is a benchmark administered by the European Central Bank. It is an unsecured rate that reflects wholesale euro unsecured overnight borrowing transactions with financial counterparties, details of which are provided by fifty-two reporting banks. Additionally, regulations have been introduced in the form of the EU Benchmarks Regulation (Regulation (EU) 2016/1011) of the European Parliament and of the Council of 8 June 2016 on indices used as benchmarks in financial instruments and financial contracts or to measure the performance of investment funds and amending Directives 2008/48/EC and 2014/17/EU and Regulation (EU) No 596/2014 (the 'Benchmarks Regulation'). The Benchmarks Regulation applies to a wide range of benchmarks (including Euribor), the contribution of input data to benchmarks, and the use of benchmarks within the European Union. In particular, the Benchmarks Regulation (i) requires benchmark administrators to be authorised or registered (or, if non-EU-based, to be subject to an equivalent regime or otherwise recognised or endorsed) and to comply with extensive requirements in relation to the administration of benchmarks and (ii) prevents certain uses by EU-supervised entities of benchmarks of administrators that are not authorised or registered (or, if non-EU-based, deemed equivalent or recognised or endorsed). The Benchmarks Regulation aims to ensure the reliability of benchmarks used in the EU, and to minimise conflicts of interest in the setting of benchmarks.

2.6.3 Zero and minimum floors on benchmark rates

In recent years, due to a very low interest rate environment it has become common **2.40** to include zero or minimum floors for Libor or Euribor benchmark rates in loan agreements. A zero floor means that if the benchmark rate becomes negative, it will be treated as zero for the purposes of calculating the interest rate under the loan agreement. In such a case the interest rate payable will be equal to the margin. In the case of a minimum floor (often set at the level of 1 per cent), the benchmark rate will be treated as being the minimum despite falling below that number. If the benchmark rate definitions are not supplemented in this way, the margin may be reduced if the relevant benchmark becomes negative, for example as first happened with CHF Libor in 2011 and with Euribor subsequently.[36] In

---

[36] However it may not be appropriate for such floors to be included where the transaction involves corresponding interest rate hedging. In such a case, a benchmark rate floor could lead to a

extreme cases this may raise the prospect of the borrower arguing that it ought to be paid by the lenders where the negative benchmark rate exceeds the margin. It is unlikely that a court applying English law would find that this had been the intention of the parties. Loan agreements only contemplate the borrower paying interest to the lenders, not the obverse situation. It would be difficult to argue that such a term should be implied as it would not be necessary to give business efficacy to the contract, nor would it represent the obvious but unexpressed intention of the parties.[37] If a contract does not expressly provide what happens when some event occurs, the usual inference is that nothing is to happen.[38]

2.6.4 Interbank funding conventions

2.41 There are certain conventions that apply in the London interbank market which will be mirrored in the documentation for a facility based on interbank funding. With some adaptation, the same conventions apply for lending in euros based upon the European interbank market. The conventions are as follows.

2.42 The market in London operates on the basis of borrowing funds, in neatly rounded amounts, for definite periods, being overnight, one week, one month, three months, and six months. Other periods and amounts may be available on an ad hoc basis. A day reflects the period from one day to the next.

2.43 Except in the case of sterling, which is available daily, other funds are borrowed on two business days' notice. Dealings are agreed as at 11.00am (London time) on the day that sterling is to be made available or, for other currencies, 11.00am (London time or, for a euro-denominated transaction, Brussels time) two business days prior to the funds being made available.

2.44 Payments are made on the basis that the funds will be freely available to the recipient for value on the day of intended receipt. Payments are made by transfers between bank accounts; in the case of sterling, between accounts in London and, for other currencies, between accounts in the principal financial centre of the currency concerned (or, for euros, to an account in the financial centre of a participating state in the eurozone or in London).

2.45 The period of a month ends on the same numerical day in the next month as the day on which it began (and so on for other periods of months), unless there is no such day at the end of the period, or it is not a banking business day in both London and the place for payment (or, in the case of a payment in euros, a day on

---

mismatch with the amounts payable under the hedging agreements.

[37] In *The State of Netherlands v Deutsche Bank AG* [2018] EWHC 1935 (Comm) it was held that derivatives documentation did not require a party to account for negative interest. The obligation had not been expressly included and it would not be implied.

[38] *A-G of Belize v Belize Telecom Ltd* [2009] 1 WLR 1988; *Rosserlane Consultants Ltd v Credit Suisse International* [2015] EWHC 384 (Ch).

which the TARGET2 system[39] is in operation), in which case the month will end on the immediately preceding such business day. Otherwise, payments that fall due on a day which is not a business day will be made on the next business day.

For the purpose of making per annum interest calculations, interest is calculated **2.46** on the actual number of days that have elapsed in a period, divided by a year of 360 days (or 365/366 in the case of sterling). Interest calculations and payments of interest conform to the foregoing, as do most other types of fees and commissions referable to a per annum basis of calculation.

2.6.5 Funding rollover

Loan facilities based upon interbank funding assume that the lender funds it- **2.47** self during the life of the loan by making successive borrowings in the interbank market for periods that are available in the market. The assumption is that the lender tends to fund itself short to lend long. During the life of the facility, it is assumed that it repays a borrowing that it has made in the interbank market on the last day of the period of that borrowing by using the funds it has obtained for the next period, which commences simultaneously with the ending of the previous period (this is the concept of 'rollover' of funding). The interest that the borrower pays under the facility is used by the lender to pay the interest that is due on its own funding. The interest periods and interest payment dates in the facility therefore have to correlate with the periods for which funds are assumed to have been borrowed in the interbank market (the 'matched funding' principle). The assumption is that when the facility is repaid, the merry-go-round will stop and the lender will use the repayment it receives from the borrower, together with the interest payment made by the borrower, to retire its final position in the interbank market. The assumption on which the documentation is based would be a fiction if the lender is actually funding itself from other sources.

2.6.6 Market disruption

As the underlying assumption behind the transaction structure is that the lender **2.48** is funding itself in the interbank market, it will be necessary for the loan facility agreement to cater for the possibility that funds may not be available at some point in the life of the facility because of a disruption in the market arising from events that are outside the lender's control. Examples of such events are the storms that swept through southern England in October 1987 and the tragic events that occurred in New York in September 2001. Some facility agreements provide that the borrower may not draw whilst such an event is continuing, but

---

[39] The Trans-European Automated Real-time Gross Settlement Express Transfer payment system, that operates for payments across the eurozone. TARGET was superseded by TARGET2 in November 2007.

this is not a common restriction on the borrower's rights. Nearly all facility agreements contemplate that the lender will fund itself during the period of disruption from such sources as are available to it, and that the calculation of interest will be based on the cost of such funding to the lender, unless the borrower and the lender can agree to some other arrangement. On the most common formulation of the clause, it would be necessary for the lenders to invoke the market disruption clause separately in respect of each interest period under the loan. In the case of multi-currency facilities, it is also common to provide that the borrower may not draw in a currency other than the base currency of the facility and that the facility will be sourced and maintained by the lender in the base currency during the period of any disruption that affected the lender's ability to obtain funds in other currencies. The financial crisis of 2007–2008 showed that despite a freeze in the interbank market there was considerable reluctance on the part of lenders to rely on market disruption clauses in practice, mainly for reasons of reputation and confidentiality (for example, a lender may not wish to reveal that it has entered into a sub-participation agreement).[40] Where the borrower has hedged the interest rate that it pays under the loan by reference to a particular benchmark (say Libor), the exercise by the lenders of their rights under a market disruption clause could lead to cashflow difficulties for the borrower in that the amounts it would receive under its hedging agreements by reference to Libor would now be less than what it would be required to pay to the lenders on the basis of their costs of funding which would be in excess of Libor. The borrower would no longer be effectively hedged.

2.7 Borrowing under the Facility

2.49 There are a number of expressions (which are largely interchangeable) that are used to refer to the process of borrowing or utilising a facility, including 'drawing', 'draw down', 'utilisation', 'advance',[41] and 'disbursement'. For ease of reference, the expressions 'borrowing' and 'drawing' will be used in this chapter.

2.50 A facility might provide that it may be borrowed in one single amount or it might provide for borrowings by one or more amounts until the facility limit has been reached. Normally, there will be a period that is prescribed in which the borrowing may take place, called an 'availability' or 'commitment' period. If the

---

[40] But see *Blackwater Services Ltd and ors v West Bromwich Commercial Ltd* [2016] EWHC 3083 (Ch) for an example of a situation where a bank invoked a market disruption clause and the borrower disputed that the bank had correctly certified an alternative basis for determining the interest rate, inter alia, because it had referred to its parent entity's cost of funding.

[41] In *Leibson Corporation v TOC Investments Corporation* [2018] EWCA Civ 763 the Court of Appeal held that where funds were described as being 'advanced' (with the document being silent as to repayment), the payment did not constitute a loan.

facility is a revolving facility, the borrower may draw, repay (wholly or partially), and redraw (on any number of occasions) during such a period, provided that the maximum amount borrowed and outstanding at any time does not exceed the prescribed facility limit. The borrower will signify its intention to make a drawing by providing a notice to the lender in the form that is prescribed by the facility agreement.

The facility agreement will usually specify that certain requirements must be met **2.51** before the borrower is entitled to borrow. The most important of these are the conditions precedent that must be satisfied before a borrowing can take place, which are mentioned separately later. In addition, the facility agreement will normally provide that the lender may suspend, or even cancel, the borrower's entitlement to draw under the facility if an event of default has occurred or suspend it if with the expiry of a grace period, the giving of notice, the making of any determination under the finance documents, or any combination of any of the foregoing such an event will occur. It should be noted that in facilities to finance a takeover bid and in certain other types of acquisition finance, where certainty of funding is a prerequisite for a transaction to be announced publicly and to proceed,[42] the lender might be required to remove many such requirements from the facility agreement or to agree that the borrower may draw under the facility notwithstanding the occurrence of non-core events of default or some other technical ground on which the facility might otherwise be unavailable. By contrast, if the facility is an uncommitted (as opposed to a committed) facility, the lender will not have any obligation to make any advance at any time under the facility and the borrower must take its chances that the funds will be provided when it makes a request to borrow.[43] For obvious reasons, a lender will charge less to provide an uncommitted facility and there will also be regulatory benefits to a lender if it has the right at any time to terminate and cancel the facility.[44]

In the case of revolving facilities that are predicated on interbank funding, the **2.52** borrower will be permitted to borrow drawings during the commitment or availability period, each of which will be for the duration of an interest period. The borrower will be required to repay a drawing at the end of the interest period to which it relates, but with the right to re-draw immediately if it so wishes, so that

---

[42] See rr 2.7(d) and 24.8 of the City Code on Takeovers and Mergers (<http://www.thetakeoverpanel.org.uk/the-code>).

[43] A loan will be uncommitted if it provides that the lender's decision whether to the make the advance will be made at the lender's 'sole discretion'. Such a discretion to make or refuse an advance must be exercised consistently with the purposes of the contract and in accordance with the reasonable expectations of the parties so as not to subvert the basis of the contract; it ought not to be exercised in a manner that is irrational, arbitrary, or in bad faith: *McKay v Centurion Credit Resources LLC* [2012] EWCA Civ 1941.

[44] See eg art 78 of and Annex II to Directive 2006/48/EC [2006] OJ L177/1 and para 3.7.2 of the BIPRU block of the Financial Conduct Authority's *Handbook*.

the proceeds of the new drawing can be used to fund the repayment of the previous drawing. Alternatively, the borrower may have other funds that it may wish to use to make the repayment.

2.53 Multi-currency facilities are usually structured on a model that is similar to that just described for revolving facilities. The borrower is permitted to make a drawing in a permitted currency (being, basically, a currency that is freely available to the lender in the interbank market) for the duration of an interest period, at the end of which it is obliged to repay that drawing. It may choose to fund that repayment from the proceeds of a new drawing in the same currency or from other sources that it may have, in which case it may decide to make a new drawing in another currency. The borrower will usually be permitted to maintain drawings in more than one currency at the same time, with some limit on the number to meet administrative requirements. The interest periods need not be the same. An alternative structure to that just described is that drawings which are made by the borrower are not treated as being repaid at the end of each interest period, but the borrower is given the right to have them re-denominated in another currency at the end of each such period if it so wishes, with payments being made between the borrower and the lender to reflect the choice that the borrower has made. At the conclusion of the facility, the borrower will repay in the currency or currencies in which the facility is then outstanding. Whichever method is used, it is necessary to have a measuring stick against which the value of amounts drawn can be assessed, so that the overall facility amount is not exceeded. This is achieved by one currency being nominated as the base currency, in which the total amount of the facility is expressed. Drawings in other currencies are then notionally valued back against the base currency (usually at the beginning of each interest period), and adjusting payments may have to be made by the borrower, so as to ensure that the facility amount is not exceeded.

2.8 A Wrongful Refusal to Lend

2.54 The question arises as to the borrower's rights in a situation where the lender was contractually obliged to lend but has wrongly refused to make an advance, even though the borrower may have fulfilled all the requirements to entitle it to borrow. Lord Scott in *Concord Trust v Law Debenture Trust Corporation plc*[45] agreed with a suggestion that such a lender might be at risk of incurring a liability in damages for breach of contract. It used to be said that the borrower could not obtain a mandatory order against the lender for performance of the contract, such as by way of an order for specific performance.[46] However, it seems contrary

---

[45] [2005] UKHL 27, [2005] 1 WLR 1591 [41].
[46] See *South African Territories Ltd v Wallington* [1898] AC 309, but contrast with *Loan Investment Corp of Australasia v Bonner* [1970] NZLR 724 (PC). Also note the position under s 740 of the

to principle to maintain that this is categorically impossible.[47] The availability of specific performance of an obligation to lend would depend on the particular circumstances of a given case, in particular whether damages would provide an adequate remedy and this may depend on the delay and expense involved in finding an alternative lender, the practical consequences for the borrower, and the difficulty of assessing damages. Nonetheless, other remedies are more likely to be available to the borrower and these will be considered in turn.

2.8.1 Repudiatory breach

Given its seriousness, the breach might be considered as constituting a repudiatory breach of contract by the lender. The borrower may then elect to treat the contract as at an end, with the consequence, in broad terms, that its own obligations for future performance would also be terminated. As will be seen below, the contract is not treated as terminated *ab initio*, nor does it mean that the parties are discharged for all purposes by the termination. The borrower would also be entitled to claim damages for the loss it has suffered in consequence of the breach and termination of the contract (see further below). **2.55**

2.8.2 The obligation to repay after termination

It is an interesting question as to whether the borrower would be entitled to claim, in consequence of its election to bring the contract to an end, that it was relieved of its liability to repay any money that had already been advanced to it before the termination, where the facility agreement had provided for repayment at some future date or dates.[48] **2.56**

At first blush, support for such a view might be drawn from what Lord Diplock said in *Moschi v Lep Air Services Ltd*.[49] He said that the election by the innocent party to bring the contract to an end: **2.57**

Companies Act 2006 (previously s 195 of the Companies Act 1985) which provides that a contract to subscribe for debentures to be issued by a company may be specifically enforced; in *Fons HF v Corporal Ltd* [2015] 1 BCLC 320 the Court of Appeal held that a loan agreement could constitute a debenture in the context of the particular contract before it. In *Rogers v Challis* (1859) 27 Beavan 175 the Court of Chancery refused to order specific performance to compel a borrower (who had found a better deal with a different lender) to borrow money.

[47] In *Battlebridge Group Ltd v Amala Equity Ltd* [2006] EWHC 2982 (Comm), David Steel J ordered a lender to furnish the funds to a borrower which the lender had wrongly refused to lend. It would appear, however, that *South African Territories Ltd v Wallington* was not cited to the judge and the lender did not dispute that such an order could be made against it. See also *Wight v Haberdan Pty Ltd* [1984] 2 NSWLR 280.

[48] But even if such an argument succeeded in respect of contractual obligations arising from the loan agreement, the borrower would still be faced with an unjust enrichment claim for the return of the funds advanced by the lender.

[49] [1973] AC 331, 350.

[p]uts an end to the primary obligations of the party not in default to perform any of his contractual promises which he has not already performed by the time of [the termination]. It deprives him of any right as against the other party to continue to perform them. It does not give rise to any secondary obligation [on his part] in substitution for a primary obligation which has come to an end. The primary obligations of the party in default to perform any of the promises made by him and remaining unperformed likewise come to an end as does his right to continue to perform them. But for his primary obligations there is substituted by operation of law a secondary obligation to pay to the other party a sum of money to compensate him for the loss he has sustained as a result of the failure to perform the primary obligations. The secondary obligation is just as much an obligation arising from the contract as are the primary obligations that it replaces.

2.58 There are, however, limits on the apparent width of that statement. In the first place, as Lord Diplock explained in *Moschi*, matters which are of an ancillary or secondary nature to the main purpose of the contract will survive the termination of the parties' primary obligations. It is a matter of construing the contract to determine which provisions the parties intended should be regarded as falling within that category so that they will continue to apply.[50] It has been held that provisions relating to choice of law and jurisdiction and arbitration clauses could survive the termination of the contract.[51] It is submitted that a number of the other provisions in a loan agreement, such as those dealing with set-off and the various 'boiler-plate' provisions, might fall into this category as well.

2.59 Secondly,[52] the election by the innocent party to terminate the contract does not have the effect of discharging the rights, and the corresponding obligations, of either party which have accrued or been 'unconditionally acquired' prior to the date of termination. This was succinctly expressed by Sir Owen Dixon in the High Court of Australia in *McDonald v Dennys Lascelles Ltd*,[53] when he said:

> When a party to a simple contract, upon a breach by the other contracting party of a condition of the contract, elects to treat the contract as no longer binding upon him, the contract is not rescinded as from the beginning. Both parties are discharged from further performance of the contract, but rights are not divested or discharged which have been unconditionally acquired. Rights and obligations which arise from partial execution [ie partial performance] of the contract and causes of action which have accrued from its breach alike continue unaffected.

2.60 That statement was expressly approved by Lord Wilberforce in *Johnson v Agnew*.[54] It was followed by Lord Brandon in *Bank of Boston Connecticut v European Grain*

---

[50] *Duffen v Frabo SpA* [2000] 1 Lloyd's Rep 180, 194. See also *Plantation Holdings (FZ) LLC v Dubai Islamic Bank PJSC* [2017] EWHC 520 (Comm) [243].
[51] *Heyman v Darwins Ltd* [1942] AC 356; *Yasuda Fire & Marine Ins Co of Europe Ltd v Orion Marine Insurance Underwriting Agency Ltd* [1995] QB 174.
[52] John Whittle SC of the NSW Bar provided illuminating insight on this point.
[53] (1933) 48 CLR 457, 476–77.
[54] [1980] AC 367, 396.

& Shipping Ltd.[55] It might well be argued that the obligation of the borrower to repay the amount already advanced to it under the loan agreement, albeit that the date for repayment had not fallen due, should be seen as a right that had vested in the lender prior to the termination of the contract and which therefore should survive the election by the borrower to terminate the contract. This is demonstrated by the *Bank of Boston* case. That case concerned a charterparty where the voyage had commenced. The charterer had an obligation under the contract to pay the freight, but the date for payment had not arisen prior to the date when the charterer terminated the contract because of the owner's default during the voyage. The House of Lords held that the right to be paid the freight had been 'unconditionally acquired' before the termination of the contract, even though the date for payment was postponed in the contract to a later date and so had not arisen. Lord Brandon said[56] that '[t]he postponement of payment was an incident attaching to the right acquired, but it was not a condition of its acquisition'. A similar approach was taken by Rix LJ in *Explora Group plc v Hesco Bastion Ltd*[57] in relation to commission earned under an agency agreement prior to the termination of the agreement due to the agent's repudiatory breach of the agreement.

2.8.3 Set-off claim

The borrower, as the innocent party, should be entitled to assert as an equitable **2.61** set-off against any amount so payable by it to the defaulting party, the value of its entitlement to damages for the consequences of the repudiatory breach. This entitlement would be subject to any provision in the contract which prevented the claim to set-off from arising,[58] although that, in turn, would depend upon whether the provisions of the contract dealing with set-off had survived the termination of the contract, as referred to earlier.

2.8.4 Damages

It is now appropriate to consider the borrower's claim for damages for the loss it **2.62** has suffered in consequence of the lender's breach of contract,[59] particularly for

---

[55] [1989] AC 1056, 1098–99.
[56] At 1098–99.
[57] [2005] EWCA Civ 646, [82]–[90].
[58] The courts apply such clauses in accordance with their terms: *FG Wilson (Engineering) Limited v John Holt & Company (Liverpool) Limited* [2012] EWHC 2477 (Comm); *Deutsche Bank SA v Khan* [2013] EWHC 482 (Comm). Such clauses in non-consumer contracts may be subject to a test of reasonableness under the Unfair Contract Terms Act 1977, see eg *United Trust Bank Limited v Dalmit Singh Dohil* [2012] 2 All ER (Comm) 765. However, it may be difficult to prove that the parties contracted on the lender's standard terms so as to engage the reasonableness test under the Act: *African Export-Import Bank v Shebah Exploration & Production Company and ors* [2017] EWCA Civ 845. Unfair terms in consumer contracts are now subject to Part 2 of the Consumer Rights Act 2015.
[59] See further the discussion on remedies for breach and claims for damages in section 1.5.

loss of credit in not having the funds that it expected to be made available to it and for damage to its business reputation. It may also wish to claim more generally for economic loss, such as for the loss of profit on a transaction that was to be funded by the facility, damages it may have to pay if it defaulted on that transaction, and the loss of the opportunity to gain further business. In general, damages for breach of contract are awarded in English law to compensate for the loss of its contractual bargain that was suffered by the innocent party in consequence of the breach.[60] To succeed in such a claim, a number of hurdles have to be overcome. The innocent party must prove the loss it has suffered (which could be the loss of a chance) and that the loss was caused by the lender's breach of contract,[61] it has a duty to mitigate its loss and, as mentioned below, the recoverable loss for which damages are sought must fall within the rules as to remoteness.

2.63 In establishing its claim for damages, the borrower must bring itself within the rules as to remoteness, as set down originally by *Hadley v Baxendale*[62] (thus often referred to as the rule in *Hadley v Baxendale*) and more recently qualified by the House of Lords in the case of *Transfield Shipping Inc v Mercator Shipping Inc (The Achilleas)*.[63] In the latter case, Lord Hoffman (and Lord Hope) suggested that the rules as to remoteness are not only concerned with foreseeability but also whether the defendant could reasonably be regarded as having assumed responsibility for the kind of loss in question.

2.64 Nonetheless, as a starting point, it is necessary to consider the rule in *Hadley v Baxendale*. There are two limbs to this rule, which is applied as at the time of contracting and relates to the type of loss that could have been envisaged as at the time of contracting. Under the first limb of the rule, a claimant will be able to claim damages for the type of loss that could reasonably be expected to have arisen in the normal course of things. Under the second limb of the rule, the claimant may claim for those losses which may reasonably be supposed to have been in the contemplation of the parties, at the time they made the contract, as would probably result from the breach. The discussion that follows will begin by looking at the position before the decision of the House of Lords in *Sempra Metals Ltd v*

---

[60] The House of Lords indicated in *Attorney General v Blake* [2001] 1 AC 268 that, in exceptional circumstances where normal remedies were inadequate to compensate for a breach of contract, the court may be prepared to order the defendant to account for the profits it had received or to which it was entitled.

[61] *Jackson v Royal Bank of Scotland plc* [2005] UKHL 3, [2005] 1 WLR 377. The loss will be irrecoverable if an intervening cause (such as a third party's conduct) has broken the chain of causation: *Galoo Ltd v Bright Grahame Murray* [1994] 1 WLR 1360 (CA). As to a loss of chance see *Wellesley Partners LLP v Withers LLP* [2015] EWCA Civ 1146.

[62] (1854) 9 Exch 341. See the discussion of the rule in *Jackson v Royal Bank of Scotland plc* [2005] UKHL 3, [2005] 1 WLR 377.

[63] [2009] 1 AC 61. It was a difficult case and although argued on the basis of remoteness, it may have been better decided on the basis of an implied term restricting liability based on market practice.

HM Commissioners of Inland Revenue[64] and then by discussing how the decision in that case may have changed the approach that might be taken in this type of situation.[65] Finally, it is necessary to consider what impact *Transfield Shipping Inc v Mercator Shipping Inc (The Achilleas)* as explained in subsequent cases may have on the outcome.

In *Kpohraror v Woolwich Building Society*,[66] the Court of Appeal awarded dam-   **2.65**
ages, within the first limb of the rule, for loss of perceived credit worthiness and damage to business reputation[67] that was suffered by a bank's customer in consequence of the bank having wrongly bounced the customer's cheque when there were funds available in the customer's account to meet the cheque. Although that case concerned a situation where the customer had a sufficient credit balance in his current account to meet the cheque, the same conclusion should have been reached if the cheque could have been met within an agreed facility which had not been terminated. By analogy, similar considerations should apply when a lender wrongly refuses to make funds available to a borrower under a committed lending facility with the consequence that a third party is not paid by the borrower when it should have been paid.

It is not clear, however, if the borrower could claim under the first limb of the rule   **2.66**
in its traditional application for more general economic loss. Although the House of Lords allowed a claim under the first limb for loss of the customer's profit on future transactions (which were cancelled in consequence of the bank's wrongful actions) in *Jackson v Royal Bank of Scotland plc*,[68] the facts were rather different in that case. Generally speaking, however, the courts have been unwilling in the past to award substantial damages under the first limb of the rule for a failure to make funds available because the loss is treated as being too remote from what was foreseeable at the time of contracting. The assumption has been that an intended

---

[64] [2009] 1 AC 61.
[65] Although that case was recently departed from in respect of restitutionary awards in *Prudential Assurance Co Ltd v Revenue and Customs Commissioners* [2018] UKSC 39, the Supreme Court made it clear that this does not affect when compound interest may be awarded as damages, at [44] and [79].
[66] [1996] 4 All ER 119.
[67] The computation of a claim for such a loss is problematic. In *Kpohraror*, the Court of Appeal said that there was a presumption that some damage to reputation arose, but it is not clear how the amount that was awarded was calculated, other than that 'some allowance, though not very great' was made for the loss to the claimant's reputation. In *Anglo-Continental Holidays Ltd v Typaldos Lines (London) Ltd* [1967] 2 Lloyd's Rep 61, the Court of Appeal allowed an award of damages for loss of goodwill and business reputation. Lord Denning MR (with whom Davies LJ agreed) was prepared to uphold the award that the judge had made, as it was permitted to award a 'reasonable sum as damages' without proof of specific loss. Russell LJ felt there was proof of specific loss on the facts to justify the sum that the judge had awarded.
[68] [2005] UKHL 3, [2005] 1 WLR 377. See also *John Grimes Partnership Ltd v Gubbins* [2013] EWCA Civ 37 where falls in market value caused by a delay in the performance of services were held to be recoverable, although the conclusion may be different in the case of a highly volatile market.

recipient of funds is not impecunious and that alternative facilities should be available from another provider of finance.

2.67   Assuming that the type of loss that the borrower wished to claim did not fall within the first limb of the rule, as it was traditionally applied, the borrower would have had to establish its claim for more general loss under the second limb of the rule in *Hadley v Baxendale*. To do this, it would need to show that the defendant lender was aware, when it granted the facility, of special circumstances relating to the borrower and its business which gave rise to the loss claimed. For instance, the borrower would have to show that the lender was aware, when it contracted, that the borrower was dependent upon the facility, that finance was not readily available from elsewhere within applicable time limits, and that the borrower would suffer substantial loss if the funds were not provided as agreed under the contract.[69] Although it would not be an easy task, it may be possible that the borrower could show this, given that most lenders undertake extensive investigations before they agree to provide facilities and would be aware of the borrower's actual circumstances, its plans for the future, and its reliance on the facility that is to be provided.

2.68   It is now relevant to consider if the borrower's task might be any easier in light of the decision of the House of Lords in *Sempra Metals Ltd v HM Commissioners of Inland Revenue*.[70] It is submitted that that task has been made easier. Lord Nicholls, who delivered the leading opinion of the majority in the case, made it clear[71] that the usual principles relating to damages for breach of contract would apply where the breach consisted in the failure to pay money or in the late payment of money. The ordinary remoteness rules would apply and there was no special rule which would deny a claimant the opportunity to recover its losses simply because of this type of breach. The losses that were claimed must have been reasonably foreseeable and the court would not presume what was foreseeable but, subject to that and the rule as to mitigation, it would always be open to the claimant to plead and prove its actual loss. His Lordship envisaged that such loss could include interest, including compound interest, for the loss of the use of the money. In addition, in his Lordship's words,[72] it might be:

---

[69] See, by analogy, *Trans Trust SPRL v Danubian Trading Co Ltd* [1952] 2 QB 297 and *Wadsworth v Lydell* [1981] 1 WLR 598.

[70] [2007] UKHL 34. This case has been departed from in respect of unjust enrichment in *Prudential Assurance Co Ltd v Revenue and Customs Commissioners* [2018] UKSC 39 where it was held that simple, rather than compound, interest is to be awarded in respect of such claims. However, the Supreme Court did not reconsider the principles relating to compound interest being awarded as damages that had been laid down in the *Sempra Metals* case, see [44]. The court said at [79] that it was unnecessary to consider the reasoning in that case so far as it concerned the award of interest as damages, and nothing in its judgment was intended to question that aspect of the decision.

[71] At [92]–[96].

[72] At [95].

the loss of an opportunity to invest the promised money. Here again, where the circumstances require, the investment loss may need to include a compound element if it is to be a fair measure of what the [claimant] lost by the late [or non-existent] payment. Or the loss flowing from the [default] may take some other form. Whatever form the loss takes the court will, here as elsewhere, draw from the proved or admitted facts such inferences as are appropriate ... There are no special rules for the proof of facts in this area of the law.

Finally it is necessary to consider *Transfield Shipping Inc v Mercator Shipping Inc* **2.69**
(The Achilleas)[73] and subsequent cases which qualify the rule in *Hadley v Baxendale* by focusing on whether the defendant had assumed responsibility for the loss. The additional test based on 'assumption of responsibility' or 'scope of duty undertaken' can override the rule in *Hadley v Baxendale* by either curtailing its application or extending it.[74] First, the defendant may be able to avoid liability for a type of loss, notwithstanding that it was reasonably foreseeable, on the basis that the defendant did not assume responsibility for it.[75] Secondly, it is possible for the defendant to have assumed responsibility for a type of loss on the particular facts, even if it was not reasonably foreseeable.[76] Whether the defendant assumed responsibility for a particular type of loss may turn on the general market practice and expectations of participants in a particular market,[77] and whether the purpose of the obligation was to prevent the risk that actually eventuated.[78] Therefore, in the context of a wrongful refusal to lend, arguments would arise as to whether there was an understanding in the City that a particular type of loss was or was not the lender's responsibility and the nature and scope of the purpose of the lending transaction in the particular case.

Another rule that would limit the amount of damages recoverable by the bor- **2.70**
rower for a failure to lend would be the requirement that the innocent party take reasonable steps to mitigate its loss.[79] A borrower could not sit back and watch its losses mount due to lack of finance. It would have to endeavour to obtain finance from other creditors, perhaps on worse terms than were offered by the defaulting lender. It should then be able to recover the difference between them from the defaulting lender.

---

[73] [2009] 1 AC 61.
[74] *Siemens Building Technologies FE Ltd v Supershield Ltd* [2010] EWCA Civ 7.
[75] *Transfield Shipping Inc v Mercator Shipping Inc (The Achilleas)* [2009] 1 AC 61.
[76] *Siemens Building Technologies FE Ltd v Supershield Ltd* [2010] EWCA Civ 7.
[77] *Transfield Shipping Inc v Mercator Shipping Inc (The Achilleas)* [2009] 1 AC 61; *Sylvia Shipping Co Ltd v Progress Bulk Carriers Ltd, The Sylvia* [2010] EWHC 542 (Comm).
[78] *Siemens Building Technologies FE Ltd v Supershield Ltd* [2010] EWCA Civ 7.
[79] *British Westinghouse Electric Manufacturing Co Ltd v Underground Electric Rlys Co of London Ltd* [1912] AC 673.

2.9 Conditions Precedent

2.71 A loan facility agreement usually specifies a number of conditions precedent that must be satisfied before the borrower is entitled to draw under the facility. They are required for the benefit of the lender and it is often stated that they must be fulfilled 'in form and substance' to the satisfaction of the lender. If extensive, the list of requirements will probably be set out in one of the schedules to the agreement, which requirements are incorporated by virtue of a reference to them in one of the clauses of the agreement. Sometimes, there may be conditions precedent to be fulfilled at intervals during the life of the facility, before further drawings can take place, as may be the case in a facility which is intended to provide the finance in stages for a construction, engineering, or infrastructure project.

2.9.1 The list

2.72 The list of conditions precedent usually relates to documentary evidence and other matters that must be produced to the lender, such as copies of resolutions of the directors and shareholders of the borrower approving the transaction and the relevant documentation, the provision of guarantees and security in support of the borrower's obligations, other documentation that is relevant in the context of the transaction, certificates that might be required as to factual matters, information that the lender requires for regulatory purposes, including money laundering and knowledge of customer checks, and legal opinions confirming the enforceability of the transaction. In leveraged acquisition finance and project finance transactions, which usually involve extensive due diligence by the lenders, specific conditions precedent are likely to be included in respect of problems that the lender's advisors have identified.

2.9.2 Conditions precedent and conditions subsequent

2.73 As a matter of general contract law, a distinction is drawn between conditions precedent and conditions subsequent.[80] The latter concern events that might occur after the contract has become binding upon the parties and which the contract contemplates would have the effect of discharging the parties from the obligation to make further performance under the contract after the event has occurred. The former are conditions that the contract lays down and which must be satisfied before one or other, or both, of the parties is obliged to perform under the contract. In the context of a loan facility agreement, the conditions precedent are intended to be requirements that must be satisfied by the borrower before the lender is obliged to advance funds under the agreement, although it is also normally intended

---

[80] See eg the discussion in *Total Gas Marketing Ltd v Arco British Ltd* [1998] 2 Lloyd's Rep 209.

that, irrespective of whether or not the conditions are satisfied, the borrower will have certain secondary obligations that it must meet, such as in the payment of fees to the lender. It must also be noted that the phrase 'conditions subsequent' is also used in a commercial sense to refer to obligations of the borrower to deliver documents or to resolve problems, usually by a specified deadline, which have been identified as part of the lender's due diligence. Consequently a set of such undertakings is often found in loan agreements under the heading 'Conditions Subsequent'. Whereas conditions precedent are conditions for the borrower to receive funds under the loan agreement, conditions subsequent (in this sense) are obligations which the borrower must perform to avoid triggering an event of default and hence the risk of being compelled to repay the principal before the scheduled dates for repayment.

The agreement will also normally provide that the lender is to be the arbiter of **2.74** whether the conditions precedent have been met.[81] It is also worth making the point that as the conditions precedent are intended to be for the benefit of the lender, it is always free to waive any one or more of the conditions, so that the borrower is then permitted to draw under the facility.[82] Alternatively, the lender might agree with the borrower that the fulfilment of a condition might become a condition subsequent in the commercial sense, so that the borrower would be permitted to draw under the facility but may be required to repay if the condition was not met by some later date.

Questions might arise in relation to the apparent width of a lender's discretion in **2.75** determining if the borrower has satisfied the conditions precedent.

One question concerns the limits, if any, that might be imposed upon the lender **2.76** in making its determination that the conditions precedent have been met to its satisfaction, in the absence of some explicit requirement that the lender should act reasonably or in some other objective manner.[83] As mentioned earlier, the agreement will often state almost the opposite to any objective requirement, by stating that the conditions precedent must be met in a manner which, in form and substance, is satisfactory to the lender within its own discretion or opinion.[84] It might

---

[81] However, in the case of syndicated facilities, it is usually the facility agent (possibly acting on the instructions of a majority of the lenders) who makes the decision as to whether the conditions precedent are satisfied. Consequently an individual lender may be outvoted and forced to lend despite not being convinced that the conditions precedent have been satisfied.

[82] Eg as in *Bank of Ireland v AMCD (Property Holdings) Ltd* [2001] 2 All ER (Comm) 894.

[83] As to the application of an express requirement to act reasonably see para 1.58.

[84] This clearly imposes a subjective test which does not import an obligation to act reasonably. In *Docker v Hyams* [1969] 1 WLR 1060 (CA) 1065 Harman LJ stated that 'where the condition is that something is to be done to A.'s approval or to his satisfaction, then he is the judge, and as long as he is honest, he need not be reasonable'. *LBI EHF v Raiffeisen Bank International AG* [2018] EWCA Civ 719 concerned a contractual determination to be made in a party's 'reasonable opinion'. This required no more than for the decision-maker to act 'rationally and not arbitrarily or perversely'.

be argued that some limit should be implied on the apparent width of such a discretion. This could be done by arguing that there was an implied term of the agreement to that effect.[85] At the least, it might be said that the discretion should be exercised in good faith and not capriciously, arbitrarily, perversely, irrationally, or for a collateral purpose which was outside the legitimate scope of the contract.[86] In *Deutsche Bank (Suisse) SA v Khan*[87] the above principles were applied specifically in the context of a condition precedent which required that a bank 'shall have received in form and substance satisfactory to it the documents' listed in the loan agreement, which included a valuation report. Hamblen J held that what was 'satisfactory' to the bank indicated subjectivity rather than objectivity but such a decision could not be made capriciously, perversely, irrationally, or arbitrarily.[88] This appears to leave quite a measure of subjective decision-making in the hands of the lender.

2.77 In this context it is also necessary to note that the Court of Appeal has drawn a distinction between binary choices under a contract—such as the choice whether to exercise an absolute right to make a price deduction in accordance with a pre-agreed formula or to terminate a contract—where constraints ought not to be implied and a contractual choice from a range of options where such constraints ought to apply.[89] Whether a condition precedent has or has not been satisfied may appear at first sight to be a binary choice on the part of the decision-maker. However, that view was not adopted in *Novus Aviation Ltd v Alubaf Arab International Bank BSC*.[90] A bank's commitment to provide the equity portion of an aircraft acquisition and leasing deal provided that it 'shall be conditional upon satisfactory review and completion of documentation for the purchase, lease and financing'. Leggatt J held that the condition gave the bank a contractual discretion and as such it was subject to the implied restrictions already discussed. These

---

[85] As to the modern approach for the implication of terms see *Marks & Spencer plc v BNP Paribas Securities Services Trust Co (Jersey) Ltd* [2015] UKSC 72, [2015] 3 WLR 1843.

[86] *Paragon Finance plc v Nash & Staunton* [2001] EWCA Civ 1466, [2002] 1 WLR 685; *Paragon Finance plc v Pender* [2005] EWCA Civ 760, [2005] 1 WLR 3412; and *Socimer International Bank Ltd v Standard Bank London Ltd* [2008] EWCA Civ 116, [2008] 1 Lloyd's Rep 558 [66] and [106] (Rix LJ); *Braganza v BP Shipping Ltd* [2015] UKSC 17, [2015] 1 WLR 1661. See also the discussion on this point in section 1.2.9. It may be arguable that an implied term may also require a bank to make its decision 'in accordance with proper banking procedures': *The Office of Fair Trading v Abbey National plc* [2008] EWHC 875 (Comm) [79].

[87] [2013] EWHC 482 (Comm).

[88] See also *Astra Trust Ltd v Adams and Williams* [1969] 1 Lloyd's Rep 81, 87.

[89] *Mid Essex Hospital v Compass* [2013] EWCA Civ 200 [83]–[92]. See also *Sucden Financial Ltd v Fluxo-Cane Overseas Ltd and anor* [2010] EWHC 2133 (Comm) [50]. The distinction was applied in *Myers v Kestrel Acquisitions Ltd* [2015] EWHC 916 (Ch) where the court refused to imply a term that a power to modify loan notes unilaterally to match another instrument should be exercised in good faith. The discretion was characterised as one whether or not to exercise a contractual right, rather than a choice among a range of options.

[90] [2016] EWHC 1575 (Comm). A decision to lend or not to lend was also said to be subject to the *Socimer*-based implied term in *McKay v Centurion Credit Resources LLC* [2012] EWCA Civ 1941.

were breached because the bank's sole reason for deciding not to proceed with the transaction was that it had considered that it was not in its commercial interests; its decision was not based on any dissatisfaction with the relevant documentation which had been provided.

It might also be said that, by implication, the lender should not act in a way which **2.78** deliberately prevented the conditions precedent from being met[91] or that it would not wrongfully impede them from being met,[92] particularly in relation to matters that were within its own control as, for instance, in approving legal opinions from its own lawyers.[93] It has even been held that a discretion not to lend had to be exercised consistently with the purposes of the contract and in accordance with the reasonable expectations of the parties; the discretion could not be used so as to subvert the basis of the contract in which it was contained.[94] It remains to be seen whether such a departure from the more conservative approach to business judgements traditionally taken by the courts will find support in subsequent cases.

Arguments made on behalf of borrowers in this area sometimes draw upon a con- **2.79** cept that has been advanced in a number of cases, which is in turn based upon the supposition that parties enter into contracts that they wish to perform, that a term might be implied that the parties will cooperate to ensure the proper performance of the contract,[95] or that neither party will prevent the other from being able to perform the contract and enjoy its rights under the contract.[96] However, attempts at arguing for such additional general forms of limitation have failed.[97] Authorities implying terms of this nature in respect of the performance of existing contractual obligations have been distinguished in the context of conditions precedent because the latter are only conditions for bringing obligations into effect.[98]

---

[91] See *Blake & Co v Sohn* [1969] 1 WLR 1412.

[92] See *Thompson v ASDA-MFI Group plc* [1988] Ch 241. In *Richco International Ltd v Alfred C Toepfer International GmbH* [1991] 1 Lloyd's Rep 136 Lord Diplock noted in a slightly different context that it is a rule of construction of contracts that '[a] man cannot be permitted to take advantage of his own wrong'.

[93] Bearing in mind that it is very unlikely, if not unheard of, for a legal opinion to give merely positive assurances and contain no qualifications.

[94] *McKay v Centurion Credit Resources LLC* [2012] EWCA Civ 1941.

[95] *Mackay v Dick* (1881) 6 App Cas 251 (but see n 98 below); *James E McCabe Ltd v Scottish Courage Ltd* [2006] EWHC 538 (Comm) [17]–[18]; *General Trading Co (Holdings) Ltd v Richmond Corp Ltd* [2008] EWHC 1479 (Comm).

[96] *Stirling v Maitland* (1864) 5 B&S 840 (but see n 98 below); *Southern Foundries (1926) Ltd v Shirlaw* [1940] AC 701; *Schindler v Northern Raincoat Co Ltd* [1960] 1 WLR 1038; *Equitable Life Assurance Society v Hyman* [2002] 1 AC 408; *Crastvell Trading Ltd v Bozel SA* [2010] EWHC 166 (Comm) [30]; *Plantation Holdings (FZ) LLC v Dubai Islamic Bank PJSC* [2017] EWHC 520 (Comm) [158].

[97] *Lee-Parker v Izzet (No 2)* [1972] 1 WLR 775; *Astra Trust Ltd v Adams and Williams* [1969] 1 Lloyd's Rep 81; *Stabilad Ltd v Stephens & Carter Ltd (No 2)* [1999] 2 All ER (Comm) 651; *Law Debenture Trust Corp plc v Ukraine* [2018] EWCA Civ 2026 [207].

[98] *Mackay v Dick* (1881) 6 App Cas 251 was held not to be applicable to a classic condition precedent in *Ouais Group Engineering and Contracting v Saipem SpA* [2013] EWHC 990 (Comm). See

2.80　In the end, it comes down to the construction of the agreement and whether a court would be prepared to imply a term, but it is possible to prevent the implication of a term by a provision to the contrary in the agreement.[99] It is submitted that this might be achieved by using the formula referred to earlier, which is that meeting the conditions precedent is subject to the lender being satisfied with the materials presented to it, both as to form and substance. This must be subject to the reservation that a lender would still most likely have an implied duty to act in good faith and that it should not act capriciously, arbitrarily, perversely, irrationally, or for a collateral purpose which was outside the legitimate scope of the contract. Such a term is extremely difficult to exclude, and has been implied even where the contract expressly provided that the relevant party was entitled to make the relevant decision in its 'sole and absolute discretion'.[100]

2.81　If the lender does have some type of obligation as to the way in which it acts concerning the conditions precedent and is found to be in breach of that obligation, there will then be an issue as to the remedy that should be granted to the borrower. For the reasons discussed earlier in this chapter, it is unlikely that a mandatory order (for instance, an order for specific performance or for an injunction) would be made against the lender. On the other hand, and also for the reasons already discussed, the borrower may have difficulty in proving a recoverable loss should it seek damages.[101]

2.82　Another question is whether the secondary obligations of the borrower (to pay fees and the like) can be enforced where the lender is given a wide and unrestricted element of discretion in its right to make its determination, at least in the period before the lender has confirmed its complete satisfaction and, consequently, before the facility has become available for drawing by the borrower. It might be argued that the lender has, in effect, a right of veto upon the borrower's enjoyment of the facility and that, until it gives its confirmation, it has not undertaken any binding commitment on its own part, with the consequence that there cannot be an effective and binding contract between the parties.[102] However, it would be difficult for such an argument to succeed because the parties' intention is usually for the contract to become effective immediately on signing whereupon

---

also *Swallowfalls Limited v Monaco Yachting & Technologies SAM and anor* [2014] EWCA Civ 186 where *Stirling v Maitland* (1864) 5 B&S 840 was construed narrowly so as not to be applicable.

[99] See *Micklefield v SAC Technology Ltd* [1990] 1 WLR 1002; *BNP Paribas SA v Yukos Oil Company* [2005] EWHC 1321 (Ch).

[100] *Westlb AG v Nomura Bank International plc* [2012] EWCA Civ 495. See also *Mid Essex Hospital v Compass* [2013] EWCA Civ 200 [83].

[101] However, see *Novus Aviation Ltd v Alubaf Arab International Bank BSC* [2016] EWHC 1575 (Comm) where damages were awarded for a wrongful refusal to proceed with a transaction on the basis of a condition precedent.

[102] *Watson v Watchfinder.co.uk Ltd* [2017] EWHC 1275 (Comm).

it creates mutual rights and obligations, albeit conditional obligations to lend in the case of the lender.[103]

2.9.3 Role of the borrower

It is now relevant to consider the role of the borrower and whether it has any ob-   **2.83**
ligation to bring about the satisfactory achievement of the conditions precedent. An obvious point to make is that the borrower can hardly be expected to undertake that it will meet whatever the lender happens eventually to decide might be required within its own unfettered discretion. In other situations, it will be a question of whether a term might be implied under which such an obligation is undertaken by the borrower; for instance, that the borrower will use its reasonable endeavours to meet and satisfy the conditions precedent. Such a term has been implied in cases involving contracts for the sale of an asset where the sale has been subject to the fulfilment of a condition, with one of the parties being responsible for seeking to bring it about.[104] It is submitted that a court would not imply such a term in relation to a loan facility agreement, because it is not necessary to give efficacy to the contract, which can work perfectly well without the term. If the borrower fails to satisfy the conditions precedent then the lender has no obligation to lend. Subject to the fulfilment of any pre-existing secondary obligations on the part of the borrower, the contract will simply fall away.[105]

2.10 Repayment

2.10.1 Limited and non-recourse lending

In most cases, the obligation of the borrower to repay will relate to the full amount   **2.84**
that has been lent to it, so that the borrower undertakes an unqualified covenant for repayment. It is possible, however, for the obligation to repay to be limited or qualified,[106] so that it is made conditional upon certain circumstances being met (eg prescribed cash flow requirements).[107] The borrowing may even be expressed

---

[103] The Court of Appeal had no doubt that a contract had been entered into despite the fact that the lender's obligation to make any advance was in its sole discretion: *McKay v Centurion Credit Resources LLC* [2012] EWCA Civ 1941.

[104] *Re Anglo-Russian Merchant Traders and John Batt & Co (London) Ltd* [1917] 2 KB 679; *Hargreaves Transport Ltd v Lynch* [1969] 1 WLR 215.

[105] However, the contract should not generally be treated as at an end before the deadline set for the expiry of the conditions has elapsed: *Smith v Butler* [1900] 1 QB 694.

[106] As opposed to being entirely negated, as it would then cease to be a loan and would be a gift. The negation of any stipulation for repayment of a loan (as opposed to a gift) would equate to a proviso that was wholly repugnant to a loan: *Williams v Hathaway* (1877) 6 ChD 544.

[107] An example is the so-called 'flawed asset' provision which limits the obligation of a bank to repay a deposit: see *Re Bank of Credit and Commerce International SA (No 8)* [1996] Ch 245 (CA) 262–63 and [1998] AC 214 (HL) 225.

as being without recourse to the borrower, in that it is limited to the proceeds of realisation of an asset or the income derived from that asset.[108] Hence, the liability of a trustee for moneys it borrows can be limited to the funds available to it from the trust assets and, in any event, expressed only to apply to the trustee of the trust for the time being so that a person who occupied that position will have no liability once it has ceased to be trustee.[109] The same points may be made in relation to other types of payment obligation, including as to interest, fees, or commission. The following discussion will be based on the assumption that the borrower has a full personal obligation to make payment.

2.10.2 Repayment on demand

2.85 The obligation to repay may be expressed to be an obligation to repay on demand.[110] An overdraft facility is a typical example of a facility that normally is repayable on demand.

2.86 Generally speaking, the underlying principle in contract law is that it is not necessary to make a demand upon a debtor before commencing proceedings to recover a debt that was expressed to be payable on demand.[111] However, there is an exception to that underlying principle in the case of the relationship between banker and customer, which is that (in the absence of agreement to the contrary, as, for instance, in the case of a term deposit or a term loan) a demand is necessary before either is entitled to require payment from the other, although the issuance of proceedings will normally serve as a sufficient demand if an express demand has not already been made.[112]

2.87 Under English law as it currently stands, the right of the lender to make demand (where the facility gives it that right) is exercisable at any time and without

---

[108] *Mathew v Blackmore* (1857) 1 H&N 762; *De Vigier v IRC* [1964] 1 WLR 1073; *Levett v Barclays Bank plc* [1995] 1 WLR 1260, 1271–72.

[109] *Williams v Hathaway* (1877) 6 ChD 544.

[110] There may be a question as to whether the facility is repayable on demand as a matter of construction of the facility agreement and the conduct of the parties: *Titford Property Co Ltd v Cannon Street Acceptances Ltd* (unreported, 22 May 1975); *Bank of Ireland v AMCD (Property Holdings) Ltd* [2001] 2 All ER (Comm) 894: *Swallowfalls Limited v Monaco Yachting & Technologies SAM and anor* [2014] EWCA Civ 186. In *SRM Global Master Fund v Treasury Commissioner* [2009] EWHC 227 (Admin) [139] it was concluded that '[i]t is settled law that where a facility letter provides that a loan is "repayable on demand", that provision prevails even though there are other provisions in the facility agreement indicating that the bank intends to make the facility available until a specific date.' See also *Carey Group plc v AIB Group (UK) plc* [2011] EWHC 567 (Ch), [2012] Ch 304 [39].

[111] *Bradford Old Bank Ltd v Sutcliffe* [1918] 2 KB 833.

[112] As to deposits made by the customer with its bank, see *Joachimson v Swiss Bank Corp* [1921] 3 KB 110. As to overdrafts granted by the bank to its customer, see *Cripps v Wickenden* [1973] 1 WLR 944; *Williams and Glyn's Bank Ltd v Barnes* [1981] Com LR 205; *Lloyds Bank plc v Lampert* [1999] 1 All ER (Comm) 161; and *Bank of Ireland v AMCD (Property Holdings) Ltd* [2001] 2 All ER (Comm) 894.

reason.[113] The borrower must repay without delay; it is not entitled to any more time than is necessary to allow for the mechanics of making payment.[114] In one decision the Court of Appeal left open the possibility that the law might be changed so that a debtor which is able to raise funds from another lender to enable it to make the repayment should be given a reasonable time to do so.[115] However, cases such as *Nicholson v HSBC Bank plc* reaffirm the traditional approach where Rix LJ concluded that 'there is clear authority that "on demand" means "on demand"'.[116] There is no special wording that must be used in making the demand for repayment, so long as it clearly requires repayment,[117] and the demand need not specify the precise amount that is due.[118] Of course any notice requirements specified in the loan contract ought to be complied with.

The lender does not need to make inquiries or investigations before making the demand. In one case the borrower argued that a bank could not demand repayment of an overdraft without having given fair consideration to a financial report concerning it or in circumstances where to its knowledge the bank had not obtained an accurate or competently prepared report. The court held that no such duty of care was owed as it would be inconsistent with the bank's unqualified contractual right to demand repayment.[119] **2.88**

2.10.3 Term facilities

A term facility is a facility where the date or (if repayment is to be made by instalments) dates for repayment are fixed by the facility agreement. In such a situation, there is no inherent right upon the lender to demand earlier repayment[120] unless the facility specifically provides for such a right, as through the operation of an events of default clause[121] or in other defined circumstances.[122] If the whole debt **2.89**

---

[113] *Williams and Glyn's Bank Ltd v Barnes* [1981] Com LR 205; *Bank of Baroda v Panessar* [1987] Ch 335; *Lloyds Bank plc v Lampert* [1999] 1 All ER (Comm) 161; *Bank of Ireland v AMCD (Property Holdings) Ltd* [2001] 2 All ER (Comm) 894.

[114] *Bank of Baroda v Panessar* [1987] Ch 335. In *Sheppard & Cooper Ltd v TSB Bank plc* [1996] 2 All ER 654, it was said that some minimum time should be allowed, unless the debtor admits that it cannot repay. In that case, one hour was held to be sufficient where the demand was made in business hours. These decisions were followed in *Su-Ling v Goldman Sachs International* [2015] EWHC 759 (Comm).

[115] *Lloyds Bank plc v Lampert* [1999] 1 All ER (Comm) 161.

[116] [2001] EWCA Civ 748.

[117] *Re Colonial Finance Mortgage Investment and Guarantee Corp Ltd* (1905) 6 SRNSW 6, approved in *In Re A Company* [1985] BCLC 37.

[118] *Bunbury Foods Pty Ltd v National Bank of Australasia Ltd* (1984) 153 CLR 491; *Bank of Baroda v Panessar* [1987] Ch 335.

[119] *Chapman v Barclays Bank* [1998] PNLR 14. This case was followed in *Hall v Royal Bank of Scotland plc* [2009] EWHC 3163.

[120] *Cryne v Barclays Bank plc* [1987] BCLC 548.

[121] See further section 2.18.

[122] For instance, by the operation of an illegality clause, which is a clause which purports to give the lender the right to demand early repayment if it becomes unlawful for the lender to maintain the facility in a relevant jurisdiction. It has also become common in facility agreements for the lender to

is repayable on one date, it is sometimes colloquially referred to as a 'bullet' repayment. Where the debt is repayable by instalments, the debt is said to amortise over the period for the payment of the instalments. Where the debt is repayable in instalments with a larger final instalment, this is referred to as a 'balloon' repayment.

2.10.4 No agreed date for repayment

2.90 If there is no agreement as to the date for repayment of a debt and (in the case of a loan by a bank) it has not been agreed that it should be repayable on demand, then the debt will be treated as having become repayable immediately after it was incurred.[123] This may give rise to problems in recovering the debt as the limitation period under the Limitation Act 1980 will begin to run from the date the debt was incurred.

2.10.5 Clogs on the equity of redemption

2.91 In equity, it is not permitted to prevent a secured borrower from redeeming its security; for instance, by providing that the security may never be redeemed. The debtor is entitled to redeem its security on payment of the secured obligations and a provision which is intended to prevent that entitlement (called a 'clog on the equity of redemption') is void and unenforceable.[124] The parties may agree that the right of redemption should be postponed for the period of the facility,[125] provided that is not an unreasonably long period.[126] The position has been changed by legislation in relation to companies, which can issue perpetual debentures.[127]

2.10.6 Early repayment

2.92 Failing a provision in the agreement which allows it to make early repayment, a debtor has no right to make early repayment of a term facility.[128] The lender is

---

have the right to require the borrower to make early repayment where there has been a substantial change in the ownership of the borrower or of its parent company, usually referred to as a change of control. Other so-called 'mandatory prepayment events' may also be agreed depending on the particular deal. For example, the loan considered in *Aston Hill Financial Inc v African Minerals Finance* [2013] EWCA Civ 416 contained a clause requiring the borrower to prepay from the proceeds of any new debt raised by it.

[123] *Bradford Old Bank Ltd v Sutcliffe* [1918] 2 KB 833; *Longstaff International Ltd v Evans* [2001] All ER (D) 283 (Jul).

[124] *Noakes & Co Ltd v Rice* [1902] AC 24; *Kreglinger v New Patagonia Merat and Cold Storage Co Ltd* [1914] AC 25; *Jones v Morgan* [2001] EWCA Civ 995, [2002] 1 EGLR 125.

[125] *Teevan v Smith* (1882) 20 ChD 724; *Williams v Morgan* [1906] 1 Ch 804. As to the relationship between a contractual provision for redemption and the equitable right to redeem, especially in the context of contingent and future liabilities due to the mortgagee, see *Re Rudd and Son Ltd* (1986) 2 BCC 98,955 and *Law Debenture Trust Corp plc v Concord Trust* [2007] EWHC 1380 (Ch).

[126] *Morgan v Jeffreys* [1910] 1 Ch 620.

[127] S 739 of the Companies Act 2006 (previously s 193 of the Companies Act 1985). See *Knightsbridge Estates Trust Ltd v Byrne* [1940] AC 613.

[128] *Hyde Management Services Pty Ltd v FAI Insurance* [1979] HCA 22, (1979) 144 CLR 541, quoting, inter alia, Luxmoor J in *Knightsbridge Estates Trust Ltd v Byrne* [1938] Ch 741. But contrast

entitled to rely on the contract and its right to earn interest for the full term. If the debtor does make early repayment it may be in breach of contract and liable in damages for the loss the lender suffers, but the lender will be obliged to mitigate its loss by re-deploying the funds. For this reason, it is common for a borrower to negotiate a right in the contract to make early repayment of the whole or part of the loan that has been advanced to it, usually referred to as a 'prepayment'. The borrower will usually be given, as well, a right to cancel the whole or part of the facility so as to defray any commitment charges that would otherwise accumulate on the undrawn portion of the facility. The agreement will probably provide that if repayment is made otherwise than at the end of the relevant interest period, the borrower will compensate the lender for any loss it suffers which is not covered by its redeployment of the funds it receives on repayment.[129]

Premiums or fees on early repayments are sometimes agreed to compensate the lenders for the loss of their anticipated return, especially in project finance and real estate loans. Such fees are usually imposed only in the case of voluntary pre-payments, particularly if made in the earlier years of the term, and are usually based on a percentage of the amount prepaid.[130] Where such early repayments are permitted by the terms of the loan agreement, there is no question of the early repayment being a breach of contract. Accordingly any prepayment fee imposed in respect of such payment does not engage the penalty doctrine because it is not an imposition of a punishment for a breach of contract.[131] **2.93**

2.11 Interest

Almost without exception, commercial loan transactions that take place in western cultures will be expressed to bear interest.[132] The position relating to Islamic finance and the alternative ways of structuring financial transactions to meet Sharia law are examined separately elsewhere.[133] **2.94**

Lancashire Waggon Co v Nuttall (1879) 61 LT 18 where it was held that a buyer under a hire-purchase agreement could prepay, and hence acquire title early, by paying all amounts that would have fallen due until maturity.

[129] Eg *K/S Preston Street v Santander UK plc* [2012] EWHC 1633 (Ch).

[130] *TAEL One Partners Ltd v Morgan Stanley & Co International plc* [2015] UKSC 12 involved a prepayment make-whole fee calculated to ensure that the lender achieved a target rate of return of 17 per cent to 20 per cent per annum. *Edgeworth Capital (Luxembourg) Sarl v Ramblas Investments BV* [2016] EWCA Civ 412 concerned a fee amounting to €105 million.

[131] *Holyoake v Candy* [2017] EWHC 3397 (Ch) [468].

[132] As Sir William Blackstone wrote in *The Commentaries on the Laws of England* (1765–1769 Vol II, xxx, 456): 'Unless money … can be borrowed, trade cannot be carried on: and if no premium were allowed for the hire of money, few persons would care to lend it.' (Cited in *Tael One Partners Ltd v Morgan Stanley & Co International plc* [2013] EWCA Civ 473.)

[133] See Sarah Paterson and Rafal Zakrzewski (eds), *McKnight, Paterson, & Zakrzewski on the Law of International Finance* (2nd edn, OUP 2017) ch 3, para [3.13]ff.

2.95 Interest is a charge for the use of money over time. It is usually calculated at a rate per cent per annum and accrues for each day on which a loan is outstanding. Most facilities provide for interest to be paid periodically on interest payment dates which are the last days of successive interest periods. As previously explained, those periods and payment dates correlate with the funding arrangements that the lender is assumed to have entered into in the interbank market.[134] The borrower is given some say in the process, as the facility agreement will provide that it may choose the length of each interest period (and thereby it also chooses the length of the relevant funding period that the lender is assumed to obtain in the interbank market), so long as its choice conforms with the normal practices in the interbank market and certain other mechanical and practical requirements are met (eg as to conforming the last day of an interest period with a repayment date for principal).

2.11.1 Agreement to pay interest

2.96 The traditional position at common law (which has recently changed in relation to interest on amounts in default, as mentioned below) is that interest is not payable on a loan or a debt unless it had been agreed between the parties or arose under a course of dealing or custom.[135] Such an agreement should normally be express but it will be implied in the case of an overdraft.[136] The agreement can cover the position both before and (subject to it not amounting to a penalty) after default. To prevent the covenant for payment of interest merging in any judgment that the creditor might obtain should the debtor default in making payment, the obligation to pay interest at the contractual rate should be expressed as being payable 'after as well as before any judgment'.[137]

2.11.2 Rates of interest

2.97 In commercial agreements not involving consumers, there is very little restriction upon the interest rate that the parties may choose as the rate of interest that the borrower can agree to pay for the period prior to default. The usury laws were repealed in the middle of the nineteenth century[138] and subsequent legislation in the

---

[134] However, as noted previously, this may be a fiction as the bank may fund itself from sources other than the interbank market.

[135] *Page v Newman* (1829) 9 B&C 378; *London Chatham & Dover Ry Co v South Eastern Ry Co* [1893] AC 429; *President of India v La Pintada Compania Navegacion SA* [1985] AC 104; *Al Jaber v Al Ibrahim* [2018] EWCA Civ 1690.

[136] *Lloyds Bank plc v Voller* [2000] 2 All ER (Comm) 978; *Emerald Meats (London) Ltd v AIB Group (UK) plc* [2002] EWCA Civ 460. But see also *Financial Institutions Services Ltd v Negril Holdings Ltd* [2004] UKPC 40.

[137] *Economic Life Assurance Soc v Usborne* [1902] AC 147. See also *Director General of Fair Trading v First National Bank plc* [2001] UKHL 52, [2002] 1 AC 481 (as to the use of such a clause in consumer lending). In *Standard Chartered Bank v Ceylon Petroleum Corp* [2011] EWHC 2094 (Comm) it was held that an agreed post-judgment rate did not cap the 8 per cent rate of interest that the claimant was entitled to on a judgment debt under the Judgments Act 1838.

[138] Usury Laws Repeal Act 1854.

form of the Moneylenders Acts 1900 and 1927 has also been repealed.[139] There remains, however, the provision concerning 'extortionate credit transactions' in section 244 of the Insolvency Act 1986, which gives a liquidator or administrator the power to challenge such a transaction if it was entered into within a period of three years preceding the onset of the relevant insolvency proceedings.[140]

2.11.3 Interest as a share of profits

It should be noted that if the loan agreement provides that the lender is to receive **2.98** a share of the borrower's profits or that the interest on the loan is to vary dependent upon those profits, the claim of the lender for repayment of the loan will be subordinated in the borrower's insolvency behind the claims of its unsecured creditors.[141] However, to the extent that the loan is secured, the lender may have recourse to its security and so it will not be affected by such a subordination.[142] It is submitted that if the lender holds share capital in the borrower separately from its loan, and the loan is expressed to carry interest in the normal way, the lender's rights under the loan will not be subordinated, as the relevant legislation specifically provides that it is the loan contract which must contain the profit sharing agreement, although this must be subject to the overall arrangement not being seen as a sham to disguise the true nature of the loan.

2.11.4 Interest for default in payment

Traditionally (but subject as explained below), interest was not normally awarded **2.99** by way of damages at common law for failure to pay a debt on the due date with respect to the period from the due date to the date of judgment.[143] However, interest could be awarded on the unpaid amount where interest was agreed to be paid on the loan, even though it was not expressly agreed that interest would continue to accrue after default, although it may not have been awarded at the

---

[139] Repealed by s 192(4) of the Consumer Credit Act 1974. An example of the application of such legislation in other parts of the Commonwealth is provided by the decision of the Privy Council in *Palmer v Cornerstone Investments & Finance Co Ltd* [2007] UKPC 49.

[140] The meaning of the expression 'extortionate credit transaction' was considered in *Paragon Finance plc v Staunton* [2001] EWCA Civ 1466, [2002] 1 WLR 685, in which the Court of Appeal quoted from Goode, *Consumer Law and Practice*, para 47.26, that: 'the concepts of extortion and unconscionability are very similar. "Extortionate", like "harsh and unconscionable", signifies not merely that the terms of the bargain are stiff, or even unreasonable, but that they are so unfair as to be oppressive. This carries with it the notion of morally reprehensible conduct on the part of the creditor in taking grossly unfair advantage of the debtor's circumstances.'

[141] S 3 of the Partnership Act 1890, which is of general application and applies in the administration or winding up of companies, as well as in bankruptcy: see r 12.3(2A)(c) of the Insolvency Rules 1986. See also *Re Theo Garvin Ltd* [1969] 1 Ch 624, which concerned a related point under s 317 of the Companies Act 1948. It does not matter if the loan was made under a written or an oral agreement: *Re Fort, ex p Schofield* [1897] 2 QB 495.

[142] *Re Lonergan, ex p Sheil* (1877) 4 ChD 789; *Badeley v Consolidated Bank* (1888) 38 ChD 238, which concerned the predecessor of s 3 that was found in s 5 of Bovill's Act 1865.

[143] *London Chatham & Dover Ry Co v South Eastern Ry Co* [1893] AC 429.

contract rate.[144] Furthermore, interest might be awarded under the second limb of the rule in *Hadley v Baxendale*[145] as damages if it was in the reasonable contemplation of the defendant at the time of contracting that the creditor would itself suffer an interest charge if the debt was not paid on the due date.[146]

2.100 The rule at common law was partially relaxed by statute. Under section 35A of the Supreme Court Act 1981,[147] the High Court has power to award simple interest on an unpaid debt provided that the debt remained unpaid at the time that proceedings were commenced for its recovery.[148] The courts are prepared to award such interest at a commercial rate.[149] There is also an entitlement to interest under various other statutory provisions, such as that under the Late Payment of Debts (Interest) Act 1998 relating to the late payment of debts arising for the supply of goods or services,[150] where the purchaser and supplier are both acting in the course of a business.

2.101 In *Sempra Metals Ltd v HM Commissioners of Inland Revenue*[151] the House of Lords changed the law and held that interest may be awarded at common law as damages for late payment of a debt within the first limb of the rule in *Hadley v Baxendale*,[152] subject to the usual rule in awarding damages that the claimant must prove its loss. Furthermore, it held that compound interest could be awarded at common law within such damages, as that is consistent with everyday practice in the lending of money. It also held that interest, including compound interest, could be awarded on a tortious claim and, by majority,[153] that such interest could be awarded upon a restitutionary claim for money paid under a mistake.[154]

---

[144] *Cook v Fowler* (1874) LR 7 HL 27.
[145] (1854) 9 Exch 341.
[146] *Wadsworth v Lydell* [1981] 1 WLR 598, approved by the House of Lords in *President of India v La Pintada Compania Navegacion SA* [1985] AC 104.
[147] See also the Judgment Act 1838, s 74 of the County Courts Act 1984, and s 49 of the Arbitration Act 1996. The latter also permits an award of compound interest to be made.
[148] See *President of India v La Pintada Compania Navegacion SA* [1985] AC 104 (Lord Brandon).
[149] *Tate & Lyle Food Distribution Ltd v Greater London Council* [1982] 1 WLR 149, 154; *Kuwait Airways Corp v Kuwait Insurance Co SAK (No 2)* [2000] 1 All ER (Comm) 972.
[150] Financial services, such as lending money, would not be considered the supply of a service: see *R v Preddy* [1996] AC 815, 840 (Lord Goff).
[151] [2007] UKHL 34.
[152] (1854) 9 Exch 341.
[153] Lords Hope, Nicholls, and Walker. Lord Scott and Lord Mance dissented on this point. Lord Scott said that such interest should only be awarded to the extent that it could be shown that the defendant had been unjustly enriched by itself receiving interest on the amount mistakenly paid to it. Lord Mance said there should be no entitlement to interest on such a claim but, if there were, it should be on the basis put forward by Lord Scott.
[154] Thereby overruling the position, as to compound interest, as it had applied since the earlier decision of the House of Lords in *Westdeutsche Landesbank Girozentrale v Islington LBC* [1996] AC 669. Their Lordships were divided as to whether a restitutionary award of interest would arise in equity or at common law (compare Lords Nicholls and Hope, who would award such interest as a matter of the common law, with Lord Walker, who would award it within the court's equitable jurisdiction. Lord Scott and Lord Mance would also have confined it to a jurisdiction at common law).

However, the last conclusion has now been overruled by the Supreme Court in *Prudential Assurance Co Ltd v Revenue and Customs Commissioners*[155] where it held that simple, rather than compound, interest is to be awarded in respect of restitutionary claims.

It might be argued that the decision in the *Sempra Metals* case was obiter dicta, in **2.102** so far as it related to contractual damages for an unpaid debt. The case concerned a claim for interest as damages in tort or as a restitutionary award. However, the decision on the contractual issue was unanimous and their Lordships felt that it was necessary to deal with that issue as it was part of the background to the conclusions that they reached on the tortious and restitutionary claims.

2.11.5 Interest in equity

In certain circumstances interest might be awarded in equity despite there being **2.103** no agreement for payment of interest. For instance, equity will award interest on a mortgage debt,[156] a surety is entitled to interest under its indemnity from the principal debtor,[157] a fiduciary may be liable to pay interest on funds of its beneficiary that are in its hands,[158] a trustee may have to pay compound interest on any wrongful profit it makes for itself,[159] and interest is payable on fraudulently obtained money.[160]

2.11.6 Compound interest

The right to charge compound interest will arise either by agreement[161] or by **2.104** custom, such as by the practice of bankers.[162] Compound interest may also be awarded as damages for late payment of a debt or for a claim in tort.[163] Compound interest is interest that is charged on unpaid interest, which is usually achieved by capitalising the unpaid interest (adding it to principal) so that it becomes part

---

[155] [2018] UKSC 39.
[156] *Re Kerr's Policy* (1869) LR 8 Eq 331; *Al Wazir v Islamic Press Agency Inc* [2001] EWCA Civ 1276, [2002] 1 Lloyd's Rep 410.
[157] *Re Fox Walker & Co* (1880) 15 ChD 400.
[158] *Brown v IRC* [1965] AC 244.
[159] *Attorney-General v Alford* (1855) 4 De GM&G 843, 851.
[160] *Johnson v The King* [1904] AC 817, 822.
[161] In *FBN Bank (UK) Ltd v Leaf Tobacco A Michailides SA* [2017] EWHC 3017 (Comm) it was held that the usual formulation of the default interest clause included in LMA recommended form documents did not entitle the lenders to charge compound interest for late payments.
[162] *National Bank of Greece SA v Pinios Shipping Co* [1990] AC 637. Clauses imposing compound interest cannot be challenged as penalties where they do not operate on breach of contract: *Holyoake v Candy* [2017] EWHC 3397 (Ch).
[163] *Sempra Metals Ltd v HM Commissioners of Inland Revenue* [2009] 1 AC 61. In *JSC BTA Bank v Ablyazov* [2013] EWHC 867 (Comm) it was held that to recover compound interest as damages the loss had to be pleaded and proved. However, in *Equitas Ltd v Walsham Brothers & Co Ltd* [2013] EWHC 3264 (Comm) it was held that compound interest could be awarded without this requirement being met.

of the principal on which interest is charged. It is not yet clear how frequently the practice of bankers would apply the 'rests', being the dates for capitalising of interest.[164] The right of a banker to compound interest continues until payment, notwithstanding that the banker has made demand for repayment.[165]

2.12 Penalties

2.105 Fairly typically, a loan facility agreement will provide for an additional rate of interest to be payable on any amount that is in default of payment; that is, a rate which is additional to the normal contractual rate that applied prior to default. Such a rate is often referred to as the 'default rate'.[166] A different category of contract may provide for some other type of additional amount to be payable if there has been a breach, sometimes called a 'liquidated damages clause'. Such provisions, however, run the risk that they might be struck down by the courts as being an unenforceable penalty.[167] In such a case, the court will make its own assessment of the damages to which the claimant will be entitled in consequence of the default that has occurred, based upon the normal rules for the assessment of damages, including the rules as to remoteness.

2.106 A provision will be characterised as being a penalty if it was intended to punish the borrower for a breach of contract.[168] The term will be a penalty where it imposes a detriment on the contract breaker 'out of all proportion to any legitimate interest of the innocent party' in enforcing its rights under the contract.[169] Thus

---

[164] Quarterly rests were conceded in *National Bank of Greece SA v Pinios Shipping Co* [1990] AC 637 and were permitted in *Kitchen v HSBC Bank plc* [2000] 1 All ER (Comm) 787.

[165] ibid.

[166] In *FBN Bank (UK) Ltd v Leaf Tobacco A Michailides SA* [2017] EWHC 3017 (Comm) the court considered the usual formulation of the default interest clause included in LMA recommended form documents.

[167] Most commentaries on this subject traditionally began with the speech of Lord Dunedin in *Dunlop Pneumatic Tyre Co Ltd v New Garage & Motor Co Ltd* [1915] AC 79, particularly at 87–88. However, the doctrine was recently recast by the Supreme Court in *Cavendish Square Holding BV v Talal El Makdessi; ParkingEye Limited v Beavis* [2015] UKSC 67 in a manner that narrows its application. Cf the broader approach taken in Australia in *Andrews v Australia and New Zealand Banking Group Ltd* [2012] HCA 30, (2012) 247 CLR 205 and *Paciocco v Australia and New Zealand Banking Group Limited* [2016] HCA 28.

[168] The modern approach is to refer to whether the clause is intended to punish a breach, rather than the older formulation of whether it was intended to deter a breach from occurring (see *Murray v Leisureplay* [2005] EWCA Civ 963, [2005] IRLR 946 [111] (Buxton LJ)) or to act 'in terrorem' (see Colman J in *Lordsvale Finance Ltd v Bank of Zambia* [1996] QB 752, 762).

[169] *Cavendish Square Holding BV v Talal El Makdessi; ParkingEye Limited v Beavis* [2015] UKSC 67 [32], [152], [255], and [293]. In *Hayfin Opal Luxco 3 SARL and anor v Windermere VII Cmbs plc and ors* [2016] EWHC 782 (Ch) Snowden J stated by way of obiter that the imposition of interest rates applying to a structured instrument (which exceeded several thousand per cent per quarter for certain periods) for breach in failing to make payment of a sum due under that instrument would be a penalty as it was exorbitant, if not extortionate.

a default interest provision will not be a penalty if it protects a legitimate interest of the lender in the performance of the payment obligations under the contract and is not out of all proportion in doing so. Legitimate interests of the lender would include the securing of a higher rate of interest for providing finance to a person who has now proved to be a less creditworthy borrower, compensating the lender for the inconvenience and detriment that it suffers due to the late receipt of payment (particularly if it has entered into matched-funding arrangements to obtain the funds to make loans), encouraging the borrower to perform its payment obligations strictly on time, and incentivising the borrower to rectify promptly defaults that had already occurred. The question in any particular case will be whether the detriment imposed on the borrower by the default rate is out of all proportion to such legitimate interests.

The circumstances in which the contract was made will be taken into account in **2.107** applying the above test. Where the contract was negotiated between represented parties with comparable bargaining power, the strong initial presumption will be that the provision is to be upheld as the parties are the best judges of what is legitimate in a provision dealing with the consequences of breach.[170] The resources that a particular contract-breaker possesses to pay the specified amount are not a factor that is to be taken into consideration.[171]

Each case depends on its facts, so a provision that may be acceptable in the circum- **2.108** stances of one contract may not necessarily be enforceable in the circumstances of another. However some examples may be cited as benchmarks. It was held in one case that a 'modest increase' of 1 per cent per annum above the normal pre-default rate, which was payable during the period of default, could be justified.[172] Given that the statutory interest rate currently applicable to the late payment of commercial debts[173] is 8 per cent plus the Bank of England base rate (currently 0.75 per cent) and the rate applicable to the late payment of judgment debts[174] is 8 per cent, it may be extremely difficult to argue successfully that default rates which do not significantly exceed these statutory thresholds are penal. Recently a default rate of 15 per cent per annum compounded monthly was not considered to be a penal rate for a commercial agreement.[175]

---

[170] *Cavendish Square Holding BV v Talal El Makdessi; ParkingEye Limited v Beavis* [2015] UKSC 67.
[171] *Hayfin Opal Luxco 3 SARL and anor v Windermere VII Cmbs plc and ors* [2016] EWHC 782 (Ch).
[172] *Lordsvale Finance Ltd v Bank of Zambia* [1996] QB 752, in which it was held that an additional 1 per cent per annum over the normal pre-default contractual rate payable by the borrower under that loan agreement would not be a penalty.
[173] Late Payment of Debts (Interest) Act 1998.
[174] S 17 Judgments Act 1838.
[175] *Holyoake v Candy* [2017] EWHC 3397 (Ch).

2.109   In the past various situations have been examined by the courts and held to fall outside the scope of the doctrine of penalties entirely, including the following.

2.110   A practice that has traditionally been used in mortgages is to provide for a normal rate which will be reduced for prompt payment. In effect, the mortgage provides that the normal rate will be x per cent per annum but if the mortgagor pays an instalment of interest on or before the due date, the mortgagee will accept a payment equal to a lower specified rate. Despite the apparent artificiality of such an arrangement, it has been upheld as not amounting to a penalty, because the mortgagor is not being charged an extra amount in consequence of a default but is being allowed a concessionary benefit for paying on time. Hence, the full or higher rate may be legitimately charged if the mortgagor defaults in due and punctual payment.[176] There is no reason why this approach should be confined to mortgages; it can be applied to other types of credit or finance arrangements.[177]

2.111   An obligation on a party to a principal contract to indemnify a third party for a payment due by the third party under a guarantee or a bond is not a penalty, even though the guarantee or bond relates to the indemnifier's own breach of its contractual obligations under the principal contract. This is because the obligation under the indemnity is not one arising due to a breach of the indemnity.[178]

2.112   A premium or fee that is payable by a contracting party if it wishes to exercise a right of early termination of the contract is not a penalty. It is regarded as the legitimate consideration that is payable for the exercise of a contractual right.[179]

2.113   It has also been held that a right to accelerate the repayment of a loan on the occurrence of an event of default and to receive payment of the interest that had accrued up to the date of payment does not amount to a penalty.[180] Similarly, a right to terminate a hire-purchase or equipment lease agreement for breach by the hirer

---

[176] See *Wallingford v Mutual Society* (1880) 5 App Cas 685, 702 (Lord Hatherley). But note the obiter dicta in *Cavendish Square Holding BV v Talal El Makdessi; ParkingEye Limited v Beavis* [2015] UKSC 67 [258] which suggest that 'disguised penalties' may be brought within the ambit of the rule by focusing on the substance of the contractual term rather than its form.

[177] *Lordsvale Finance Ltd v Bank of Zambia* [1996] QB 752, 762; *Holyoake v Candy* [2017] EWHC 3397 (Ch).

[178] *Export Credits Guarantee Department v Universal Oil Products Co* [1983] 1 WLR 399.

[179] *Bridge v Campbell Discount Co Ltd* [1962] AC 600. As that case demonstrates, a court may strain to find that the relevant party did not intend to exercise its right to terminate but, instead, indicated its unwillingness to be bound by the contract if such a finding would result in a lesser amount being payable by way of damages than under the exercise of the contractual right. In *Edgeworth Capital (Luxembourg) Sarl v Ramblas Investments BV* [2016] EWCA Civ 412 a fee of €105 million was upheld as not being a penalty because it was payable on the happening of a specified event rather than on a breach of contract. See also *Holyoake v Candy* [2017] EWHC 3397 (Ch) where an arrangement whereby, on early repayment, the debtor had to pay all the interest that would have accrued by the end of the term of the loan was not a penalty as it did not operate on breach.

[180] *The Angelic Star* [1988] 1 Lloyd's Rep 122 and *County Leasing Ltd v East* [2007] EWHC 2907 (QB).

or lessee will not be a penalty.[181] However, it may be a penalty if a loan agreement additionally provided for the lender to receive all of the interest to which it would have been entitled had the loan run its full course.[182]

It has been held that a compromise agreement is enforceable[183] if the creditor agrees **2.114** to forgo payment of the whole of a debt should the debtor pay a lesser sum but that if such lesser sum is not paid the whole debt will be payable. The revived obligation to pay the whole debt is not regarded as a penalty but merely as a reservation of the creditor's pre-existing right to be paid the whole debt.[184] The same principle will apply where the stipulated residual or revived amount represents a bona fide calculation of what would have been due, even if it was not the precise amount.[185] However, the principle will not apply if the creditor acquired new or additional rights under the settlement agreement that it did not have previously.[186]

If a provision is struck down as a penalty, it cannot be partially enforced. The gen- **2.115** eral law as to the assessment of damages applies.[187]

2.13 Payments under a Loan Facility Agreement

A finance transaction involves payments as between the lender and the borrower, **2.116** not infrequently involving international payments between different jurisdictions. The lender disburses the drawing to the borrower[188] and the borrower makes payment of principal, interest, and other amounts to the lender. Various questions may arise that relate to such payments, including the method and finality of making payment, the effect of rights of set-off, and the conclusiveness of the lender's determination of amounts that are payable by the borrower. The common law rules relating to those matters will be addressed in the following paragraphs.[189]

---

[181] *Transag Haulage Ltd v Leyland Daf Finance plc* [1994] 2 BCLC 88. For the position concerning conditional sale, see ss 48(3) and (4) of the Sale of Goods Act 1979.

[182] *The Angelic Star* [1988] 1 Lloyd's Rep 122; *County Leasing Ltd v East* [2007] EWHC 2907 (QB). But such an obligation will need to be triggered by a breach for the penalty doctrine to be engaged; it will stand where it is conditional on another event: *Holyoake v Candy* [2017] EWHC 3397 (Ch).

[183] Subject, of course, to being supported by consideration or being made by way of a deed.

[184] *Thompson v Hudson* (1869) 4 HL 1.

[185] *Society of Lloyd's v Twinn* The Times, 4 April 2000.

[186] *Donegal International Ltd v Republic of Zambia* [2007] EWHC 197 (Comm).

[187] *Cavendish Square Holding BV v Talal El Makdessi; ParkingEye Limited v Beavis* [2015] UKSC 67 [83]–[87].

[188] It should be noted that a bank owes its customer a duty to refrain from executing a payment request if the bank has reasonable grounds for believing that the request is an attempt to misappropriate the funds of the company: *Barclays Bank plc v Quincecare* [1992] 4 All ER 363 and *Singularis Holdings Ltd (In Liquidation) v Daiwa Capital Markets Europe Ltd* [2017] EWHC 257 (Ch). This principle could potentially apply to the drawdown of a loan facility.

[189] The EC Directive on payment services (EU 2015/2366), implemented in its previous form by the Payment Services Regulations 2009, could, depending on the facts, affect some of the rules as

Conflict of laws issues may also arise relating to the currency of account for calculating the obligations of the parties, the currency of payment in which payments should be made, the requirements for effecting performance, and the effect of illegality in a place that is relevant to performance and payment. The conflict of laws issues are addressed elsewhere in this book's parent work, *McKnight, Paterson, & Zakrzewski on the Law of International Finance*.[190] It should also be noted that damages may be awarded under English law for currency exchange losses that arise in consequence of making late payment.[191]

2.13.1 Methods of payment

2.117 The common methods for making a payment (or the equivalent to making a payment) are by cash, by cheque, bill of exchange, promissory note or similar instrument, by a barter through the exchange of goods or by some other method of payment in kind,[192] by netting and set-off of liabilities, or by transfers between bank accounts.[193] For practical purposes, payments in cash are unlikely to occur in transactions of any size[194] and payments by cheque or a similar instrument are also unlikely to occur in commercial finance transactions. Barter transactions and payments in kind are confined to specialist transactions that are outside the scope of the present discussion. Set-off and netting will be referred to separately later.

2.118 The most likely method of payment in finance transactions, being that which is commonly stipulated in loan facility agreements, is by payment to the credit of a bank account which will probably involve payment transfers across the accounts of different banks. For instance, a payment in US dollars by a payer situated in London to a payee whose account is in New York will probably be effected by the payer instructing its bank in London to effect the payment, if necessary

---

they had been developed at common law. The Directive, now amended by PSD2 (Revised Payment Service Directive), has relevance to electronic payments and payment systems throughout the EC and the EEA. It deals with matters such as the authorisation of entities that may provide payment services, transparency, and the provision of information relating to payments; the rights and obligations of users and providers of payment services; and liabilities for incorrectly executed payment orders.

[190] (2nd edn, OUP 2017) ch 4. Importantly it should be noted that an English law governed debt can only be discharged in accordance with English law: *Antony Gibbs & Sons v La Société Industrielle et Commerciale des Metaux* (1890) 25 QBD 399. English-law rights of creditors are not discharged by a foreign insolvency proceeding, if the creditors have not submitted to the jurisdiction of the foreign court: *Bakhshiyeva v Sberbank of Russia and ors* [2018] EWHC 59 (Ch).

[191] *President of India v Lips Maritime Corp* [1988] 1 AC 395.

[192] For instance, by the provision of services, by issuing equity or further debt, or by off-taking or transferring products, rights, or benefits that might have been generated by, or resulted from, the subject matter of the financing.

[193] For a judicial consideration of the mechanics of making payments by the clearing houses automated payment system (CHAPS) see *Tidal Energy Ltd v Bank of Scotland plc* [2014] EWCA Civ 1107.

[194] Although they may be available when other methods of payment cannot be used: see *Libyan Arab Foreign Bank v Bankers Trust Co* [1989] QB 728.

after having converted sterling into US dollars. That bank will instruct its correspondent bank in New York[195] (or its own branch in New York) to make the payment to the payee's bank in New York,[196] which, on receipt, will credit the payment to the payee's account. Whilst commercially the various steps are seen as payments, in fact they do not involve any physical payments of money but, instead, involve a series of successive credits and debits to bank accounts, each representing debtor–creditor relationships. Thus, the receipt of payment by the payee will be constituted by a credit entry on its account with its bank, which represents a debt due by that bank to the payee. The payment to the payee's bank will be represented by debit and credit entries in the payment system of which the correspondent bank and the payee's bank are members, the payment effected by the payer's bank to the correspondent bank will be effected on the accounts between them, and the whole process will be begun by the payer's bank debiting the payer's account with the amount it has been instructed to pay.

2.13.2 Effectiveness of payment

Under English law, an obligor with a payment obligation is obliged to make payment in cash (ie legal tender by the use of notes and coins) unless the parties have agreed to another method of payment or the payee accepts an alternative method of payment.[197] Where the contract specifically provides for a different method of payment (eg by a transfer to a specified bank account) that will constitute effective payment if it is made in accordance with the requirements (eg as to time) of the contract.[198] If such a method is the only method of payment that is permitted by the contract then payment must be made by the contractually agreed method. Otherwise, a debtor is entitled to pay in cash in addition to any alternative method specified by the contract; indeed, the debtor may be obliged to pay in cash if the alternative method is unavailable.[199] In other cases, the debtor must

2.119

---

[195] Eg by sending an instruction through the SWIFT system (the Society for Worldwide Interbank Financial Telecommunications).

[196] Unless agreed otherwise between the payer and its bank, the latter is entitled to determine the method of transfer and to make payment within a reasonable time, although it does owe the payer a duty of care and skill in carrying out the payer's instruction: *Royal Products Ltd v Midland Bank Ltd* [1981] 2 Lloyd's Rep 194. See also *Dovey v Bank of New Zealand* [2000] NZLR 641. Generally speaking, the payer's bank owes no duty to the payee, nor does the correspondent bank owe a duty to either the payer or the payee: *Royal Products Ltd v Midland Bank Ltd*. Where the bank suspects a customer of money laundering, an implied term in the bank-customer contract permits the bank to refuse to execute a payment instruction pending permission from the National Crime Agency under the Proceeds of Crime Act 2002: *Shah v HSBC Private Bank (UK) Ltd* [2013] 1 All ER (Comm) 72. See also *N v S* [2015] EWHC 3248 (Ch) which provides an example of a mandatory injunction being granted requiring a bank to comply with a customer's instructions.

[197] *Libyan Arab Foreign Bank v Bankers Trust Co* [1989] QB 728, 764.

[198] *TSB Bank of Scotland v Welwyn Hatfield DC* [1993] 2 Bank LR 267, 272; *Royal Products Ltd v Midland Bank plc* [1981] 2 Lloyd's Rep 194, 198; *Hosni Tayeb v HSBC Bank plc* [2004] EWHC 1529 (Comm), [2004] 4 All ER 1024 [80]–[82].

[199] *Libyan Arab Foreign Bank v Bankers Trust Co* [1989] QB 728, 764.

tender payment but payment will not be effective unless the tender is accepted by the creditor or its authorised agent. If a tender of payment is rejected, the tenderer can protect itself if it is subsequently sued by paying the money into court and raising a defence of tender.[200] In cases of money transfers that are not made pursuant to, and in conformity with, an agreed requirement in the contract between the payer and payee, the payee's bank may not be authorised as agent to accept payment (eg where the payment is late) so as to bind its customer and prevent the customer from rejecting the purported payment and exercising its rights arising in consequence of late payment.[201] Accordingly, there is no general authorisation for a bank to accept payment on behalf of its customer where the customer has not agreed to the receipt,[202] either in the contract between the payer and the customer or as between the customer and the bank (for instance, in the bank's mandate, as will often be the case). An unauthorised payment by a third party will not bind the debtor unless it is ratified.[203]

2.13.3 Receipt of payment

2.120   Where a payment is received by the payee's bank and it is received within the bank's mandate, payment is treated (as between the payee and its bank and also as between the payer and payee) as received by the payee, and cannot be countermanded, when its account is credited with the payment, unless it is merely credited conditionally (eg a cheque awaiting clearance of funds), in which case it will be treated as finally received when the condition has been satisfied; effective receipt by the payee in accordance with the foregoing is not dependent upon the bank notifying the receipt to the payee.[204] Where a conditional payment is accepted by a payee pending clearance (eg a cheque), the payment will be treated, as between payer and payee, as being effective from the date of receipt of the conditional payment, provided clearance is effected.[205] If such a payment is received by the payee but it fails to seek clearance of the payment, it will not be able to claim

---

[200] *HM Customs & Excise v National Westminster Bank plc* [2002] EWHC 2204 (QB) [9]; *RSM Bentley Jennison v Ayton* [2015] EWCA Civ 1120.

[201] *Mardorf Peach & Co Ltd v Attica Sea Carriers Corp, The Laconia* [1977] AC 850.

[202] *TSB Bank of Scotland v Welwyn Hatfield DC* [1993] 2 Bank LR 267; *HM Customs & Excise v National Westminster Bank plc* [2002] EWHC 2204 (QB).

[203] *Owen v Tate* [1976] QB 402. But a payment by a third party to a creditor under legal compulsion on account of a debt owed by a debtor (eg due to a contractual obligation under a letter of credit) automatically discharges the debtor's debt and questions of agency, authority, and ratification do not arise: *Ibrahim v Barclays Bank plc* [2013] Ch 400.

[204] *The Brimnes, Tenax SS Co Ltd v The Brimnes (Owners)* [1975] QB 929; *Mardorf Peach & Co Ltd v Attica Sea Carriers Corp, The Laconia* [1976] QB 835 (reversed by HL on other grounds); *Momm v Barclays Bank International Ltd* [1977] QB 790; *Libyan Arab Foreign Bank v Manufacturers Hanover Trust Co (No 2)* [1989] 1 Lloyd's Rep 608; *Hosni Tayeb v HSBC Bank plc* [2004] EWHC 1529 (Comm); *Tidal Energy Ltd v Bank of Scotland plc* [2014] EWCA Civ 1107.

[205] *Holmes v Smith* [2000] Lloyd's Rep Bank 139.

it has not received payment.[206] Where a conditional payment is received pending clearance and clearance fails, the payment is ineffective (unless it was agreed that it would be an absolute payment).[207]

2.13.4 Drafting of payments provisions

A loan facility agreement should take account of the issues just outlined, as well **2.121** as the associated conflict of laws issues. Subject to one point that arises in consequence of the experience in the *Libyan Arab Foreign Bank* litigation,[208] the agreement should provide for all calculations and payments to be made in the relevant currency or currencies of account, to be made unconditionally for value on the due date, and that the payments should be made to nominated bank accounts. As payments have to be settled by transfers via the relevant payments systems, they should be made for settlement in the principal financial centre of the relevant currency (or, in the case of payments in euros, in a financial centre of a participating Member State in the eurozone or in London). The point raised by the exception is that it would be sensible for the contract expressly to give the lender the right to direct that payments by the borrower (and, perhaps, by the lender) should be made in an equivalent amount in a different currency to the currency of account and in a different place if it becomes unlawful or impossible for them to be made in the normal way. Otherwise, a borrower under an agreement governed by English law might be excused from having to make a payment if it becomes unlawful for it to make the payment under the law stipulated by the agreement as the place of payment.[209]

2.13.5 Unlawfulness

Such unlawfulness or, indeed, illegality on a broader scale may mean that it is not **2.122** feasible for the lender to continue with the facility. For instance, the lender's regulator or other authorities in its home jurisdiction may prohibit it from maintaining the facility or having dealings with the borrower. Strictly speaking, if all of those dealings and any payments it has to make take place outside its home jurisdiction, so that the transaction is not unlawful in its intended place of performance, the lender may not be excused by English law from its contractual obligations under the facility,[210] unless it could argue that the contract had been frustrated.[211]

---

[206] *Fusion Interactive Communication Solutions Ltd v Venture Investment Placement Ltd* [2005] EWHC 736 (Ch), [2006] BCC 187.
[207] *Re Romer & Haslam* [1893] 2 QB 286; *Bolt & Nut Co (Tipton) Ltd v Rowlands Nicholls & Co Ltd* [1964] 2 QB 10.
[208] *Libyan Arab Foreign Bank v Bankers Trust Co* [1989] QB 728 and *Libyan Arab Foreign Bank v Manufacturers Hanover Trust Co (No 2)* [1989] 1 Lloyd's Rep 608.
[209] See the discussion in Sarah Paterson and Rafal Zakrzewski (eds), *McKnight, Paterson, & Zakrzewski on the Law of International Finance* (2nd edn, OUP 2017) ch 4.
[210] ibid.
[211] See section 1.4.

To cover the possibility that the lender may be at risk in such circumstances, the agreement should contain a provision which gives the lender the right to terminate the facility and call for repayment of any amounts that it might have lent in the event that it becomes unlawful for it to maintain the facility.

2.123 A borrower's obligations to pay under a loan agreement will not be suspended or frustrated because the borrower's funds are frozen pursuant to sanctions legislation if the loan agreement could still be performed if the borrower obtained a licence to permit payment. If there is no possibility of obtaining a licence, the borrower would still have to repay the loan on the basis of section 1 of the Law Reform (Frustrated Contracts) Act 1943.[212] Similarly, a sanctions law applying to payments to a lender will not necessarily release a borrower from its payment obligations.[213]

2.13.6 Conclusive evidence clauses

2.124 Loan facility agreements, security documents, and the like often contain a provision to the effect that a certificate provided by the creditor or one of its officers as to the amount due by the borrower at any time should be treated as conclusive evidence of that fact, save for any error that is manifest on the face of the certificate. Similar provisions will also be found in guarantees with respect to the amount of the guaranteed liabilities. It has been held that such a certificate will be binding upon the borrower or the guarantor and cannot be challenged in proceedings to enforce payment of the amount of the relevant liability in the absence of manifest error.[214] In the context of such a clause, a 'manifest error' is one which is obvious or easily demonstrable without extensive investigation.[215] However, a party does not have to be able to demonstrate the error immediately and conclusively for it to be regarded as manifest for such purposes.[216] Extrinsic evidence can be considered to establish this.[217] Conclusive evidence clauses may be subject to review, as to whether they meet the requirement of reasonableness, if the Unfair Contract Terms Act 1977 applies to the particular contract.[218]

---

[212] See *DVB Bank SE v Shere Shipping Company Limited and ors* [2013] EWHC 2321 (Comm).

[213] *Melli Bank plc v Holbud Limited* [2013] EWHC 1506 (Comm).

[214] *Bache & Co (London) Ltd v Banque Vernes et Commerciale de Paris SA* [1973] 2 Lloyd's Rep 437, which was a case concerning a guarantee. See also *ABN Amro Commercial Finance plc v McGinn* [2014] EWHC 1674 (Comm).

[215] *Van Der Merwe v IIG Capital LLC* [2008] EWCA Civ 542.

[216] *North Shore Ventures Ltd v Anstead Holdings Inc* [2011] EWCA Civ 230; *Amey Birmingham Highways Ltd v Birmingham City Council* [2018] EWCA Civ 264; cf *ABN Amro Commercial Finance plc v McGinn* [2014] EWHC 1674 (Comm).

[217] *IG Index v Colley* [2013] EWHC 478 (QB) [813]; *Amey Birmingham Highways Ltd v Birmingham City Council* [2018] EWCA Civ 264.

[218] *AXA Sun Life Services plc v Campbell Martin Ltd* [2011] EWCA Civ 133; *United Trust Bank Limited v Dalmit Singh Dohil* [2011] EWHC 3302 (QB).

On the other hand, it has been held that a clause in a bank's terms and conditions **2.125** with its customer, by which the customer agreed that any statement of account produced by the bank would be binding upon the customer and that the bank would not be responsible for any loss suffered by the customer if it contained any error, unless the customer queried the statement within a defined period after it received the statement, should be construed as only relating to areas of computation. It was designed as a form of release by the customer of the bank for claims for consequential loss that the customer might suffer as a result of a customer being misinformed about its financial position. It did not serve to validate items wrongly debited to the account, such as an invalid interest charge.[219]

2.13.7 Set-off provisions

One of the ways in which a party's liabilities may be settled is through the oper- **2.126** ation of netting or set-off. Those matters are dealt with substantively elsewhere.[220] For present purposes, it is relevant to observe that under English law rights of set-off may be enhanced or restricted[221] by contract. However, set-off is mandatory in the insolvency of either of the parties between whom there have been mutual dealings and it is not possible to contract out of set-off in insolvency.[222] Contractual provisions which advance and restrict rights of set-off are frequently to be found in a loan facility agreement. The rights are enhanced in favour of the lender, so that it can set off any liability it may have to the borrower against the borrower's obligations to it, such as by the application of a credit balance in the borrower's favour against the borrower's liability under the loan agreement. The right of the borrower to assert a claim to set-off is restricted. This rather unevenly handed approach may appear to be unfair. The justifications from the lender's perspective are, first, that such a right would hinder the ability of the lender to trade the loan participation in the secondary market and, second, that it relies upon receiving payments from the borrower to meet its own obligations for payment in the interbank market or to its creditors with respect to the funding it has obtained for the purposes of the facility. Precluding a right of set-off does not mean that

---

[219] *Financial Institutions Services Limited v Negril Holdings Limited* [2004] UKPC 40.

[220] See Sarah Paterson and Rafal Zakrzewski (eds), *McKnight, Paterson, & Zakrzewski on the Law of International Finance* (2nd edn, OUP 2017) ch 14.

[221] *Coca-Cola Financial Corp v Finsat International Ltd* [1998] QB 43; *FG Wilson (Engineering) Limited v John Holt & Company (Liverpool) Limited* [2012] EWHC 2477 (Comm); *Deutsche Bank SA v Khan* [2013] EWHC 482 (Comm). This is subject to the possible operation of the Unfair Contract Terms Act 1977: see *Stewart Gill Ltd v Horatio Meyer & Co Ltd* [1992] QB 600; *Rohlig (UK) Ltd v Rock Unique Ltd* [2011] EWCA Civ 18; *AXA Sun Life Services plc v Campbell Martin Ltd* [2011] EWCA Civ 133; *United Trust Bank Limited v Dalmit Singh Dohil* [2011] EWHC 3302 (QB); *Deutsche Bank SA v Khan* [2013] EWHC 482 (Comm); and in the case of consumer cases Part 2 of the Consumer Rights Act 2015 which covers unfair terms in consumer contracts.

[222] *National Westminster Bank Ltd v Halesowen Presswork & Assemblies Ltd* [1972] AC 785; *Re Maxwell Communications Corp plc (No 2)* [1993] 1 WLR 1402; *Re West End Networks Ltd* [2004] UKHL 24, [2004] 2 AC 506.

the counter-claim on which it would have been based is lost. The counter-claim can still be pursued independently but the cash-flow advantage of the set-off is lost, as the debt must be paid in full and the counter-claim sought elsewhere and probably paid at a later date.

2.13.8 Payments made by mistake[223]

2.127 It is relevant to consider, briefly, the position under English law where a payment is made in consequence of a mistake made by the payer concerning a matter of fact[224] or of law.[225] The payer has a prima facie right to recover the payment from the recipient, even if the mistake is only held by the payer and is not shared by the payee.[226] The claim for recovery may fail, however, if the payer intends that the payee should have the money at all events.[227] It may also fail if the payment was made for good consideration, in particular if the money is paid to discharge a debt owed to the payee (or the payee's principal on whose behalf the payee is authorised to receive payment), such debt being due by the payer (or the payer's principal in a case where the principal had authorised the payment).[228] In addition, the right to recovery will fail if the payee has changed its position in good faith, or is deemed in law to have done so,[229] even if the payee had paid away the money voluntarily, provided it did so in good faith.[230] A change of position defence (eg that the payee had paid away the money it had received from the payer) will not be available if the payee had acted in bad faith, for instance, if it paid away the money with knowledge of the mistake, or if the payment it made was for expenditure that it would have incurred in any event.[231] Nor will the defence be available to the extent that the payee had retained the benefit of its expenditure of the money.[232] It would appear that a defence of change of position can only apply where the change occurred after the receipt by the payee of the money.[233]

---

[223] These matters can be affected by the EC Directive on payment services (2015/2366), implemented in its previous form by the Payment Services Regulations 2009, which concerns electronic payments within the EU and the EEA. The Regulations contain provisions (eg reg 75) relating to obligations on a payment service provider to give refunds for incorrectly executed payment orders.

[224] *Barclays Bank Ltd v WJ Simms Son & Cooke (Southern) Ltd* [1980] QB 677.

[225] *Kleinwort Benson Ltd v Lincoln City Council* [1999] 2 AC 349; *Pitt v Holt* [2013] 2 AC 108.

[226] *National Westminster Bank Ltd v Barclays Bank International Ltd* [1975] QB 654; *Barclays Bank Ltd v WJ Simms Son & Cooke (Southern) Ltd* [1980] QB 677; *Pitt v Holt* [2013] 2 AC 108.

[227] *Barclays Bank Ltd v WJ Simms Son & Cooke (Southern) Ltd* [1980] QB 677.

[228] ibid; *Lloyds Bank plc v Independent Insurance Co Ltd* [2000] QB 110.

[229] *Gowers v Lloyds and National and Provincial Bank Ltd* [1938] 1 All ER 766; *Barclays Bank Ltd v WJ Simms Son & Cooke (Southern) Ltd* [1980] QB 677.

[230] *Lipkin Gorman v Karpnale & Co* [1991] 2 AC 548.

[231] ibid.

[232] *Scottish Equitable plc v Derby* [2001] EWCA Civ 369; *National Westminster Bank plc v Somer International (UK) Ltd* [2001] EWCA Civ 970, [2002] QB 1286.

[233] *South Tyneside Metropolitan BC v Svenska International plc* [1995] 1 All ER 545.

It has been held that if a paying bank which has paid by mistake (eg it made the **2.128** payment without authority) is unable to recover payment from the payee, it may be entitled to recover from its own customer where the payment it made had the effect of discharging a genuine liability that the customer owed to the payee or its principal. This was on the basis that the paying bank should be treated as being subrogated to the claim of the payee (or its principal) against the customer.[234] This has been doubted in later cases, except where it could be said that the customer had ratified the payment.[235]

2.14 Protecting the Lender's Financial Position and Its Rate of Return

As previously explained, a lender may obtain the money to provide a facility by **2.129** borrowing the funds that are required from other lenders in the interbank market, in the case of a bank lender from retail deposits that have been placed with it by its customers, or from other sources such as the capital markets, for which it must bear a cost. It agrees to lend to the borrower on the basis of making a rate of return calculated by reference to that cost. As has also been seen, the lender expects to receive full payment from the borrower of interest during the life of the loan and (at the due date for repayment) principal, so that the lender can meet its own obligations to pay interest and, ultimately, to repay its own funding. The borrower benefits from this as the cost to the lender of obtaining the funds reflects the lender's own financial standing and the advantageous rate that it can usually obtain for the funds provided to it.[236] If something occurs which increases the lender's cost base and the underlying cost of funds to the lender, which would have the result of eroding the return that the lender has bargained to receive or which would mean that the lender does not receive in full on the due date the gross amount of interest and principal that it expects to receive from the borrower, then the lender will expect the borrower to meet the extra cost or to make up the diminished return or amount.

Matters along those lines might typically arise in consequence of regulatory or li- **2.130** quidity costs or fees that may be imposed on a lender in connection with a facility or its funding of the facility. They may also arise because of withholding taxes on interest payments that are made (or other taxes imposed in relation to amounts receivable by the lender) or in consequence of a default by the borrower or due

---

[234] *B Liggett (Liverpool) Ltd v Barclays Bank Ltd* [1928] 1 KB 48.
[235] *Re Cleadon Trust Ltd* [1939] Ch 286; *Crantrave Ltd v Lloyds Bank plc* [2000] QB 917 followed in *Liverpool Freeport Electronics Ltd v Habib Bank Ltd* [2007] EWHC 1149 (QB) and *Swotbooks.com Ltd v Royal Bank of Scotland plc* [2011] EWHC 2025 (QB).
[236] The position was sorely tested in the crisis that enveloped the financial markets in the second part of 2007, in which interbank lending rates exceeded domestic deposit rates.

to a currency loss that the lender suffers in enforcement proceedings against the borrower.

2.14.1 Increased costs

2.131 The loan facility agreement usually contains provisions which require the borrower to compensate the lender for a diminution that it might suffer in its rate of return due to changes in law. Such provisions are found in the 'Increased Costs' clause, which covers additional costs or diminished returns to the lender (or an entity affiliated with the lender) arising from the introduction of or any change in (or in the interpretation, administration, or application of) any law or regulation or compliance with any law or regulation made after it has entered into the facility agreement. An example of an increased cost would be where a lender or an affiliate of the lender[237] suffers an increased regulatory capital cost because of an adverse change during the life of a facility in the capital adequacy treatment of the facility.[238] There may be some negotiation of what should be covered by the Increased Costs clause when the facility documentation is being prepared, and a number of exceptions may be made which limit its scope.[239]

2.132 Protections that are routinely included for the protection of borrowers usually include the following. First, the borrower is given a right to prepay or require the transfer of the participation of any lender who makes an increased costs claim. Secondly, the lender is required to take reasonable steps to mitigate the claim, eg by changing its lending office or transferring its loan participation to an affiliate in another jurisdiction, unless the lender considers that the action would be prejudicial to it. Thirdly, assignments and transfers only give rise to liability under this clause to the extent that the clause would also have protected the transferor lender. Fourthly, taxes imposed on the overall net income of the lender are excluded. Fifthly, the borrower must be notified promptly of any potential claim. Sixthly, costs caused by a lender wilfully failing to comply with a regulation are excluded.

2.133 Borrowers with more negotiating power might obtain a time limit on the lender's right to claim so that the claim must be made within a certain period of time (eg within 180 days) or a limitation that only costs that were not reasonably foreseeable at the date of the loan agreement may be recovered. Borrowers may also negotiate for a right to receive a documented calculation of the increased costs attributable to their particular loan facility (which may be difficult for the lender to provide in practice), or a requirement that the costs cannot be claimed from

---

[237] For instance, as may arise under consolidated supervision of the bank and the affiliate.

[238] For a description of such matters, see Sarah Paterson and Rafal Zakrzewski (eds), *McKnight, Paterson, & Zakrzewski on the Law of International Finance* (2nd edn, OUP 2017) ch 2.

[239] For instance, as to the implementation of the revised capital standards under Basel 3.

the borrower unless they are also claimed on the same basis from other borrowers of the lender in order to prevent discrimination against that particular borrower.

2.14.2 Mandatory costs

In facilities that were based upon interbank funding in London, the loan facility **2.134** agreement used to contain mandatory cost provisions which required the borrower to compensate the lender for certain reserve or regulatory costs. Such provisions used to be part of the mechanism for calculating and charging interest, where the 'Mandatory Costs' element of the interest rate reflected the continuing regulatory and liquidity fees that were charged to the lender from the inception of the facility and which were referable to the facility. In syndicated loans, the Mandatory Costs were calculated by reference to a formula which was set out in one of the schedules to the agreement. Such an approach was generally abandoned after the Loan Market Association (LMA) ceased publishing its Mandatory Costs schedule on 1 April 2013. This was due to the difficulties experienced by agent banks in calculating mandatory costs. It was thought to be too inflexible for syndicates of lenders with different levels of mandatory costs. The LMA suggested that Mandatory Costs could be calculated for the syndicate based on the agent's costs or incorporated into the loan pricing as part of the margin. The latter approach has prevailed in practice.

2.14.3 Third party issues

Traditionally, difficulties arose at general law when it was sought to apply the **2.135** benefit of an Increased Costs clause in favour of a person other than the original lender, such as an assignee of the loan or an affiliate of the lender.[240] In the case of the former, if the assignee sought to enforce the benefit of the agreement as assignee, it might be met by an argument that the clause only applied to the personal circumstances of the assignor, being the original lender.[241] By force of the assignment, the assignor was no longer in the position where it would suffer the costs and impositions covered by the clause.[242] An assignee could not be in a better position than the assignor, nor should the borrower be required to meet claims that did not relate to the rights of the original lender.[243] If the assignee

---

[240] See generally the discussion on these issues in section 1.2.7.

[241] However, the argument that the right to an indemnity is a personal one is rendered more difficult by the Court of Appeal's decision in *Shaw v Lighthousexpress Ltd* [2010] EWCA Civ 161 [16] and [19] where it was held that there was nothing inherent in the nature of an indemnity which required it to be unassignable.

[242] Eg *Pendal Nominees Pty Ltd v Lednez Industries (Australia) Ltd* (1996) 40 NSWLR 282. Of course, if a claim under the clause had already accrued in favour of the original lender, it could assign the right to be paid.

[243] *Dawson v Great Northern & City Ry Co* [1905] 1 KB 260. But it was pointed out in *Offer-Hoar v Larkstore Ltd* [2006] EWCA Civ 1079, [2006] 1 WLR 2926 [42] that the purpose of the principle that the assignee cannot recover more than the assignor is to protect the debtor from being prejudiced by the assignment (eg by requiring it to make a payment to the assignee which the debtor

tried, in the alternative, to argue that the clause was intended to benefit it personally and not just as an assignee seeking to assert the assignor's rights, it might be met by a privity of contract point; that is, that it was seeking to enforce the contract in that regard as a stranger to the contract. A privity of contract point might also be raised against an affiliate which sought on its own behalf to enforce the contract. It was a stranger to the contract with no right to enforce it for its own benefit (unless, of course, it was a contracting party to the contract).

2.136   In an attempt to defeat those arguments, the original lender might seek to enforce the contract itself on behalf of those persons. If it did so, it would be met by an argument that it was seeking to enforce the agreement for the benefit of a non-contracting party so that the loss it suffered if the borrower failed to pay was merely a nominal loss. One possible counter to this, although it seems rather far-fetched, would be for the contracting party to obtain an equitable mandatory order requiring the payment to be made because damages would clearly be an inadequate remedy.[244] Another possibility would be for the original lender to argue that it had contracted, with respect to the benefit of the provision, as the agent or trustee of such other persons, although such a role is not commonly acknowledged in loan facility agreements.[245] Another way around the problem from the perspective of a potential assignee would be to novate the facility agreement in favour of the assignee/transferee, so that it would obtain a direct contractual relationship with the borrower, as is commonly done in the case of syndicated facilities.

2.137   The problems as just described can now be overcome. Under the Contracts (Rights of Third Parties) Act 1999, it is possible for a third party which was intended to benefit under a contract to enforce the intended benefit of the contract in its own right, provided that the application of the Act has not been disapplied by the contract and the other requirements of the Act have been met. This means that it is now possible for a person in the position of an assignee or an affiliate of the lender to enforce a clause like an Increased Costs clause for its own benefit, so long as it can be demonstrated that the clause was not intended to be solely for the benefit of the original lender.[246] For example, in the LMA recommended form documentation, a 'Finance Party' includes its successors in title, permitted assigns,

---

would not have had to make to the assignor, had the assignment never taken place) but the principle is not intended to allow the debtor to rely on the fact of the assignment to escape all legal liability. See also *Pegasus Management Holdings SCA v Ernst & Young* [2012] EWHC 738 (Ch) where it was held that the disposal of an asset to which a loss related did not mean that the loss was avoided. The loss in respect of the transferred asset could still be the subject of an assigned cause of action. It should still be treated as a loss of the assignor which the assignee can recover.

[244]   *Beswick v Beswick* [1968] AC 58.

[245]   Consider also whether any other exceptions to the general rule that a third party's loss cannot be recovered may apply: Hugh Beale (ed), *Chitty on Contracts* (32nd edn, Sweet & Maxwell 2015) [18-046]ff.

[246]   See further section 1.2.7. A similar analysis and outcome may also be relevant in the case of the Grossing Up clause that is discussed later.

and permitted transferees.[247] Therefore, a permitted assignee of an original lender should be treated as a Finance Party for the purposes of the Increased Costs clause.

2.14.4 Grossing Up clauses

To protect the lender against the effect of the imposition of withholding taxes **2.138** (and similar types of mandatory deductions from payments that are to be made by the borrower), the agreement will contain a 'Grossing Up' clause, to which further reference is made later. The expression 'withholding tax' is used to describe a requirement that is imposed by law on a person that makes a payment (typically a payment of a revenue nature, such as an interest payment). The payer is required to deduct from the payment an amount being a tax charge referable to the amount payable to the recipient of the payment. The amount deducted is then paid over by the payer to the relevant taxing authority. A withholding tax is usually imposed by the country in which the payer is resident or from which it is to make the payment. In effect, the payer is acting as the tax collection agent of the relevant country. The nature and incidence of withholding taxes differs from one jurisdiction to the next but, in some instances, the charge may be imposed without reference to the taxable status, residence, or affairs of the recipient. In other cases, the incidence of a withholding tax charge can be avoided, such as by reference to the residence and status of the recipient (eg the recipient has a tax residence in the relevant country and so is subject to its normal tax rules) or through the operation of a double tax treaty between the country where the deduction would have to be made and the country of residence of the recipient.

In the UK, the relevant statutory provisions dealing with the equivalent of with- **2.139** holding tax on interest payments are to be found in section 874 of the Income Tax Act 2007 (ITA 2007). It imposes a withholding or deduction obligation on the payer with respect to 'yearly interest' (basically, interest on a loan which may exist for more than a year), if the payer is a company or a partnership of which a company is a member, or if the recipient's usual place of residence is outside the UK. The interest must have a UK source or the payer must be subject to UK tax. Where such a deduction is required then the payer must account to HM Revenue & Customs for the amount so withheld. There are a number of exceptions to the withholding requirement. One exception applies to interest that is payable on an advance from a UK bank,[248] where the person beneficially entitled to receive it (which could be an assignee of the UK bank which advanced the loan) is within

---

[247] Likewise a 'Party' includes its successors in title, permitted assigns, and permitted transferees. Consequently, the provision which provides that a person who is not a Party has no right under the Contracts (Rights of Third Parties) Act 1999 to enforce or enjoy the benefit of any term of this Agreement does not to apply to restrict the rights of third parties who are permitted assigns and therefore 'Parties'.
[248] As defined by s 991 ITA 2007.

the UK charge to tax with respect to the interest.[249] Another set of exceptions[250] applies to interest paid by a local authority, a company, or a partnership which includes a company to a payee that is either UK tax resident or which carries on a trade in the UK through a permanent establishment in the UK and brings the interest into its UK tax account or which meets certain other criteria. Yet another exception applies to interest that is paid by a UK bank in the ordinary course of its business.[251] There are also exceptions that will apply in consequence of double tax treaties between the UK and other countries.

2.140 A Grossing Up clause is to the effect that if the borrower is required by the law of any relevant jurisdiction to make a deduction from any amount payable to the lender, it will pay to the lender a total sum which comprises both the original amount as so reduced and such an additional amount (after taking account of any further deduction that might be attracted to the grossed up amount) as will ensure that the lender receives in total the full gross amount it would have received had such a deduction not been required. It can be seen that, from the borrower's perspective, the effect of having to gross up the payment is that the borrower will find that it has to pay far more than the original amount, as it will have to pay the deducted amount to the relevant tax authority and it will have to pay an additional amount to the lender so as to ensure that the lender receives the full amount it should have received without the deduction.

2.141 A well-advised borrower may seek certain qualifications to the operation of a Grossing Up clause, particularly to reflect the scope of statutory exceptions that would normally be available to a lender had it met the relevant criteria as, for instance, outlined earlier under UK legislation. The borrower may also seek a right of reimbursement from any additional amount that it has paid to the lender where the lender obtains a tax credit referable to the amount that was withheld and paid over to a taxing authority. In theory, the amount withheld and paid over to the tax authority should be applied as a credit against the lender's own tax liability; in effect, it amounts to a pre-payment of the lender's tax liability. Most lenders will concede the point in principle but hedge it about with various conditions; for instance, that the concession should only apply if the lender would normally be subject to tax in the relevant jurisdiction and that its application should not prejudice the freedom of the lender to arrange its tax affairs in the manner it wishes, such as by the utilisation of other credits available to the lender. In practice, it is difficult for the borrower to gain much advantage from the point.

---

[249] S 879 ITA 2007.
[250] Ss 933–937 ITA 2007.
[251] S 878 ITA 2007.

2.14.5 Tax indemnity

Loan facility agreements also often contain more general tax indemnities which **2.142** seek to protect the lenders from a decreased return on the facility caused by the imposition of taxes, other than income taxes imposed by the jurisdiction in which the lender is located. Such a provision places the risk of non-income taxes in relation to sums received or receivable under the loan agreement on the borrower. Similar protections as in relation to Increased Costs claims are usually included in loan documentation for the benefit of the borrower to apply in the event of tax indemnity claims.[252]

2.14.6 Other indemnity provisions

A loan facility agreement is also likely to contain indemnity provisions in favour **2.143** of the lender which apply in relation to a default by the borrower or a currency loss that the lender suffers in enforcement proceedings against the borrower. The provisions concerning default usually apply to cover losses that the lender may suffer because it does not receive a payment on its due date or where an anticipated drawing does not proceed. The type of losses will include losses on funding that the lender has obtained or contracted to obtain and which cannot be recouped. Where the facility contemplates that the lender will enter into hedging arrangements with respect to currency or interest rate exposures associated with the facility, the indemnity will extend to cover associated losses that the lender may suffer if the borrower fails to fulfil its obligations under the facility; for instance, because the lender has to break or retire the hedging arrangements ahead of their normal expiry date.[253] Currency losses may be suffered by the lender where it has to convert a claim into a local currency for the purposes of bringing a claim or enforcing a judgment or so as to lodge a proof in an insolvency of the borrower.[254] Whether an indemnity extends to prospective losses or only covers losses already incurred will turn on the wording of the particular provision.[255] The indemnities will also usually cover professional fees incurred or to be incurred by the lender in respect of the loan transaction.[256]

---

[252] See section 2.14.3 above.

[253] For an example of the type of loss that may be suffered, see the Scottish case of *Bank of Scotland v Dunedin Property Investment Co Ltd* [1999] SLT 470.

[254] See the discussion in Sarah Paterson and Rafal Zakrzewski (eds), *McKnight, Paterson, & Zakrzewski on the Law of International Finance* (2nd edn, OUP 2017) ch 4.

[255] In *K/S Preston Street v Santander UK plc* [2012] EWHC 1633 (Ch) the bank had made a loan under a short-form facility letter and the borrower's voluntary prepayment triggered the following indemnity: 'the [borrower] shall indemnify the bank on demand against any ... loss ... the bank incurs as a result of the repayment of the loan during the fixed rate period.' Judge Pelling QC held that the wording only justified a demand for losses that had actually been suffered. The lender could not recover its prospective, extrapolated losses but had to wait until they were already incurred. See also *Barnett Waddington v RBS* [2015] EWHC 2435.

[256] In *Bank of New York Mellon v GV Films Ltd* [2009] EWHC 3315 (Comm) Blair J rejected the argument that there was an implied term that a demand for reimbursement of legal costs was

2.15 The Monitoring and Minding Provisions in a Loan Facility Agreement

2.144 The description of clauses in a loan facility agreement as the 'monitoring and minding' provisions of the agreement is used here merely for convenience to describe the clauses of the agreement which, together with the events of default clause, relate to the legal and commercial circumstances and state of affairs of the borrower (and, often, those affiliated with it) and its or their financial affairs, business, assets, and legal status. The relevant provisions comprise the representations and warranties clause and the covenants or undertaking clauses. The former contains the representations and warranties that are stated as being given by the borrower so as to induce the lender to grant and maintain the facility. The latter sets out the 'do's' and 'don'ts' of what the borrower (and its affiliates) will do and will not do during the course of the facility so as to preserve and maintain the economic, commercial, and legal state of affairs, and the flow of information relating to the borrower (and its affiliates) that the lender expects to receive for the duration of the facility. There is often some degree of overlap in the subject matter of the provisions (particularly as between the subject matter of the representations and warranties, on the one hand, and the covenants and undertakings, on the other) and it is necessary to ensure that the overlap does not lead to any inconsistency between them.

2.145 As just indicated, the provisions are likely to refer to both the borrower and those that are affiliated within the same corporate group as the borrower. A group in this sense will probably fall within much the same definition as a consolidated group for accounting purposes, although it may also be relevant to include other companies or entities in which a member of the group has a participating interest or which, for purely technical reasons, may not fall within the consolidation. Although as a strict matter of law a borrower is regarded as a separate legal entity from the other members of its group (assuming, that is, that the borrower is a corporation or other form of separate legal entity), as a matter of economic and commercial reality, it is likely that there will be some fairly close degree of connection and inter-dependence between them. The relationship may be reflected explicitly if other members of

---

not valid (and hence there was no corresponding non-payment event of default) if the costs incurred were not reasonable. Where the indemnity expressly provided that costs must be 'reasonably incurred', the Court of Appeal's decision in *Waaler v Hounslow LBC* [2017] EWCA Civ 45 provides useful guidance on how that is to be determined. See also *UBS AG, London Branch v Glas Trust Corp Ltd* [2017] EWHC 1788 (Comm) which considered whether a note trustee's costs were 'properly incurred'.

the group are to give a guarantee or security for the borrower's obligations under the facility. Even without that formal recognition, it is likely that the connection will be important in relation to the borrower's business, assets, and resources. For instance, if the borrower is the holding company of a group of companies, their affairs are of immediate relevance to it. Similarly, there may be a trading or financial dependence between the members of the group, they may share or supply assets or stock to each other, and so forth. Exceptions may be made for companies that are entirely irrelevant to the fortunes of the borrower, such as non-trading companies with no assets. If the borrower is not the parent company of the group, it might be felt to be more appropriate that the parent should make statements and give undertakings about the group members and their affairs, in which case the parent will need to be a party to the loan facility agreement, or its involvement will have to be incorporated in some other legally binding manner.

These provisions fit in with the remainder of the agreement in that the agreement will provide that if they are breached or not observed (or, indeed, if such a state of affairs is likely to occur) the borrower may be denied the right to avail itself of the facility or the remainder of it that has not been drawn. If a breach actually occurs the same may also constitute an event of default which entitles the lender to suspend or terminate the facility and accelerate the borrower's obligation to repay the total amount that has been drawn, although sometimes the borrower may be given a second chance if it can rectify the position before the lender has taken the step of terminating the facility. The borrower may also be required to certify its proper observance of these provisions before it may make a drawing and at various times during the life of the facility. Because of the fact that they are tailored to the particular borrower, their importance in the context of the agreement and the availability of the facility and the effect that they will have on the continuing affairs of the borrower and its affiliates during the life of the facility, the monitoring and minding provisions of the agreement, together with the events of default clause, usually give rise to most of the contentious discussion that may take place during the negotiations that lead to settling the wording of the agreement. **2.146**

As previously noted, in facilities to finance a takeover bid and in certain other types of acquisition finance, where certainty of funding is a prerequisite for a transaction to be announced and to proceed, the lender might be required to permit a drawing to take place and so to provide funds even if there has been a breach of the representations and warranties clause or a default in the borrower's observance of the covenants and undertaking. **2.147**

Due to their importance and content, the representations and warranties clause, on the one hand, and the provisions containing the covenants and undertakings, on the other, will be examined separately. **2.148**

2.16 Representations and Warranties

2.16.1 Preliminary observations

2.149 In traditional legal analysis, a representation is a statement of fact (rather than opinion) that is made prior to or at the time of the making of a contract; it is made by one party to the other party so as to induce that other party to enter into the contract.[257] In this context, a warranty is a promise to similar effect that has become a term of the contract.[258] Prior to the Misrepresentation Act 1967, the making of a misrepresentation (whether fraudulently, negligently, or innocently made) gave rise to a right in the recipient to rescind the contract *ab initio*, provided it could show that the representation was substantially untrue and that it had relied on the representation in deciding whether it should enter into the contract, but that right was easily lost. There was no claim for damages available to the recipient of an innocent misrepresentation. A breach of a warranty gave rise to a claim for damages but there was no right to rescind or to terminate.[259] The deficiencies in the law concerning innocent misrepresentations and warranties were largely rectified by sections 1 and 2 of the Act, although section 2(1) does give the representor a defence to a claim for damages for a misrepresentation if it can show that it was not negligent in making the representation and section 2(2) gives the court the power to award damages in lieu of a right to rescind. On the other hand, if the representation was made fraudulently or negligently, there was a claim for damages at general law, as a claim in deceit or for a negligent misrepresentation, which right remained after the passing of the Act.[260]

2.150 Such legal niceties are not of great importance to the lender in the context of the representations and warranties clause of a loan facility agreement. The lender is not really very interested in having a claim for damages against the borrower[261] or,

---

[257] For a detailed consideration of what constitutes a misrepresentation see chapter 4 of Dominic O'Sullivan, Steven Elliott, and Rafal Zakrzewski, *The Law of Rescission* (2nd edn, OUP 2014).

[258] The distinction is explored in detail in Rafal Zakrzewski, 'Representations and Warranties Distinguished' (2013) 6 Journal of International Banking and Financial Law 341. See also *Idemitsu Kosan Co Ltd v Sumitomo Corporation* [2016] EWHC 1909 (Comm).

[259] Rescission involves a retroactive extinguishment of the parties' contractual rights and duties; the contract is wiped away as if it had never existed. Termination on the other hand operates only proactively to release the parties from their future obligations and corresponding rights; any accrued rights remain enforceable. See Dominic O'Sullivan, Steven Elliot, and Rafal Zakrzewski, *The Law of Rescission* (2nd edn, OUP 2014) [1.06]–[1.34].

[260] See further the discussion of these matters in ch 3.

[261] However, in the case of knowingly false representations, it may give the lender some comfort that the individuals who execute the loan agreement on behalf of the borrower will be personally liable to the lenders in fraud if they knew that the representations were untrue: *Standard Chartered Bank v Pakistan National Shipping Corp (No 2)* [2002] UKHL 43, [2003] 1 AC 959.

more tenuously, a claim for rescission.[262] Nor is the lender likely to be interested in the distinction between matters of fact (for which the law gives remedies if they were incorrectly represented) and matters of opinion (for which no remedy is available[263]). What the lender needs, and what a well drafted agreement should provide, is the right to refuse to make advances to the borrower if the terms of the clause (whether relating strictly to factual matters or concerning matters of opinion) have been breached or if such a breach is likely to occur (which right will usually be found in the provisions relating to drawings). In addition, the lender will wish to have the right, where the clause has been breached, to suspend or terminate the facility and to demand repayment of any amounts already advanced to the borrower, perhaps with some opportunity being afforded to the borrower to rectify the breach before the lender takes such drastic action. Such a right is conferred by the events of default clause.

To achieve those aims, the clause also departs from a traditional legal analysis by providing that the statements that are made by the borrower under it are stated as being made not just as at the time of the signing of the agreement but are also to be treated as being repeated at various intervals during the life of the facility. So as to keep the statements that are made by the borrower up to date, the clause will provide that each repetition will be expressed to be by reference to the facts and circumstances prevailing at the time of the repetition, with specific exceptions being provided in the clause for matters that the borrower was only prepared to represent and warrant at the date the agreement was signed.[264]   **2.151**

It follows that the role of the representations and warranties clause in a facility agreement is partly preliminary to the facility being made available and, in that sense, acts as an inducement to the lender to enter into the agreement and provide the facility, and partly continuing as to the availability of drawings during the commitment or availability period of the facility and as to the continuance of the facility once the drawings have been made. From a practical perspective, the proposed wording of the clause also has another role even before the agreement is signed. Once the wording of the clause has been produced in the negotiations prior to the signing of the agreement, it should flush out any potential difficulties that then exist or which may be anticipated, as the borrower should be encouraged to indicate those matters where it cannot accurately give the statements that the wording requires. It is always far better that these matters are brought out into the open and addressed at that stage (perhaps by providing for exceptions by   **2.152**

---

[262] A rescission of the loan contract *ab initio* is almost invariably against the interests of the lender who would thereby lose the benefit of carefully crafted indemnities and other protections that are likely to be present in the loan agreement.

[263] With the rather fine distinction that a statement of opinion might be taken to imply the fact that the maker genuinely held the opinion: see *Edgington v Fitzmaurice* (1885) 29 ChD 459.

[264] See *Grupo Hotelero Urvasco SA v Carey Value Added SL* [2013] EWHC 1039 (Comm).

reference to a statement of disclosures that is made by the borrower), rather than giving rise to difficulties because of a breach occurring later on.

2.16.2 Types of provision

2.153 For explanatory purposes, the representations and warranties may be divided into two categories. The description that follows refers to the borrower but the same issues will also concern other members of the borrower's group, particularly those that might be giving guarantees or security for the transaction, where reference is made to them in the clause.

2.154 The first category concerns matters relating to legal issues, such as:

(1) the due existence, status, powers, and authority to contract of the borrower and those who act on its behalf;[265]
(2) the legal validity and enforceability of the documentation and the transaction overall;[266]
(3) the ranking of the lender's rights as a creditor;[267]
(4) the tax treatment of the transaction (particularly as to payments to be made under the facility);
(5) that the transaction will not contravene the rights of third parties;[268]
(6) that the borrower has all the necessary consents and permits that are required for it to own its assets and carry on its business; and
(7) that the borrower intends and will use the proceeds of the facility for lawful and legitimate purposes.[269]

2.155 The second category concerns commercial and factual matters, such as:

---

[265] As a matter of English law, a company may be unable to give a representation that it has power to enter into a transaction when it lacked the corporate capacity to enter into that transaction: see *British and Commonwealth Holdings plc v Barclays Bank plc* [1996] 1 WLR 1, 24 (Aldous LJ). However, in *Credit Suisse International v Stichting Vestia Groep* [2014] EWHC 3103 (Comm) it was held that a representation and warranty made in a contract which the entity had capacity to enter into gave rise to a contractual estoppel which prevented it from escaping liability on other contracts which it did not have capacity to enter into. It also gave rise to a claim in damages.

[266] This may be expanded to cater for sanctions laws and regulations. For example, US and EU sanctions laws may prohibit a lender from providing funds to targets of any relevant sanctions authority.

[267] See the discussion of the *pari passu* provisions in section 2.17.7 below.

[268] This may go some way in protecting the lender from claims that it had committed an economic tort such as interference with contractual relations. This is an intentional tort and representations of this nature provide evidence that the lender did not intend to interfere with any third party's contractual rights. See point (4) at para 2.182 below.

[269] The last of these representations and warranties may be helpful to the lender in resisting an argument that it knowingly participated (by providing the finance) in an unlawful scheme or activity in which the borrower was engaged. Of course, if the lender was aware of the facts, the representation and warranty will be of no avail.

(1) the absence of litigation which might adversely affect the borrower, its business or assets, and its ability to perform its obligations under the facility;
(2) that no events of default have occurred under the facility and that no similar events have occurred under other transactions to which the borrower is a party;
(3) that the financial and accounting statements that it has supplied to the lender give a true and fair view of it and its assets as at the date and for the period to which they relate, do not omit any matters that were material and had been prepared in accordance with the requisite accounting standards;
(4) that there has been no material adverse change in the circumstances of the borrower and its assets since the date of those statements;[270]
(5) that other information which has been supplied to the lender was true and accurate and did not omit any material matters; and
(6) that opinions that have been expressed to the lender concerning the borrower and its affairs were held on reasonable grounds.

There may also be additional representations and warranties relating to matters that are specific to the borrower's business and its assets (for instance, as to environmental matters if that is relevant to the business), the facility, and the use of the finance provided under it. **2.156**

2.16.3 Negotiating points

Needless to say, a well-advised borrower will scrutinise the wording that has been presented to it as part of the negotiating process before the agreement is signed and seek to ameliorate the strictness represented by that wording before it is prepared to proceed. Qualifications to the wording that may be sought might be along the following lines: **2.157**

(1) where the representations and warranties concern other members of its group, the borrower may seek to exclude references to companies that are not directly involved in the transaction and are of no material significance to the group taken as a consolidated whole;
(2) it may seek to qualify the statements concerning legal matters by reference to the types of qualification that appear in legal opinions. A lender needs to be careful in accepting such a qualification where it relates to matters that concern questions of reasonableness, best knowledge, or that a certain factual situation existed when the facility was signed;
(3) in relation to the commercial and factual statements contained in the representations and warranties, the borrower might wish to qualify them by reference to a test of materiality and the likely effect that such matters may have on the lender's rights and the borrower's state of health and its ability

---

[270] See the discussion of what constitutes material adverse change in section 2.18.3 below.

to perform its obligations under the facility. After all, no business is run perfectly and many events may occur which have no significance to its long-term operations and viability; and

(4) as previously indicated, the borrower might also seek exceptions to the statements by reference to specific disclosures that it has made to the lender.

2.17 Covenants and Undertakings

2.17.1 Preliminary observations

2.158 The words 'covenants' and 'undertakings' these days are used interchangeably, although a traditionally trained English lawyer would prefer to see the use of the word 'covenant' confined so that it describes obligations that are created by deed. In a loan facility agreement, the covenants and undertakings clause (sometimes there is more than one clause in the agreement dealing with this subject) contains the obligations undertaken by the borrower in favour of the lender relating to what the borrower will do and will not do during the period of the facility. From the lender's perspective, the intention behind the clause is to require that the economic, commercial, and legal state of affairs of the borrower should not deteriorate during the term of the facility, as well as to provide for a flow of information relating to the borrower that the lender expects to receive in that period. Essentially, the covenants and undertakings reflect the agreement between the parties that the state of affairs concerning the borrower on which the lender made its decision to proceed with the facility should be maintained by the borrower for the duration of the facility (or even improved), as well as to provide the lender with relevant information so that it can assess and check the position from time to time. As previously mentioned, these provisions may extend to cover the affairs of other members of the borrower's group. If the borrower wishes to depart from the legislated position as it was agreed in the facility agreement then it must seek the lender's consent.

2.159 As with the position concerning the representations and warranties clause, a lender's objective in relation to a breach by the borrower of the covenants and undertakings is not to pursue the remedies that might be available at general law,[271] but, rather, that it should have the right to refuse to make advances to the borrower if the clause has been breached or if such a breach is likely to occur (which right will usually be found in the provisions relating to drawings). This should be viewed together with the right of the lender (under the events of default

---

[271] Such as by way of a claim for damages and, perhaps, a claim to terminate the agreement for a repudiatory breach of contract. The one exception to this may be where the lender might seek an injunction to restrain a threatened breach by the borrower of the negative pledge clause or the clause which limits the disposal of assets, as discussed further later.

clause), where the clause has been breached, to suspend or terminate the facility and to demand repayment of any amounts already advanced to the borrower, perhaps with some opportunity being afforded to the borrower to rectify the breach before the lender takes such drastic action. Of course, no sensible lender would enter into an agreement with a borrower if it thought it likely that the borrower would default under its obligations or, worse, deliberately breach those obligations. The whole point of the undertakings and covenants is to lay down a set of rules which the borrower is able and willing to observe, which can only be achieved as a result of a sensible negotiation between the parties before the agreement is signed. It also means that the parties should act sensibly during the currency of the agreement in an attempt to overcome difficulties that may arise before they turn into insuperable problems.

When the markets experience high liquidity and hence greater competition **2.160** among debt providers, lenders are often prepared to limit the extent of the covenants and undertakings in high yield[272] facilities granted to borrowers with lower credit ratings who are raising more risky finance, particularly in facilities designed to finance the acquisition activities of private equity groups. To some extent, this reflects an easy flow of credit and the fact that a great deal of the debt arising under such facilities is held by creditors which are not banks. Whilst the relevant loan facility agreements retain some of the obligations and restrictions traditionally imposed upon borrowers, they often relax the usual forms of financial covenants resulting in 'covenant light' or 'cov-lite' facilities or some permutation thereof.[273] In particular, the most significant loosening of covenants occurs in the area of the ability to raise additional debt. In addition, such facilities often contain a relaxation of the more traditional restrictions on the potential activities of borrowers in matters such as those relating to acquisitions and disposals of assets and the granting of security. They also make provision for processes under which a borrower might be assisted in obtaining consents and waivers if it wishes to depart from the requirements of the remaining undertakings and covenants in an agreement, as well as procedures for dissenting creditors to be removed from the facility and replaced by more compliant successors.

2.17.2 Shadow directors

At the opposite end of the scale, there is a risk that a lender which becomes too **2.161** closely involved in the affairs of its borrower and which has the effective power to control or direct its activities and its decision-making processes, may find itself accused of being in the position of a 'shadow director' of the borrower. This is a particular concern in a situation where a borrower might be in financial difficulties,

---

[272] Ie bearing a higher rate of interest than would apply for a less risky transaction. These are usually leveraged acquisition facilities.
[273] See para 2.171 below.

in pursuance of which the lender might have imposed strict conditions as to the conduct of the borrower's business, as well as onerous monitoring and supervision of the borrower, as a requirement for its continued support of the borrower. Under English law, the consequences to a lender of being found to be a shadow director are serious. It may, for instance, find itself exposed to disqualification proceedings under the Company Directors Disqualification Act 1986[274] or to misfeasance proceedings under the Insolvency Act 1986,[275] and such circumstances might also be relevant to the continuance of its authorisation under the Financial Services and Markets Act 2000 (FSMA) and any licence that it may hold under the Consumer Credit Act 2006. In addition, transactions between a borrower and a shadow director may require the observance of the special procedures provided for transactions with directors and related parties under Chapter 3 and Chapter 4 of Part 10 of the Companies Act 2006.[276] A shadow director could also owe fiduciary duties to the borrower.[277] Any such transaction may also attract the additional disadvantages that are relevant to connected persons who have entered into transactions with the borrower in a period before the onset of insolvency under the Insolvency Act 1986.[278] There may also be adverse consequences under tax and environmental legislation.

2.162 A 'shadow director' of a company is defined[279] to mean:

a person in accordance with whose directions or instructions the directors of the company are accustomed to act (but so that a person is not deemed a shadow director by reason only that the directors act on advice given by him in a professional capacity).

2.163 It had been said that for the definition to apply there must have been an element of subservience by the directors to the will of the other person; such a person should be like a puppet master pulling the strings behind the curtain.[280] Accordingly, it used to be thought that if the lender did not engage in active intervention in the borrower's day-to-day affairs, but simply imposed conditions in the contract between it and the borrower which the borrower had to observe if it wished the lender to continue providing its facilities, that would not make the lender a shadow director. The borrower could decide whether it wished to accept the terms

---

[274] See s 6(3C) of the Act.
[275] For instance, for fraudulent trading under s 213 of the Act (where, strictly speaking, it is not necessary for the liquidator to prove that the person knowingly concerned in the fraudulent carrying on of the company's business was a shadow director of the insolvent company) or for wrongful trading under s 214 of the Act.
[276] See ss 187 and 223 of the Act.
[277] *Vivendi SA v Richards* [2013] EWHC 3006 (Ch), [2013] BCC 771.
[278] Under ss 238, 239, and 245 of the Act.
[279] By s 251 of the Insolvency Act 1986. Similar definitions are to be found in s 22(5) of the Company Directors Disqualification Act 1986 and in s 251 of the Companies Act 2006.
[280] *Re Unisoft Group Ltd (No 3)* [1994] 1 BCLC 609, 620.

of the facility or decline to use the facility, even where there was financial dependency of the borrower on the lender for the borrower's continued existence.[281]

The position became less certain in view of the decision of Morritt LJ in *Secretary* **2.164**
of State for Trade and Industry v Deverell[282] and subsequent cases. His Lordship
made a number of observations as to the meaning of the concept of shadow directorship, which could mean that third parties, such as lenders, might be held
to be shadow directors. His Lordship said that the definition should not be construed narrowly but, rather, in the normal way in light of an intention to protect
the public against the consequences of directors acting on the directions or instructions of a shadow director. There was no need for the person to have been 'in
the shadows'; his involvement could be public and obvious.[283] It was not necessary to show that the directors acted in a subservient role or that they surrendered
all of their discretions to that person. Such a person should be shown to have real
influence over the affairs of the company but it need not be over the whole field
of its activities.[284] It was necessary to ascertain objectively whether the person's
words or conduct amounted to directions or instructions, but it was not necessary
to prove any understanding or expectation on the part of the giver or recipients
of those directions and instructions that they would be followed. Although the
definition excludes advice given in a professional capacity, non-professional advice could be caught. Ultimately whether or not someone is a shadow director is
a question of fact and degree.[285]

It is submitted that in light of those observations, a lender should be very careful **2.165**
before it becomes too involved in the affairs of a borrower, such as in a situation
where it might wish to monitor the borrower closely, particularly if the borrower
is in financial difficulties. The imposition of covenants and undertakings along
the usual lines in a loan facility agreement is a normal fact of life and should not
lead to any difficulties in this area. However, if the agreement is too prescriptive
so that it has the effect of controlling to a large degree the conduct of the affairs
and activities of the borrower, that could be a problem, particularly if there was a
dependence upon the lender for the continued survival of the borrower. It would
be even more damning if the lender had actively become involved in the conduct
of the business, such as where the borrower was required to obtain the lender's
consent before it could make payments and deal with everyday matters.

---

[281] *Re PFRZM Ltd* [1995] BCC 280. See also Sir Peter Millett, 'Shadow Directorships—A Real
or Imagined Threat to the Banks' [1991] Insolvency Practitioner 14.
[282] [2001] Ch 340 [24]–[36]. See also the judgment of Finn J in the Australian case of *Australian
Securities Commission v AS Nominees Ltd* (1995) 133 ALR 1.
[283] See also *HMRC v Holland* [2010] UKSC 51, [2010] 1 WLR 2793.
[284] See also *Mckillen v Misland (Cyprus) Investments Ltd* [2012] EWHC 521 (Ch) [67] and
Smithton Ltd v Naggar [2014] EWCA Civ 939 [32].
[285] *Smithton Ltd v Naggar* [2014] EWCA Civ 939 [45].

2.166 Having made those preliminary observations, it is now relevant to examine the types of covenants and undertakings that will usually be found in a loan facility agreement.

2.17.3 Information undertakings

2.167 The undertakings to provide information to the lender usually relate to matters along the following lines:

(1) an obligation to furnish accounting information at specified intervals during the life of the facility, together with obligations as to the manner in which that information will be compiled and presented, reflecting the consistent application of relevant accounting standards, as well as the necessity for at least the yearly accounts to be audited by auditors of repute. There also used to be some further stipulation as to the identity or suitability of the auditors, however EU Regulation 537/2014 and UK regulations implementing EU Directive 2014/56/EU prevent the use of such terms restricting a borrower's choice of auditor;[286]

(2) a requirement that the lender should be sent the same information as is supplied to the borrower's creditors and shareholders generally or which is disclosed to stock exchanges and the like;

(3) an obligation to provide information that the lender may require for the purpose of meeting regulatory requirements that are imposed upon the lender, including information that is relevant to the assessment of risk weightings for capital adequacy purposes and information to meet customer knowledge and money laundering requirements;

(4) the borrower may be required to produce other information that may be relevant to the affairs of the borrower and other relevant entities, either when it becomes known to the borrower[287] or when requested by the lender;[288]

(5) the borrower may be obliged to provide information relating to the occurrence of an event of default or the likelihood of such an event occurring; and

(6) the borrower may be required to supply certificates at various times, signed by its directors, confirming compliance by the borrower with the covenants and undertakings in the agreement.

---

[286] The EU Regulation requires publicly listed companies to report any attempts by lenders to impose a prohibited auditor clause (or otherwise improperly influence the choice of auditor) to national authorities. The Directive was implemented in reg 12 of The Statutory Auditors and Third Country Auditors Regulations 2016 and extends the ban to all companies. Consequently any contractual clause which restricts the borrower's choice of auditor by reference to 'certain categories or lists of statutory auditors or audit firms' is null and void.

[287] See the discussion as to the attribution to a corporate borrower of knowledge that was held by one of its directors in *Jafari-Fini (Mohammad) v Skillglass Ltd* [2007] EWCA Civ 261.

[288] See the discussion of such a requirement in *Milner Laboratories Ltd v Citibank NA* (Morison J, 18 December 2001).

2.17.4 Financial covenants

Financial covenants are intended to monitor, regulate, and preserve the financial **2.168** and economic position of the borrower (and, where relevant, its group). By them, the lender wishes to be assured that, provided the borrower observes the covenants, the borrower is likely to have sufficient resources to meet its obligations to the lender as they become due for payment. These types of covenant have the effect of requiring the borrower usually to ensure the maintenance and, perhaps, the improvement of that position during the life of the facility.[289] If the borrower has difficulty in meeting the covenants, or breaches them, that should serve as a warning that all is not well, although the value of such a warning mechanism is open to doubt, for the reasons mentioned in what follows. Some of the covenants relate to successive periods and provide that during such periods, a certain state of affairs will be maintained. Other covenants speak of the circumstances as at the end of each such period, because they relate to the cumulative position at the end of the period. The formulation and measurement of the covenants and what they require is based upon the financial statements of the borrower (and its group), including the profit and loss account and the balance sheet, but it is common for the loan facility agreement to provide for adjustments to be made to what is contained in those financial statements, so as to take into account additional material or to ignore certain other matters. Such financial statements will normally include the annual audited accounts, as well as half yearly accounts and, not infrequently, quarterly and monthly accounts.

As a method of monitoring the borrower's observance of the covenants, the loan **2.169** facility agreement will almost invariably provide for certificates to be provided by the borrower at the end of each of the relevant periods. The certificates are intended to confirm that the borrower has complied with the covenants for the period and as at the date to which the certificate relates or, alternatively, state that it has been unable to do so and give an explanation of the reasons for the failure to comply. The certificates should be signed by one or more of the directors of the borrower on its behalf. Sometimes a loan facility agreement may also require that the auditors of the borrower should confirm the accuracy of what is stated by reference to the borrower's audited accounts, although auditors are increasingly reluctant to undertake such a task because of the responsibilities that might be associated with such a role.[290] It should also be remembered that such certificates

---

[289] But see paras 2.171 and 2.172 for a discussion of non-maintenance-based financial covenants.

[290] For instance, it might be argued that they have accepted responsibility towards the lender for the accuracy of what is stated in such a way that the lender may argue that they owed it a duty of care in the tort of negligence on the basis of claim under *Hedley Byrne & Co Ltd v Heller & Partners Ltd* [1964] AC 465. If there were such an acceptance of responsibility, the position of the auditors in *Caparo Industries plc v Dickman* [1990] 2 AC 605 would be overcome (see eg the approach taken by the Outer House of the Court of Session in *Royal Bank of Scotland v Bannerman Johnstone Maclay* [2003] SLT 181 and compare with *Al Saudi Banque v Clarke Pixley* [1990] 1 Ch 313).

speak historically so that the grounds for a breach of the covenants may already have occurred or be accumulating prior to the date on which the certificate is to be provided. In such a case, the borrower would probably have been obliged to alert the lender to the looming problem in pursuance of its obligations under the fifth of the obligations to provide information (as to actual or potential defaults) as set out above. Whether it did so, of course, is another matter, which may well have depended upon its appreciation of the significance of the potential problem.

2.170 Some of the traditional types of financial covenant that are contained in a loan facility agreement are as follows:

(1) there may be a leverage covenant, which measures financial indebtedness as against earnings for the relevant period. The concept of financial indebtedness is usually drafted widely, to encompass all of the various ways in which debt or credit may be raised and remain outstanding, including debt or credit arising under or concerning borrowing facilities, acceptance credit and other types of banking facilities, debt instruments, the deferred price for the provision of goods and services, advance payment arrangements, redeemable capital, recourse receivables purchase facilities, certain types of derivatives transactions and option arrangements, equipment finance facilities, and suretyship obligations. Earnings is taken as the bottom line figure on the profit and loss account, after ignoring any interest earned for the period and adding back any deductions for interest and taxation[291] and (sometimes) adding back the amount referable to any depreciation or amortisation of assets;[292]

(2) there may be a cash flow cover covenant, which measures outgoings (including some or all of debt service costs for interest and principal, tax payments, and other expenditure) over a period against earnings and movements in working capital for that period;

(3) there may be a requirement that the worth or balance sheet value of the borrower (and its group) will be maintained at not less than a certain stated amount in each of the periods. The requirement may be expressed to vary (usually upwards) from one period to a later period. Adjustments may be required in ascertaining the amount of such worth by ignoring the value (if any) ascribed in the accounts to intangible assets, such as intellectual property[293] and goodwill, by adjusting the value of holdings in companies that are not wholly owned and by moderating or ignoring upwards revaluations of assets (particularly if they cannot be justified on objective grounds), in which

---

[291] Often referred to as 'EBIT'.
[292] Often referred to as 'EBITDA'.
[293] The valuation of these matters has always been difficult and often ignored in preparing financial statements. However, if the borrower's business is reliant upon intellectual property, such as trade marks, patents, design rights, and copyright, there may be a strong commercial case to recognise their value in determining the worth of the borrower.

case the covenant will relate to the tangible net worth of the borrower. An adjustment in the opposite direction may permit subordinated debt to be treated as if it were equity share capital, where that debt is subordinated in right of payment behind the debt due to the lender under the loan facility agreement;

(4) there may be a gearing covenant, which limits the amount of financial indebtedness of the borrower when compared with its worth or tangible net worth at any time in each of the periods;

(5) there may be an interest cover covenant, under which the amount of interest payable by the borrower for a period is compared against its earnings for the period. Interest is defined widely to include all payments in the nature of interest, howsoever called;

(6) there may be restrictions on capital expenditure in each of the periods; and

(7) if security is to be given, there may be a security cover covenant, by which the value of the secured assets must exceed a certain multiple of the amount of principal and interest outstanding under the facility.

Traditionally financial covenants in loans made on the European market are **2.171** 'maintenance' based. This means that they are tested at regular time intervals and the borrower is obliged to conduct its business so as to ensure that they are not infringed. The policy behind this arrangement is that a covenant breach will then provide an objectively ascertained early warning that the borrower may not be able to service its debt in the future. This then allows the lenders to take pre-emptive action to force a consensual restructuring of the loan facilities. Loans are commonly said to be 'covenant light' or 'cov-lite' if they have no such maintenance financial covenants. In such loans the financial covenants are instead tested on an 'incurrence' basis. This means that they are only tested when the borrower wishes to take a specified action such as incurring more debt, paying a dividend, or making an acquisition or disposal. Such incurrence-based covenants were traditionally included in New York law governed high yield bonds. This was because the bondholders received a higher rate of return. They comprised a disparate group from whom it would be difficult to obtain waivers of more restrictive maintenance covenants and the bonds were very liquid allowing bondholders to dispose of them if the borrower's financial condition worsened. Over time the investor base in loans has developed to include entities which have experience of investing in high yield bonds and European issuers have acquired experience in raising finance in the form of such bonds. These reasons, combined with increased competition among loan providers and the search for higher yields, have led to incurrence-based covenants being utilised more widely in the loan markets.

'Covenant-loose' usually refers to leveraged acquisition loans which include at **2.172** least one maintenance financial covenant, usually leverage (ie that the borrower must not exceed a maximum debt to earnings ratio), but not the traditional full set of financial covenants. 'Quasi covenant-lite' refers to loans where at least one maintenance financial covenant is included but that covenant only benefits the lenders under the revolving facility, not lenders under the term facilities. Such a covenant would only be tested on a 'springing basis'; that is, when the revolving facility is more than 15–25 per cent utilised on the relevant testing date. 'Fall-away covenants' are financial covenants that cease to apply, or are tested less frequently, if the borrower becomes publicly listed, if it reduces the level of its debt, or if the borrower obtains an investment grade rating from a credit rating agency.

2.173 Borrowers may be able to negotiate for remedy or cure rights in respect of financial covenants to be included in the loan agreement. An 'equity cure' permits a related company to provide additional funds to the borrower in the form of equity capital or subordinated debt to cure a breach of a financial covenant. These fresh funds may be used to make a prepayment under the loan agreement or, more rarely, may be added to the earnings or cashflow calculations with the relevant financial covenants being recalculated on the basis of the new figures. It is important that any such provisions are carefully drafted so as not to prejudice the lenders. In *Strategic Value Master Fund Ltd v Ideal Standard International Acquisition SARL*[294] funds were lent to the borrower by a related entity to cure a breach of an interest cover ratio and were then immediately on-lent by the borrower to a related entity (the operation being described as 'round-tripping'). Because of the way in which the relevant provisions had been drafted, the funds were counted for the purposes of the relevant equity cure provision even though they had not actually improved the financial strength of the borrower. Equity cure rights are most commonly included in private equity sponsored transactions and real estate financings.

2.17.5 Other covenants and undertakings

2.174 The remaining undertakings and covenants in a loan facility agreement impose various restrictions on the scope of the borrower's activities during the period of the facility, and are also designed to maintain and preserve the position of the lender vis-à-vis the other creditors of the borrower. There may also be particular obligations that are undertaken by the borrower with respect to the particular purpose or project for which the facility has been provided which will be of relevance, for instance, in the financing of construction and infrastructure projects and in acquisition finance. The discussion that follows will refer to the covenants and undertakings that are normally found in loan facility agreements and which concern changes in the nature and scope of the borrower's business, the ranking of the lender's claims as against those of the other creditors of the borrower, and the negative pledge and anti-disposals clauses.

---

[294] [2011] EWHC 171 (Ch).

2.17.6 Maintenance of business

The borrower will undertake to carry on its business as it was undertaken at the **2.175** commencement of the facility and that it will not vary the nature of its business.[295] The point behind this covenant is that the lender will have made its decision to grant the facility to the borrower on the strength of the borrower's business as it existed when the decision was made. If the borrower undertakes a different type of business, that may expose it to risks that it does not understand and which may imperil its financial position. A bank may also be subject to limits on how much of its funds it may commit to a particular sector of the economy to prevent a downturn in a particular industry from having a disproportionate effect on the financial condition of the bank. There may also be a covenant to maintain all agreements, licences, and consents that are necessary for the relevant business and the holding and use of its assets. There will probably also be an undertaking to maintain adequate insurance in connection with such business and assets.

2.17.7 Ranking—the *pari passu* clause

The lender will be concerned as to its ranking as a creditor of the borrower, particularly in an insolvency of the borrower. This concern will be manifested in two sets of undertakings by the borrower. The first, which is particularly relevant if the lender is providing the facility on an unsecured basis, will be that the borrower should ensure that the lender's claims will rank in an insolvency of the borrower *pari passu*[296] with the claims of all of the other unsecured creditors of the borrower, except for those mandatorily preferred by law.[297] Whilst that is the general position under English law,[298] there are some jurisdictions where it is possible for an unsecured creditor's claim to gain priority in an insolvency over the claims of other unsecured creditors by following certain procedures.[299] In the case of

---

[295] In *Decura IM Investments LLP v UBS AG* [2015] EWHC 171 a contract relating to financial services provided that a termination event would occur if UBS 'ceases to carry on a material part of its UBS IB business at any time' and 'such cessation ... has a material adverse effect on UBS IB's ability to market the [relevant services]'. Burton J followed *Grupo Hotelero Urvasco SA v Carey Value Added SL* [2013] EWHC 1039 (Comm) holding that 'material' here meant significant or substantial. His Lordship also held that in the absence of words such as 'in the opinion of' the matter was to be assessed objectively.

[296] Ie rateably in proportion that each claim bears to the total.

[297] Under English law, the statutorily preferred claims in a liquidation are referred to in s 175 of, and are set out in sch 6 to, the Insolvency Act 1986. As to the ranking of liquidation expenses ahead of the claims of floating charge holders and other claims, see s 176ZA of the Insolvency Act 1986 and rr 4.180 and 4.218 of the Insolvency Rules 1986.

[298] S 107 of the Insolvency Act 1986 (voluntary winding up), s 328(3) of that Act (bankruptcy), and r 4.181 of the Insolvency Rules 1986 (compulsory winding up).

[299] Eg this was possible in Spain and the Philippines through notarization of the loan agreement in a prescribed manner: Lee C. Buchheit and Jeremiah S. Pam, 'The Pari Passu Clause in Sovereign Debt Instruments' (2004) 53 Emory Law Journal 869, 903–04.

sovereign debt,[300] a sovereign borrower may change its laws to prefer certain unsecured creditors over others, which would constitute a clear breach of a *pari passu* undertaking. If the lender is taking security then the clause should provide that, to the extent of the security, the lender's claims will have a first claim on such security (assuming that is intended to be the case) and, otherwise, that its residual unsecured claim will rank *pari passu* with the claims of the other unsecured creditors.

2.177   It has sometimes been argued that a *pari passu* clause prevents the borrower from making any payment to another creditor, even before the onset of insolvency, unless it will also make payment to the lender under the facility which contains the clause.[301] This is an incorrect interpretation of the purpose of such a clause, which is to provide for the position upon insolvency.[302] Of course, the interpretation of the clause will depend upon its drafting but a well-advised borrower should ensure that the effect of a *pari passu* clause is confined in the manner suggested. The position as to payments to other creditors outside insolvency should be dealt with, if at all, in other provisions that are specifically tailored to meet a particular objective.

2.178   It may be suggested that recent case law in the USA lends support to the wider 'rateable payment' interpretation. In 2001 Argentina defaulted on US$95 billion of its external debt. In 2005 and 2010 two restructurings were carried out allowing bondholders to exchange old bonds for new bonds. Some hedge funds purchased the defaulted Argentine debt on the secondary market and refused to take part in the restructurings. They sued for the full amount of the original bonds and sought an injunction to prevent Argentina from making payments on the exchange bonds without making rateable payments to the holdout creditors by reason of a breach of the *pari passu* clause. They argued that no payment of interest could be made on the exchange bonds without making a rateable payment of the amount due on the holdout creditors' bonds. In 2012, the District Court granted the injunction sought by the holdout creditors.[303] The decision was subsequently upheld on appeal by the Court of Appeals for the Second Circuit.[304]

---

[300] The history and evolution of the *pari passu* clause in the sovereign debt context (where the clause originated) is traced in detail in Lee C. Buchheit and Jeremiah S. Pam, 'The *Pari Passu* Clause in Sovereign Debt Instruments' (2004) 53 Emory Law Journal 869.

[301] This argument was made but not ruled on in *Kensington International Ltd v Republic of the Congo* [2003] EWHC 2331 (Comm), approved by the Court of Appeal at [2003] EWCA Civ 709. It appeared to have been accepted in obiter by the Singapore Court of Appeal in *DBS Bank Ltd v Tam Chee Chong* [2011] SGCA 47 [52].

[302] Philip R. Wood, 'Pari Passu Clauses—What Do They Mean?' (2003) 18 Butterworths Journal of International Banking & Financial Law 4; Financial Markets Law Committee, 'Issue 79—Pari Passu Clauses' (March 2005) <http://fmlc.org/wp-content/uploads/2018/02/Issue-79-Pari-Passu-Clauses.pdf> accessed 21 July 2018, reaffirmed in 2015 <http://fmlc.org/wp-content/uploads/2018/03/fmlc_paper_analysing_the_role_use_and_meaning_of_pari_passu_clauses_in_sovereign_debt_obligations_as_a_matter_of_english_law.pdf> accessed 21 July 2018.

[303] *NML Capital, Ltd v Republic of Argentina*, No 08 Civ 6978 (TPG) (SDNY 23 February 2012). But contrast *White Hawthorne LLC v The Republic of Argentina* (22 December 2016).

[304] *NML Capital, Ltd v Republic of Argentina*, 699 F.3d 246 (2d Cir 2012).

The US Supreme Court declined to hear an appeal against the application of the *pari passu* clause.[305] However, this line of cases may be of limited precedential value before English courts and is unlikely to be applied in the UK for the reasons set out in the preceding paragraphs. Additionally the US courts did not have to decide, and did not clearly decide, between the narrow and the wide interpretations. Argentina had changed its law to effectively subordinate the holdout creditors' bonds by imposing a legislative ban on payments to or settlements with the holdouts. Consequently the *pari passu* clause was breached even on the orthodox narrower 'equal ranking' interpretation. The most controversial aspect of the case may be the injunction which was granted by way of remedy. At any rate, the practical effect of the decision on future bonds restructurings has been mitigated by the increased use of collective action clauses which will make such holdout situations less likely in the future.[306]

2.17.8 Negative pledge and disposals of assets

The second set of undertakings relating to the lender's position as a creditor is **2.179** contained in the negative pledge clause and, allied to that, the clause against disposals of assets.[307] These clauses are designed to ensure that, to the maximum extent possible, the borrower's assets will be available to meet the claims of its unsecured creditors (including that of the lender) in an insolvency of the borrower. If the lender is taking security, the clauses serve the alternate function of seeking to preserve the rights of the lender in the secured assets ahead of others seeking to assert a proprietary interest (whether by way of security, purchase, or other disposition) in the assets. As a matter of English law, if the lender wishes to assert that it has taken fixed security, rather than a floating charge, it is also important to have the clauses so as to prevent the borrower from having the right to deal with the assets which are the subject of the lender's security (again, by way of security, sale, or other disposition) as it could do under a floating charge.[308]

The negative pledge clause is an undertaking by the borrower not to create se- **2.180** curity (or permit security to subsist[309]) in its assets in favour of a third party. The concept of security is usually extended, for this purpose, to include quasi-security

---

[305] But the Supreme Court upheld the injunction in *Republic of Argentina v NML Capital, Ltd* 134 S Ct 2250 (2014). The cases were subsequently settled by Argentina.

[306] See paras 7.4.4 and 7.4.5 of Sarah Paterson and Rafal Zakrzewski (eds), *McKnight, Paterson, & Zakrzewski on the Law of International Finance* (2nd edn, OUP 2017) for a discussion of collective action clauses.

[307] For a fuller discussion of this subject, see Andrew McKnight, 'Restrictions on Dealing with Assets in Financing Documents' [2002] JIBL 193.

[308] *Agnew v Commissioner of Inland Revenue* [2001] UKPC 28, [2001] 2 AC 710; *National Westminster Bank plc v Spectrum Plus Ltd* [2005] UKHL 41, [2005] 2 AC 680.

[309] This is important because the borrower may acquire an asset that is already subject to security or an asset may be subject to a statutory charge or the security may arise by operation of law, such as under an equitable lien.

and other devices which have the effect of conferring upon a creditor a preferred right in an asset of the borrower or a right to apply the asset in discharge of a liability of the borrower. It is intended, therefore, to address traditional concepts of security under English law, such as mortgages, charges, and possessory security (liens and pledges), as well as rights under title finance and rights of set-off, and similar concepts under other systems of law. A clause against the disposition of assets is intended to apply to methods of outright disposal of assets and more limited forms of divestment of possession or title, such as by way of lease or the grant of an equitable interest.

2.181 A well-advised borrower will seek various exceptions to the restrictions contained in these clauses. For instance, it will seek exceptions from the negative pledge clause to cover rights of set-off that arise by operation of law,[310] or in the ordinary course of carrying on its business,[311] or which arise in favour of its bankers, repairers' liens, and other liens arising by operation of law,[312] or in the ordinary course of its business, security over assets which it acquires or security granted by a company which it acquires (usually subject to the security being discharged within a certain period after the acquisition), security that is given in connection with non-recourse lending where repayment of the lending will be taken from the sale of the secured assets and not by recourse to a personal covenant of the borrower,[313] security as disclosed when the loan facility agreement was signed, security up to a certain level of secured obligations during the term of the loan facility agreement, and other security which is likely to arise in the context of its business.[314] Exceptions to the disposals clause would be intended to allow the borrower to make payments and to acquire and dispose of assets in the ordinary course of trading,[315] as well as being able to do other things that a business might ordinarily undertake.

---

[310] Such as under rr 2.85 and 4.90 of the Insolvency Rules 1986.

[311] Care needs to be taken when considering the concept of the ordinary course of business, given the wide construction given to it by the courts in relation to the inherent liberty to deal with assets in the ordinary course of business under a floating charge: see the review in *Ashborder BV v Green Gas Power Ltd* [2004] EWHC 1517 (Ch) [192]–[227]. In older cases the concept was construed very widely. In *Re HH Vivian & Co Limited* [1900] 2 Ch 654 a sale of one of the borrower's three businesses could not be stopped by floating charge holders as being outside its ordinary course of business. See also *Foster v Borax Company* [1901] 1 Ch 326 (CA).

[312] Such as an equitable lien: see *Re Molton Finance Ltd* [1968] Ch 325; *London & Cheshire Insurance Co Ltd v Laplagrene Property Co Ltd* [1971] Ch 499; *Burston Finance Ltd v Speirway Ltd* [1974] 1 WLR 1648; *Orakpo v Manson Investments Ltd* [1978] AC 95; *International Finance Corp v DSNL Offshore Ltd* [2005] EWHC 1844 (Comm), [2007] 2 All ER (Comm) 305.

[313] If such an exception is agreed then there is an argument that the value of the asset and the amount of the borrowing should be ignored in the constituent elements of the gearing covenant.

[314] For instance, margin payments that may be required under commodities and derivatives contracts or pledges over imported goods that have been paid for under a letter of credit.

[315] This is a narrower concept than the ordinary course of business. By way of example, if a manufacturer of widgets sells a factory, this may be done in its ordinary course of business but is unlikely to be in its ordinary course of trading.

The question arises as to the remedies that might be available to the lender if **2.182** the negative pledge or disposals clauses are breached. In this instance, the lender might not be content to rely upon its usual rights to suspend the facility and demand repayment under the events of default clause in the loan facility agreement. If it learns of a threatened breach, it may seek an injunction to restrain the borrower from proceeding with the threatened breach[316] but it is unlikely that the lender would find out before the breach occurred. More importantly, the lender might wish to prevent the third party from benefiting from the borrower's breach of contract and relying upon the rights it has gained in the borrower's assets in consequence of the breach. Accordingly, the lender might seek an injunction against the third party, so as to prevent it from relying upon the interest it has gained in the assets[317] (although, if the lender is merely an unsecured creditor, this will not have the result in itself of giving the lender an interest in those assets). To do so, the lender would need to show that it had a cause of action against the third party for the tort of inducing or procuring a breach of contract,[318] and to do that it would need to establish the following:[319]

(1) that there had been a breach by the borrower of the contract between it and the lender, which may be difficult to establish if there is a broad spectrum of exceptions to the restrictions in the clause;

(2) the third party must have known that it was inducing a breach by the borrower of its contract with the lender. It is not enough that the third party ought reasonably to have appreciated the likely effect nor that it should have realised, but did not, that the act done by the borrower would, as a matter of law or construction of the contract, amount to a breach of its contract with the lender. The issue is purely subjective;

---

[316] Under the principle propounded by Lord Cairns LC in *Doherty v Allman* (1878) 3 App Cas 709. See also *Pullen v Abelcheck Pty Ltd* (1990) 20 NSWLR 732.

[317] As discussed by Browne-Wilkinson J in *Swiss Bank Corp v Lloyds Bank Ltd* [1979] Ch 548.

[318] Apart from a common law action in tort, it has been suggested that a claim based on equity could also be brought against a creditor who takes security with knowledge of a negative pledge on the basis of the principle in *de Mattos v Gibson* (1858) De G&J 276, 45 ER 108. There the court held that 'where a man ... acquires property from another, with knowledge of a previous contract, lawfully and for valuable consideration made by him with a third person, to use and employ the property for a particular purpose in a specified manner, the acquirer shall not, to the material damage of the third person, in opposition to the contract and inconsistently with it, use and employ the property in a manner not allowable to the giver or seller'. If this principle applied, the acquirer could be restrained by an injunction from acting inconsistently with the previous contract of which it had actual knowledge. It is unclear whether this principle applies to contracts generally or whether it is confined to the facts of the *de Mattos* case. See Eilis Ferran and Look Chan Ho, *Principles of Corporate Finance Law* (2nd edn, OUP 2014) 289–90.

[319] The requisite elements of the tort, as set out here, are taken from the review of the tort conducted by Lord Hoffmann in *OBG Ltd v Allan; Douglas v Hello! Ltd; Mainstream Properties Ltd v Young* [2007] UKHL 21. In *DBS Bank Ltd v Tam Chee Chong* [2011] SGCA 47 the Singapore Court of Appeal recognised that the tort may apply to a breach of a negative pledge.

(3) there is the question of what would amount to sufficient knowledge on the part of the third party of the contract, its terms and their breach, apart from actual knowledge. Actual knowledge is sufficient and a reckless indifference to the facts could constitute a sufficient degree of knowledge.[320] Negligence, even gross negligence, such as by negligently making the wrong enquiries, would not be sufficient to ground the tort. It is also submitted that merely having constructive knowledge would be insufficient knowledge for these purposes,[321] when taken in conjunction with the second of the matters that must be established.[322]

(4) the third party must possess an intention to procure the breach of contract. If the breach of contract is merely a foreseeable consequence of some other intended action and is not in itself the end or intended consequence of the action taken by the third party, nor the means of achieving some other intended consequence, then there will not be an intention on its part to cause the breach of contract. Furthermore, if the third party, knowing of the contract, has been assured by the borrower that it will not be breaching its contract with the lender because it has the lender's consent or because an exception applies, and the third party honestly believes that answer, it will lack the necessary intention.[323]

2.183 Taking those various requirements together, the lender may find that it has an uphill struggle in making out its claim against the third party.[324] If it cannot prevail against the third party then the latter will be able to assert its interest in the relevant assets despite the objections of the lender. If the lender is unsecured, it will be unable to prevent the third party resorting to its security.

2.184 With those difficulties in mind, an unsecured lender may wish to provide in the loan facility agreement that the borrower would be obliged to create equivalent

---

[320] As, for instance, was held to be the case by Sir John Donaldson MR in *Merkur Island Shipping Corpn v Laughton* [1983] 2 AC 570 at 591(whose judgment was approved on appeal by Lord Diplock in the same case, at 608–09), when he held that 'almost certain knowledge' of the existence of the contract, its relevant terms and the breach thereof would amount to sufficient knowledge.

[321] *Swiss Bank Corp v Lloyds Bank Ltd* [1979] Ch 548.

[322] It was previously held that constructive knowledge of the existence of a charge by virtue of its registration in the Companies Registry did not give constructive knowledge of the contents of the charge instrument: see *Siebe Gorman & Co Ltd v Barclays Bank Ltd* [1979] 2 Lloyd's Rep 142, 160 and the cases therein mentioned. However, at that time the existence of a negative pledge contained in a floating charge was not a registrable particular. This detail is now registrable under s 859D of the Companies Act 2006, so presumably due registration will constitute constructive notice of the negative pledge.

[323] These were the facts in *Mainstream Properties Ltd v Young* [2007] UKHL 21. For this reason in nearly all loan agreements the borrower represents and warrants that its entry into the transaction does not conflict with any other agreement binding upon it.

[324] However, in *Slocom Trading Ltd v Tatik Inc* [2012] EWHC 3464 (Ch) [332]ff, upheld on appeal [2014] EWCA Civ 831, the tort of inducing a breach of contract was made out in the context of a disposal of a substantial asset that, to the knowledge of the acquirer, was contrary to the covenants of a loan agreement.

security in favour of the lender if the borrower granted security to a third party (sometimes referred to as 'springing security'). To avoid an argument that the provision failed at the outset for uncertainty, it would be essential that the provision was drafted so that there could be no doubt at the time the provision came into effect as to which assets were to be the subject of the agreement, the type of security that was to be given, and how it was to rank. Even so, there would be considerable obstacles under English law in enforcing such a provision, which may be summarised as follows, not to mention the difficulties that might also arise under the laws of other relevant jurisdictions:

(1) it has been said that such a provision is registrable under Part 25 of the Companies Act 2006[325] as an agreement to give a floating charge.[326] Failure to meet the registration requirements would mean that the agreement was void as against a liquidator, administrator, or secured creditors of the borrower;

(2) the borrower may be unable to cooperate in giving the security because of a negative pledge in the third party's or some other creditor's documentation and they may intervene;

(3) if the borrower does give the security to the lender, the security may be vulnerable to attack under the avoidance provisions of the Insolvency Act 1986[327] or similar enactments and claw-back provisions under the laws of other jurisdictions;

(4) if the security is over future property, it may fail because it is not supported by valuable consideration provided at the time or subsequent to its creation;[328]

(5) if the borrower failed to cooperate in giving the security once the relevant circumstances had arisen, it is very unlikely that the lender would be able to obtain recognition of the original agreement as having the automatic effect of giving it the security. The lender would be seeking recognition in equity, on the basis that the borrower should be treated as having done that which it promised to do. The reasons why it would be unable to gain such recognition would be that, in the first place, the original agreement was conditional upon the will of the borrower in creating the circumstances under which the agreement took effect. Equity will not enforce such conditional arrangements. Secondly, to enforce the agreement the lender must show that it provided new value in return for its reliance on the security. Whilst it may have provided value when it made its advances, that will have been spent by the time

---

[325] Previously Part XII of the Companies Act 1985.

[326] See *Smith (Administrator of Cosslett (Contractors) Ltd) v Bridgend CBC* [2001] UKHL 58, [2002] AC 336 [59]–[64] (Lord Scott).

[327] Particularly ss 127, 238, 239, and 245 of the Act. See also art 4(2)(m) of the EC Insolvency Regulation (1346/2000/EC [2000] OJ L160/1) which is to be replaced by a recast Insolvency Regulation in 2017.

[328] See *Tailby v Official Receiver* (1888) 13 App Cas 523 (Lord Macnaghten). Such value could include a realistic agreement by the lender to forbear from taking enforcement action against the borrower: *Glegg v Bromley* [1912] 3 KB 474.

it claims that its proprietary rights arose under the security. Thirdly, the same problems may arise under the Insolvency Act 1986 as already mentioned.

2.18 Events of Default and Acceleration

2.185 As explained earlier in this chapter, a lender under a term loan does not have an inherent right to demand early repayment of its loan.[329] It can only do so if the loan facility agreement gives it that right.[330] This will normally be done in accordance with the provisions of a clause in the agreement, usually referred to as the 'events of default' clause, under which a series of possible events will be specified.[331] Such a clause provides that if any of the stated events occurs, the lender will have the right to suspend or terminate the facility and demand repayment.[332] The clause may also provide that the lender is entitled to convert a term loan or a revolving loan into a loan repayable 'on demand'. An acceleration clause does not, in the absence of express language to that effect, allow the lenders to give notice of a future acceleration, or one conditional on future events.[333] It has been held that acceleration clauses are enforceable and will not amount to a penalty, so long as they do not also set out to punish the borrower by providing for the payment of all amounts of interest and such like that would have accrued due in the future, had the facility run its normal course.[334] Upon acceleration, any repayment schedule will necessarily fall away.[335] Loan agreements usually do not require that the events of default relied on be specified in the acceleration notice,[336] but it is common practice to include them.[337]

---

[329] *Cryne v Barclays Bank plc* [1987] BCLC 548.

[330] *The Angelic Star* [1988] 1 Lloyd's Rep 122.

[331] There may be other clauses as well which give rise to a right to require early repayment, such as those described in n 122 above.

[332] 'The loan is not automatically cancelled or accelerated on the happening of an event of default': *Habibsons Bank Ltd v Standard Chartered Bank (Hong Kong) Ltd* [2010] EWHC 702 (Comm) [30]. This should be contrasted with US loans where automatic acceleration provisions may be added because of local insolvency laws.

[333] *African Export-Import Bank v Shebah Exploration & Production Company and ors* [2016] EWHC 311 (Comm) (upheld on appeal [2017] EWCA Civ 845) where a notice which purported to accelerate a loan at a specified date in the future if all sums had not been paid and other events of default remedied at that date was ineffective to accelerate the loan.

[334] *The Angelic Star* [1988] 1 Lloyd's Rep 122. But contrast *Holyoake v Candy* [2017] EWHC 3397 (Ch).

[335] *Dubai Islamic Bank PJSC v PSI Energy Holding Company BSC* [2013] EWHC 3781 (Comm) [157]. In *Strategic Value Master Fund Ltd v Ideal Standard International Acquisition Sarl* [2011] EWHC 171 (Ch) Lewison J held that placing the principal of an amortising term loan 'on demand' in accordance with the terms of the loan agreement did not permanently erase the repayment schedule; withdrawal of the notice was possible. As to the exercise of a right to payment on demand see section 2.10.2 above.

[336] *TFB Mortgages Limited v Pimlico Capital Limited* [2002] EWHC 878 (Ch) [39].

[337] The lender can justify its acceleration by reference to other events of default which existed at the relevant time even if they were not referred to, see para 2.205 below.

For the reasons expressed elsewhere in this book, it is submitted that there is no **2.186** other fetter on the ability of the lender to determine if it wishes to exercise its rights under the clause.[338] The lender is free to exercise its rights as it wishes and the courts will not imply a term requiring it to act reasonably.[339] It is irrelevant that the lender has suffered no loss, or that it is acting to escape an unprofitable contract, or that the borrower later remedies its breach.[340] Motive is irrelevant in the exercise of a lender's rights.[341] There is no room for implied terms to control the lender's exercise of its powers to accelerate and demand repayment.[342] This might be contrasted with the position under New York law, where there is an obligation of good faith and fair dealing in determining if a power to accelerate payment should be exercised.[343]

The making of such a demand is said to 'accelerate' the repayment obligation of **2.187** the borrower and the process is referred to as 'acceleration' of the loan. The decision of a lender that an event of default has occurred is sometimes referred to as a 'declaration of default'. The expression 'events of default' is a bit of a misnomer. Some of the events specified in the clause are in the nature of defaults or breaches of contract but others of them may arise in other circumstances, they may relate to different persons, and they may even be outside the control of the borrower.[344] For instance, in cross-border and international lending, it may be relevant for the clause to refer to the circumstances of the country in which the borrower is incorporated or established. As with the monitoring and minding provisions of the agreement, the events of default clause is normally the product of negotiation between the parties before its final form is settled.

Loan agreements often specify that events of default have contractual effect only **2.188** while they are continuing.[345] A borrower with negotiating strength may be able

---

[338] See para 1.57 above.

[339] *BNP Paribas v Yukos* [2005] EWHC 1321 (Ch) [23].

[340] Furthermore it seems that a creditor who is itself in default can still exercise contractual rights granted to it in respect of its counterparty's events of default: *Grant and ors v WDW3 Investments Ltd and anor* [2017] EWHC 2807 (Ch).

[341] *Çukurova Finance International Ltd v Alfa Telecom Turkey Ltd* [2013] UKPC 2 [78].

[342] In *Sucden Financial Ltd v Fluxo-Cane Overseas Ltd and anor* [2010] EWHC 2133 (Comm) [50]. Blair J stated: 'the authorities relied upon by [the defendant] are concerned with contracts which give one party a discretion as to how it is to be performed. In certain cases, the courts will treat such discretion as subject to limits … These authorities, in my judgment, have no application to the termination of a financial contract upon an Event of Default.' This is consistent with the distinction later drawn by the Court of Appeal between binary choices under a contract where constraints ought not to be implied and a contractual choice from a range of options which may be subject to implied limitations: *Mid Essex Hospital v Compass Group UK and Ireland Ltd* [2013] EWCA Civ 200 [83]–[92]. See para 2.77 above.

[343] See § 1-208 of the New York Uniform Commercial Code.

[344] Events of default which do not involve a breach of contract will not be enforceable by means of a claim for damages or an injunction. The distinction is also relevant when considering potential causes of action against third parties who interfere with the performance of the loan contract: there is no tort of inducing an event of default.

[345] See also 2.203 and 2.204.

to negotiate successfully for an event of default to be defined as 'continuing' only where it has not been either remedied by the borrower or waived by the lender. On the other hand lenders generally prefer to define continuing events of default as those that have not been waived by the lenders. If this narrower formulation is agreed it follows that a borrower cannot deprive an event of default of its potential contractual effect by unilaterally remedying it. In that case, the borrower would still formally need a waiver of the now cured event of default from the lenders.

2.18.1 The events

2.189 The list of events of default typically includes the occurrence of matters along the following lines (references to the borrower might be extended to include other members of its group):

(1) non-payment on the due date of amounts falling due under the agreement (perhaps with a one or two business day period of grace in which the position may be rectified, particularly if it has arisen because of difficulties in the mechanics for transmission of payment);[346]

(2) other breaches of the agreement or defaults by the borrower, such as under the representations and warranties clause or the covenants and undertakings (perhaps with a period of grace to allow the breach or default to be cured);[347]

(3) a cross-default concerning payment due by the borrower to another creditor;

(4) enforcement action against the borrower by other creditors under security or by enforcement of judgment;

(5) insolvency[348] events relating to the borrower;[349]

---

[346] If a payment default occurs, that is an event of default. There is no further requirement as regards materiality, or that the failure to pay has to be repudiatory or really serious. See *Bank of New York Mellon v GV Films Ltd* [2009] EWHC 3315 (Comm).

[347] In determining whether a breach is curable or capable of remedy, 'the proper approach ... should be practical rather than technical': *Akici v LR Butlin Ltd* [2005] EWCA Civ 1296. In *Telchadder v Wickland Holdings Ltd* [2014] UKSC 57 the Supreme Court reaffirmed that this is a practical inquiry as to whether the mischief caused by the breach can be redressed. See also *Dubai Islamic Bank PJSC v PSI Energy Holding Company BSC* [2013] EWHC 3781 (Comm) where it was held that a bank could not be precluded from serving notices in respect of events of default by the fact that its counterparties had been rendered incapable of curing the default, provided that the bank has not itself prevented such performance.

[348] Insolvency does not necessarily entail an anticipatory repudiation of a contract (see *Re Agra Bank* (1867) LR 5 Eq 160) and therefore it is almost always expressly included as an event of default. An insolvency event of default was found to have occurred within the terms of the relevant clause (which were wider than the general law test) in *TMT Asia Limited v Marine Trade SA* [2011] EWHC 1327 (Comm). In the case of borrowers who are incorporated overseas, insolvency would be determined according to the jurisdiction relevant to that company, not necessarily English law as the governing law of the loan agreement (unless the agreement provided to the contrary): *Strategic Value Master Fund Ltd v Ideal Standard International Acquisition Sarl* [2011] EWHC 171 (Ch).

[349] Sometimes a restructuring event of default is defined to occur if, by reason of actual or anticipated financial difficulties, the borrower enters into negotiations with any creditor for the rescheduling of its indebtedness. In *Grupo Hotelero Urvasco SA v Carey Value Added SL* [2013] EWHC 1039 (Comm) the High Court accepted that the term 'rescheduling' required a degree of formality but that the commencement of negotiations with creditors generally was not required. Negotiations

(6) the loss of security or of a guarantee relating to the facility;

(7) events relating to third parties which are relevant to the circumstances of the facility or the borrower; and

(8) an adverse change in the borrower's circumstances.

Two of those provisions (often called 'clauses') call for further comment, namely the cross-default clause and the material adverse change clause.

2.18.2 Cross-default

A cross-default clause is likely to be along the following lines (with alternative   **2.190** wording placed in squared brackets):

(i) Any [Financial] Indebtedness of the Borrower [or any other member of its Group] [in an amount cumulatively exceeding []] is not paid when due (taking into account any applicable grace period); or

(ii) any such Indebtedness is [validly] declared to be or otherwise becomes due and payable prior to its originally stated date of maturity (except in consequence of the exercise of a voluntary right of the Borrower [or such other member of its Group] to make early payment of it)[350] [;or

(iii) the creditor to whom such Indebtedness is due becomes entitled to declare it to be due and payable prior to its stated date of maturity in consequence of an event of default (howsoever described)].

The clause relates to defaults in payment (and, in the case of subparagraphs (ii)   **2.191** and (iii) of other obligations), whether on the due date or in consequence of acceleration, by the borrower (or other members of its group) to other creditors, particularly financial creditors (as opposed to trade suppliers). The idea behind the clause is that if another such creditor (or the same creditor under a different facility)[351] has not been paid or otherwise becomes entitled to take action against the borrower to recover its debt,[352] the lender under the present facility wishes to be in the same position to make recovery. Otherwise, the other debt may be repaid first, leaving little or nothing available for the lender when it does eventually have the right to demand early repayment from the borrower.

---

with one creditor would be sufficient provided the financial difficulties in question were substantial. That approach was also taken in *Torre Asset Funding v RBS* [2013] EWHC 2670 (Ch). See also *Fomento De Construcciones Y Contratas SA v Black Diamond Offshore Ltd* [2016] EWCA Civ 1141.

[350] The provision in this subparagraph is referred to as a cross-acceleration clause. In contradistinction to a cross-default clause which is triggered as soon as a default occurs under another facility, a cross-acceleration clause requires the debt under the other facility to be accelerated before the cross-acceleration clause is triggered.

[351] *Rahman v HSBC Bank* [2012] EWHC 11 (Ch) [278].

[352] Either by formal proceedings or by exerting pressure.

2.192 Cross-default events of default have been applied in accordance with their plain meaning in derivatives transactions. In *Abu Dhabi Commercial Bank PJSC v Saad Trading, Contracting & Financial Services Co*,[353] the High Court held that reading down such a clause to cover only events of default which are similar to those included in the principal contract would be uncommercial and very difficult to apply in practice. The same would apply to loan agreements.

2.193 A problem from the borrower's perspective is that the operation of the clause, in conjunction with similar clauses in its other financial agreements, may cause its collapse because all of its financial creditors may pursue it at the same time, should it fail to pay any one of its financial creditors, whether on normal maturity or because of acceleration of that creditor's debt. Similarly, such a provision has the effect of allowing the borrower's creditors to take advantage of more onerous terms in one creditor's agreement with the borrower, even if such terms are not contained in their own agreements or are expressed differently.

2.194 Given those disadvantages, a borrower would be well advised to resist an attempt to extend the operation of a cross-default clause (such an extension being represented by paragraph (iii) in the example given) to a situation where another creditor has obtained a right to accelerate (for instance, because an event of default has occurred under its agreement) but has not yet done so. After all, that other creditor may be content to let the matter rest for the time being and not accelerate the borrower's payment obligations. In addition, a well-advised borrower should seek to include the word 'validly' where it is shown in the earlier example, to prevent an argument that even a wrongful attempt at acceleration by another creditor might lead to the triggering of the right to accelerate under the cross-default clause.

2.18.3 Material adverse change

2.195 A material adverse change (MAC) clause in a loan agreement is likely to be along the following lines (with alternative wording placed in squared brackets):

> Any event or series of events occurs, whether or not related (including, without limitation, an adverse change in the business, revenues, profits, assets, [prospects] or other [financial] condition of the borrower [or any other member of its Group]) which [would] [is reasonably likely to] [might][in the [reasonable] opinion of the lender] affect [materially and] adversely the ability of the Borrower [or the Guarantor] to comply with its [respective] obligations under this Agreement [or the Guarantee] or the rights of the Lender hereunder [or under the Guarantee].[354]

---

[353] [2010] EWHC 2054 (Comm).

[354] For additional analysis of legal issues arising out of MAC clauses see: Rafal Zakrzewski, 'Material Adverse Change and Material Adverse Effect Provisions: Construction and Application' (2011) 5 Law and Financial Markets Review 344 and 'When is a Material Adverse Change Clause a Force Majeure Clause?' (2012) 9 Journal of International Banking and Financial Law 547.

The material adverse change clause is most likely to be used by a lender to stop **2.196** or suspend a drawdown under the conditions precedent clause or to force a re-negotiation of the terms of the loan agreement where changed circumstances have increased the risks faced by the lender. Negotiating points (highlighted by the alternative wording above) commonly include: what the material adverse changes should impact so as to trigger the clause,[355] in particular whether the clause should be forward-looking by extending to changes in the borrower's 'prospects'; whether it should be concerned only with the financial condition[356] and payment obligations of the borrower; the probability of the MAC impacting on the borrower—whether the effect should be certain ('would' have the effect), probable ('is likely to' or 'is expected to'), or only possible ('might'); and whether the occurrence of the event should be determined in the opinion of the lender (ie subjectively) or objectively.

In *Çukurova Finance International Ltd v Alfa Telecom Turkey Ltd*[357] the Privy **2.197** Council considered whether the following MAC event of default had occurred: 'an event or circumstances which in the opinion of [the lender] has had or is reasonably likely to have a material adverse effect on the financial condition, assets or business of [the borrower]'. It concluded that this clause entitled the lender to be a judge in its own cause. The event did not need objectively to have an adverse effect.[358] What was required was that the lender believed that it has such an effect provided that the belief was honest and rational.[359] For the reasons mentioned in section 1.2.9, even if the lender has an apparently unfettered discretion in determining whether an adverse change has occurred, some limitation is likely to be implied as to the manner in which it might exercise that discretion, along the lines that it should not be exercised arbitrarily, capriciously, for some unwarranted collateral purpose, or in a way that no comparable lender, acting reasonably, would act. A negative consequence for a lender of a subjective formulation is that in the event of litigation it will only be able to point to matters indicating a MAC of which it was aware at the time it formed its opinion, and not to matters

---

[355] In *Ipsos SA v Dentsu Aegis Network Ltd* [2015] EWHC 1726 (Comm) Blair J held that it was not arguable that financial forecasts that had been significantly revised downwards were a 'fact, matter, event or circumstance' within the meaning of a MAC clause under a share purchase agreement.

[356] Financial condition is assessed primarily by reference to the borrower's financial information, but other evidence, such as non-payment of debts, can be considered: *Grupo Hotelero Urvasco SA v Carey Value Added SL* [2013] EWHC 1039 (Comm).

[357] [2013] UKPC 2.

[358] In the absence of 'in the opinion of the lender' MAC will be assessed objectively: *Decura IM Investments LLP v UBS AG* [2015] EWHC 171.

[359] See also *Grupo Hotelero Urvasco SA v Carey Value Added SL* [2013] EWHC 1039 (Comm) [344]. The bank must hold the relevant opinion at the relevant time in order to be able to exercise the rights that stem from the relevant event of default: *Plantation Holdings (FZ) LLC v Dubai Islamic Bank PJSC* [2017] EWHC 520 (Comm) [232].

which subsequently came to light.[360] In the case of an objectively formulated MAC clause, the lender would not be restricted in this way and could adduce evidence which supported the existence of a MAC which it had discovered after invoking the clause.

2.198 The clause is rather general in its wording. Given its apparent generality, it might be thought that the courts would approach a material adverse change clause rather sceptically and read it down within the context of the events of default clause overall, particularly as the other provisions in most events of default clauses are extensive and should cover nearly anything that could go wrong. It might be said that it was difficult to envisage adverse events which might occur that would not cause one of those other provisions to be triggered or, alternatively, that the parties did not contemplate that any further events that were not so specified might be considered as having a material effect. On that basis, the *ejusdem generis* rule might be applied in construing the material adverse change clause, under which the more general wording of the material adverse change clause would be restricted to things of the same nature as the more specific matters dealt with in the events of default clause. However, when a material adverse change clause has come before them, the courts have followed a more independent approach. They have considered the clause on its own merits and, taking a practical approach, have determined whether the events that occurred fell within the wording of the clause taken in its ordinary meaning.[361] The leading case is *Grupo Hotelero Urvasco SA v Carey Value Added SL*.[362] Blair J held that an adverse change would be material if it substantially or significantly affected the borrower's ability to repay the loan in question.[363] It was also clarified that in order to be material, the change must be more than merely temporary[364] and, somewhat controversially, that a lender cannot trigger the clause on the basis of circumstances which it was aware of at the date of the loan agreement.[365]

---

[360] Another problem which the subjective formulation poses for the lender is that it may neuter the borrower's representation and warranty that no MAC has occurred. The borrower's assertion that 'in the lender's opinion no MAC has occurred' is likely to be construed as no more than a statement of its honest perception of what the lender has communicated to it.

[361] *BNP Paribas SA v Yukos Oil Company* [2005] EWHC 1321 (Ch); *Pan Foods Company Importers & Distributors Pty Ltd v Australia & New Zealand Banking Group Ltd* [2000] HCA 20, (2000) 74 ALJR 791; *Çukurova Finance International Ltd v Alfa Telecom Turkey Ltd* [2013] UKPC 2.

[362] [2013] EWHC 1039 (Comm).

[363] This formulation was subsequently applied in *Decura IM Investments LLP v UBS AG* [2015] EWHC 171 and in Australia in *Kupang Resources Ltd v International Litigation Partners Pte Ltd* [2015] WASCA 89.

[364] This is consistent with the interpretation adopted in the US case of *IBP Inc v Tyson Foods Inc* 789 A2d 14 (Del Ch 2001) 65 where it was held that the change must affect the relevant party in a durationally significant manner.

[365] [2013] EWHC 1039 (Comm) [352]. A different position was taken on this point in *Levison v Farin* [1978] 2 All ER 1149, a decision not cited in the *Grupo Hotelero* case.

2.18.4 Construction of the events of default clause

Such an approach in reading separately the various provisions within an events of **2.199**
default clause and giving them a literal effect was reflected in the judgment of Hart
J in *Law Debenture Trust Corporation plc v Elektrim Finance BV*.[366] The judgment
is of interest in relation to two provisions in the events of default clause that his
Lordship considered. Whilst the case concerned the conditions of a bond issue,
there is no reason to believe that the same approach to construction would not
have been taken in construing the similar provisions of a loan facility agreement.

The first of those provisions was in the following terms: **2.200**

> All or any part of the undertaking, assets or revenues of the Guarantor, the Issuer or
> [any material subsidiary of the Guarantor] is condemned, seized or otherwise appro-
> priated by any person acting under the authority of any national, regional or local
> government or any political sub-division thereof.

The tax authorities of the relevant country, Poland, had carried out an execution
against the bank accounts of such a material subsidiary to satisfy alleged substantial tax liabilities. The validity of the execution was being contested before
the courts in Poland. It was argued by the issuer and the guarantor that an event
within the wording above had not occurred on essentially two grounds. First, it
was said that any such seizure etc had to be material when taken in the context
of the undertaking and assets of the whole group which, it was said, was not the
case on the facts. Although there was no direct reference to such a requirement
of materiality in the wording, it was claimed that this was imported from the
wording of another provision in the events of default clause which was apt to refer
to the same events but which was qualified by the materiality test. Secondly, it was
argued that the wording should be construed as if it was intended to catch only
lawful seizures etc. As the execution was being contested, its lawfulness was in
doubt and so it was not possible to proceed on the basis that an event within the
wording had occurred. His Lordship rejected both arguments. There was nothing
in the wording to suggest that it should be qualified on either basis. It was perfectly possible that the same set of facts might fall within separate provisions in
the events of default clause and there was nothing in the clause to indicate that
one provision should be read down so as to conform with the wording of another
provision.[367] Each provision depended upon its own wording. Furthermore, the

---

[366] [2005] EWHC 1999 (Ch). See also *BNP Paribas SA v Yukos Oil Company* [2005] EWHC
1321 (Ch); *TMT Asia Limited v Marine Trade SA* [2011] EWHC 1327 (Comm); *LB Re Financing
No. 3 Ltd (In Administration) v Excalibur Funding No. 1 plc* [2011] EWHC 2111 (Ch); and *Grupo
Hotelero Urvasco SA v Carey Value Added SL* [2013] EWHC 1039 (Comm).
[367] Similarly in *Abu Dhabi Commercial Bank PJSC v Saad Trading, Contracting & Financial
Services Co* [2010] EWHC 2054 (Comm) the court refused to read down a cross-default clause to
only cover events of default similar to those included in the principal agreement.

wording as set out above did not justify any conclusion that the seizure etc had to be lawful to fall within the compass of the provision.

2.201 The other provision which is relevant for present purposes provided as follows:

> If ... proceedings shall have been initiated against ... the Guarantor under any applicable bankruptcy, reorganisation or insolvency law.

An application for the bankruptcy of the guarantor had been filed before the courts in Poland, which was then contested by the guarantor. The application was subsequently withdrawn without any order being made against the guarantor. The expert evidence as to Polish law showed that such a filing on its own had no legal implications upon the guarantor's contractual relations with third parties, and that such a filing was only a preliminary step in bankruptcy proceedings and had no legal significance where it had been withdrawn. Nonetheless, Hart J held that the fact of the filing fell within the wording of the paragraph and so an event of default had occurred.[368] The proceedings had been initiated. The subsequent withdrawal of the filing did not detract from the fact that proceedings had been initiated.

2.202 The conclusion to be drawn from these findings is that an issuer or a borrower should ensure that the wording of each provision within an events of default clause contains qualifications to give protection against the harshness of the operation of the provisions in circumstances such as those that have been described. It would also be sensible to provide that action against the issuer or the borrower can only be taken in reliance upon the occurrence of an event of default if the relevant circumstances are still present and continuing at the time that the relevant creditors, or their representatives, purport to take the action.

2.203 As already noted, a borrower with negotiating strength may be able to argue successfully for an event of default to be defined as 'continuing' where it has not been either remedied by the borrower or waived by the lender. Lenders prefer to restrict this only to events that have not been waived by the lenders. If this formulation is adopted it follows that a borrower cannot deprive an event of default of its potential contractual effect by purporting to remedy it. In such a case, the borrower would still need to obtain a waiver from the lenders.

2.204 *LB Re Financing No. 3 Ltd (In Administration) v Excalibur Funding No. 1 plc*[369] involved a wide interpretation of when an event of default was 'continuing' which resulted in the cure of a breach of a poorly drafted financial covenant. The covenant required the debtor to ensure that the value of the securities it held on the

---

[368] The same plain meaning approach was taken in *Grupo Hotelero Urvasco SA v Carey Value Added SL* [2013] EWHC 1039 (Comm) in respect of an event of default triggered by negotiations to reschedule financial indebtedness.
[369] [2011] EWHC 2111 (Ch).

testing date did not exceed its indebtedness. It sold some of the securities and, on the testing date, held cash to be used for the repayment of part of its indebtedness which was to occur only three days later. On a literal interpretation of the coverage ratio, the debtor was in breach on the testing date but Briggs J found that the event of default ceased to be continuing when the repayment was made three days later.

2.18.5 An invalid declaration of default

Despite the courts not construing widely worded events of default clauses against the lender, there may still be circumstances in which a lender purports to declare that an event of default has occurred on incorrect grounds or where no grounds exist at all. The case law indicates that if the lender specifies the wrong grounds for its declaration,[370] but other valid grounds did exist, the declaration will be valid and the lender will be entitled to exercise its right to accelerate the borrower's obligations and enforce any security that it may hold.[371] The position is more complicated if no grounds existed on which the declaration might have been based.[372] **2.205**

In the leading case in the House of Lords, *Concord Trust v Law Debenture Trust Corp plc*,[373] it was held that, in the absence of an explicit provision by which a creditor undertook not to make an invalid declaration of default,[374] there was no term that should be implied by which the relevant creditor undertook such an obligation. The contract worked perfectly well on its own, so it was unnecessary to imply such a term. As there was no such term, an invalid declaration would simply be a nullity and of no effect;[375] it could not give rise to a breach of contract by the creditor. The case concerned the events of default clause in the conditions of a bond issue and an assumed invalid declaration of default by the trustee for the bondholders, but the same consequence would apply with respect to a loan facility agreement.[376] **2.206**

---

[370] Unless the loan agreement provides otherwise, the lender is not actually required to specify any grounds in its acceleration notice, see *TFB Mortgages Limited v Pimlico Capital Limited* [2002] EWHC 878 (Ch) [39].

[371] *Byblos Bank SAK v Al Khudhairy* (1986) 2 BCC 99549; *Anglo Petroleum Ltd v TFB (Mortgages) Ltd* [2003] EWHC 3125 (QB) [42]; *Brampton Manor (Leisure) Ltd v McClean* [2006] EWHC 2983 (Ch).

[372] For a fuller discussion than that which follows, see the note written by McKnight at [2006] JIBLR 117–124.

[373] [2005] UKHL 27, [2005] 1 WLR 1591. Lord Scott gave the leading judgment, which was supported by the four other members of the House who sat on the appeal.

[374] In *Dubai Islamic Bank PJSC v PSI Energy Holding Company BSC* [2013] EWHC 3781 (Comm) [155], the bank had assumed a positive obligation in a restructuring agreement to refrain from exercising its rights unless there had been an event of default.

[375] A demand for payment made without any basis for it is not a demand at law, it is simply a request for payment that can be refused: *Verizon UK Ltd (formerly MCI WorldCom Ltd) v Swiftnet Ltd* [2008] EWHC 551 (Comm).

[376] Jonathan Parker LJ had arrived at the same conclusion when considering the position under a bilateral loan facility agreement in *Bournemouth & Boscombe AFC Ltd v Lloyds TSB Bank plc*

2.207 It is submitted that a borrower which was faced with such a situation could obtain a declaration from the court that the lender's purported determination was invalid and an injunction to restrain the lender from taking further action in pursuance of its invalid determination. It could also plead the matter by way of a defence if the lender brought proceedings against it. If the lender was holding security, particularly over goods or land, and purported to enforce the security following upon an invalid demand then the creditor (or a receiver appointed by it) may be exposed to an action in conversion or for trespass. Such an action in conversion could not be brought for wrongful interference with the borrower's contractual rights,[377] and, in the absence of proof of a subjective intention to cause the borrower harm, it is doubtful if any other claim in tort would be available to the borrower.[378] If the lender, in reliance upon its wrongful determination, refused to make further advances to the borrower, the borrower may have rights against the lender, along the lines previously discussed.[379]

2.208 It was also held in *Concord Trust v Law Debenture Trust Corp plc*[380] that the trustee did not owe any duty of care in the tort of negligence towards the issuer and so there could be no liability for any loss (eg commercial or financial loss) that the issuer might have suffered in consequence of the invalid declaration of default. The position of a trustee for the bondholders is different from that of a lender under a loan facility, as the trustee has explicit fiduciary duties towards the bondholders which might well be inconsistent with any alleged duty of care towards the issuer.[381] A bank may owe its customer a duty of care in consequence of the contractual relationship[382] and there is no reason why a duty of care may not also arise in tort.[383] Whether the duty would extend to the circumstances under discussion

---

[2003] EWCA Civ 1755 [49]–[50]. Evans-Lombe J in *BNP Paribas SA v Yukos Oil Company* [2005] EWHC 1321 (Ch) applied the decision of the House of Lords in *Concord Trust v Law Debenture Trust Corp plc* in relation to a syndicated loan facility agreement, as did the Court of Appeal in relation to a bilateral loan facility agreement in *Jafari-Fini (Mohammad) v Skillglass Ltd* [2007] EWCA Civ 261. See also *Dubai Islamic Bank PJSC v PSI Energy Holding Company BSC* [2013] EWHC 3781 (Comm).

[377] *OBG Ltd v Allan; Douglas v Hello! Ltd; Mainstream Properties Ltd v Young* [2007] UKHL 21.

[378] ibid.

[379] See section 2.8 above.

[380] [2005] UKHL 27, [2005] 1 WLR 1591.

[381] A similar view could be taken concerning the position of an agent bank in a syndicated facility. The agent acts on behalf of the syndicate of lenders and its duties towards them would be inconsistent with an assertion that it had a duty of care towards the borrower. The same could not be said, however, of the lenders themselves, on whose behalf the agent acted, particularly if the lenders had instructed the agent to act. If they had not instructed it, they might (depending upon the facts) be able to argue that the agent had acted outside the scope of its authority and they were not liable for its actions.

[382] See s 13 of the Supply of Goods and Services Act 1982 and *Selangor United Rubber Estates Ltd v Cradock (No 3)* [1968] 1 WLR 1555, 1592–1610.

[383] See Lord Goff in *Henderson v Merrett Syndicates Ltd* [1995] 2 AC 145, 184–94, in which he approved the decision of Oliver J in *Midland Bank Trust Co Ltd v Hett Stubbs & Kemp* [1979] Ch 384 and disapproved the decision of the Privy Council in *Tai Hing Cotton Mill Ltd v Liu Chong Hing Bank Ltd* [1986] AC 80.

is another matter and would have to be tested in accordance with established rules.[384] It might be argued that the immediacy of the relationship between the parties and the foreseeability of loss supported the existence of the duty. On the other hand, in entering into the agreement the parties acted on their own behalf and they clearly had divergent interests. In deciding to act, the lender was entitled to have regard to its own interests. If the borrower wanted protection (and had the bargaining power to obtain it), it could have stipulated for it by insisting upon an explicit term in the contract under which the lender undertook not to make an invalid declaration of default.

---

[384] In particular, those discussed by the House of Lords in *Commissioners of Customs and Excise v Barclays Bank plc* [2006] UKHL 28, [2007] 1 AC 181.

3

SYNDICATED LENDING

3.1 Introduction

3.01 Syndicated lending was developed to enable loan finance to be provided for large amounts that could not readily be made available by a single bank acting on its own, due to factors affecting such a bank, including its assessment of the risk and exposure to a single borrower (and its group), capital adequacy considerations, and the limits on the bank's own resources and sources of funding. Syndicated lending evolved as economic conditions in the period after the Second World War led to a requirement for ever larger amounts of finance to fund the activities of borrowers, with the borrowers ranging from corporate entities to public authorities and states and their instrumentalities. The rather ad hoc alternative involved a borrower obtaining a series of individual bilateral loans from various different banks, which was a cumbersome procedure that was not really to the advantage of either the banks or the borrower. From the borrower's perspective, it meant finding the banks and attracting them to enter into discussions with the borrower, and, thereafter, negotiating with each bank separately, with the possibility of different terms and conditions applying to each loan, in both a commercial and a documentary sense. Thus the borrower might find that the period, interest rate, and the contractual provisions concerning undertakings, events of default and the like for each loan differed, dependent upon the outcome of its negotiations with the separate banks. From the perspective of the banks, they would not necessarily be aware of the position concerning the other banks, and each of them would have to undertake its own preliminary credit and other investigations, and then negotiate separately with the borrower. Syndicated lending obviated a great deal of the unnecessary duplication associated with separate bilateral lending by each bank. It provided a mechanism by which a group of banks could be found that were prepared to advance funds to the borrower in a coordinated fashion on the same terms and through the mechanism of the same facility.

3.02 Although those requiring large amounts of debt finance may now often prefer to raise funds through an issuance of debt instruments in the capital markets, syndicated lending is still used in many large financing transactions. For instance, it remains a common mechanism for project financing. There are also occasions where it might not be possible or convenient for a capital markets transaction to take place, as might be the case if it is desired to keep the matter confidential (eg to finance a hostile takeover bid, where the facility must be arranged before the bid is made), where the flexibility under a multicurrency facility is required, where a borrower desires to have a revolving facility for short-term advances, or where the borrower does not have a sufficient reputation to make it an attractive proposition to investors in the capital markets. Another benefit of a syndicated facility is that it is possible to structure the facility so that the borrower is given a range of different options that it may utilise under the facility, and thus, for example, the facility arrangements may comprise not just a loan facility but also an acceptance credit facility and a bonding and guarantee issuance facility. Such a facility is normally referred to as a multi-option facility.

3.03 In basic outline, a syndicated facility involves a group of lenders being brought together to form a syndicate, which will provide funds to the borrower within the compass of a single facility. In a relatively straightforward syndication, which will provide the basis for the discussion in this chapter, the syndicate of lenders will be present from the outset when the transaction is signed and entered into. In other situations, the facility documentation may contemplate the mechanics of a syndicated loan, but the wider syndicate will be brought together at a later stage, by virtue of a 'selling down' exercise, under which the bank or small group of banks that initially entered into the transaction with the borrower (often referred to as 'underwriters' or 'co-arrangers') will transfer participations of their commitments and exposures to the larger syndicate at some time after the facility agreement has been entered into between the borrower and the initial bank or banks.[1] In the latter case, the method of effecting the syndication will involve a transference of the participations, using the techniques for transferring loan and facility participations, most probably by the use of transfer certificates to effect novations, as discussed in chapter 4. Nonetheless, many of the issues that are discussed in this chapter will also be relevant in relation to that situation and the position that follows during the remaining life of the transaction.

3.04   The cast list of entities involved in a syndicated transaction will include the following:

(1) The borrower needs no particular introduction, but in some cases there may be more than one borrower and other entities that are linked to it may also be involved, such as in acting as guarantors. The guarantee could be given as a separate document or it may be included within the provisions of the facility agreement, in which case the guarantor would be a party to that agreement. There may even be mechanisms so that borrowers and guarantors can be added in or removed from the cast list.

(2) The arranger is the financial institution that is commissioned by the borrower to arrange or put the transaction together, which will include finding the syndicate and taking the transaction through to the stage where the facility documentation is signed or, in a 'selling down' exercise, the later date when the syndicate is brought in to the contractual arrangements. There will usually be one principal arranger, which may be called the lead manager, but other entities may be accorded a similar sounding status, such as co-arranger, co-lead manager, underwriter, manager, or book runner, which may reflect their assistance in finding syndicate members or the relative proportions of the facility that they have taken or were prepared to take onto their own books (ie to underwrite) if other syndicate members could not be found.[2]

---

[1] When there is an initial group of lenders which formally agree to provide the facility and a later syndication to a wider group, this two-stage process is sometimes referred to as the 'primary syndication' and 'secondary syndication'.

[2] Such titles have been said to suffer from 'fluidity and lack of definition', see *Golden Belt 1 Sukuk Co BSC(c) v BNP Paribas* [2017] EWHC 3182 (Comm) [40], [61], and [67].

(3) The agent bank, sometimes called the facility agent, is the coordinator of the facility once it has been formalised by the signing of the documentation. Its role begins upon execution of the facility agreement and will continue, unless it is replaced by another agent, until the conclusion of the transaction. Its role is crucial to the management and effective coordination of the arrangements between the lenders and as between them and the borrower. The facility agent may be assisted in a complicated facility by other entities which perform specific roles. If security is to be taken, there may be a separate security agent, failing which, the facility agent will also hold the security, usually as trustee on behalf of the lenders.[3]

(4) The syndicate of lenders will provide the lending to the borrower, with each of them having a specified commitment to provide a set proportion of the overall facility amount. They may comprise a small group of relationship banks who intend to hold their loan participations to maturity (in which case it may be referred to as a 'club' loan) or a more disparate group of banks, insurance companies, pension funds, and specialised loan funds who may intend to hold their loan participations to maturity or to trade them in the secondary market.

3.2 The Obligations and Rights of the Lenders and the Relationship between Them

3.2.1 The dichotomy

The concept of a syndicated transaction involves certain dichotomies. On the **3.05** one hand, the lenders agree to provide their participations in the facility in a coordinated fashion under the umbrella of a single facility agreement, they agree to majority voting on many (although not all) of the matters that might

---

[3] If the security agent is based in a jurisdiction that does not recognise trusts, a parallel debt structure can be used instead of a security trust. Under a parallel debt clause the borrower acknowledges a separate and additional debt owed by it to the security agent. This debt exists simultaneously (in parallel) with the debt owed by the borrower to the lenders, and is equal to the amount owed by the borrower to the lenders at any time during the term of the loan. The borrower grants security in favour of the security agent to secure this parallel debt. Consequently the holder of security and the beneficiary of the parallel debt obligation continue to be the same entity even if the identity of particular lenders changes. Therefore, if there is an assignment or transfer of a participation by a lender, it is not necessary to release and re-establish security. If the security agent receives any monies in respect of the parallel debt, it is required to share them with the lenders under the sharing provisions of the loan or intercreditor agreement. One disadvantage of the parallel debt structure as compared to a traditional security trust is that the lenders take a credit risk on the security agent, whereas in the case of a security trust, the insolvency of the security trustee will not prejudice the lenders' security. An argument that the parallel debt structure was in effect a fiction and that its true character was different to what had been provided for in the documentation was rejected in *Law Debenture v Elektrim Finance NV* [2006] EWHC 1305 (Ch) [48]–[51].

arise for their decision, and they agree that they should be treated on a *pari passu* basis with respect to repayment. If security is taken, it is usually taken in a composite manner on behalf of all the lenders. Each of those matters tends to emphasise the collective nature of a syndicated transaction.[4] On the other hand, the facility agreement usually provides that each lender's respective obligations are limited to its specified participation, so that no lender accepts responsibility for the liabilities of any other members of the syndicate to provide their share of the facility. Thus, the facility agreement makes it clear that if one lender defaults in making its participation available, the other lenders should not be obliged to make up the shortfall;[5] each of them is owed separately a debt for the money it has advanced to the borrower and the lenders do not wish to share the profits that they earn from the transaction. The facility agreement also provides that their rights, as against the borrower, should be separate and not joint. Accordingly, if payments are not made by the borrower, each lender can sue to recover its own debt.[6] However, a single lender cannot unilaterally accelerate its loan and demand early repayment due to an event of default. Such acceleration will usually require a decision to be made by the requisite majority of lenders.

3.06 What follows will begin by addressing the provisions in a facility agreement that tend to emphasise the collective nature of a syndicated transaction, namely the provisions that provide for the *pari passu* distribution of receipts as between the lenders and the provisions relating to the making of decisions. It will then be necessary to examine the possible legal consequences that might arise from the nature of a syndicated transaction and the relevant provisions in a facility agreement that address them.

3.2.2 *Pari passu* distribution and the sharing clause

3.07 It is a standard principle of syndicated facilities that payments which are to be made by the borrower (or another person, such as a guarantor) and the recoveries from enforcement action should be paid to and received by the agent, which will then distribute them on a pro rata basis amongst the lenders (except in the unusual case where only one lender is entitled to receive the payment). This is reflected in the payment clauses in the facility agreement.

---

[4] Each of these matters is something that could be regulated in a separate intercreditor agreement. Conceptually, a syndicated loan can be viewed as a number of bilateral loans advanced on identical terms which are bound together by an embedded intercreditor agreement.

[5] This should be contrasted with the usual position under a subscription agreement in a bond issue, under which the managers who agree to subscribe for the issue contractually undertake a joint and several liability to subscribe for the whole of the issue.

[6] But contrast *Charmway Hong Kong Investment Ltd v Fortunesea (Cayman) Ltd* [2015] HKCFI 1308 and see the discussion at para 3.34 below.

A sharing clause deals with the situation where that procedure is bypassed, so that **3.08** a particular lender receives or recovers payment directly when the other lenders have not been paid or, alternatively, where it receives or recovers more than its fair share with respect to a payment that is due by the borrower. The clause requires such a lender to pay to the agent the amount in excess of its pro rata share, so that the agent can then distribute the excess amongst the other lenders. The effect of the clause is to achieve the *pari passu* position as to the distribution of payments amongst the syndicate of lenders as originally laid down by the contract, which would have been bypassed by the direct payment or recovery received by the individual lender.[7] The clause usually applies both to payments made to the relevant individual lender and to other means of recovery by that lender, such as by the exercise of set-off rights or the enforcement of security. It is usually expressed, however, not to apply to recoveries obtained through litigation or arbitration proceedings where the recipient lender has invited the other lenders to join those proceedings and they have declined to do so.

If the sharing clause simply provided for the receiving lender to pay over the excess **3.09** amount to the agent then that lender might be at a disadvantage, as the borrower could claim that it had paid, or should be treated as having paid, the full amount (including the excess) to that lender, so that the state of the account as between them had been reduced by the full amount rather than by the lesser amount that the lender has been able to retain in consequence of the operation of the sharing clause. To overcome such an argument, the clause will provide for one or more mechanisms that are intended to restore to the lender the right to claim from the borrower an amount equivalent to the excess that it has paid over to the agent. One such mechanism is to provide that the receiving lender will be subrogated to the rights of the other lenders against the borrower to the extent that they have participated in a distribution by the agent of the excess.[8] Another mechanism is for the clause to state that the receiving lender is to be treated as if it had never

---

[7] But note that the provisions only catch payments due under the loan agreement, not every payment made to the lenders. In *Azevedo and anor v Importacao Exportacao E Industria De Oleos Ltda and ors* [2013] EWCA Civ 364, [2015] QB 1 it was held that a payment promised to the noteholders who voted in favour of an amendment to the notes (a 'consent payment') fell outside of the contractual provisions that required *pari passu* treatment of the noteholders.

[8] This would be a form of contractual subrogation, as distinguished from subrogation to prevent unjust enrichment which can operate outside a contractual agreement: see *Banque Financière de la Cité v Parc (Battersea) Ltd* [1999] 1 AC 221 (Lord Hoffmann). Contractual subrogation is based on agreement: *Pickenham Romford Ltd v Deville* [2013] EWHC 2330 (Ch). Contractual subrogation is similar to an assignment, whereas subrogation to prevent unjust enrichment does not involve an assignment of rights but comprises the creation of new rights: *Day v Tiuta International Ltd* [2014] EWCA Civ 1246 [43]. If there is the possibility that a lender may wish to be subrogated to any security held by or for the benefit of the other lenders, it would be sensible to provide for that in the relevant clause, as it has been held that the mere fact that money is provided to discharge a secured debt does not, of itself, entitle the provider to be subrogated to the security: see *Paul v Speirway Ltd* [1976] Ch 220, 230 (Oliver J) and *Orakpo v Manson Investments Ltd* [1978] AC 95, 105 (Lord Diplock).

received the amount of the excess, so that the outstanding account as between it and the borrower will only be reduced by the amount the lender has been able to retain. The agreement will go on to provide that, in consequence, the accounts as between the borrower and the other lenders will be treated as reduced by the amount of the excess that they have received via the agent. A third mechanism is for the other lenders, to the extent that they have received a payment out of the excess, to assign their rights against the borrower to the original receiving lender.[9]

3.10 The sharing clause will also contain other safeguards for the lender that originally received or recovered the payment. If the mechanisms referred to above are not effective as a matter of law or if the lender is under an obligation to return the excess to the borrower then the obligation of the lender under the clause to pay over the excess to the agent will not apply or the sharing will be unwound, as the case may be.

3.2.3 Voting and decision-making by lenders

3.11 The facility agreement is likely to state that in some circumstances the consent of all of the lenders is required before a decision can be made, such as in making amendments to the basic economic elements of the facility, including as to the rate of interest, the amount or date of any payment that should be made by the borrower, any change in the financial obligations of the lenders, as well as in making any change in the method of ascertaining the requisite majority of the lenders that can make decisions where the agreement provides for decisions being made by the majority.[10] Otherwise, the facility agreement is likely to provide that decisions may be taken by a majority vote of the lenders.[11] The method of ascertaining what constitutes a majority of the lenders will be specified in the facility agreement. It is normally determined as amounting to a two-thirds majority of the lenders, judged by the amount (by value) of their participations in the facility. Some of the more important decisions that may be taken by a majority include waivers of conditions precedent, waivers or amendments of undertakings, and events of default and decisions to accelerate the loan following an event of default.

---

[9] This last mechanism was used in the original forms of syndicated facility agreements but is rarely used nowadays. It was thought that it might give rise to a liability to pay stamp duty or other documentary taxes, potentially on the whole amount of the facility, and there might also be conflict of laws difficulties in achieving recognition of the assignment, for instance, in the borrower's jurisdiction.

[10] Whether something requires unanimous or majority lender consent can pose difficult questions of construction. Eg *Bank of New York Mellon (London Branch) v Truvo NV* [2013] EWHC 136 (Comm) concerned a dispute whether a change to a mandatory prepayment waterfall required only majority lender consent or unanimous consent as an amendment to the order of priority or subordination.

[11] As explained later in relation to the role of the facility agent, in the absence of a decision by the majority, the agent will be able to exercise its own discretion in determining matters that relate to the facility, except for those matters that are reserved for a unanimous decision of all of the lenders.

In leveraged acquisition facilities, a 'super majority' concept is often included to **3.12** facilitate future restructurings of the facilities. Amendments such as an extension of time for payment, a reduction in the amount payable, the extension of existing commitments, or the introduction of new tranches (*pari passu* or junior) may be carried out with the consent of the lenders whose rights are to be amended and an overall 75–85 per cent majority. This makes it difficult for a particular lender to block such an amendment in order to have its participation prepaid early or at a premium.

Even in the absence of super majority provisions, a sufficient majority of lenders **3.13** may be able to force through amendments which would otherwise require unanimous consent by means of a scheme of arrangement. A scheme of arrangement is a statutory procedure under the Companies Act 2006[12] whereby a company may, subject to court approval, make a compromise or arrangement backed by a majority in number and at least 75 per cent in value of its creditors, which is then binding on all creditors of that class. A scheme can be used in respect of English companies and non-English borrowers provided there is a sufficient connection with England, such as the choice of English law as the governing law of the loan agreement.[13]

A facility agreement sometimes gives the borrower a power to force a transfer by a **3.14** lender who does not consent to a waiver or amendment that requires unanimous consent and which is approved by a majority of the other lenders. This is colloquially called a 'yank-the-bank' provision. A facility agreement may also provide that the lenders are required to submit their votes within a specified time and, if they fail to do so, their participation is disregarded for the purposes of calculating who voted in favour and who voted against an amendment or waiver. This is called a 'snooze-you-lose' or 'use-or-lose' provision.

The voting provisions may provide that the votes of members of the borrower's **3.15** corporate group or other lenders which are connected with the group are to be disregarded.[14] In *Strategic Value Master Fund Ltd v Ideal Standard International Acquisition SARL*[15] the loan contained no such provisions and lenders connected

---

12 See pt 26 of the Companies Act 2006.
13 *Re Rodenstock* [2011] EWHC 1104 (Ch). This even extends to situations where the governing law and jurisdiction clauses are amended to give the English courts jurisdiction: *Re Apcoa Parking Holdings GmbH* [2014] EWHC 3849 (Ch).
14 Such disenfranchisement clauses were given effect in the context of a bond restructuring in *Assenagon Asset Management v Irish Bank Resolution Corp* [2012] EWHC 2090 (Ch) cf *Citicorp Trustee Co Ltd v Barclays Bank plc* [2013] EWHC 2608 (Ch). In *Citibank v Oceanwood Opportunities Master Fund and ors* [2018] EWHC 448 it was held that 'control' of the debtor which would trigger disenfranchisement provisions had to be control arising other than under the finance documentation. Consequently a majority creditor was not disenfranchised just because under the finance documentation it could replace the debtor's management and direct the enforcement process following a default.
15 [2011] EWHC 171 (Ch).

with the borrower were able to acquire a majority stake in the loan participations enabling them to waive events of default effectively and to withdraw an acceleration notice.

3.16 The fact that a lender votes in accordance with the instructions of a third party, for example, because it has entered into a contract that may require it (such as a funded or risk participation), does not mean that it is exercising its contractual discretion dishonestly, for improper purposes, capriciously, arbitrarily, wholly unreasonably, or on the basis of extraneous considerations.[16]

3.17 If lenders provide each other with information or explanations as to why a particular vote is proposed or whether consent ought to be given or refused, they may assume responsibility for the accuracy of the explanations given and hence come under a duty to take reasonable care as to their accuracy.[17] The agent and arranger protections in a typical syndicated loan agreement will usually be inapplicable in this context as they do not allocate the respective responsibilities of lenders in respect of such communications between them.[18]

3.18 If a loan agreement contains several different facilities and the lenders do not participate in the facilities pro rata (or if transfers of participations can be made such that the lenders cease to participate pro rata in each of the facilities) then it should be considered at the drafting stage whether consents, waivers, and amendments are to be voted on by all the lenders as a whole or whether the lenders under each facility are to be treated as a separate class for voting purposes. If the former option is chosen, conflicts may arise between the interests of lenders under one facility and the interests of those under another.[19]

3.2.3.1 Constraints on the majority's power to bind the minority

3.19 Some constraints on the ability of a majority to bind a dissenting minority through a vote of those concerned may be implied into the relevant agreement.[20] They are as follows.

3.20 There must be a power conferred by the relevant contractual documentation for a decision to be made by the relevant majority and the vote must concern a matter

---

[16] *Carey Group plc v AIB Group (UK) plc* [2011] EWHC 567 (Ch), [2012] Ch 304.

[17] *Torre Asset Funding v RBS* [2013] EWHC 2670 (Ch) [185].

[18] ibid.

[19] As occurred in *Redwood Master Fund Ltd v TD Bank Europe Ltd* [2002] EWHC 2703 (Ch) where a conflict of interest arose between the lenders under a drawn term facility and some lenders under an undrawn revolving facility as to whether an event of default should be waived.

[20] The propositions that are stated in what follows are largely derived from the judgment of Rimer J in *Redwood Master Fund Ltd v TD Bank Europe Ltd* [2002] EWHC 2703 (Ch), [2006] 1 BCLC 149 and from cases concerning bond issues, including *Azevedo and anor v Importacao Exportacao E Industria De Oleos Ltda and ors* [2013] EWCA Civ 364, [2015] QB 1 and *Assenagon Asset Management v Irish Bank Resolution Corp* [2012] EWHC 2090 (Ch), [2013] 1 All ER 495.

upon which a decision may be made.[21] If the matter is outside the subject matter on which a vote may be taken and a majority decision made, then the vote will be ineffective.[22] The power must be exercised within its proper scope and for its proper purpose. This is a question of construction of the power, that is, the rights conferred by the terms agreed by the parties. It is necessary for the vote to be passed by the requisite majority as laid down in the facility documentation.

As a general matter (but subject as already stated), the majority can bind the minority and those forming the majority may vote in their own interests.[23] This is particularly the case where, from the outset of the transaction, there is an obvious potential for a conflict in the interests of those who may be called upon to vote and where the identity of those who could be involved is likely to change from time to time.[24]   **3.21**

If there is a special or secret advantage that is to be given to or conferred upon a voting participant to secure its vote within the majority, that must be disclosed. If it is not disclosed, the vote will be invalid.[25] However, if the advantage is fully disclosed, the participant may vote in favour of the decision and the vote will be valid.[26] In *Azevedo and Another v Importacao Exportacao E Industria De Oleos Ltda and ors*,[27] the Court of Appeal held that an inducement openly and equally promised to those who vote in favour of a resolution was not a bribe and that it does not mean that the resolution is oppressive or an abuse of power.[28]   **3.22**

The court may intervene if there has been some other unfairness or oppression, in the sense of some deliberate intention on the part of the majority to damage   **3.23**

---

[21] *Hay v Swedish & Norwegian Ry Co* (1889) TLR 460; *Mercantile Investment & General Trust Co v International Co of Mexico* [1893] 1 Ch 484.

[22] Eg where the facility agreement provides that a matter may only be decided by a unanimous vote of all of the lenders.

[23] *British America Nickel Corp Ltd v MJ O'Brien Ltd* [1927] AC 369. See also *Law Debenture Trust Corp plc v Concord Trust* [2007] EWHC 1380 (Ch). Rimer J in *Redwood Master Fund Ltd v TD Bank Europe Ltd* [2002] EWHC 2703 (Ch) said that a borrower should be entitled to rely on this principle unless it was on notice that the vote of the majority was tainted by one of the matters that will shortly be mentioned, where the vote by the majority may be upset.

[24] See Rimer J in ibid, who followed the approach taken by the High Court of Australia in *Peters American Delicacy Co v Heath* (1938–39) 61 CLR 457 and the Privy Council in *Howard Smith Ltd v Ampol Petroleum Ltd* [1974] AC 821.

[25] *British America Nickel Corp Ltd v MJ O'Brien Ltd* [1927] AC 369.

[26] *North-West Transportation Co v Beatty* (1887) 12 App Cas 589; *Goodfellow v Nelson Line* [1912] 2 Ch 324.

[27] [2013] EWCA Civ 364, [2015] QB 1.

[28] The *Azevedo* case differed from the exit consent situation in the *Assenagon* case because an exit consent involves a sanction (a resolution that will make the minority's position worse as compared to the majority) and not a positive inducement (a payment that will make the majority financially better off). Secondly, in the *Azevedo* case the debtor offered the inducement; in the exit consent scenario the majority would take steps to worsen the minority's situation. In the *Azevedo* case the amendments benefited all noteholders as they would lead to a restructuring; in the *Assenagon* case the aim was simply to destroy the value of the notes of the holdout noteholders, not to enhance it.

or oppress the interests of the minority. Evidence of this may be difficult to obtain, but the court may be prepared to conclude that there was a lack of good faith along those lines if the outcome of the vote is so manifestly disadvantageous, discriminatory, or oppressive towards the minority that the only reasonable conclusion which the court could draw is that the majority must have been motivated by dishonest considerations that were inconsistent with a proper exercise of its powers.[29] However, in a case where negotiations between the borrower and a committee of the lenders had been openly conducted and involved proposals put forward by the borrower, it was held that allegations of unfairness and oppression could not be substantiated.[30]

3.24   On the other hand, a different conclusion was reached in respect of a vote taken under a financial instrument in *Assenagon Asset Management v Irish Bank Resolution Corp*.[31] This case involved a technique used by bond issuers in restructurings of their indebtedness to persuade creditors to exchange existing defaulted bonds for new ones with a lower nominal value. Creditors are invited to offer bonds for exchange but on terms that by doing so they will commit to vote for a resolution (an 'exit consent') amending the existing bonds so as to seriously damage or destroy the value of the rights arising from those bonds. In this case, the amendment to the existing bonds would allow the debtor to redeem them for nominal consideration. Creditors are thereby strongly incentivised by means of a sanction not to end up as part of a dissenting minority. The claimant argued that the resolution was an abuse of power of the majority and that it was oppressive and unfairly prejudicial to the minority. Briggs J concluded on the particular facts, by way of obiter dicta as the case was decided on other grounds, that such an exit consent was a coercive threat which the debtor invited the majority to levy against the minority. In his Lordship's opinion, the only function it had was to intimidate the potential minority into agreeing to the debtor's proposal. This was at variance with the purposes for which majorities were given contractual power to bind minorities and was oppressive of the minority. What level of coercion will be considered to be oppressive in litigation relating to future exit consents remains to be seen. Presumably this will depend on matters such as the extent of the threatened abrogation of the rights of the minority creditors weighed against the commercial objectives that are being sought to be achieved, namely, the rescue of the troubled debtor for the benefit of all of its creditors.

3.25   Possibly, and also by analogy with case law concerning bonds, if the facility agreement provides that a separate vote is required of a special class or section of the lenders, it could be argued that the vote must be exercised for the benefit of the class as a whole and not merely so as to benefit individual members of that

---

[29] See *Redwood Master Fund Ltd v TD Bank Europe Ltd* [2002] EWHC 2703 (Ch) (Rimer J).
[30] *Redwood Master Fund Ltd v TD Bank Europe Ltd* [2002] EWHC 2703 (Ch).
[31] [2012] EWHC 2090 (Ch), [2013] 1 All ER 495.

class.[32] It is not entirely clear, in such a situation, how the benefit of the class as a whole should be identified. It would appear that if the minority's interests (ie a minority within the class) are being interfered with then that would not be to the benefit of the class as a whole.[33] It has also been suggested that the test might be assessed by reference to what would be in the interests of an individual hypothetical member of the class,[34] but it may be rather difficult to identify such a mythical person amongst a divergent body of lenders. Ultimately, the conclusion which best reflects commercial reality may be that the lenders are entitled to have primary regard to their own interests, with the line being drawn at actions which are manifestly oppressive of the minority.

3.2.4 Partnership

In light of the collective provisions as just described, it is relevant to discuss if **3.26** the lenders, by joining in a syndicated facility, may be considered as constituting a partnership. The primary consequences, should they be a partnership, are that they would have joint and several liability for the defaults of any of their members and they would owe fiduciary duties to one another. Section 1(1) of the Partnership Act 1890 defines a partnership as the 'relation which subsists between persons carrying on a business in common with a view to profit'. The elements of the definition are, first, that the persons should be carrying on a business in common, and, secondly, that they should be doing so with a view to profit. Those elements will be examined in turn, following which mention will be made of the provisions that are commonly to be found in the syndicated facility documentation aimed at displacing any risk that the lenders may be responsible for each other's obligations.

By joining in the facility, the lenders undoubtedly are acting in common. In add- **3.27** ition, they agree to act on many matters through their collective agent and to be bound by a majority vote on many of the matters on which a decision is required. The question then turns to whether by doing so they are carrying on a business in common. Section 45 of the Partnership Act 1890 defines 'business' to include 'every trade, occupation or profession' which, in effect, means that any commercial activity or venture could be considered as a business. At first sight, the concept of carrying on a business in common might be thought to imply the necessity of there being some element of continuity in carrying on the business. A syndicated loan is an isolated transaction entered into for that transaction alone, rather than with a view to establishing an ongoing business intended to grant loans and facilities under several different transactions. The lenders which join the syndicate do so simply for that transaction. Hence it might be argued

---

[32] *British America Nickel Corp Ltd v MJ O'Brien Ltd* [1927] AC 369.
[33] ibid.
[34] See *Greenhalgh v Arderne Cinemas Ltd* [1951] Ch 286, 291 (Sir Raymond Evershed MR).

that the lenders are not carrying on a business so as to constitute a partnership. The need for some element of continuity was mentioned by Brett LJ in *Smith v Anderson*[35] in relation to the prohibition that then existed under the Companies Act 1862, which prevented more than twenty persons from carrying on a business for gain. Support for this view might also be drawn from cases relating to the Moneylenders Act 1900 (now repealed), in which it was said that the concept of 'carrying on business as a moneylender' required a 'repetition of acts, the sum of which constitutes the "business"'.[36] Similarly, Slade J said in *Skelton Finance Co Ltd v Lawrence*[37] that two isolated loan transactions by a lender 'did not import the necessary element of system, repetition and continuity necessary to constitute a moneylending business'. That was doubted, however, by the Court of Appeal in *Conroy v Kenny*[38] in which Kennedy LJ said[39] that a lender who sets himself up as a licensed moneylender may still be regarded as having a moneylending business even if he only makes one loan. Furthermore, Lord Keith said in *Davies v Sumner*[40] that a 'one-off adventure in the nature of trade, carried through with a view to profit' could constitute a course of trade or business within the Trade Descriptions Act 1968. Perhaps the distinction between these various approaches lies in gauging whether the relevant person or persons has set himself or have set themselves up with the intention of carrying on a business, even if he or they only enter into one transaction, as opposed to intending from the outset only to enter into an isolated transaction. This is consistent with the approach that was taken by Moore-Bick LJ in *GE Capital Bank Ltd v Rushton*[41] when considering the provisions of Part III of the Hire Purchase Act 1964.

3.28 In relation to the Partnership Act, however, it has been held that a single trading venture entered into by two or more persons may constitute a partnership.[42] This is reinforced by section 32(b) of the Act which provides that a partnership which is entered into for a single adventure or undertaking will be dissolved upon the termination of that adventure or undertaking, so quite clearly the Act itself contemplates the possibility that a partnership may be constituted by a single venture. In addition, a syndicated transaction is intended to continue for the period of the facility, so it will be carried on over a period of time, rather than being merely an entirely isolated incident. There must, therefore, be a risk that the lenders may

---

[35] (1880) 15 ChD 247.
[36] *Kirkwood v Gadd* [1910] AC 422, 431 (Lord Atkinson).
[37] (1976) 120 SJ 147.
[38] [1999] 1 WLR 1340. In *Masters v Barclays Bank plc* [2013] EWHC 2166 (Ch) it was recognised that a single transaction could constitute the carrying on of business but, on the facts, signing one guarantee document and incurring a continuing liability did not amount to carrying on a business.
[39] At 1346–47.
[40] [1984] 1 WLR 1301, 1305.
[41] [2005] EWCA Civ 1556, [2006] 3 All ER 865 [39]–[40].
[42] *Mann v D'Arcy* [1968] 1 WLR 893.

be held to be carrying on a business in common by virtue of them joining in the syndicate.

It is next relevant to consider if what the lenders are doing is with a view to profit **3.29** or, to put it more fully, with a view to sharing the profits.[43] By profit is meant the net amount received from the receipts of the business after deducting the expenses and outgoings incurred in the business.[44] This should be contrasted with the concept of merely agreeing to share the 'gross returns' of a venture, under which each party bears its own expenses and losses connected with its participation in the transaction and receives its own share of the receipts generated by the transaction. In this connection, section 2 of the Partnership Act 1890 provides that, in determining if a partnership exists, regard shall be had to various rules, including the following:

> (2) The sharing of gross returns does not of itself create a partnership, whether the persons sharing such returns have or have not a joint or common right or interest in any property from which or from the use of which the returns are derived.

A syndicated loan looks very much like a transaction under which the lenders **3.30** intend that they will each separately bear their own expenses and losses of the transaction and that they will only share the gross returns, that is, the receipts from the borrower that are passed on by the facility agent to the lenders.[45] Each lender has to find the amount of its own contribution to the facility and, if the borrower defaults in making repayment of the amount advanced by that lender, it will suffer on its own the loss attendant upon that default. Further, the profit that a lender makes on the amount it has lent, that is, the yield that it receives by way of interest, fees, and commission, will depend upon its own cost base and, in particular, the cost to it of providing the money it has lent. Thus the profit of each lender depends on its own individual circumstances, as contrasted with the position in a partnership where the partners share the profits remaining after taking into account any losses and net of the expenses incurred in earning the profits.

It might also be added that a scheme which permits any lender to transfer its **3.31** rights and obligations to a new entity, as is commonly the case in consequence of the transfer provisions in syndicated facility documentation, is rather inconsistent with the concept of a partnership. In partnership terms, if such provisions operated then they would have the effect of causing a dissolution of the existing

---

[43] See *Mollwo, March & Co v Court of Wards* (1872) LR 2 PC 419 (Lord Lindley).

[44] Lord Herschell in *Gresham Life Assurance Soc v Styles* [1892] AC 309, 322–23, expressed it as follows: 'When we speak of the profits or gains of a trader we mean that which he has made by his trading. Whether there be such a thing as profit or gain can only be ascertained by setting against the receipts the expenditure or obligations to which they have given rise.' The approach taken by Lord Herschell was referred to with approval by Lord Templeman in *Beauchamp v FW Woolworth plc* [1990] 1 AC 478, 489.

[45] It is submitted that the sharing clause (which is described above) does not destroy this concept. The lenders will still individually suffer the loss, if any, on their ultimate recoveries.

partnership and the commencement of a new partnership. It is inconceivable that this could be the case, especially as such provisions often operate without the necessity of any approval being given by the other lenders. The lack of any requirement for such approval would stretch to breaking point the concepts of good faith and fair dealing that underlie the concept of partnership and the duties of good faith that are owed as between prospective partners.[46]

3.32 It is submitted that the position as just described is not weakened by the fact that the lenders may find themselves having to bear some of the expenses of the facility agent connected with the operation and management of the facility. The facility documentation will usually provide that the borrower should bear the expenses incurred by the facility agent but that if the borrower fails to do so, the lenders will indemnify the facility agent for its outstanding expenses. It has been held that the parties to a venture may agree that they will share the gross receipts and the running expenses of the venture without thereby constituting themselves as a partnership.[47]

3.33 To resolve any residual doubt, the facility documentation will usually provide that the obligations of the lenders are several and that no lender will be responsible for the failure of any other lender to perform its obligations. It is further provided that the amount advanced by each lender shall be regarded as a separate and independent debt due to that lender by the borrower and that the rights attached to that debt are separately vested in the lender. As a party to the agreement, the borrower will be bound by such provisions.[48]

3.34 In *Charmway Hong Kong Investment Ltd v Fortunesea (Cayman) Ltd*,[49] a Hong Kong court held that an individual lender under a syndicated loan based on the

---

[46] As to such duties, see *Conlon v Simms* [2006] EWHC 401 (Ch), [2006] 2 All ER 1024 (Lawrence Collins J), approved on appeal at [2006] EWCA Civ 1749, [2007] 3 All ER 802.

[47] *French v Styring* (1857) 2 CBNS 357, which involved the two joint owners of a racehorse, who agreed to share their winnings and the expenses of keeping, feeding, and training the horse. See also *Ketteringham v Hardy* [2011] EWHC 162 (Ch).

[48] It is an interesting question whether the borrower could pray in aid the provisions of s 3 of the Unfair Contract Terms Act 1977 (described further below, at section 3.5.4.2), to challenge the effect of such provisions, by seeking to argue that they have the effect of excusing the lenders from the obligations that they would otherwise have as partners. Consider whether it could be argued that the lenders were dealing on their standard terms of business. The use of recommended forms for syndicated lending has become widespread in the London financial market. Even though there will usually be some variation of the forms in consequence of the negotiations for each transaction, that does not entirely destroy the possibility that the documentation might still be considered as constituting standard terms of business: see *St Albans City & District Council v International Computers Ltd* [1996] 4 All ER 491. However, an argument that a Loan Market Association (LMA) recommended form constituted a bank's standard form failed on the facts in *African Export-Import Bank v Shebah Exploration & Production Company and ors* [2017] EWCA Civ 845. In this context, a further question would arise as to whose terms are represented by the contract, given that the documentation will have been propounded in the first instance by the arranger rather than by the lenders and will have been sent to the lenders in draft form at the request of the borrower. See further later as to the role of the arranger and as to s 3.

[49] [2015] HKCFI 1308.

Loan Market Association (LMA) recommended form, and thus containing provisions such as those mentioned in the previous paragraph, did not have the right to take independent enforcement action to recover a debt under the loan agreement but that collective enforcement action was required. This conclusion seems incorrect and contrary to the generally held understanding of the position of lenders under syndicated loans. The orthodox view is that if the debt to an individual lender is due and payable, the lender can sue to recover its debt individually. However, it must be kept in mind that for an individual lender's right to obtain early repayment of its principal to become enforceable (and hence for the corresponding debt to become due and payable) collective action, in the form of acceleration, will usually be a necessary precondition. To remove any doubts, the *Charmway* decision led to a revision of the relevant clause in LMA recommended form agreements to make it even clearer that individual lenders may separately enforce the debts and other obligations owed to them.

3.2.5 Collective investment schemes

It is arguable that syndicated lending might come within the definition of a 'collective investment scheme' within section 235(1) to (4) of the Financial Services and Markets Act 2000 (FSMA) unless it falls into one of the exemptions to the definition that is provided, through delegated legislation, by virtue of section 235(5) of FSMA. If the definition does catch syndicated lending then the consequence would be that those involved in 'establishing' or 'operating' the transaction would have to be authorised under FSMA to do so.[50] That would be apt to catch the activities of the arranger and others in arranging the transaction and the activities of the facility agent during the lifetime of the transaction.[51] Furthermore, lenders which intended to transfer their participations would have to consider if they might be dealing in a security,[52] which would also need to be authorised under FSMA.[53] **3.35**

Section 235 of FSMA provides as follows: **3.36**

> (1) 'collective investment scheme' means any arrangements with respect to property of any description, including money, the purpose or effect of which is to enable persons taking part in the arrangements (whether by becoming owners

---

[50] See arts 4 and 51ZE of the Financial Services and Markets Act 2000 (Regulated Activities) Order 2001, SI 2001/544, as amended (the Regulated Activities Order).

[51] There is also a restriction on promoting a collective investment scheme by virtue of s 19 of FSMA, which itself is subject to exemptions contained in the Financial Services and Markets Act 2000 (Promotion of Collective Investment Schemes) (Exemptions) Order 2001, SI 2001/1060, as amended.

[52] A unit (which is defined by s 237(2) of FSMA) in a collective investment scheme is a 'security' within art 81 of the Regulated Activities Order and so would fall within art 14 of the Regulated Activities Order (which concerns dealing in such a security), subject to any applicable exemptions, such as under art 15 of the Regulated Activities Order.

[53] See art 14 of the Regulated Activities Order.

of the property or any part of it or otherwise) to participate in or receive profits or income arising from the acquisition, holding, management or disposal of the property or sums paid out of such profits or income.

(2) The arrangements must be such that the persons who are to participate ('participants') do not have day-to-day control over the management of the property, whether or not they have the right to be consulted or to give directions.

(3) The arrangements must also have either or both of the following characteristics—

    (a) the contributions of the participants and the profits or income out of which payments are to be made to them are pooled;

    (b) the property is managed as a whole by or on behalf of the operator of the scheme.

(4) If arrangements provide for such pooling as is mentioned in subsection 3(a) in relation to separate parts of the property, the arrangements are not to be regarded as constituting a single collective investment scheme unless the participants are entitled to exchange rights in one part for rights in another.

(5) The Treasury may by order provide that arrangements do not amount to a collective investment scheme—

    (a) in specified circumstances; or

    (b) if the arrangements fall within a specified category of arrangement.

3.37 Arden LJ (with whom Ward LJ and Collins J agreed) provided some guidance as to the definition of 'collective investment scheme' in *Financial Services Authority v Fradley & Woodward*.[54] Her Ladyship said that the wording used in section 235, including 'arrangement' and 'property of any description', should be given a wide interpretation and that the application of the section depended upon the specific facts of each case. She said that there was no formality required for there to be an 'arrangement', although she did not decide if it had to be a legally binding arrangement. There was no requirement for a participant's contributions to be invested in some investment. It was also immaterial that the scheme involved bets which were null and void by virtue of section 18 of the Gaming Act 1845. She also said that 'profits' could include winnings on such bets. However, she did qualify her comments by saying that, with its criminal context if there should be a breach of the requirements of the FSMA, the section should not be interpreted to include matters that were not fairly within it. Arden LJ went on to say that[55] there could be more than one operator of a scheme but if two or more services were offered together, it did not necessarily follow that they formed only one set of arrangements. There can still be a collective investment scheme even if only some of the participants have transferred day-to-day control to the operator of the scheme, whilst others may have not done so,[56] and there can be a pooling of the participants' moneys despite the fact that there might be a trust of such moneys in their favour, with each participant's entitlement being separately identified, thus

---

[54] [2005] EWCA Civ 1183. See, in particular, [32]–[33]. See also *Financial Conduct Authority v Capital Alternatives Ltd and ors* [2015] EWCA Civ 284.

[55] *Financial Services Authority v Fradley & Woodward* [2005] EWCA Civ 1183 [37].

[56] ibid [46].

giving each of them a proprietary right in the pooled fund.[57] It would follow from the last point that the case would be even stronger if such an entitlement did not exist. In *Financial Services Authority v Asset LI Inc (t/a Asset Land Investment Inc)*[58] the Supreme Court endorsed the above approach and adopted a broad interpretation of what constitutes 'property' and 'control' for the purposes of determining whether there was a collective investment scheme within the meaning of section 235(1).

It will be seen that section 235(1) provides a basic definition of a collective invest- **3.38** ment scheme, which is further refined by the requirements of section 235(2) to (4). Looked at from the perspective of the lenders which participate in a syndicated loan, the transaction appears to fall within the definition. When the lenders make an advance under the facility, they do so by paying their respective contributions to the facility agent which, having received the contributions into its account, then disburses the combined amount as one sum to the borrower. When the borrower makes a payment of interest or principal under the facility, it pays the relevant amount as one sum to the facility agent which, having received the amount in its account, then distributes the proceeds amongst the lenders. The lenders are thus participating in the amount lent under the pooled facility and they are receiving income from the facility, which is payable by the borrower on the amount that has been lent to it through the facility agent. The facility agent deals on behalf of the lenders with the borrower and has the management of the facility. Whilst the lenders may be consulted by the agent and have the right to give it directions, the facility agent remains in effective day-to-day control of the facility.

As previously mentioned, syndicated lending will not come within the definition **3.39** of a collective investment scheme if it falls within one or more of the exemptions that are specified by virtue of section 235(5) of FSMA. The exemptions are to be found in the Financial Services and Markets Act 2000 (Collective Investment Schemes) Order 2001.[59] Article 3 of the Order specifies that the kinds of arrangements, as set out in the Schedule to the Order, will not amount to a collective investment scheme. There are two relevant exemptions that arise by virtue of the Schedule.

The first exemption is contained in paragraph 6 of the Order, which provides as **3.40** follows:

> Arrangements do not amount to a collective investment scheme if—
>
> (a) they are arrangements under which the rights or interests of participants are rights to or interests in money held in a common account; and

---

[57] ibid [47].
[58] [2016] UKSC 17.
[59] SI 2001/1062, as amended.

(b) that money is held in the account on the understanding that an amount representing the contribution of each participant is to be applied—
  (i) in making payments to him;
  (ii) in satisfaction of sums owed by him; or
  (iii) in the acquisition of property for him or the provision of services to him.

It is submitted that paragraph 6 is apt to describe the position with respect to the money (ie the credit balance) from time to time held by the facility agent in its account, which is to be applied either in making payments to the borrower or in making payments to the lenders.

3.41 The second exemption is contained in paragraph 9 of the Order, which provides as follows—

(1) Subject to sub-paragraph (2), arrangements do not amount to a collective investment scheme if each of the participants—
  (a) carries on a business other than the business of engaging in any regulated activity of the kind specified by any of articles 14, 21, 25, 37, 40, 45, 51 to 53 or, so far as relevant to any of those articles, article 64 of the Regulated Activities Order;[60]
  (b) enters into the arrangements for commercial purposes related to that business.
(2) Sub-paragraph (1) does not apply where the person will carry on the business in question by virtue of being a participant in the arrangements.

Where the relevant business of each of the lenders is that of taking money on deposit (an activity that is regulated by Article 5 of the Regulated Activities Order), or borrowing money in the inter-bank market or raising it from other sources and lending that money to borrowers (the activity of lending, per se, is not a regulated activity within the FSMA), each of the lenders enters into the syndicated facility for the purpose of that business, that is, as a method of lending money that it has taken through deposits or by borrowing from others or raising it from other sources. Except for lenders whose only activity or, perhaps, principal activity is entering into syndicated lending transactions, the qualification in sub-paragraph (2) should not be relevant.

3.3 Arrangement of the Facility by the Arranger

3.42 The arranger is the financial institution that is commissioned by the borrower to arrange the transaction, that is, put the transaction together. This will include finding the syndicate (and the underwriters, if required) and taking the negotiations for the transaction through to the stage where the facility documentation is signed or, in a 'selling down' exercise, the later date when the wider syndicate

---

[60] Ie the Regulated Activities Order as defined earlier.

is brought into the contractual arrangements. As noted previously, there may be more than one entity performing such functions; but, for the purposes of this chapter, it will be assumed that there is only one arranger; however the issues that are discussed will be just as relevant if there is more than one entity involved in fulfilling that role.

3.3.1 The mandate

After negotiations between the arranger and the borrower, the arranger is awarded **3.43** a mandate by the borrower to assemble and bring the transaction to fruition. The documentation that forms the mandate or which accompanies it will describe the proposed transaction (and its principal economic and other terms) in outline, probably in the form of a term sheet. It will specify, possibly in a separate letter, the fees or commission that will be paid to the arranger and the others involved in the arrangement, underwriting, and syndication exercises. The arranger will undertake to use its reasonable, or its best, endeavours[61] to achieve the transaction.[62] Nonetheless, there is likely to be a provision which will permit the arranger to withdraw[63] or to amend the terms,[64] particularly those relating to the financial return that the lenders will receive and the more significant other terms, in the event of the occurrence (after the date of the mandate) of an adverse change in general economic and other conditions affecting the financial markets and the availability of finance for the transaction or if an adverse change should occur in the circumstances of the borrower and its affiliate group of companies.[65] The underwriters (if any) will also wish to see that the arranger has such rights and they may be keen to reach an understanding with the arranger that it will take their interests into account in deciding if it will exercise the rights.

3.3.1.1 Market flex provisions

It is worth considering in a little more detail the provision in the mandate which **3.44** permits the arranger to amend the basic terms of the transaction (as originally set out in the mandate and the term sheet) in the event that there is an adverse change in general economic conditions affecting the financial markets and the availability of finance for the transaction. This is usually referred to as a 'market flex' provision. The intention behind such a provision is that the arranger should be able to 'sweeten' the terms, so as to make them more attractive to the lending

---

[61] See the discussion in section 1.2.10.

[62] See the discussion in section 1.2.3 as to whether the arrangements as agreed between the arranger and the borrower would be considered sufficient to constitute a binding contractual agreement between them.

[63] Usually referred to as a 'material adverse change' provision.

[64] Usually referred to as a 'market flex' provision.

[65] As to a provision that relates to material adverse change which affects the circumstances of the borrower, see the further discussion of such provisions in section 2.18.3.

community, if the arranger considers that it would not be possible to conclude the transaction on the original terms because of the occurrence of such an adverse change. The most likely amendment would be to the financial terms of the transaction, such as in relation to the interest rate, fees, the overall facility amount, or the period of the facility. The arranger may also consider that other amendments may be required, such as in relation to guarantees and security cover or to financial and other covenants.

3.45 The provision is usually worded (at least in the form as initially presented by the arranger in its first draft of the mandate) so as to invest the arranger with a considerable amount of discretion in determining if the relevant conditions have arisen and as to the nature and extent of the amendments that will be required. It also normally provides that the discretion may be exercised at any time up to the date when the lenders (or at least the initial syndicate) have entered into the formal legal documentation representing the facility agreement and so have become legally obliged to provide the facility. Quite obviously, a borrower should be concerned as to the apparent width of the discretion that the arranger wishes to reserve to itself, and the borrower may wish to limit the discretion.[66] The borrower may, for instance, wish to stipulate that it may terminate the mandate if it is unhappy with the way in which the discretion has been exercised. It may also wish to have the right to be consulted before the discretion is exercised. Neither of those stipulations will be of much value if the borrower is in the position where it has no real option but to accept what the arranger proposes. The borrower may wish, therefore, to insert some more precise definition of the circumstances in which the discretion may arise, as well as placing restrictions upon the extent to which the arranger may amend the terms. On the other hand, the arranger will resist limits being placed upon its discretion, arguing that it must be a matter for the exercise of its own judgement in deciding if the discretion should be exercised and what amendments should be made so that the transaction will proceed. As with many aspects of commercial life, the parties will have to resolve the debate by negotiation.

3.3.2 The role of the arranger

3.46 The role that the arranger undertakes in consequence of having been awarded the mandate is usually threefold, although it does depend upon the cooperation of the borrower.

---

[66] *ACP Capital Ltd and ACP Mezzanine Ltd v IFR Capital plc and ING Bank NV* [2008] EWHC 1627 (Comm) involved a dispute as to the exercise of a market flex clause allowing the margin under a loan facility to be increased by up to 2.5 per cent. The lenders sought an injunction requiring the borrower to consent to a change in the pricing of the facility and damages. However, the court did not consider the merits of this claim as the case ultimately turned on the effect of an exclusive jurisdiction clause.

First, the arranger agrees to assist the borrower in compiling the information that **3.47** will be required to enable the lenders to assess the proposed transaction and decide if they wish to take part in it. Most of the information will have to be provided by the borrower and the arranger's task will mainly involve it in advising the borrower on what has to be provided and in assembling the information in a readable and acceptable form of presentation. That information will include financial and commercial material concerning the borrower and its affiliated entities, such as copies of accounts (both audited and, if available, more up-to-date unaudited accounts) together with earnings and cash flow statements, information about immediate and long-term liabilities, information about the business and assets of the relevant entities, the markets and conditions in which they operate, and projections of future prospects and activities. A copy of the term sheet summarising the transaction will also be included. The package of information will usually be assembled in an information memorandum, which the arranger will then distribute to the lenders. The nature of an information memorandum (or 'IM') was summarised by Christopher Clarke J in *Raiffeisen Zentralbank Österreich AG v Royal Bank of Scotland plc* as follows:[67]

> Within [the syndicated loans] market Information Memoranda are commonly used to provide to would-be participants in a given loan a summary of the loan transaction in which they are being invited to participate together with information on the principal credit issues arising in relation to the loan and details of the pricing structure, as the basis upon which potential lenders *start* their credit process (i.e. the process within the bank by which they decide whether to participate and if so to what extent) ... [E]xactly what is included in the IM is for the Arranger and the Borrower and their advisers to decide. The IM is a summary prepared by the Arranger of what it regards as relevant. Whilst a bank could reasonably expect that the principal credit issues were addressed, it could not reasonably assume that the IM contained everything that anyone might think relevant (even on credit issues); nor that everything relating to what was stated or referred to in the IM had been said, particularly in the case of a part of the overall transaction other than the debt or any security therefor.

Secondly, the arranger agrees to use its reasonable (or its best) endeavours to ap- **3.48** proach the lenders (including, if required, underwriters) that it believes would be interested in the transaction and to obtain their agreement in principle to participate in the syndicate. This will depend, to a large extent, on the attractiveness of the proposal that is put to them, not just in the profitability of the proposed transaction but also in terms of the risk that they will undertake as it is disclosed in the information memorandum and any other information that is sent to the lenders. The arranger may be assisted in this task by other lenders who have agreed to act as underwriters, that is, that they undertake to provide up to a certain proportion of the total facility in the event that other lenders cannot be found to complete a wide syndication of the risk.

---

[67] [2010] EWHC 1392 (Comm) [92]–[93].

3.49 Thirdly, the arranger will prepare the facility documentation, having appointed lawyers to assist it in that task. The documentation will reflect the outline represented by the term sheet. The procedure that is usually followed is that the lawyers appointed by the arranger will prepare a draft of the documentation for review by the arranger, following which it will be sent to the borrower and reviewed by the borrower and its lawyers, and then discussed between the arranger, the borrower, and their respective lawyers. Once they have generally agreed on the form of the documentation, the arranger will send copies to the lenders for their review. The arranger will receive any comments that the lenders may wish to make, discuss them with the borrower, and, perhaps after further negotiation, the documentation will be settled in an agreed final form for signature by all concerned.

3.50 In a straightforward syndication, where the full complement of the lenders is present from the date of signing the facility agreement, the arranger's role comes to an end once the facility documentation has been finalised and entered into by the parties. Where syndication to a wider syndicate is to take place through a 'selling down' process after the documentation has been signed, the arranger's role will be completed once the full syndicate has been brought into the transaction by accession to the documentation. Although the arranger will usually be named as a party to the principal facility agreement and will enter into it as such,[68] that is done so that it can gain various contractual protections, as will be discussed further later, rather than to cater for any further role of a contractual nature.

3.4 Areas of Risk to the Arranger

3.4.1 A claim by the borrower

3.51 One possible area of risk to the arranger would be where the borrower is unhappy with the performance of the tasks undertaken by the arranger in attempting to put the transaction together, in particular, where the arranger fails to bring about the syndicated facility. This will depend upon the terms of the mandate that was agreed between the borrower and the arranger and whether the arranger has complied with the obligations that it undertook in the mandate. If the borrower wishes to bring a claim against the arranger, it is likely that the claim would be framed against the arranger for breach of contract in failing to meet the obligations imposed upon the arranger by the contract. There may also be a claim framed in the tort of negligence. For present purposes, it will be assumed that the contract and any tortious claim would be governed by English law, so that law would apply to the contractual and any tortious claim, including as to whether it had been

---

[68] Additionally, it will probably be a party to the facility agreement as a lender within the syndicate, as it would be difficult for it to sell the transaction to other lenders if it did not intend to take a participation in the facility for itself. It may also fulfil the role of being the facility agent.

performed or breached its obligations and, in broad terms, the consequences of the breach. So long as the arranger has approached its task competently and exercised reasonable care and skill, it is unlikely that the borrower would be able to pursue a successful claim against the arranger.[69]

3.4.2 Claims by the syndicate members

Of greater concern to the arranger will be its possible exposure to claims that the **3.52** members of the lending syndicate may bring against it in the event that the facility had been entered into and the borrower had made drawings under it but then defaulted in meeting its obligations. If it turns out that the transaction was more risky than the lenders had thought when they agreed to join the syndicate and that they were not fully appraised of all of the factors that were relevant in deciding to join the transaction, they may wish to visit their discontent by claiming against the arranger for the loss they have suffered.[70] They may well, of course, have a claim against the borrower, but that may be worth little if the borrower is insolvent and unable to satisfy its obligations. In such a case, it is not inconceivable that the lenders may wish to consider the possibility of bringing a claim against the arranger, bearing in mind its involvement from the outset in arranging the transaction and the likelihood that it will have the financial resources to meet any claim that was successfully brought against it. It is unlikely that any such claim could be founded in contract as, at the time the arranger was performing its role, there would have been no contractual relationship between the arranger and the lenders that it approached to join the syndicate. Furthermore, in respect of the lenders who did join the syndicate and therefore subsequently entered into a

---

[69] In *Finch v Lloyds TSB Bank plc* [2016] EWHC 1236 (QB) claims of breach of contract (based on an implied term of reasonable care and skill under s 13 of the Supply of Goods and Services Act 1982) and negligence in relation to a bank's alleged failure to advise the borrower of a potentially onerous clause in a loan agreement were unsuccessful. See also *Deslauriers and anor v Guardian Asset Management Ltd (Trinidad and Tobago)* [2017] UKPC 34 which reaffirmed that the relationship between a bank and a commercial borrower is arm's length and not advisory. Similarly in *Carney v NM Rothschild and Sons Ltd* [2018] EWHC 958 (Comm) [58] it was held that here is no duty on a lending bank to give advice about the prudence of the transaction which the loan is intended to fund. Further there was no 'general' duty on a bank to give information on all aspects and risks of a product, referred to as a 'mezzanine' duty (less onerous than the duty to give advice but more onerous than the duty not to misstate); instead a bank's duty was simply not to misstate any information which it did give. See also *Property Alliance Group Ltd v Royal Bank of Scotland plc* [2018] EWCA Civ 355. Although the foregoing authorities considered the position of banks vis-à-vis borrowers, the conclusions should apply equally to arrangers unless, on the particular facts, an arranger assumed greater duties towards the borrower.

[70] In *NatWest Australia Bank Ltd v Tricontinental Corp Ltd* (Supreme Ct of Victoria, 26 July 1993). Unreported on this issue but noted and reported, on a different point, at (1993) ATPR (Digest) 46–109), a bank successfully obtained judgment against the arranger for damages amounting to the whole of the bank's participation in the syndicated facility, based upon a claim against the arranger for a negligent misstatement. Contrast the less generous assessment of damages for negligence made against the arranger in *Golden Belt 1 Sukuk Co BSC(c) v BNP Paribas* [2017] EWHC 3182 (Comm).

contractual relationship with the arranger, any such contract is unlikely to contain any relevant undertakings by the arranger that these lenders could point to. The claim will have to be based on some other ground. It may be conceived on the basis that the arranger owed a wide duty of care towards the lenders to ensure that the transaction was a good credit risk or, at least, a duty to point out to the lenders any deficiencies which they should have taken into account in deciding to proceed. In the alternative, it may be put more narrowly and concentrate on a failure to perform a specific task or on the inaccuracy in some particular information that was supplied to the lenders, for instance in the information memorandum, on which the lenders relied in deciding to enter into the transaction.

3.53   Before proceeding to examine the bases of the possible claims against the arranger under English law, it is relevant to keep in mind the conflict of laws issues that may arise concerning those claims. This is because of the jurisdictional and conflict of laws issues that might arise when considering a claim, namely, the possibility that a claimant might commence proceedings in a foreign jurisdiction, and, in addition to that matter or separately, the need to identify the applicable law that a court (whether an English or a foreign court) would apply as the law governing the issue or issues in dispute. This could well be relevant where there is a cross-border element in the situation; for instance, where one or more of the lenders was dealing from an office situated outside England and received the relevant information on which its claim is based in that office. The English rules relating to conflict of laws are discussed in chapter 4 of *McKnight, Paterson, & Zakrzewski on the Law of International Finance* and the reader is referred to that chapter for further consideration of the conflicts issues that may arise.[71]

3.54   Assuming that the issues will be determined in accordance with English law, it is now necessary to state more precisely the possible causes of action on which the claims of the lenders may be based. The claims might be framed as follows: first, as a claim in the tort of negligence, based either upon an alleged wide duty of care owed by the arranger to the lenders or, more narrowly, for a negligent misstatement that it made in relation to the information that it provided to them (as this is the most likely basis of a claim against the arranger and because it is also relevant in the context of various other relationships that may be found in financing transactions, it will be given a greater degree of examination than the other possible bases of claim); secondly, as a claim in the tort of deceit with respect to a misstatement that was made by the arranger; thirdly, as a claim for misrepresentation within sections 2(1) or 2(2) of the Misrepresentation Act 1967 (as amended), concerning an incorrect (albeit not deliberate) representation that was made by the arranger; fourthly, as a claim that the arranger was in the position of

---

[71] Sarah Paterson and Rafal Zakrzewski (eds), *McKnight, Paterson, & Zakrzewski on the Law of International Finance* (2nd edn, OUP 2017).

a fiduciary towards the lenders and that it breached its fiduciary duties towards them in failing to act in their best interests, which would be a fairly broad basis of claim. Each of those bases of claim will now be examined. After that, it will be relevant to see if the arranger can successfully avoid or limit any duty or responsibility that it may have by the use of appropriately worded disclaimers of responsibility, whether set out in a contractual form or by another means.

3.4.3 A claim in the tort of negligence

A claim by the lenders against an arranger in the tort of negligence will almost **3.55** certainly be one to recover for pure economic loss, rather than being dependent upon physical injury or damage. The decision of the House of Lords in *Hedley Byrne & Co Ltd v Heller & Partners Ltd*[72] established the possibility that a claimant could bring a claim in the tort of negligence for pure economic loss that was not dependent upon the claimant suffering physical injury or damage to its property. Such a claim may relate to the negligent giving of advice or information or the negligent performance of other services,[73] and it may cover negligent acts and omissions. The relationship giving rise to the duty may arise by express words or by implication from the circumstances, such as where the defendant had some special expertise or knowledge which he should have appreciated would be relied upon by the claimant.[74]

In outline, the matters which must be established if a claimant is to succeed in a **3.56** claim in negligence are set out in what follows. Whilst they are set out as distinct steps, in practice they will usually be inter-dependent, in that they cannot be taken in pure isolation and the same issue may transcend several of the steps. The matters are, first, that the defendant owed the claimant a duty of care; secondly, that the scope of that duty must be shown; thirdly, that the defendant failed to act reasonably within the scope of its duty of care to the claimant; fourthly, that the claimant reasonably relied upon the defendant in the exercise of that duty towards it; fifthly, that the loss which was suffered arose in consequence of the breach of the duty, that is, that it was caused by the breach; finally, to the extent that it has not already fallen to be considered in establishing the existence of a duty of care, that at the time the breach occurred, the loss was a reasonably foreseeable consequence of the breach of the defendant's duty of care. As this is still a developing area, those matters will now be examined in more detail by looking at their constituent elements in theory and, once that has been done, by then applying

---

[72] [1964] AC 465. The basic principles were recently reaffirmed by the Supreme Court in *Playboy Club London Ltd and others v Banca Nazionale del Lavoro SPA* [2018] UKSC 43.
[73] See *Henderson v Merrett Syndicates Ltd* [1995] 2 AC 145, 180 (Lord Goff of Chieveley).
[74] See *Hedley Byrne & Co Ltd v Heller & Partners Ltd* [1964] AC 465, 502–03 (Lord Morris of Borth-y-Gest) and *Henderson v Merrett Syndicates Ltd* [1995] 2 AC 145, 180 (Lord Goff).

the theory to the position of an arranger to see whether a case could be made out against it.

3.4.3.1 *The existence of a duty of care*

3.57 The tests for establishing in any particular situation the existence of a duty of care or, more accurately, a duty to exercise reasonable care, hark back to a passage in the famous speech of Lord Atkin in *Donoghue v Stevenson*,[75] in which his Lordship said:

> The rule that you are to love your neighbour becomes in law, you must not injure your neighbour; and the lawyer's question, Who is my neighbour? receives a restricted reply. You must take reasonable care to avoid acts or omissions which you can reasonably foresee would be likely to injure your neighbour. Who, then, in law is my neighbour? The answer seems to be—persons who are so closely and directly affected by my act that I ought reasonably to have them in contemplation as being so affected when I am directing my mind to the acts or omissions which are called into question.

3.58 Despite such an auspicious beginning, there have been divergent approaches in the case law over the years, particularly in the House of Lords, in determining the circumstances under which a duty of care may arise in cases involving a new situation where the claim has been for pure economic loss. The divergence of approach is reflected in the review of the case law that was conducted by the House of Lords in *HM Commissioners of Customs and Excise v Barclays Bank plc.*[76] Three possible tests, as outlined below, have been put forward in the case law to determine if a duty of care exists in a situation that is not covered by existing authority, although no one of those tests will be determinative in every situation.[77] To a large extent, the House of Lords signalled in the *Barclays Bank* case that the tests should be applied on a pragmatic, rather than a theoretical, basis and that the concepts that are used in the tests are not precise but should be seen as guides rather than definitive tests.[78] What is important is to discover what could reasonably be inferred from the defendant's conduct against the background of all of the circumstances of the case, and that this was not just a question of fact, as questions of fairness and policy would also enter into the decision.[79] In the *Barclays Bank* case

---

[75] [1932] AC 562, 580.

[76] [2006] UKHL 28, [2007] 1 AC 181.

[77] See eg the review conducted by Lord Mance in the *Barclays Bank* case and his summary at the end of his review, at [93]. More generally see also *Michael v The Chief Constable of South Wales Police* [2015] UKSC 2. In *Golden Belt 1 Sukuk Co BSC(c) v BNP Paribas* [2017] EWHC 3182 (Comm) the three tests were applied to determine whether an arranging bank owed a duty to the creditors under a financing transaction to take reasonable care to ensure that the transaction documentation was properly executed.

[78] The Court of Appeal has stressed that the three tests are complementary and usually lead to the same answer; they should be used as cross-checks and not considered in isolation from each other: *Property Alliance Group Ltd v Royal Bank of Scotland plc* [2018] EWCA Civ 355 [62].

[79] See the *Barclays Bank* case [35] (Lord Hoffmann).

the decision was largely based upon whether, as a matter of policy, it was fair, just, and reasonable to impose a duty of care upon the defendant. None of this makes it easy to say how the courts will deal with any particular set of new circumstances when they arise.

The first test is that of an 'assumption of responsibility', that is, whether the de-   **3.59** fendant voluntarily assumed responsibility for what he said and did vis-à-vis the claimant, or is to be treated by the law as having done so. This test was championed by Lord Goff of Chieveley in three cases: *Spring v Guardian Assurance plc*,[80] *Henderson v Merrett Syndicates Ltd*,[81] and *White v Jones*.[82] Lord Goff based the test, in particular, on Lord Devlin's speech in *Hedley Byrne & Co Ltd v Heller & Partners Ltd*.[83] Lord Walker said in the *Barclays Bank* case[84] that the concept of a 'voluntary' assumption meant a conscious, considered, or deliberate decision on the part of the defendant. Lord Bingham said in the *Barclays Bank* case[85] that in some cases a party can be said to have assumed responsibility and that can be seen as a sufficient condition of liability, but such an assumption should never be regarded as a necessary condition of liability. The paradigm situation where such an assumption may exist is where there is a relationship having an equivalence to the characteristics of a contract, save for the presence of consideration.[86] Lord Bingham said that this was the position in *Hedley Byrne & Co Ltd v Heller & Partners Ltd*,[87] in *White v Jones*,[88] and in *Henderson v Merrett Syndicates Ltd*.[89] Presumably the same could be said in cases where a claim in tort is brought as an alternative to a claim in contract.[90] The reference to an equivalence to the characteristics of a contract should not be taken too literally,[91] as an assumption of responsibility has also been found in situations that were some way removed from

---

[80] [1995] 2 AC 296.
[81] [1995] 2 AC 145, 178.
[82] [1995] 2 AC 207, 268.
[83] [1964] AC 465, 528–29.
[84] [2006] UKHL 28 [73].
[85] At [4].
[86] Eg see *Calvert v William Hill Credit Ltd* [2008] EWHC 454 (Ch), upheld on appeal [2008] EWCA Civ 1427.
[87] [1964] AC 465.
[88] [1995] 2 AC 207.
[89] [1995] 2 AC 145.
[90] See *Henderson v Merrett Syndicates Ltd* [1995] 2 AC 145, 184–94 (Lord Goff).
[91] In *Playboy Club London Ltd and others v Banca Nazionale del Lavoro SPA* [2018] UKSC 43 an undisclosed principal argued that, by analogy with contract, it could step into the shoes of its agent and therefore it was owed the same duty of care by a bank in respect of a reference that was owed to its agent. The Supreme Court rejected this argument based on 'equivalence to contract' as fallacious. The relationship between the bank and the undisclosed principal was not sufficiently proximate to give rise to a duty of care.

any equivalence to a contract between the claimant and defendant, as in *Smith v Eric S Bush*,[92] *White v Jones*,[93] and *Phelps v Hillingdon London Borough Council*.[94]

3.60 Lord Bingham also said in the *Barclays Bank* case[95] that the assumption of responsibility test is to be applied objectively and not just by a consideration of the defendant's subjective thoughts or intentions.[96] The concept of a subjective assumption of responsibility might still be relevant in cases where it could be demonstrated that a defendant had intended to accept responsibility or had expressly disavowed an acceptance of responsibility.[97] Lord Bingham also said that the further the assumption test is removed from subjective considerations, so that the more it becomes a notional assumption of responsibility, the less of a distinction will exist between this test and the threefold test, which is the second test as outlined in what follows.

3.61 Lord Mance said in the *Barclays Bank* case[98] that the concept of an assumption of responsibility may be particularly useful in two situations concerning special relationships that had been identified by Lord Browne-Wilkinson in *White v Jones*[99] namely, where the defendant had a fiduciary duty towards the claimant and where the defendant had voluntarily assumed responsibility when it knew or ought to have known that the claimant would rely upon the defendant. In that situation, the test of voluntary assumption may effectively subsume all of the aspects of the threefold test.[100]

3.62 **The second test** is the 'threefold' test, which was outlined by Lord Bridge of Harwich in *Caparo Industries plc v Dickman*.[101] The three elements of the test are

---

[92] [1990] 1 AC 83. However, it ought to be noted that this decision has been heavily distinguished, and described as the high water mark in this area in eg *Scullion v Bank of Scotland plc* [2011] EWCA Civ 693.
[93] [1995] 2 AC 207.
[94] [2001] 2 AC 619.
[95] [2006] UKHL 28 [5].
[96] See *Smith v Eric S Bush* [1990] 1 AC 831, 862 (Lord Griffiths); *Caparo Industries plc v Dickman* [1990] 2 AC 605, 637 (Lord Oliver); and *Phelps v Hillingdon LBC* [2001] 2 AC 619, 654 (Lord Slynn). See also *Henderson v Merrett Syndicates Ltd* [1995] 2 AC 145, 181 (Lord Goff).
[97] Although such a disavowal should be considered as an attempt to exclude or restrict liability for negligence and so should be subject to the need to satisfy the requirement of reasonableness in s 11 of the Unfair Contract Terms Act 1977. See *Smith v Eric S Bush* [1990] 1 AC 831, 873 (Lord Jauncey).
[98] [2006] UKHL 28 [92]–[93].
[99] [1995] 2 AC 207, 273–74.
[100] For examples of the application of this test in the context of the provision of information, see *Patchett v Swimming Pool & Allied Trades Association Ltd* [2009] EWCA Civ 717; *HSBC Bank plc v 5th Avenue Partners Ltd* [2009] EWCA Civ 296; *Arrowhead Capital Finance Ltd (In Liquidation) v KPMG LLP* [2012] EWHC 1801 (Comm); *Barclays Bank plc v Grant Thornton UK LLP* [2015] EWHC 320 (Comm); and *Playboy Club London Ltd and others v Banca Nazionale del Lavoro SPA* [2018] UKSC 43.
[101] [1990] 2 AC 605, 617–18; *His Royal Highness Okpabi v Royal Dutch Shell plc* [2018] EWCA Civ 191.

(a) whether the loss to the claimant was a reasonably foreseeable consequence of what the defendant did or failed to do; (b) whether the relationship between the defendant and the claimant was one of sufficient proximity; and (c) whether in all the circumstances it was fair, just, and reasonable to impose a duty of care on the defendant towards the claimant.[102] Although Lord Bingham in the *Barclays Bank* case said[103] that this test may not provide a straightforward answer in a novel situation to whether a duty exists, Lord Hoffmann said in *Sutradhar v Natural Environment Research Council*[104] that the threefold test provides the 'standard framework' within which the question of whether a duty of care exists will usually be examined. He went on to say in that case (albeit in the context of a case which involved physical injury alleged to have arisen in consequence of a negligent state-ment) that the concept of proximity involved the defendant in having 'a measure of control over and responsibility for' the situation giving rise to the loss, in dis-tinction to the loss merely being foreseeable but outside that element of control and responsibility.[105]

Lord Goff said in *Henderson v Merrett Syndicates Ltd*[106] that in a situation where there has been a voluntary assumption of responsibility by the defendant towards the claimant, it is unnecessary to show that it would be 'fair, just and reasonable' to impose liability. See also Lord Steyn in *Williams v Natural Life Health Foods Ltd*.[107] Lord Hoffmann made a similar point in the *Barclays Bank* case.[108] **3.63**

---

[102] Which, Lord Bingham noted with approval in the *Barclays Bank* case [2006] UKHL 28 [4], Kirby J had labelled as 'policy' in *Perre v Apand Pty Ltd* [1999] HCA 26, (1999) 198 CLR 180 [259]. For failures to satisfy this requirement see *Arrowhead Capital Finance Ltd (In Liquidation) v KPMG LLP* [2012] EWHC 1801 (Comm); *Smeaton v Equifax plc* [2013] EWCA Civ 108 [74]–[76]; *Barclays Bank plc v Grant Thornton UK LLP* [2015] EWHC 320 (Comm) [49]; and *CGL Group Ltd v RBS plc* [2017] EWCA Civ 1073 (not satisfied because imposing a duty of care on banks would cut across the applicable regulatory regime). In *Hall v Royal Bank of Scotland plc* [2009] EWHC 3163 (QB) it was held that, in the absence of an assumption of responsibility, the courts ought not to impose a duty on a bank where the exercise of that duty would create a conflict of interest between the bank's interests and the interests of its counterparties.

[103] At [6].

[104] [2006] UKHL 33 [32].

[105] *Sutradhar v Natural Environment Research Council* [2006] UKHL 33, [2006] 4 All ER 490 [38]. See also Lord Brown of Eaton-under-Heywood in the same case, at [48]. In *Taberna Europe CDO II plc v Selskabet (Formerly Roskilde Bank A/S) (In Bankruptcy)* [2016] EWCA Civ 1262 [11], Moore-Bick LJ stated that the mere placing of a presentation to original loan note purchasers on a website would not of itself create the proximity necessary to create a duty of care to subsequent purchasers of the notes in the secondary market. However, on the facts of this case such a duty did arise as the company was found to have intended that purchasers in the secondary market could rely on the presentation. See also *Golden Belt 1 Sukuk Co BSC(c) v BNP Paribas* [2017] EWHC 3182 (Comm).

[106] [1995] 2 AC 145, 180–81.

[107] [1998] 1 WLR 830, 834.

[108] [2006] UKHL 28 [35]–[36].

3.64 In *Caparo Industries plc v Dickman*[109] it was held that the auditors of a public company did not owe a duty of care in the conduct of their audit towards potential investors in the company, whether such investors were shareholders who were considering making a further investment on the strength of the audited accounts of the company, or members of the public at large who might invest on the strength of such accounts. The relationship was not sufficiently proximate between such investors and the auditors. The auditors performed their functions pursuant to a statutory duty, for the more limited purpose of enabling the body of the shareholders to exercise informed control of their company rather than enabling potential investors, whether they might already be shareholders or not, to decide if they wished to make an investment by acquiring shares in the company.[110] It was similarly held in *Al Saudi Banque v Clark Pixley*[111] that the auditors of a company did not owe a duty of care to banks which were contemplating the provision or continuance of facilities to a company. Even if it was foreseeable that a copy of the audited accounts might be provided to the banks which might rely on them in deciding to provide or continue facilities, there was not a sufficiently close or direct relationship to establish the necessary degree of proximity to give rise to a duty of care. That case was distinguished, however, in the later Scottish case of *Royal Bank of Scotland plc v Bannerman Johnstone Maclay*[112] where the auditors were aware that a copy of the audited accounts would be made available to a bank as a condition to the making available or continuance of a facility, the auditors had requested sight of the facility documentation to confirm that the facility would be available to the company, subject to the satisfaction of that condition, and so were specifically aware of the fact that the bank would place reliance upon the audited accounts in making the facility available to the company. It was not necessary also to prove, additionally, an intention on the part of the auditors that the accounts would be relied upon by the bank for that purpose. Similarly in *Golden Belt 1 Sukuk Co BSC(c) v BNP Paribas*[113] a duty was held to be owed by an arranger to participants in a financing transaction who had purchased their participations on the secondary market. The duty required the arranger to exercise reasonable care to ensure that the original documentation was properly executed. The purchasers were dependent on the bank for the proper execution of the promissory note and had no means of checking whether the promissory note had been

---

[109] [1990] 2 AC 605. The basic principles of this case were recently reaffirmed by the Supreme Court in *Playboy Club London Ltd and others v Banca Nazionale del Lavoro SPA* [2018] UKSC 43.

[110] For a different approach to the problem, where it was said that in certain specific circumstances, an auditor might be held to owe a duty of care to shareholders and potential investors, see *Man Nutzfahrzeuge AG v Freightliner Ltd* [2007] EWCA Civ 910.

[111] [1990] 1 Ch 313. See also *Barclays Bank plc v Grant Thornton UK LLP* [2015] EWHC 320 (Comm).

[112] [2003] SLT 181, [2003] PNLR 6 (Lord MacFadyen in the Outer House of the Court of Session).

[113] [2017] EWHC 3182 (Comm).

properly executed. There was no principled reason why as a matter of policy the arranger should not owe such a duty to purchasers in the secondary market.

The third test is the 'incremental' test and is based upon the observation of **3.65** Brennan J in *Sutherland Shire Council v Heyman*,[114] which was approved by Lord Bridge in *Caparo Industries plc v Dickman*,[115] to the effect that the law should develop new categories of negligence incrementally and by analogy with established categories and not by extending the categories in a massive manner with only limited and ill-defined restraints. Lord Bingham said in the *Barclays Bank* case[116] that the incremental test is of little value in itself and will only be of use when combined with one of the other tests. The closer the case is to the facts of a previous case where a duty of care has been found to exist, the more willing the court will be, by use of the incremental test, to find a duty of care based on one of the other two tests. The converse will also be true.[117]

Tripartite situations involving an agent It is important to note, however, that **3.66** in *Williams v Natural Life Health Foods Ltd*[118] the House of Lords held that in a tripartite situation where an agent acted on behalf of a principal in dealing with the claimant, then whilst the principal may have a duty of care towards the claimant, the agent will not be liable unless it can be shown, on an objective basis, that the agent had undertaken its own personal duty of care by an assumption of responsibility towards the claimant and, in addition, that it was reasonable for the claimants to place reliance upon the agent.[119] That case involved an allegation that a director of a company, who was its moving force, should be made liable for the financial loss that the claimants had suffered through the negligence of the company. Whilst the case involved a company director, Lord Steyn, who gave the leading speech in the House of Lords, said that the same principle would apply generally in situations involving an agent acting on behalf of or representing a natural or corporate principal.[120] A similar approach has been taken in cases where claims have been brought against sub-contractors who supplied services or gave advice to the claimant pursuant to a contract with a head contractor who had contracted with the claimant for the provision of such services or advice.[121]

---

[114] (1985) 157 CLR 424, 481.
[115] [1990] 2 AC 605, 618.
[116] [2006] UKHL 28 [7].
[117] *Patchett v Swimming Pool & Allied Trades Association Ltd* [2009] EWCA Civ 717 [39].
[118] [1998] 1 WLR 830.
[119] See Lord Steyn, 835–36. See also *Roberts v Egan* [2014] EWHC 1849 (Ch) [56]; *Bush v Summit Advances Ltd* [2015] EWHC 665 (QB); and *First Bespoke Ltd Partnership v Hadjigeorgiou* (HHJ Raeside QC, 12 June 2015). However, if a tort is committed by an individual tortfeasor, he is personally liable for it, even if he was a director of a limited company, which might also be liable for that tort: *Yeeles v Benton* [2010] EWCA Civ 326.
[120] [1998] 1 WLR 830, 835. See also Lord Hoffmann in *Standard Chartered Bank v Pakistan National Shipping Corp (No 2)* [2003] 1 AC 959, 969.
[121] For instance, in *Henderson v Merrett Syndicates Ltd* [1995] 2 AC 145, *Riyad Bank v Ahli United Bank (UK) plc* [2006] EWCA Civ 780, [2006] 2 Lloyd's Rep 292, and *BP plc v AON Ltd*

In the *Williams* case the House declined to hold the director liable, as there was no objective basis on which it could be said that he had assumed responsibility towards the claimants; nor was there any evidence that the claimants had relied upon the director or that it would have been reasonable for them to have done so.[122] Lord Hoffmann made the additional point in the *Barclays Bank* case[123] that in determining if a relationship has arisen in cases of loss caused by the provision of information (and also, presumably, advice), it was critical to determine if it was the defendant, as opposed to someone else, who had assumed the responsibility from which the alleged relationship arose,[124] to whom the obligation had been assumed,[125] and for what purpose the information had been provided.[126]

3.4.3.2 *The scope of the duty*

3.67 Assuming that it can be shown that the defendant owed a duty of care towards the claimant, it is then necessary to establish the scope or the extent of that duty, because a defendant cannot be made liable for loss which was suffered by the claimant if it arose from a matter that was outside the ambit of the defendant's duty of care.[127] In relation to an arranger, this issue will be important in distinguishing between (a) whether the arranger owed the lenders a wide duty of care, essentially to use reasonable care so as to ensure that the transaction was suitable for them or, alternatively, so as to ensure that the lenders were correctly appraised of all the risks associated with the transaction that could reasonably have been investigated by the arranger (a duty to advise),[128] and (b) a more limited duty to use reasonable care to ensure that the information that was supplied to them by the arranger was accurate and not misleading or that any specific task which it undertook was performed to the appropriate standard of care and skill. If the duty is limited to the second category then the arranger will not be liable for a loss that might have been

---

[2006] EWHC 424 (Comm), [2006] 1 All ER (Comm) 789, in each of which the sub-contractor was found to be liable to the claimant because it had assumed responsibility. See also *Webster v Liddington* [2014] EWCA Civ 560.

[122] See Lord Steyn's comment that even if there was reliance, it had to be reasonable to place reliance on the agent or employee, at [1998] 1 WLR 830, 837. See also Lord Steyn's reference to the decision of La Forest J in Supreme Court of Canada in *Edgeworth Construction Ltd v ND Lea & Associates Ltd* [1993] 3 SCR 206, 212.

[123] [2006] UKHL 28 [35].

[124] Cf *Williams v Natural Life Health Foods Ltd* [1998] AC 830 and the discussion concerning liability in a case where there are 'chains' of contractual relationships, in the Court of Appeal in *Riyad Bank v Ahli United Bank (UK) plc* [2006] EWCA Civ 780, [2006] 2 Lloyd's Rep 292.

[125] Cf *Smith v Eric S Bush* [1990] 1 AC 831; *Henderson v Merrett Syndicates Ltd* [1995] 2 AC 145; and *White v Jones* [1995] 2 AC 207.

[126] Cf *Caparo Industries plc v Dickman* [1990] 2 AC 605.

[127] *South Australia Asset Management Corp v York Montague Ltd* [1997] AC 191. See section 3.4.3.5 below for further discussion of this case and the intertwined element of causation.

[128] The mere fact that information was selected and offered by a bank does not give it the status of advice: *Marz Ltd v Bank of Scotland plc* [2017] EWHC 3618 (Ch) [357].

suffered despite the accuracy of the information that it supplied to the lenders or the satisfactory performance of the task it undertook.[129]

The importance of the distinction is illustrated by the decision of the House of **3.68** Lords in *Aneco Reinsurance Underwriting Ltd v Johnson & Higgins Ltd*[130] which was a case concerned with the liability of insurance brokers in placing excess of loss cover on behalf of the claimant reinsurance company. If the duty of the brokers had been limited to placing cover for the claimant, their liability would have been limited to some US$11m, which was the amount of cover that they were asked to place and which they failed to do. However, it was held that the duty of the brokers extended more widely to advising the reinsurance company on what course it should adopt in entering into its commitments, and they had failed to advise that reinsurance cover was generally unavailable in the market. Had the brokers properly advised the claimant, it would not have proceeded with the transaction. Accordingly, the claimant was awarded damages for a loss of US$35m, being the amount of loss that it suffered in consequence of entering into the transaction.

The distinction is also illustrated by *Torre Asset Funding v RBS*.[131] A bank breached **3.69** a voluntarily assumed duty to use reasonable care to ensure that the information that was supplied by it to the other lenders was accurate. It did so by providing an inaccurate explanation as to why consent to an amendment was being sought. However, the claim against the bank failed because of the limited scope of the relevant duty of care. The duty of care only extended to loss that might be suffered as a result of giving the consent that was sought. The claimant did not suffer such loss as the proposal did not garner enough votes and did not come into effect. The information was not provided for the purpose of conducting an overall review of the desirability of the recipient remaining as a participant in the transaction; losses caused by such a decision were outside of the scope of the duty of care that had been assumed.

3.4.3.3 *Reasonable care*

The fact that a person or entity has a duty of care does not mean that it will be **3.70** obliged to prevent any and all loss that may be suffered for matters that may fall within the scope of that duty. The duty is to exercise reasonable care, not to provide absolute protection, and loss may still be suffered even where reasonable care has been exercised.[132] The reasonableness test is normally to be judged by the

---

[129] The distinction is further explained in detail in *Hughes-Holland v BPE Solicitors (Gabriel v Little)* [2017] UKSC 21.
[130] [2001] UKHL 51, [2002] 1 Lloyd's Rep 157.
[131] [2013] EWHC 2670 (Ch) [184]–[188]. See also para 3.74 below.
[132] See eg *Stafford v Conti Commodity Services Ltd* [1981] 1 Lloyd's Rep 466, 474–75 (Mocatta J) with respect to the provision of advice concerning investments in volatile markets. His Lordship pointed out that advice may have been given with the exercise of reasonable care concerning the making of such investments which, with the benefit of hindsight, may turn out to have been

standard of the ordinary man in the street or on the famous Clapham omnibus, that is, whether the ordinary man or woman, faced at the same time with the same circumstances, would have acted in the way in which the defendant acted. It has been held, however, that a professional person or entity which purports to have specialist skill and knowledge will have a higher duty than might be expected of the ordinary man in the street. In such a case, the test is the standard of the ordinary skilled person exercising and professing to have that special skill.[133] This does not require that the defendant should exercise the highest level of expertise and skill of a person in his position, just that of an ordinary competent person in that position or, to put it another way, consistently with the reasonable average.[134] However, it has also been held that acting in accordance with a common practice in a profession or trade is not necessarily sufficient to discharge the duty of care if that practice is inherently negligent, in that there was a foreseeable risk that could have been avoided.[135]

3.4.3.4 Reasonable reliance

3.71 The claimant must show that it reasonably relied upon the defendant in the exercise of the duty of care towards it.[136] There are two facets to this issue.[137] First, the claimant must show that it did in fact rely upon the defendant to exercise reasonable care towards the claimant. If, for instance, the claimant placed no store in the competence of the defendant or on what it was told by the defendant, then it will not have relied upon the defendant.[138] Secondly, even if it asserts that it did rely upon the defendant, a claimant can only recover if, in the circumstances, it was reasonable for it to place such reliance upon the defendant.[139]

3.72 Situations may arise, however, in which it may be held that a defendant had a duty of care towards the claimant where, at the time the duty was breached, the

---

incorrect as the markets may not have performed in the manner that was expected when the advice was given.

[133] *Bolam v Friern Hospital Management Committee* [1957] 1 WLR 582. A similar approach has been taken in the case of professional trustees: Brightman J in *Bartlett v Barclays Bank Trust Co Ltd* [1980] Ch 515, 534. However, the *Bolam* test does not apply in the context of investment advice given by a bank where there is overlap with applicable regulatory rules: *O'Hare v Coutts* [2016] EWHC 2224 (QB).

[134] *Eckersley v Binnie* [1988] 18 Con LR 1.

[135] *Edward Wong Finance Co Ltd v Johnson Stokes & Master* [1984] AC 296 (PC).

[136] See eg the references to reliance made by Lord Morris and by Lord Hodson in *Hedley Byrne & Co Ltd v Heller & Partners Ltd* [1964] AC 465, 503 and 514.

[137] See Lord Steyn in *Williams v Natural Life Health Foods Ltd* [1998] 1 WLR 830 and his discussion of two Canadian cases that are relevant to this issue: *London Drugs Ltd v Kuehne & Nagel International Ltd* (1992) 97 DLR (4th) 261 and *Edgeworth Construction Ltd v ND Lea & Associates Ltd* [1993] SCR 206.

[138] In *HSBC Bank plc v 5th Avenue Partners Ltd* [2009] EWCA Civ 296, although a bank had acted in breach of a duty of care by issuing a particular document, the claimant's action failed because it had relied on assurances of fraudsters in making a payment, and not on that document.

[139] *Steel v NRAM Ltd* [2018] UKSC 13.

claimant was unaware of the defendant and of the task undertaken by it. In such a situation, it will be difficult, if not impossible, to demonstrate reliance as a matter of fact by the claimant upon the defendant. This is demonstrated by the decision of the House of Lords in *White v Jones*[140] in which a solicitor, who was negligent through inexcusable delay in failing to prepare a will before the testator died, was held liable to intended beneficiaries who did not receive bequests that the testator had intended to confer upon them. In many such cases, an intended beneficiary may be unaware of the proposed bequest and, perhaps, even of the existence of the testator, so the claimant can hardly claim any deliberate or overt reliance on its part. Nonetheless, Lord Browne-Wilkinson was prepared to allow such claimants to recover.[141] In such cases, the reliance may be said to arise by implication from the claimant's ignorance of the existence of the relevant relationship and its total dependence upon the claimant in the absence of being in a position to make any judgement of its own.

3.4.3.5 Causation

The claimant must show that the loss which it has suffered was caused by the defendant's breach of duty, which is a matter closely connected with the scope of the defendant's duty.[142] Lord Hoffmann explored this issue in *South Australia Asset Management Corp v York Montague Ltd*[143] (the *SAAMCO* case), in which he gave the graphic example of the mountaineer who goes to his doctor about his knee before embarking upon a mountaineering expedition. The doctor negligently pronounces his knee to be fit. Had the doctor correctly diagnosed the faulty knee, the claimant would not have gone on the expedition. He suffers injury whilst on the expedition but it has nothing to do with his knee. He has not suffered a loss which can be recovered against the doctor. The *SAAMCO* case involved a case against a valuer which negligently valued a property for a lender that was proposing to take a mortgage of the property, which it duly did in reliance upon the valuation. The borrower subsequently defaulted and the lender enforced the mortgage, but recovered substantially less upon enforcement than the amount of the valuation. However, this was partly due to a general fall in the market value of property. The lender argued that it would not have entered into the transaction at all if it had received a correct valuation.[144] The House of Lords held that the scope

3.73

---

[140] [1995] 2 AC 207.

[141] See Lord Browne-Wilkinson, 275–77. It is arguable, on the facts of the case, that there was reliance as a matter of fact, as the intended beneficiaries had been informed of the testator's intentions and that the solicitor had been instructed to prepare the will.

[142] Already discussed in section 3.4.3.2 above.

[143] [1997] AC 191. See also *Haugesund Kommune v Depfa ACS Bank* [2011] EWCA Civ 33 and *Astle v CBRE Ltd* [2015] EWHC 3189 (Ch).

[144] In *Arrowhead Capital Finance Ltd (In Liquidation) v KPMG LLP* [2012] EWHC 1801 (Comm) the court held that making a loan which a lender would not otherwise have made did not necessarily amount to damage; this depended on a comparison between the amount of the loan and the value of the rights which the lender acquired.

of the defendant's duty had been to report on the true value of the property and so the lender could only recover the amount of its loss that was attributable to the negligent valuation, that is, the loss attributable to the information provided by the valuer being incorrect (ie the difference between the proper market value and the reported value at the date of the valuation), not for the loss which would have been suffered in any event, even if the valuation had been correct (ie the loss attributable to the fall in the property market). Twenty years later, the Supreme Court has reaffirmed this approach in *Hughes-Holland v BPE Solicitors*.[145]

3.74 Similarly in *Torre Asset Funding v RBS*[146] it was held that the primary purpose of an agent bank's duties to provide information under loan documentation was to ensure that the lenders would receive information regarding the performance of the loans and the underlying business of the borrower to allow them to consider how to exercise their rights by accelerating or calling in security. It was not to assist them in making investment decisions as to whether to sell their participations in the loans. Consequently, any loss caused by a lender's decision to maintain its participation was outside the scope of the duty to provide information; in other words, such a loss would not be considered to be caused by a breach of that duty. The cause of such a loss was that the lenders had made a loan to a borrower who became unable to repay them and whose secured assets were insufficient to cover its debts.[147] In any event, the claim would have failed on the facts because the claimants could not prove that they would have sold their loan participations if they had been provided with the relevant information at the relevant time.

3.75 As can be seen from both the *SAAMCO* case and the *Torre* case, the question of causation is inter-mixed with the issue as to the scope of the defendant's duty, as is also apparent from the *Aneco Reinsurance* case.[148] In that case, the defendants were held liable for the whole loss suffered because of the breach of their duty to give the claimant general advice as to the transaction, rather than merely to carry out the more limited task of arranging specific excess of loss cover. Hence, in that case, the loss that the claimant was able to recover reflected the wider scope of the duty owed by the defendants to the claimant.

---

[145] (Also known as *Gabriel v Little*) [2017] UKSC 21. The burden of proof is on the claimant to prove that the loss would not have occurred even if the information provided by the defendant had been correct. See also *Lloyds Bank plc v McBains Cooper Consulting Ltd* [2018] EWCA Civ 452.

[146] [2013] EWHC 2670 (Ch) [213].

[147] ibid [216].

[148] [2001] UKHL 51, [2002] 1 Lloyd's Rep 157; see also *Torre Asset Funding v RBS* [2013] EWHC 2670 (Ch). The question of causation is also inter-mixed with questions of reasonable reliance as demonstrated by *HSBC Bank plc v 5th Avenue Partners Ltd* [2009] EWCA Civ 296 [94] and remoteness of damage as in *Rubenstein v HSBC Bank plc* [2012] EWCA Civ 1184.

3.4.3.6 *Foreseeable loss*

The defendant can only be made liable for the loss that was reasonably fore- **3.76**
seeable by the defendant at the time the breach of duty occurred. This requirement is mentioned by Lord Atkin in the passage of his speech in *Donoghue v
Stevenson* quoted previously.[149] The relevance of a test based upon foreseeability
was laid down by the Privy Council in *Overseas Tankship (UK) Ltd v Morts Docks
Engineering Co Ltd*,[150] which is usually referred to as *Wagon Mound (No 1)*.[151] The
requirement as to foreseeability is referred to in most of the cases dealing with
recovery for economic loss, such as in *Hedley Byrne* and in *Caparo*. In fact, it comprises the first part of the three criteria for establishing a duty of care as formulated
in *Caparo*. Foreseeability is also closely linked with causation and with the scope
of the defendant's duty of care, as the defendant can only be liable for the loss that
was reasonably foreseeable and which arose from the breach of duty. Thus, if the
scope of the defendant's duty was limited then loss will not be recoverable, even if
it was foreseeable, where the loss falls outside the matters for which the defendant
was responsible. Similarly, if the loss which occurred was not reasonably foreseeable by the defendant, it will not be recoverable,[152] despite the fact, if such it be,
that the loss might otherwise have arisen in consequence of the breach of duty.[153]

3.4.4 The position of the arranger in an action in negligence

A useful starting point in examining the position of the arranger in a claim in **3.77**
negligence is to determine the existence and scope of any possible duty of care
that it might be alleged to owe to the lenders. This will depend upon all the circumstances, including any disclaimers.[154] It will be recalled that the possible duty
of care could be framed either as a wide duty to take care of the interests of the
lenders or as a more limited duty with respect to particular information that it
supplies to the lenders or other tasks that it might undertake on their behalf. It
is then relevant to consider if the lenders placed reliance upon the arranger with
respect to the exercise of that duty and, if so, if it was reasonable for them to do
so. It must also be remembered that the duty is to take reasonable care; it is not
an absolute obligation to prevent any and all loss from being suffered. It may be

---

[149] See para 3.57.
[150] [1961] AC 388.
[151] However, where there is concurrent liability in contract and tort, the stricter contract measure
of remoteness will apply: *Wellesley Partners LLP v Withers LLP* [2015] EWCA Civ 1146.
[152] In *Camerata Property Inc v Credit Suisse Securities (Europe) Ltd* [2012] EWHC 7 (Comm) the
loss was irrecoverable as it was caused by the bankruptcy of Lehman Brothers which, at the time the
relevant investment advice was given, was completely unforeseeable.
[153] The Privy Council in *Wagon Mound (No 1)* said that *Re Polemis and Furness, Withy & Co
Ltd* [1921] 3 KB 560 had been wrongly decided. In *Re Polemis* it had been held that the defendant
would be liable for all of the direct consequences of its negligence, no matter how remote.
[154] Difficult questions may arise as to whether a disclaimer prevents a duty of care from arising or
only limits liability for breach of such a duty. This impacts on whether the Unfair Contract Terms
Act 1977 may apply. See paras 3.116 and 3.126.

that, despite exercising reasonable care, a loss may still be suffered. For instance, the arranger may have made reasonable efforts to check the information that was provided, yet the information may turn out to be incorrect. Similarly, the arranger may have done its best to assess projections as to the future prospects of the borrower's business, which cannot guard against unforeseen hazards that may arise in the future. Further, the loss that was suffered may not (either in part or in whole) be attributable to any breach of the duty on the part of the arranger, or it may not have been foreseeable as at the time the alleged breach of the duty occurred.

3.4.4.1 A wide duty of care

3.78 In examining the question whether an arranger owes a wide duty of care to the lenders and if the necessary elements of reliance can be made out, it is convenient to examine its role in two stages. The first stage covers the period up until the lenders commit in principle to participate in the transaction, during which the arranger invites the lenders to participate and is involved in supplying them with information relevant to their decision, in principle, to join the syndicate. The second stage relates to the period in which the arranger is involved in the preparation and negotiation of the formal facility documentation.

3.79 **The first stage** It is submitted that in respect of its role in the first stage, an arranger of a syndicated loan, which is acting in pursuance of a mandate granted to it by the borrower, should usually be in the position as addressed by *Williams v Natural Life Health Foods Ltd*, in that it is acting on behalf of the borrower rather than purporting to accept its own independent responsibility towards the lenders. On that basis, it will not have a duty of care towards the lenders unless it can be shown, judged objectively on the basis of what it said and the actions that it took, that it had accepted responsibility towards the lenders and the consequential duty of care to them. In the normal case, the arranger would clearly have been acting on behalf of the borrower, rather than on behalf of the lenders. This should be fairly obvious, not least because it is usually stated in communications between the arranger and the lenders that the arranger acts on behalf of the borrower, pursuant to a mandate granted by the borrower, and that any information that it distributes is sent to the lenders at the borrower's request, was prepared from material supplied by the borrower, and had not been verified by the arranger.[155] In *Raiffeisen Zentralbank Österreich AG v Royal Bank of Scotland plc*[156] Christopher Clarke J concluded that:[157]

---

[155] See eg the statements that accompanied the syndicate information memorandum in *IFE Fund SA v Goldman Sachs International* [2007] EWCA Civ 811 and *Raiffeisen Zentralbank Österreich AG v Royal Bank of Scotland plc* [2010] EWHC 1392 (Comm). It was accepted that this was fairly typical of the position in arranging syndicated facilities.

[156] [2010] EWHC 1392 (Comm). See text to n 319.

[157] ibid [95].

in the syndicated loans market, it was ... standard for the Arranger to disclaim in the [information memorandum] any responsibility for its contents, and for potential participants to sign a confidentiality agreement under which they would receive information about or relevant to the proposed loan on the basis that the Arranger made no representations or warranties of any kind as to the accuracy or completeness of the information with which they were being provided.

In those circumstances, a wide duty of care should not arise and, even if it did, it is **3.80** unlikely that the lenders would have placed reliance upon the arranger, nor would it have been reasonable for them to do so. As *Raiffeisen Zentralbank Österreich AG v Royal Bank of Scotland plc* demonstrates, this view is in line with accepted practice in the financial markets that operate in London.[158] The market practice is that lenders have no claim against the arrangers since each lender is treated as carrying out its own research and making its own credit decision, a position which is confirmed (or created) by the inclusion of disclaimers to that effect which are themselves market standard.

The second stage The position as to the second stage may appear to be less clear **3.81** but, in the end, it is unlikely that the arranger will be found liable to the lenders in negligence. It must, however, be conceded that it is very unlikely that the arranger could be said, in any practical sense, to be acting on behalf of the borrower once it has reached the stage of preparing and negotiating the facility documentation. Accordingly, an argument in favour of the arranger based upon *Williams v Natural Life Health Foods Ltd* is unlikely to succeed. By this stage, the arranger will have appointed lawyers to advise it in the preparation of the documentation and the borrower will have appointed its own lawyers to give it advice (the practice in the London markets is that the facility agreement itself is based on forms recommended by Loan Market Association, amended to take account of factors that are pertinent to the relevant transaction). There will often be fairly extensive, and sometimes vigorous, negotiation between the two sides (particularly of the commercial matters and security dealt with in the documentation) before a mutually acceptable draft of the documentation is settled between them. During that negotiation, the stance that the arranger usually takes is to put forward the likely views of the lenders and what they would find acceptable, because it knows that the lenders will not proceed on the basis of unacceptable documentation. These factors indicate that the arranger is no longer acting as the agent and the mouthpiece of the borrower, but has moved away from that role and towards a position that reflects its perception of the interests of the lenders, including possibly its own position as a potential syndicate member.[159] However, just because it is not acting as the agent of the borrower does not lead automatically to the conclusion

---

[158] ibid [94].
[159] See eg JRF Lehane, 'The Role of Managing and Agent Banks: Duties, Liabilities, Disclaimer Clauses' [1982] International Law Review 235.

that the arranger has accepted a duty of care towards the lenders, but it does mean that the argument is not as clear-cut as it would have been in considering its role in the first stage. Looked at objectively, the first two of the three criteria for a duty of care as outlined in *Caparo* appear to be present in examining the arranger's role in the second stage, namely, foreseeability of possible harm and proximity, as quite clearly the arranger must have the lenders in its contemplation when it is involved in the task of preparing and negotiating the documentation.

3.82 The question remains whether, in terms of the third of the criteria in *Caparo*, it would be fair, just, and reasonable to impose a duty of care upon the arranger acting in the second stage and, linked to that question, are the issues as to the scope of any duty that the arranger might owe to the lenders, and if it was reasonable for the lenders to place reliance upon the arranger in the role it undertook. It is convenient to take those various matters together, as they demonstrate collectively why it is unlikely that the arranger would be found liable in negligence. Almost invariably, the arranger distributes the documentation to the lenders in the form as negotiated with the borrower. The arranger asks the lenders for their comments on the documentation. The lenders will thus have been afforded the opportunity to review the documentation for themselves and to raise any queries or doubts that they may have following upon their own review. In relation to any commercial matters arising in the transaction, they will have been alerted to them by the term sheet and the other information distributed to the lenders and they should have been able to appreciate their significance when reading the documentation. In terms of the contents and legal enforceability of the documentation, the arranger will argue that the documentation (particularly the facility agreement itself) was largely based upon precedents commonly accepted in the London markets and that it instructed lawyers to prepare the documentation. So long as it instructed lawyers who were generally seen as being competent to fulfil their role in such transactions, the arranger had done all that reasonably could be expected of it within the scope of any duty it might have undertaken. In so far as the lawyers failed to perform their tasks, the lenders may have a claim against them. Otherwise, the lenders made their own decisions in deciding if they wished to proceed. Taking all these matters together, it can be seen that such duty as the arranger might have would be narrow in its scope and, in any event, it would be difficult for the lenders to establish that it was reasonable for them to place reliance upon the arranger. Once again, it is submitted that this view is consistent with accepted practice in the financial markets that operate in London.

3.4.4.2 A limited duty of care

3.83 Turning now to a claim based upon a more limited duty of care, the argument that might be raised is that even though the arranger may not have undertaken a wide duty of care towards the lenders, nonetheless in a more limited way the arranger had a duty of care, to one or more of the lenders, with respect to some specific task that it undertook or concerning some particular information that it supplied. In essence, the argument would be that the arranger accepted or assumed responsibility in that more limited manner. Such an argument is illustrated by four cases involving an arranger in which it was held that, in the circumstances, the arranger had assumed responsibility to the creditors.[160]

3.84 In the Australian case of *NatWest Australia Bank Ltd v Tricontinental Corp Ltd*[161] it was held that the arranger of a syndicated loan, in responding to a specific query raised by a bank that was to join the syndicate, had assumed a duty of care in the response that it gave to that bank, to ensure the accuracy of its reply. Prior to the query being made, the arranger had distributed an information memorandum which contained accounting and financial information concerning the borrower. The query that was raised by the bank concerned whether there were any contingent liabilities of the borrower, as there was no reference to any such liabilities in the information memorandum. The arranger responded that there were no such liabilities in existence, despite the fact that the arranger itself enjoyed the benefit of guarantees given by the borrower for the liabilities of another company connected to the borrower. In those circumstances, the court held that in giving its response to the bank, the arranger had assumed a duty of care towards the enquirer. It is interesting to note that the court said that, in the absence of such a specific request, a different conclusion might have been reached with respect to the possibility of a duty of care in relation to the contents of the information memorandum. Some care needs to be taken in relation to the outcome of the case, as the facts are rather extraordinary and are unlikely to arise very often, given that the arranger actually had information in its own possession which contradicted the response that it gave, and its response had the effect of denying something which already existed in its own favour. It would appear that the arranger purported to answer the specific query entirely of its own volition, without making any effort to check the accuracy of its response, without any apparent reference to the borrower for a response, and by giving the impression that it was providing the answer on its own account. In addition, it was held that the disclaimer of responsibility by the arranger contained in the information memorandum only related to the contents of that document, and it appears that there was no other attempt by the arranger to convey to the banks any limit on the role it had undertaken.

3.85 In the English case of *Sumitomo Bank Ltd v Banque Bruxelles Lambert SA*[162] the arranger put in place a mortgage indemnity insurance policy for the benefit of the

---

[160] These cases should be contrasted with *Raiffeisen Zentralbank Österreich AG v Royal Bank of Scotland plc* [2010] EWHC 1392 (Comm) where the arranger had successfully disclaimed responsibility for the information it had provided and was found to owe no wide or limited duties of care.

[161] McDonald J in the Supreme Ct of Victoria, 26 July 1993. Unreported on this issue but noted and reported on a different point at (1993) ATPR (Digest) 46–109. The relevant passages of the judgment on the matter under discussion are contained at pp 109–17 of the transcript.

[162] [1997] 1 Lloyd's Rep 487.

syndicate of banks, under which the insurer was meant to cover a certain amount of the deficiency that might arise after enforcement of security that was to be taken on behalf of the banks. When a claim was made under the policy, the insurer alleged that the policy had been avoided for the non-disclosure of a material fact by the arranger when the policy was incepted. The claim under the policy had to be compromised. The banks successfully claimed against the arranger for the loss they had suffered, in failing to receive full cover under the policy. Langley J held that the arranger had accepted or assumed a responsibility towards the syndicate with respect to the policy, when it had taken action in their interests in putting the policy in place for their benefit.

3.86 *Torre Asset Funding v RBS*[163] further illustrates the point that a limited duty of care, to one or more of the lenders, may be assumed on the facts with respect to some specific task or some particular information. There a bank (acting as a lender and a noteholder) wanted to secure the other lenders' consent to the rolling up of interest on a tranche in which it had an economic interest. It offered an inaccurate explanation for why the consent was being sought. Although the bank did not have an obligation to provide such information, it chose to do so and thereby assumed responsibility for the accuracy of the explanation given, and hence came under a limited duty of care.

3.87 In an appropriate case, it could also be argued that although in dealing with a counterparty the arranger owed no duty to explain the nature or effect of the proposed arrangement to that counterparty, if the arranger went further and provided explanations or tendered advice, then it came under a duty to give those explanations or tender that advice fully, accurately, and properly.[164] It could also perhaps be argued in a suitable case that the arranger had actually assumed a duty to provide adequate information for the lenders to make an informed decision in respect of the transaction.[165] This would be a duty less onerous than the duty to give advice but more onerous than a simple duty not to misstate.[166] However, this would require exceptional circumstances because generally a bank

---

[163] [2013] EWHC 2670 (Ch) [184]–[187]. Although this case and those cited in n 164 did not involve claims against arrangers (but rather against bank lenders), they are mentioned in this section because they provide good expositions of the principles that would apply in respect of analogous claims that could arise against arrangers.

[164] *Bankers Trust International plc v P T Dharmala Sakti Sejahtera* (No. 2) [1996] CLC 518, 533D–E; *Crestsign Ltd v National Westminster Bank plc* [2014] EWHC 3043 (Ch); *Wani LLP v The Royal Bank of Scotland plc, National Westminster Bank plc* [2015] EWHC 1181 (Ch); *Thornbridge Ltd v Barclays Bank plc* [2015] EWHC 3430 (QB).

[165] *London Executive Aviation v RBS* [2018] EWHC 74 (Ch).

[166] *Thomas v Triodos Bank NV* [2017] EWHC 314 (QB). Sometimes referred to as a 'mezzanine' duty. However, the Court of Appeal has stated that this label should be avoided as whenever such a duty is assumed it occurs on the established *Hedley Byrne* principles: *Property Alliance Group Ltd v Royal Bank of Scotland plc* [2018] EWCA Civ 355 [67].

contracting with another party owes no duty to explain the nature or effect of the transaction.[167]

A recent decision shows that an arranger may bear liability for aspects of a finan- **3.88** cing transaction to purchasers of participations in the secondary market. In *Golden Belt 1 Sukuk Co BSC(c) v BNP Paribas*,[168] BNP Paribas acted as the arranger of an Islamic financing transaction known as a sukuk (which is equivalent to a bond issuance). Repayment was secured by a promissory note governed by the laws of Saudi Arabia which an individual had purportedly signed. There was a default under the financing transaction. However creditors were not able to enforce the promissory note because the signatory had used a laser-printed signature, not a wet ink signature, rendering it unenforceable under Saudi law. Creditors who had purchased the sukuk certificates in the secondary market brought proceedings against the arranger alleging that it had failed to perform its duty to ensure the promissory note had been properly executed. The court found that the creditors were dependent on the bank for the proper execution of the promissory note and stated that the functions of an arranger 'invariably include responsibility for arranging the execution of the transaction documents'. Both the assumption of responsibility test and the threefold test were met. Consequently the arranger was held to have assumed responsibility to take reasonable care to ensure that the promissory note was properly executed. The arranger attempted to rely on a disclaimer in the offering circular, but the court held that it was not sufficient to exclude responsibility for the execution of documents.

3.4.5 A claim in the tort of deceit

Given the seriousness of such a claim it is to be hoped that the circumstances **3.89** where it may be alleged against an arranger will be very rare. For present purposes, a claim in deceit relates to a dishonestly untruthful statement that is made, usually in the context of the negotiations leading to a contract, so as induce the recipient of the statement to enter into the contract, provided that the recipient does rely upon it in deciding to enter into the contract.[169]

The grounds for dishonesty as a constituent of the claim were set out by Lord **3.90** Herschell in *Derry v Peek*[170] and can be advanced on any of three bases: first, that the maker of the false statement told a deliberate lie; secondly, that the maker of

---

[167] *Property Alliance Group Ltd v Royal Bank of Scotland plc* [2018] EWCA Civ 355 [66]. See also *Carney v NM Rothschild and Sons Ltd* [2018] EWHC 958 (Comm) and *Golden Belt 1 Sukuk Co BSC(c) v BNP Paribas* [2017] EWHC 3182 (Comm) [160].

[168] [2017] EWHC 3182 (Comm).

[169] Thus if the claimant knows that what he is being told is a lie, he is not deceived and has no claim: *Holyoake v Candy* [2017] EWHC 3397 (Ch) [388]. However, suspicions as to the truth of the representations will not necessarily have the same effect: *Hayward v Zurich Insurance Co plc* [2016] UKSC 48.

[170] (1889) 14 App Cas 337.

the false statement had no belief in the truth of the statement;[171] and thirdly that the maker of the false statement was reckless, that is, careless as to its truth or falsity.[172] The fact that the maker of the statement felt that he had some commercial justification in making the statement, or that it was unlikely that any harm would result, is no defence.[173] However, dishonesty lies at the heart of the tort of deceit and mere carelessness is not sufficient in itself to make out the claim.[174] If the maker of the statement honestly believes it to be true in the sense in which he understands it when it is made, he does not commit fraud.[175] It is not necessary to prove any intention to cheat or injure.[176]

3.91 In contrast to the position for a claim in negligence,[177] in *Standard Chartered Bank v Pakistan National Shipping Corp (No 2)*[178] the House of Lords held that an agent who makes a fraudulent or deceitful statement cannot hide behind his agency in a claim in deceit against him. He can be sued directly, even if he made the statement within the apparent course of his employment or retainer by the principal.

3.92 There is a heavy burden on the claimant in alleging a claim in deceit, as the claimant must prove a lack of honest belief on the part of the defendant, although the standard of proof is the same as in other civil claims.[179] Before a finding of fraud is made, it must be specifically pleaded with full particulars and put in cross-examination to the person said to be responsible for the fraud.[180] In

---

[171] It is difficult to know at what point it could be said that the maker of the statement might meet this test; for instance, whether a mere feeling of unease would be sufficient to say that there was a lack of belief, particularly in the case where the claim involved a statement made by a relatively junior person in an organisation who might be judged differently, in terms of knowledge and intention, from a more senior person under whose instructions he was acting: see the discussion on this point by Tugendhat J in *GE Commercial Finance Ltd v Gee* [2005] EWHC 2056 (QB), [2006] 1 Lloyd's Rep 337 [100]–[111]. This second ground was not mentioned by the Court of Appeal when it formulated a description of the tort in *Society of Lloyd's v Jaffray* [2002] EWCA Civ 1101 [49] and [62], nor was it mentioned by Potter LJ in *Twinsectra v Yardley* [1999] EWCA Civ 1290, [1999] 1 Lloyd's Rep Bank 438 [38]. In *Mortgage Express v Countrywide Surveyors Ltd* [2016] EWHC 224 (Ch) an employee valuer was found to have had no honest belief in the valuations he had made.

[172] Bowen LJ in *Angus v Clifford* [1891] 2 Ch 449, 471 said that carelessness in this context did not mean simply failing to take care. It meant 'indifference to the truth, the moral obliquity which consists in a wilful disregard of the importance of the truth'.

[173] *Standard Chartered Bank v Pakistan National Shipping Corp* [2000] 1 Lloyd's Rep 218 [2] and [3] (Evans LJ); *Jaffray v Society of Lloyd's* [2002] EWCA 1101 [66].

[174] See *Derry v Peek* (1889) 14 App Cas 337, 369 and 373 (Lord Herschell) and *Thomas Witter Ltd v TBP Industries Ltd* [1996] 2 All ER 573, 587 (Jacob J).

[175] *Akerhielm v De Mare* [1959] AC 789 (PC).

[176] *Foster v Charles* (1830) 7 Bing 105, 131 ER 40; *Derry v Peek* (1889) 14 App Cas 337 (HL) 374.

[177] As to which see *Williams v Natural Life Health Foods Ltd* [1998] 1 WLR 830 and the previous discussion at para 3.66.

[178] [2002] UKHL 43, [2003] 1 AC 959. See also *Yeeles v Benton* [2010] EWCA Civ 326.

[179] *Hornal v Neuberger Products Ltd* [1957] 1 QB 247.

[180] *Haringey LBC v Hines* [2010] EWCA Civ 1111 and *Property Alliance Group Ltd v Royal Bank of Scotland plc* [2015] EWHC 3272 (Ch) affd on appeal [2018] EWCA Civ 355.

addition, under the relevant code of conduct, lawyers may not plead fraud unless they have clear instructions to do so and have before them reasonably credible material to establish a prima facie case.[181] Furthermore, section 6 of the Statute of Frauds Amendment Act 1828 effectively provides that in a claim for fraudulent misrepresentation[182] relating to a representation as to the 'character, conduct, credit, ability, trade or dealings' of another person, which is intended to lead to the granting to that person (or his obtaining) credit, money, or goods, the representation must have been in writing signed by the maker of the statement.[183]

The remedies for deceit are rescission of the contract which was induced by the **3.93** misrepresentation and a claim for tortious damages.[184] However, the right to rescind can be lost, for instance because of delay, or because it is not possible to restore the parties to the position they were in before the contract, and/or because of the adverse effect of a rescission upon third parties.[185] Damages are at large and will be awarded for the whole loss suffered by the claimant in consequence of entering into the contract, whether the loss was foreseeable or unforeseeable.[186] A claimant has even been awarded damages to reflect the lesser profit it made after entering into a contract, as compared with the profit it would have made if the representation had been true.[187] The claimant may also be able to recover damages in respect of its loss of investment opportunity.[188]

3.4.6 A claim under section 2(1) of the Misrepresentation Act 1967

Section 2(1) of the Misrepresentation Act 1967 provides as follows: **3.94**

> Where a person has entered into a contract after a misrepresentation has been made to him by another party thereto and as a result thereof he has suffered loss, then, if the person making the misrepresentation would be liable to damages in respect

---

[181] The Code of Conduct of the Bar in England and Wales, r C9.2.c and the SRA Code of Conduct, IB(5.7). See further *Medcalf v Mardell* [2002] UKHL 27, [2003] AC 120.

[182] In *Banbury v Bank of Montreal* [1918] AC 626 it was held that the section was restricted to claims in fraudulent misrepresentation only. See, however, the Court of Appeal in *UBAF Ltd v European American Banking Corp* [1984] QB 713, where it was said that the section extended to claims for innocent misrepresentation under s 2(1) of the Misrepresentation Act 1967, because of the reference in s 2(1) to the circumstances in which a claim could be brought, had it been a claim for fraudulent misrepresentation. See also *LBI HF v Stanford* [2014] EWHC 3921 (Ch).

[183] *LBI HF v Stanford* [2014] EWHC 3921 (Ch).

[184] The claimant can recover damages in tort as well as rescind the contract: *Newbiggin v Adam* (1886) 34 ChD 582, 592. Although the rescission for deceit is *ab initio* (*Johnson v Agnew* [1980] AC 367), so that a claim for damages cannot be brought under the contract, the claim for damages is in tort which is independent of the contract.

[185] See *Thomas Witter Ltd v TBP Industries Ltd* [1996] 2 All ER 573, 588 (Jacob J). For detailed consideration of bars to rescission see Dominic O'Sullivan, Steven Elliott, and Rafal Zakrzewski, *The Law of Rescission* (2nd edn, OUP 2014).

[186] *Smith New Court Securities Ltd v Scrimgeour Vickers (Asset Management) Ltd* [1997] AC 254.

[187] *Clef Aquitaine SARL v Laporte Materials (Barrow) Ltd* [2001] QB 488.

[188] *Parabola Investments Ltd v Browallia Cal Ltd (formerly Union Cal Ltd)* [2010] EWCA Civ 486, [2011] QB 477.

thereof had the misrepresentation been made fraudulently, that person shall be so liable notwithstanding that the misrepresentation was not made fraudulently, unless he proves that he had reasonable ground to believe and did believe up to the time the contract was made that the facts represented were true.

3.95 The section was introduced to overcome the problem that at common law it was not possible to claim damages for an innocent misrepresentation.[189] Unless the representation had become a term of the contract, in which case a claim for damages would lie for breach,[190] the only remedy that was available at common law was rescission,[191] and the right to rescind could be easily lost, for instance, due to delay,[192] acquiescence, or affirmation,[193] that it was not possible to restore the parties to their pre-contractual position,[194] or where the representation had been incorporated into and become a term of the contract or the contract had been performed.[195] It is still necessary, however, to show that the representation was as to a matter of fact, as opposed to a statement of opinion, although the courts have been prepared in some instances to imply into a statement of opinion, for instance, as to a future intention, another statement that the opinion was genuinely held.[196]

3.96 It is fundamental to a claim for misrepresentation to show that a representation was made by the defendant, which was incorrect and upon which the claimant relied in deciding if it wished to enter into the contract.[197] If no such representation was made, there can be no success in claiming for misrepresentation.[198] This basic proposition is demonstrated by the decision of the Court of Appeal in *IFE Fund*

---

[189] *Heilbut, Symons & Co v Buckleton* [1913] AC 30.

[190] *Dick Bentley Productions Ltd v Harold Smith (Motors) Ltd* [1965] 1 WLR 623.

[191] It is very unlikely that rescission would be appropriate in any situation now under consideration as the claim of the lenders is based upon the fact that they have already lent their money and they are unable to recover it from the borrower. They are looking for a claim in damages against the arranger to recover the loss they have suffered having performed their part of the contract with the borrower.

[192] *Leaf v International Galleries* [1950] 2 KB 86. In that case, the delay prevented rescission even though the representee only discovered the true position shortly before it commenced proceedings.

[193] See *Peyman v Lanjani* [1985] Ch 457.

[194] At least in a substantial sense, if not precisely: see *Erlanger v New Sombrero Phosphate Co* (1878) 3 App Cas 1218, 1278–79 (Lord Blackburn). It has also been held that it is not possible to have a partial rescission: see the extensive review conducted by Colman J in *De Molestina v Ponton* [2002] 1 All ER (Comm) 587 [6.1]–[6.7], including his discussion, at [6.5]–[6.6], of the contrary decision of the High Court of Australia in *Vadasz v Pioneer Concrete (SA) Pty Ltd* (1995) 184 CLR 102 and the reference made to that case by the Privy Council in *Far Eastern Shipping Co Public Ltd v Scales Trading Ltd* [2001] 1 All ER (Comm) 319.

[195] S 1 of the Misrepresentation Act 1967 now provides for a right of rescission where the representation has become a term of the contract or the contract has been performed.

[196] *Edgington v Fitzmaurice* [(1885) 29 ChD 459.

[197] Mere silence is never sufficient: *Deslauriers and anor v Guardian Asset Management Ltd (Trinidad and Tobago)* [2017] UKPC 34.

[198] Furthermore, as a general rule, there is no duty to volunteer or disclose relevant information to a counterparty to a commercial contract: *Nextia Properties Ltd v Royal Bank of Scotland* [2013] EWHC 3167 (QB).

SA v Goldman Sachs International,[199] which concerned the arrangement of a syndicated facility.[200] In the information memorandum that was distributed by the arranger to the potential syndicate members, the arranger specifically stated that it made no representations concerning the truth or accuracy of the information contained in the information memorandum and disclaimed any responsibility to check such information or to correct it. It was held that this had the effect that what was stated in the information memorandum could not be treated or relied upon by the banks as being represented to them by the arranger.[201] The same conclusion was reached in relation to similar disclaimers included by an arranger in an information memorandum in *Raiffeisen Zentralbank Österreich AG v Royal Bank of Scotland plc*.[202]

As a general principle, the mere passing on of information might, depending on the context, not constitute a representation. For example, there would not be a representation where the recipient knows that the provider of the information is acting as a conduit. However, it will be a representation if the person passing it on adopts as his own statement of fact. It will also be a misrepresentation if he does not fairly set out the information (eg where he passes on parts of the information but omits material parts).[203]   **3.97**

A claim under section 2(1) can only be brought by a claimant which became a party to the contract in circumstances where the misrepresentation was made to it by another person who also became a party to the contract.[204] If the representor never became a party to the contract, the section will be unavailable unless it can be argued that the claimant and the defendant were parties to a collateral contract upon the strength of which the claimant entered into the principal contract, in which case there may be a claim in relation to the collateral contract.[205] Otherwise, the claimant will be thrown back on its causes of action, such as it may have, in some other area, such as for a negligent misstatement. The claimant will also be in difficulties if the representation was made by a person that was acting   **3.98**

---

[199] [2007] EWCA Civ 811.

[200] In fact, the syndication was of debt instruments, but that fact is not material to the point under discussion.

[201] The arranger did, however, concede that it had impliedly represented that it was acting in good faith in distributing the information memorandum to the potential syndicate members. The court said that it followed from such a representation that the arranger would be obliged to correct any information which had been distributed which it actually discovered (prior to syndication taking place) to be incorrect or misleading. However, it had no duty to inform the lenders if it merely became aware of the possibility that the information might be misleading or incorrect, as opposed to knowing that it was actually incorrect or misleading.

[202] [2010] EWHC 1392 (Comm). See text to n 319.

[203] *FoodCo UK LLP (t/a Muffin Break) v Henry Boot Developments Ltd* [2010] EWHC 358 (Ch) [218]; *Royal Bank of Scotland v O'Donnell* [2014] CSIH 84.

[204] *Taberna Europe CDO II plc v Selskabet (Formerly Roskilde Bank A/S) (In Bankruptcy)* [2016] EWCA Civ 1262

[205] See *Shanklin Pier Ltd v Detel Products Ltd* [1951] 2 KB 854.

as an agent for another person, provided the agent was acting within the scope of its authority on behalf of the principal. In such case, the statement should be treated as having been made by the principal, and the claimant will have to pursue its rights against the principal,[206] rather than the agent,[207] which will be of little comfort if the principal is not worth pursuing. This is obviously important in relation to the role of the arranger acting on behalf of the borrower in distributing information to the lenders.

3.99 The claimant must show that it was induced by the representation to enter into the contract and that it was incorrect. Those aspects were explored by Rix J in *Avon Insurance plc v Swire Fraser Ltd.*[208] The inducement must have played a 'real and substantial' part of the decision of the claimant to enter into the contract;[209] as opposed to something that was merely observed or considered, but had not supported or encouraged the decision. However, it need not be the sole or decisive inducement, so long as it materially contributed to the decision. A statement will be correct for these purposes if it is substantially correct, even though it may not be entirely correct.[210]

3.100 The defendant may argue that, although it had misrepresented the position, the misrepresentation had been corrected before the contract had been entered into by the parties. In such cases it is not enough for the representor to show that the recipient of the misrepresentation could have discovered the truth if it had made its own enquiries. The representor must show that the representee did discover the truth, either in consequence of a correction actually made by the representor which it had brought to the attention of the representee before contracting, or through enquiries made by the representee itself which revealed the true state of affairs before that date.[211]

3.101 It has also been said that a claim under section 2(1), in so far as it relates to a representation as to the 'character, conduct, credit, ability, trade or dealings' of a person must be in writing, as would be required for a claim in deceit, by virtue of section 6 of the Statute of Frauds Amendment Act 1828.[212]

---

[206] *Gosling v Anderson* (1972) 223 EG 1743.

[207] *The Skopas* [1983] 1 WLR 857.

[208] [2000] 1 All ER (Comm) 573 [14]–[18].

[209] *Taberna Europe CDO II plc v Selskabet (Formerly Roskilde Bank A/S) (In Bankruptcy)* [2015] EWHC 871 (Comm) revd on appeal on a different point [2016] EWCA Civ 1262.

[210] See also *With v O'Flanagan* [1936] Ch 575, 581; *Bonham-Carter v SITU Ventures Ltd* [2012] EWHC 3589 (Ch).

[211] *Redgrave v Hurd* (1881) 20 ChD 1; *Assicurazioni Generali v Arab Insurance Group* [2002] EWCA Civ 1642, [2003] 1 All ER (Comm) 140; *Flack v Pattinson* [2002] EWCA Civ 1762; *Peekay Intermark Ltd v Australia & New Zealand Banking Group Ltd* [2006] EWCA Civ 386, [2006] 2 Lloyd's Rep 511. For a relatively recent application of these principles see *Mortgage Express v Countrywide Surveyors Ltd* [2016] EWHC 224 (Ch).

[212] *UBAF Ltd v European American Banking Corp* [1984] QB 713.

If the claimant is able to make out its case that the representation was incorrect **3.102** and that it induced the claimant to enter into the contract, the burden then shifts under section 2(1) to the defendant which, if it is to escape liability, has to prove, first, that when it made the statement it had reasonable grounds to believe in the truth of the statement, and, secondly, that it continued in that belief up to the time the contract was entered into.[213] It is important to note that the defendant's belief must be based on reasonable grounds, which imports an element of objectivity and that a claim may lie under the section even though the representor may not have owed a duty of care to the representee with respect to the statement that was made,[214] although, practically speaking, the two may often coincide.

It was held by the Court of Appeal in *Royscott Trust Ltd v Rogerson*[215] that the **3.103** measure of damages for a claim under section 2(1) should be on the same basis as for a claim in the tort of deceit, namely, that the claimant should be put back in the financial position it would have been in if the contract had not been made.[216] Consequently, the claimant will usually be better off claiming damages under section 2(1) than in undertaking the more onerous burden of suing either in the tort of deceit or in the tort of negligence, which causes one to wonder whether section 2(1) was drafted as intended.

3.4.7 A claim under section 2(2) of the Misrepresentation Act 1967

Sections 2(2) and 2(3) of the Misrepresentation Act 1967 provide as follows: **3.104**

(2) Where a person has entered into a contract after a misrepresentation has been made to him otherwise than fraudulently, and he would be entitled, by reason of the misrepresentation, to rescind the contract, then, if it is claimed, in any proceedings arising out of the contract, that the contract ought to be or has been rescinded, the court or arbitrator may declare the contract subsisting and award damages in lieu of rescission, if of opinion that it would be equitable to do so, having regard to the nature of the misrepresentation and the loss that would be caused by it if the contract were upheld, as well as to the loss that rescission would cause to the other party.

(3) Damages may be awarded against a person under subsection (2) of this section whether or not he is liable to damages under subsection (1) thereof, but where he is so liable any award under the said subsection (2) shall be taken into account in assessing his liability under the said subsection (1).

---

[213] *Cassa di Risparmio della Repubblica di San Marino SpA v Barclays Bank Ltd* [2011] EWHC 484 (Comm).

[214] *Howard Marine and Dredging Co Ltd v A Ogden & Sons (Excavations) Ltd* [1978] QB 574.

[215] [1991] 2 QB 297.

[216] As to the measure of damages in a claim in deceit, see the decision of the House of Lords in *Smith New Court Securities Ltd v Citibank NA* [1997] AC 254. It should be noted that both Lord Browne-Wilkinson, at 267, and Lord Steyn, at 283, in the *Smith New Court* case declined to say if the *Royscott* case was correct on the issue of the measure of damages under s 2(1) of the Act.

3.105 As with section 2(1) of the Act, section 2(2) is concerned with a misrepresentation made by one person to another to induce that other to enter into the contract to which they both became parties. It will be of no avail if the necessary elements of representation, reliance, and falsity are not present, as previously discussed. Nor will the section be available as against an agent which made the misrepresentation within the scope of its agency. Section 2(2) gives the relevant tribunal a discretion to award damages but it does not give the representee a right to damages. The section also permits the representor to request the award of damages, within the discretion of the tribunal, in lieu of recission of the contract. The section only applies if the right to rescind continues to exist at the time of the proceedings; it is insufficient merely to show that at some time there was a right to rescind.[217] There is no defence of 'innocence' under section 2(2), so a claim under section 2(2) would be valuable to a representee which could not achieve an award of damages under section 2(1) in a case where the defence would apply under section 2(1). The tribunal has a discretion in making an award of damages under section 2(2), although it should take into account the relative difference between the loss that would be suffered by the representee if the contract were upheld as compared with the loss to the representor if the contract were rescinded.[218] It is also clear from section 2(3) that it is possible for the court to entertain claims under both section 2(1) and 2(2), although, by virtue of section 2(3), an allowance must be made in an award of damages under section 2(2) for any damages awarded under section 2(1). It has been suggested that the measure of damages under section 2(2) should normally be less than under section 2(1).[219]

3.4.8 A claim for breach of fiduciary duty

3.106 The final basis of claim that may be alleged against the arranger is that it was in the position of a fiduciary towards the lenders and that it breached its equitable fiduciary duties towards them in failing to act in their best interests, which would be a fairly broad basis of claim.[220] It is unlikely that such a claim would succeed as it is difficult to envisage how an arranger could be in such a position. Millett LJ defined a fiduciary as: 'Someone who has undertaken to act for or on behalf of another in a particular matter in circumstances which give rise to a relationship of trust and confidence. The distinguishing obligation of a fiduciary is the obligation of loyalty.'[221] His Lordship later expanded upon this when he said: 'Confidence is the very essence of the relationship. Unless a relationship is one of trust and confidence, it is not fiduciary. There are many commercial situations in which one man

---

[217] *Salt v Stratstone Specialist Ltd (t/a Stratstone Cadillac Newcastle)* [2015] EWCA Civ 745.
[218] See *Thomas Witter Ltd v TBP Industries Ltd* [1996] 2 All ER 573, 591 (Jacob J).
[219] ibid.
[220] See further the discussion in section 3.6.2.1 below.
[221] *Bristol & West Building Society v Mothew* [1998] Ch 1, 18.

undertakes to act for the benefit of another without any trust or confidence being reposed in him. In such a case there is no fiduciary relationship.'[222]

From those passages it can be seen that there must be an obligation of loyalty **3.107** owed by the fiduciary to its beneficiaries and that the latter must invest the fiduciary with their trust and confidence. In a commercial setting a mere obligation, if undertaken at all, by one person to act for the benefit of another or others will not be sufficient. As can be seen from the earlier discussion relating to a possible claim against an arranger in negligence, the elements of trust and confidence will be lacking. For most of what it does, the arranger is acting as the agent of the borrower, which can hardly be said to give rise to any obligation of loyalty towards the lenders. Even in the documentation stage of the arranger's functions, it is very unlikely that the arranger could be said to owe the lenders a duty of care, and, if it does, it is a very limited duty and there will still be a substantial question as to whether the lenders can reasonably place reliance upon the arranger. Taking those matters into account, it is submitted that an arranger should not be considered as being in the even more onerous position of a fiduciary towards the lenders.

It is submitted that the decision of the Court of Appeal in *UBAF Ltd v European* **3.108** *American Banking Corp*[223] does not alter the view expressed above. That case concerned interlocutory proceedings for leave to serve out of the jurisdiction, in a claim brought against an entity which had been the arranger of two syndicated loans and which became the agent bank (and the security trustee) for the syndicates of the banks. The proceedings had been brought by a bank in the syndicates for damages for fraudulent misrepresentation, for misrepresentation within section 2(1) of the Misrepresentation Act 1967, and for negligent misrepresentation. In considering the case, it is important to bear in mind that the defendant, which had acted as the arranger of the facilities, upon signature of the facility documentation was appointed by the banks as their facility and security agent, under which it took and then held security on behalf of the syndicates of banks. It was alleged that the defendant, when it had been the arranger, had misrepresented certain facts concerning the security, by concealment, so as to induce the claimant bank to enter into the facilities. In response, it was said by the defendant that the claim had been brought out of time so that it was barred by the Limitation Act 1980. It was held by the court that the limitation period had not begun to run until the claimant bank had discovered the concealment because the defendant, as the facility agent and trustee of the security on behalf of the banks, had been under a continuing fiduciary duty towards the claimant bank to divulge the relevant information during the lifetime of the facilities.

---

[222] *R v Chester and North Wales Legal Aid Area Office, ex p Floods of Queensferry Ltd* [1998] 1 WLR 1496, 1500.
[223] [1984] QB 713.

3.109 That finding, however, related to the defendant's alleged fiduciary position as the facility and security agent, which position it undertook once the facility documentation had been signed and under which it held security on behalf of the syndicates. If the defendant had never become the facility agent and security trustee, and its role had been confined to being merely the arranger of the facilities, then it would not have been in that position. Furthermore, even if it had been held that the arranger, as such, was in a fiduciary position in that case towards the banks that it invited to become members of the syndicates, that would not mean that the case should be taken as a general authority for the proposition that all arrangers of syndicated facilities should be considered to be in a fiduciary position towards the banks that they invite to become members of a syndicate. The facts of the case were unusual, in that the syndicated facility effected a re-financing of bilateral lending that the arranger had previously extended in its personal capacity to the borrowers. The arranger directly benefited from the re-financing arrangements, there was an allegation of fraud, and the arranger appears to have played the role of a principal rather than merely acting as the mouthpiece of the borrowers in arranging the new facilities.

3.4.9 Contributory negligence

3.110 A defence of contributory negligence, when it is available, may result in an award of damages against a defendant being reduced to take account of the claimant's own share of responsibility for the loss that arose. The defence would be raised under section 1(1) of the Law Reform (Contributory Negligence) Act 1945 which, so far as material, provides as follows:

> Where any person suffers damage as the result partly of his own fault and partly of the fault of any other person or persons, a claim in respect of that damage shall not be defeated by reason of the fault of the person suffering the damage, but the damages recoverable in respect thereof shall be reduced to such extent as the court thinks just and equitable having regard to the claimant's share in the responsibility for the damage.

Section 4 of the Act provides:

> 'Fault' means negligence, breach of statutory duty or other act or omission which gives rise to a liability in tort or would, apart from this Act, give rise to the defence of contributory negligence.

3.111 Section 1(1) applies to claims in tort, such as in negligence. It has been held, however, that it will not apply to a fraud claim or a claim for deceit.[224] The defence will apply to claims in contract where there would be a concurrent claim in tort,[225]

---

[224] *Standard Chartered Bank v Pakistan National Shipping Corp (No 2)* [2003] 1 AC 959. See also *Alliance & Leicester Building Soc v Edgestop Ltd* [1993] 1 WLR 1462.
[225] *Forsikringsaktieselskapet Vesta v Butcher* [1989] AC 852 and *UCB Bank plc v Hepherd Winstanley & Pugh* [1999] Lloyd's Rep PN 963, although a contrary view was taken in Australia in relation to similar legislation: *Astley v Austrust Ltd* [1999] Lloyd's Rep PN 758.

and to claims under section 2(1) of the Misrepresentation Act 1967[226] where there is concurrent liability for a negligent misrepresentation.[227] But even if there is such concurrent liability, it will need to be a 'very special case' before carelessness would make it just and equitable to reduce the damages otherwise payable in respect of such a claim.[228]

Where the defence is available, the court has a wide discretion to determine how much of a reduction should be made to the award of damages. The reduction should be to such an extent as the court believes to be 'just and equitable' in light of the responsibility of the claimant for the damage or loss that was suffered.[229] A failure to adhere to elementary banking principles may lead to a significant reduction of the damages that the lender may recover from the defendant.[230]   **3.112**

3.5 Protecting the Arranger

It is now appropriate to consider the protective steps that an arranger might consider taking, just in case there remains any risk that it may be held to have responsibilities towards the syndicate of lenders for the role it undertakes as the arranger. Having done that, it will then be relevant to consider how effective such steps will be as a matter of law, particularly in light of legislative restrictions upon exclusions or limitations of certain types of liability.   **3.113**

3.5.1 The means of protection

There are two levels of protection that an arranger will seek.   **3.114**

The first will be conveyed in written communications that it has with the lenders,[231] in which it will explain that it is acting at the request of the borrower in pursuance of a mandate granted to it by the borrower. The arranger will go on to   **3.115**

---

[226] Presumably the same would apply to the award of damages under s 2(2) of the Misrepresentation Act 1967.

[227] *Gran Gelato Ltd v Richcliff (Group) Ltd* [1992] Ch 560 and *Taberna Europe CDO II plc v Selskabet (Formerly Roskilde Bank A/S) (In Bankruptcy)* [2016] EWCA Civ 1262.

[228] *Gran Gelato Ltd v Richcliff (Group) Ltd* [1992] Ch 560, 574. This is because of the rule in *Redgrave v Hurd* (1881) 20 ChD 1 which provides that the maker of a misrepresentation cannot escape liability by claiming that the representee did not make use of an opportunity to discover the falsity of representation.

[229] *Platform Home Loans Ltd v Oyston Shipways Ltd* [2000] 2 AC 190; *Nationwide Building Society v Dunlop Haywards (DHL) Ltd (t/a Dunlop Heywood Lorenz)* [2009] EWHC 254 (Comm); *Bank of Ireland v Faithful & Gould Ltd* [2014] EWHC 2217 (TCC).

[230] *Lloyds Bank plc v McBains Cooper Consulting Ltd* [2018] EWCA Civ 452 where the lender's damages were reduced by two-thirds on account of its contributory negligence.

[231] A good example of this will be found in *IFE Fund SA v Goldman Sachs International* [2007] EWCA Civ 811. See also *Raiffeisen Zentralbank Österreich AG v Royal Bank of Scotland plc* [2010] EWHC 1392 (Comm) [65]. Appropriately worded standard terms or disclaimers may prevent a duty of care coming into existence at the first level.

explain that any information that it supplies has been prepared at the borrower's request and is based on information supplied by the borrower.[232] There is likely to be a statement that the arranger has not checked or verified any information supplied by the borrower, nor does it undertake to do so.[233] There is also likely to be an express statement that the arranger does not purport to act on behalf of the lenders or represent their interests, and a disclaimer of any responsibility on the part of the arranger towards the lenders.[234] This first level of intended protection will be extra-contractual,[235] but it will fall within the description of a 'notice' for the purposes of the Unfair Contract Terms Act 1977.[236]

3.116 The second level of protection will be contained in the syndicated facility agreement,[237] to which the arranger will be made a party for the purpose of gaining

---

[232] This makes it clear that the information is merely being passed on rather than represented as true facts. See para 3.97 above.

[233] *Raiffeisen Zentralbank Österreich AG v Royal Bank of Scotland plc* [2010] EWHC 1392 (Comm) [65]. Contrast *NatWest Australia Bank Ltd v Tricontinental Corp Ltd* (McDonald J in the Supreme Ct of Victoria, 26 July 1993. Unreported on this issue but noted and reported on a different point at (1993) ATPR (Digest) 46–109. The relevant passage of the judgment on the matter under discussion is at p 114 of the transcript) it was said that the disclaimer of responsibility in the information memorandum that the arranger distributed to the banks did not extend to cover the subsequent statement made by the arranger to the bank which raised a specific query with that arranger.

[234] An example of the effectiveness of such a provision in precluding the possible existence of a duty of care at common law for a negligent misstatement is to be found in *Hedley Byrne & Co Ltd v Heller & Partners Ltd* [1964] AC 465, in which it was held, on the facts, that there was an effective disclaimer of liability. Such a provision would now be subject to s 2(2) of the Unfair Contract Terms Act 1977.

[235] As it is extra-contractual, the effect of such a notice is that the reader is taken voluntarily to have assumed or assented to the risk of the loss and damage that might occur if it elects to proceed with the matter to which the notice relates or, to put the matter according to its traditional maxim, *Volenti non fit injuria*. The notice can only serve to protect a defendant if it can be shown that the claimant was aware of its contents and had a choice whether to proceed. If the claimant was obliged to proceed in any event, it could not be said voluntarily to have assumed or assented to the risk. See *McCawley v Furness Ry Co* (1872) LR 8 QB 57; *Buckpitt v Oates* [1968] 1 All ER 1145; *Bennett v Tugwell* [1971] 2 QB 267; *Birch v Thomas* [1972] 1 WLR 294; and *Burnett v British Waterways Board Ltd* [1973] 1 WLR 700. See also now the effect of s 2(3) of the Unfair Contract Terms Act 1977. In *Barclays Bank plc v Grant Thornton UK LLP* [2015] EWHC 320 (Comm) [89] an extra-contractual disclaimer in audit reports was found to preclude a duty of care arising and to satisfy the requirement of reasonableness under the Act. The effect of the disclaimer was that the claimant 'was being told expressly that it relied on the reports at its own risk'. See also *Taberna Europe CDO II plc v Selskabet (Formerly Roskilde Bank A/S) (In Bankruptcy)* [2016] EWCA Civ 1262 [16]–[22]. The Court of Appeal noted in that case that a non-contractual disclaimer may be overridden by the dealings between the parties, at [26].

[236] S 14 of the Act defines a notice to include: '[a]n announcement, whether or not in writing, and any other communication or pretended communication'. See *Taberna Europe CDO II plc v Selskabet (Formerly Roskilde Bank A/S) (In Bankruptcy)* [2016] EWCA Civ 1262.

[237] Usually within the agency clause, which is expressed in the relevant parts to be for the benefit of the arranger as well as the facility agent. Appropriately worded exclusions and limitations of liability may create a contractual estoppel or prevent a duty of care coming into existence: *Springwell Navigation Corp v JP Morgan Chase Bank (formerly Chase Manhattan Bank)* [2010] EWCA Civ 1221; *Titan Steel Wheels Ltd v Royal Bank of Scotland plc* [2010] EWHC 211 (Comm); *Raiffeisen Zentralbank Österreich AG v Royal Bank of Scotland plc* [2010] EWHC 1392 (Comm); *Standard*

the protection expressed to be given in its favour.[238] The wording of the relevant provisions in that document is likely to contain an explicit agreement or acknowledgement on the part of the lenders that the arranger owed no fiduciary or other types of duties or responsibilities towards them, as well as an exclusion of any liability that might otherwise attach to the arranger. There is also likely to be a clause by which the lenders confirm that, in deciding to enter into the agreement, they made their own enquiries and investigations, both as to factual matters and as to the meaning, scope, and contents of the facility documentation; that they did not receive,[239] nor rely upon,[240] any representations made by the arranger;[241] and that they did not otherwise rely upon the arranger in making their decision to proceed with the transaction.

3.5.2 Construction of the provisions

In considering the effect of such provisions, which are commonly referred to as exemption provisions or clauses, the first task is to determine their intended scope and meaning, as a matter of construction, to see if they cover the events as they have occurred. It is then necessary to consider if they are subject to any **3.117**

Chartered Bank v Ceylon Petroleum Corp [2011] EWHC 1785 (Comm); *Grant Estates Ltd v Royal Bank of Scotland plc* [2012] CSOH 133; *Avrora Fine Arts Investment Limited v Christie* [2012] EWHC 2198 (Ch); *Barclays Bank plc v Svizera Holdings BV* [2014] EWHC 1020 (Comm), [2015] 1 All ER (Comm) 788; *Crestsign Ltd v National Westminster Bank plc* [2014] EWHC 3043 (Ch); *Thornbridge Ltd v Barclays Bank plc* [2015] EWHC 3430 (QB); *Marz Limited v Bank of Scotland plc*[2017] EWHC 3618 (Ch); *London Executive Aviation Ltd v Royal Bank of Scotland* [2018] EWHC 74 (Ch).

[238] The importance of ensuring that these provisions are expressed to cover the arranger is demonstrated by *Sumitomo Bank Ltd v Banque Bruxelles Lambert SA* [1997] 1 Lloyd's Rep 487, in which it was held, at 493, that the protective provisions in the facility agreement were only intended to protect the agent in performing its role as the agent, rather than in also covering the role of the arranger prior to the establishment of the facility. This was despite the fact that the agent and the arranger were one and the same entity.

[239] Such a contractual acknowledgement that no representations have been made has come to be called a 'no representations' clause. Such clauses operate by giving rise to a contractual estoppel which prevents a party from arguing to the contrary: *Raiffeisen Zentralbank Österreich AG v Royal Bank of Scotland plc* [2010] EWHC 1392 (Comm) [267]; *Springwell Navigation Corp v JP Morgan Chase Bank* [2010] EWCA Civ 1221 [170].

[240] Such a contractual acknowledgement of non-reliance is usually called a 'non-reliance' clause and also operates on the basis of contractual estoppel: *FoodCo UK LLP (t/a Muffin Break) v Henry Boot Developments Ltd* [2010] EWHC 358 (Ch) [170]–[171]; *Thornbridge Ltd v Barclays Bank plc* [2015] EWHC 3430 (QB).

[241] In *Springwell Navigation Corp v JP Morgan Chase Bank* [2010] EWCA Civ 1221 the relevant terms that were given effect on the basis of contractual estoppel provided that 'no representation or warranty, express or implied, is or will be made by [the bank's entities], their representative officers, servants or agents or those of their associated companies in or in relation to such documents or information' and that 'the [counterparty] has not relied on and acknowledges that neither [of the bank's entities] has made any representations or warranty with respect to the advisability of purchasing this [instrument]'.

statutory qualifications as to their effectiveness, particularly under section 3 of the Misrepresentation Act 1967 and under the Unfair Contract Terms Act 1977.[242]

3.118 An exemption provision, by which a person seeks to avoid or restrict a liability or the consequences of such a liability, is likely to be construed fairly strictly, and the person relying upon the provision will have the burden of proving that the event which has happened falls within the provision;[243] but if the provision is expressed clearly and unambiguously, it will be read in accordance with its terms, and there is no reason why the wording should be given a strained or artificial meaning to avoid the exclusion or restriction of liability that it expresses.[244] If there is an ambiguity, the provision will be construed more stringently against the party who seeks to rely upon it.[245] In cases where there is an exception to the exemption, such as a provision which states that a party will not be liable for loss or damage arising from negligence 'except for wilful neglect or default', it is for the party which seeks to argue that the facts fall within the exception to prove that is the case.[246] But in the absence of such an exception to the exemption, it is unclear whether there is a rebuttable presumption that the exemption should not apply to a deliberate repudiatory breach of contract.[247] The so-called doctrine of

---

[242] Whilst it would not be relevant to the subject matter of this work, in contracts with consumers, it would also be necessary to consider such provisions in light of pt 2 of the Consumer Rights Act 2015.

[243] *Ailsa Craig Fishing Co Ltd v Malvern Fishing Co Ltd* [1983] 1 WLR 964, 969 and 970. For example, in *Golden Belt 1 Sukuk Co BSC(c) v BNP Paribas* [2017] EWHC 3182 (Comm) the arranger failed to show that the protective provisions included in the documentation disclaimed the particular duty of care that was found to have been breached.

[244] See *Photo Production Ltd v Securicor Transport Ltd* [1980] AC 827, 850–51 (Lord Diplock); *Transocean Drilling UK Ltd v Providence Resources plc* [2016] EWCA Civ 372; *Taberna Europe CDO II plc v Selskabet (Formerly Roskilde Bank A/S) (In Bankruptcy)* [2016] EWCA Civ 1262 [23]; and *Interactive E-Solutions JLT v O3B Africa Ltd* [2018] EWCA Civ 62 [14]. See also the discussion of contractual interpretation in section 1.2.8. In the light of this, there must be doubt about cases where it had been held that exemption clauses should be read down if they would otherwise be inconsistent with the main purpose of the contract (eg *Glynn v Margetson & Co* [1893] AC 351, 357), or if they absolved a party from all duties and liabilities. See *Swiss Bank Corp v Brink's Mat Ltd* [1986] 2 Lloyd's Rep 79, 93 (however, there may be difficulties with proving consideration if a contract absolves one party from all liability; 'to do so would be to reduce the contract to a mere declaration of intent': *Suisse Atlantique Société d'Armament SA v NV Rotterdamsche Kolen Centrale* [1967] 1 AC 361 (HL) 432). Similarly, it is submitted that the so-called 'four corners' rule, by which an exemption clause in a contract will only apply to liability falling within the four corners of the contract and not outside it (eg *Alderslade v Hendon Laundry Ltd* [1945] KB 189, 192), should really be confined to dealing with cases where, on a proper construction of the exemption provision, it was not intended to cover non-contractual liability.

[245] *Pera Shipping Corp v Petroship SA* [1984] 2 Lloyd's Rep 363, 366; *Transocean Drilling UK Ltd v Providence Resources plc* [2016] EWCA Civ 372; and *Nobahar-Cookson and ors v The Hut Group Ltd* [2016] EWCA Civ 128.

[246] *Kenyon Son & Craven Ltd v Baxter Hoare Ltd* [1971] 1 WLR 232. See paras 3.180 and 3.181ff.

[247] *Internet Broadcasting Corporation (trading as NetTV) v MAR LLC (trading as MARHedge)* [2009] EWHC 844; contrast *AstraZeneca UK Limited v Albemarle International Corporation* [2011] EWHC 1574. See also *Shared Network Services Ltd v Nextiraone UK Ltd* [2012] EWCA Civ 1171.

'fundamental breach', by which it had been said that if a contract was terminated for a repudiatory breach of contract then an exemption clause in the contract would also fall away and thus could not operate to relieve the party in breach from liability, has been held no longer to apply.[248]

It is possible for a provision to exclude or restrict liability for negligence if the   **3.119** wording that is used does so sufficiently clearly.[249] A clause that seeks to exclude liability for negligence altogether may be construed more strictly than one which only seeks to limit the damages that will be payable.[250] The approach to be taken in construing such provisions, so as to ascertain if the provision was intended to cover negligence, was summarised by Lord Morton in *Canada Steamship Lines Ltd v The King*[251] in which his Lordship set out three guidelines.[252] First, if the provision clearly exempts the defendant from negligence then effect must be given to it in accordance with its terms.[253] Secondly, if there is no express reference to negligence, the court must consider if the wording is wide enough, in its ordinary meaning, to cover negligence, with any doubt being resolved against the defendant. Thirdly, if the words are wide enough within the second guideline, the court must consider if the wording might be intended to cover some other head of damage or ground of liability apart from negligence,[254] but not if that would be so fanciful or remote as to fall outside the area of desired protection.[255] On the other hand, the courts will not permit a defendant to rely on an exclusion clause to protect it from its own fraud, as 'fraud unravels all'.[256]

---

[248] See *Photo Production Ltd v Securicor Transport Ltd* [1980] AC 827; *Ailsa Craig Fishing Co Ltd v Malvern Fishing Co Ltd* [1983] 1 WLR 964; and *George Mitchell (Chesterhall) Ltd v Finney Lock Seeds Ltd* [1983] 2 AC 803.

[249] An exclusion clause can cover both negligence and other matters: see *Photo Production Ltd v Securicor Transport Ltd* [1980] AC 827, 846 (Lord Wilberforce).

[250] See eg *Ailsa Craig Fishing Co Ltd v Malvern Fishing Co Ltd* [1983] 1 WLR 964, 970 and *George Mitchell (Chesterhall) Ltd v Finney Lock Seeds Ltd* [1983] 2 AC 803, 814.

[251] [1952] AC 192, 208.

[252] The Court of Appeal has made clear that the three principles should not be applied mechanically but only as 'guidelines'; they do not provide an automatic solution: *Mir Steel UK Ltd v Morris* [2012] EWCA Civ 1397 [35]. See also *Persimmon Homes Ltd v Ove Arup & Partners Ltd* [2017] EWCA Civ 373.

[253] For instance, 'At sole risk': *Rutter v Palmer* [1922] 2 KB 87; 'No liability of any nature': *HIH Casualty and General Insurance Ltd v Chase Manhattan Bank* [2003] UKHL 6, [2003] 2 Lloyd's Rep 61 [12]–[13]; 'Loss howsoever caused or arising': *Rutter v Palmer* [1922] 2 KB 87, 94, *White v Blackmore* [1972] 2 QB 651. However, it is still necessary to construe the wording in its context, and even wording which is superficially clear if taken on its own might, in context, not be as definite as appears at first sight.

[254] This was taken from Lord Greene MR in *Alderslade v Hendon Laundry Ltd* [1945] 1 KB 189, 192.

[255] See *Lamport & Holt Lines Ltd v Coubro & Scrutton (M&I) Ltd* [1982] 2 Lloyd's Rep 42, 50 (May LJ).

[256] See *HIH Casualty and General Insurance Ltd v Chase Manhattan Bank* [2003] UKHL 6, [2003] 2 Lloyd's Rep 61 [15]–[16] (Lord Bingham of Cornhill). His Lordship declined to determine if the same principle applied where the fraud was that of a party's agent, but he did say that, at the very least, clear wording would have to be used (see at [16]).

Fraud is usually expressly carved out from the scope of an exclusion clause.[257]

3.120 A similar approach has been taken towards clauses which seek to give a claimant an indemnity against the consequences of its own negligence, for instance if it becomes liable to a third party. Whilst there is a general inclination against construing such a provision as extending the indemnity to cover the consequences of negligence,[258] such an indemnity can be given if clear words are used and the three tests laid down by Lord Morton in *Canada Steamship Lines Ltd v The King*[259] will usually be applied.[260]

3.121 Contracts sometimes purport to extend the benefit of an exclusion clause to third parties, such as the servants or agents of a contracting party. There was previously a real difficulty at general law in achieving this as the doctrine of privity of contract would intervene to prevent the third party, which was not a party to the contract, from relying upon the provision or being able to enforce it.[261] There were, however, certain circumstances in which the protection of an exclusion clause might be enforced for the benefit of a third party, as, for instance, where an agent or trustee had contracted for the benefit of the third party.[262] A contract may also contain a promise by a party not to sue the servants or agents of the other party, and the latter should be able to prevent the promisor from breaching the contract if it sues the servants or agents.[263] It should be noted that at common law, two parties to a contract cannot impose the burden of an exclusion or limitation clause upon a third party that is a stranger to the contract.

3.122 The position at general law regarding privity of contract has been substantially affected by the Contracts (Rights of Third Parties) Act 1999,[264] although the Act

---

[257] However, construing the meaning of fraud in a carve out to an exclusion clause is often not simple, as *Interactive E Solutions JLT and anor v O3b Africa Ltd* [2018] EWCA Civ 62 demonstrates. It seems that such a reference will exclude claims where an allegation of fraud is a necessary ingredient; that is, causes of action where it is necessary to aver fraud will fall outside of such an exclusion clause.

[258] See *Smith v South Wales Switchgear Co Ltd* [1978] 1 WLR 165, 168. See also *Jose v MacSalvors Plant Hire Ltd* [2009] EWCA Civ 1329.

[259] [1952] AC 192, 208.

[260] *Smith v South Wales Switchgear Co Ltd* [1978] 1 WLR 165 and *Transocean Drilling UK Ltd v Providence Resources plc* [2016] EWCA Civ 372.

[261] See eg *Scruttons Ltd v Midland Silicones Ltd* [1962] AC 446; *Cosgrove v Horsfall* (1945) 62 TLR 140; and *Genys v Matthews* [1966] 1 WLR 758. See, generally, the discussion of this issue in section 1.2.7.

[262] See *New Zealand Shipping Co Ltd v AM Satterthwaite & Co Ltd (The Eurymedon)* [1975] AC 154 and *Port Jackson Stevedoring Pty Ltd v Salmond and Spraggon (Australia) Pty Ltd (The New York Star)* [1981] 1 WLR 138. Clauses under which a party to a contract has acted as an agent in obtaining protection for a third party, when used in a contract for the carriage of goods by sea, are often referred to as 'Himalaya clauses' after the name of the ship that was involved in *Adler v Dickson* [1955] 1 QB 158.

[263] *Snelling v John G Snelling Ltd* [1973] QB 87.

[264] Which applies to contracts made after 11 May 2000 (s 10(2) of the Act). As to the operation of the Act see, generally, para 1.39.

does not detract from any right that a third party may have at general law[265] so that if, for some reason, the third party cannot avail itself of the Act, it might still be able to fall back on one of the limited exceptions that applied at general law to the doctrine of privity of contract.[266] The Act provides that a third party which is intended to benefit from a provision of a contract[267] will be able to enforce the contract in its own right, unless on a proper construction it is apparent that the third party is precluded by the contract from doing so.[268] The Act makes it clear that the third party has the right to enforce an exclusion or limitation clause that was intended for its benefit,[269] but that right is itself subject to any restriction on the operation of such a clause that might arise by virtue of other legislation, such as the Unfair Contract Terms Act 1977.[270] However, if a third party wishes under the Act to enforce a positive obligation in its favour in the contract, its right to do so will be subject to any limitations on that right that are imposed by the contract, such as a limitation or exclusion of liability for breach of the contract that is contained in the contract for the benefit of the promisor.[271]

3.5.3 Legislative limitations upon exclusions or restrictions of liability or for damages

It is now relevant to turn to the statutory provisions that limit the effectiveness **3.123** of purported attempts to exclude or restrict liability (or the damages which flow from liability) for a tortious act, including for misrepresentation, or for a breach of contract. The two relevant pieces of legislation that will be examined are the Unfair Contract Terms Act 1977 and section 3 of the Misrepresentation Act 1967 (as amended).[272]

---

[265] S 7(1).

[266] In addition, in *Nisshin Shipping Co Ltd v Cleaves & Co Ltd* [2003] EWHC 2602 (Comm) it was held that a third party could avail itself of the Act even though at general law the contract might have been enforceable for its benefit under a trust in its favour.

[267] Ie it is expressly named as being entitled to enforce the provision, it is a member of an identified class of intended beneficiaries, or if it answers a particular description, even if it was not in existence at the time of the contract: s 1(3).

[268] S 1(2); a standard provision excluding the operation of the Act was applied in *Linnett v Halliwells LLP* [2009] EWHC 319 (TCC). In *Nisshin Shipping Co Ltd v Cleaves & Co Ltd* [2003] EWHC 2602 (Comm), it was held that the third party will be entitled to enforce the term for its own benefit unless the right to do so was contrary to the intention of the parties in the contract. Thus, if the contract is neutral on the point, s 1(2) will not operate against the third party.

[269] S 1(6). Where the contract contains an arbitration clause, see *Fortress Value Recovery Fund I LLC v Blue Skye Special Opportunities Fund LP* [2013] EWCA Civ 367.

[270] S 3(6).

[271] S 3(1)–(5). It would also appear that the provisions of the Unfair Contract Terms Act 1977 (except for s 2(1)) would not affect the rights of the promisor under ss 3(1)–(5).

[272] It is not intended here to deal with the Consumer Rights Act 2015 for, as the name implies, the provisions of the legislation will not be relevant to the types of situations that are the subject of this chapter.

3.5.4 The Unfair Contract Terms Act 1977

3.124 Despite its rather general sounding name, the Unfair Contract Terms Act 1977 has a more limited scope of application, as it does not really purport to deal with contractual unfairness in a general sense. On the other hand, it is wider in another aspect, in that it also applies to non-contractual notices in so far as they relate to negligence. It applies to attempts to exclude or restrict liability for loss or damage arising in the tort of negligence or for breach of an occupier's duty of care or in consequence of a breach of contract, and it also applies to attempts in a contract to excuse or modify performance of a party's obligations under that contract. The scheme of the Act is as follows. Part I of the Act deals with matters arising under English law and some of the provisions in Part I will be relevant in a consideration of the position of an arranger. Part II of the Act concerns matters of Scottish law, which will not be addressed in this work. Part III of the Act, together with the Schedules to the Act, are relevant to Part I and will also be mentioned. The matters that are covered in Part I concern liability in negligence, attempts to exclude or modify contractual obligations, and contracts relating to the sale or supply of goods.[273] Of those matters, the provisions concerning liability in negligence will be relevant to a consideration of the position of an arranger and will be dealt with later. It will also be relevant at a later stage in this chapter to revert to the provisions of Part I when considering the position of a facility agent. The provisions of Part I are also relevant in a consideration of equipment finance.[274]

3.125 With one limited exception,[275] Part I of the Act applies only to a 'business liability', that is, a liability arising in the course of a business.[276] There are a number of exceptions to the operation of Part I, as provided for in section 1(2) and set out in Schedule 1 (for example, with respect to contracts concerning insurance, interests in land, intellectual property rights, corporate matters, the creation or transfer of securities, employment contracts, and maritime and aircraft matters). There is also an exception for international supply contracts for the supply of goods.[277] It is further provided that Part I of the Act will not apply to a contract that is governed by English law if, but for the choice of law, the contract would be governed by the law of some place outside the UK.[278] On the other hand, it is also provided

---

[273] Provisions of the Act extending to consumers have been repealed and replaced by the Consumer Rights Act 2015.

[274] See Sarah Paterson and Rafal Zakrzewski (eds), *McKnight, Paterson, & Zakrzewski on the Law of International Finance* (2nd edn, OUP 2017) ch 15.

[275] Under s 6(4), the provisions of s 6 (which applies to implied undertakings as to title in contracts for the sale of goods or in hire-purchase agreements), apply with respect to any liability under the relevant contracts or agreements, irrespective of whether or not the liability is a business liability.

[276] S 1(3). A 'business' is defined in s 14 to include '[a] profession and the activities of any government department or local or public authority'.

[277] S 26. See further *Amiri Flight Authority v BAE Systems plc* [2003] EWCA Civ 1447, [2003] 2 Lloyd's Rep 767 and *Trident Turboprop (Dublin) Ltd v First Flight Couriers Ltd* [2009] EWCA Civ 290, [2010] QB 86.

[278] S 27(1).

that if a contract is expressed to be governed by some other law and it appears that the choice of the foreign law has been chosen to evade the operation of the Act, nonetheless the Act will apply.[279]

In considering whether a contractual provision or a notice has the effect of excluding or restricting a liability or a contractual obligation, the court will be concerned with its substance and not just its mere form.[280] This approach is also consistent with section 13(1) of the Act which provides that to the extent that Part I of the Act prevents the exclusion or restriction of any liability it also prevents: **3.126**

(a) making the liability or its enforcement subject to restrictive or onerous conditions;[281]
(b) excluding or restricting any right or remedy in respect of the liability, or subjecting a person to any prejudice in consequence of his pursuing any such right or remedy;[282]
(c) excluding or restricting rules of evidence or procedure.

Section 13(1) goes on to provide that, to the same extent, Part I of the Act also prevents an exclusion or restriction of liability by reference to terms and notices which exclude or restrict the relevant obligation or duty from arising in the first place. This would be relevant to a provision which purports to preclude a duty or obligation (as opposed to a liability for a breach of duty or an obligation) from arising at all as, for instance, by the insertion of a provision which contains a disavowal of responsibility or liability of the type that was used in *Hedley Byrne & Co Ltd v Heller & Partners Ltd*.[283]

3.5.4.1 Liability in negligence

Section 2 of the Act deals with attempts by a contractual term or a notice to exclude or restrict a liability for negligence. A 'notice' includes 'an announcement, **3.127**

---

[279] S 27(2). See *Kingspan Environmental Ltd v Borealis A/S* [2012] EWHC 1147 (Comm).

[280] See *Johnstone v Bloomsbury Health Authority* [1992] QB 333, 346 (Stuart-Smith LJ).

[281] For instance, subjecting the making of a claim to a time-limit.

[282] For instance, by precluding the exercise of a right of set-off: *Stewart Gill Ltd v Horatio Myer & Co Ltd* [1992] QB 600; *AXA Sun Life Services plc v Campbell Martin Ltd* [2011] EWCA Civ 133; *United Trust Bank Limited v Dalmit Singh Dohil* [2011] EWHC 3302 (QB); *Deutsche Bank SA v Khan* [2013] EWHC 482 (Comm); and *African Export-Import Bank v Shebah Exploration & Production Company and ors* [2017] EWCA Civ 845 but see also *Governor & Co of the Bank of Scotland v Singh* (HHJ Kershaw QC, sitting in the High Court in Manchester, 17 June 2005). Note, however, that s 13(3) provides that a written submission to arbitration is not to be treated as an exclusion or restriction of any liability.

[283] [1964] AC 465. See further *Smith v Eric S Bush* [1990] 1 AC 831, 857 (Lord Griffiths) and 873 (Lord Jauncey). Lord Griffiths referred to a 'but for' test, ie that, but for the exclusion, a liability would have arisen. It is submitted that the approach taken by the Court of Appeal on this aspect in *IFE Fund SA v Goldman Sachs International* [2007] EWCA Civ 811 was incorrect. In that case, the court said that an express disclaimer of liability had the same effect as in the *Hedley Byrne* case, that is, it meant that no liability could arise in the first place, because the defendant had disclaimed any acceptance of responsibility from arising. The *Hedley Byrne* case, of course, was decided long before the 1977 Act was passed. There was no reference in the *IFE* case to s 13 of the Act.

whether or not in writing, and any other communication or pretended communication'.[284] It would include a disclaimer of liability by an arranger in communications if sent to the potential syndicate members.[285]

3.128 'Negligence' is defined by section 1(1) to mean the breach:

(a) of any obligation, arising from the express or implied[286] terms of a contract, to take reasonable care or exercise reasonable skill in the performance of a contract;
(b) of any common law duty to take reasonable care or exercise reasonable skill (but not any stricter duty);
(c) [the statutory duty of care imposed upon occupiers of land].

3.129 It is doubtful if the definition of negligence includes the duty of care and skill that is imposed upon fiduciaries,[287] even though it is of much the same standard as that which arises in tort[288] or under section 13 of the Supply of Goods and Services Act 1982. The duty of care and skill of a fiduciary arises in equity, in consequence of the relationship of trust and confidence between the fiduciary and its beneficiary, independently of the common law or any contract.[289] This will be relevant in considering the position of the agent, which is discussed later in this chapter.

3.130 Section 2(3) provides that a person's knowledge or awareness of a contract term or notice which purports to exclude or restrict liability for negligence is not of itself to be taken as an indication of that person's voluntary acceptance of any risk.

3.131 Section 2(1) deals with the liability that would arise for death or personal injury resulting from negligence, which cannot be excluded or restricted in any circumstances. It is very unlikely that an arranger would be involved in a situation giving rise to such a liability and nothing further will be said here about section 2(1).

3.132 Section 2(2) deals with attempts by a contract term or notice to exclude or restrict liability for any other type of loss or damage resulting from negligence and would be relevant to an attempt by an arranger to protect itself from the consequences of its negligence. Section 2(2) provides that a person cannot exclude or restrict his liability for negligence except in so far as the contractual term or notice satisfies 'the requirement of reasonableness', as set forth in section 11. It should be noticed that it is the term or notice which has to satisfy the requirement of reasonableness, not the application of the term to the particular facts of a case. Section 2 will

---

[284] S 14.
[285] For an analogous situation where a disclaimer notice was included in a presentation which was disseminated, see *Taberna Europe CDO II plc v Selskabet (Formerly Roskilde Bank A/S) (In Bankruptcy)* [2016] EWCA Civ 1262.
[286] Eg by virtue of s 13 of the Supply of Goods and Services Act 1982.
[287] See the discussion on the point by Tuckey LJ in *Baker v JE Clark & Co (Transport) Ltd* [2006] EWCA Civ 464 [18]–[21].
[288] See *Henderson v Merrett Syndicates Ltd* [1995] 2 AC 145, 204–05 (Lord Browne-Wilkinson) and *Bristol & West Building Society v Mothew* [1998] Ch 1, 16–17 (Millett LJ).
[289] See further later in the chapter.

not, however, apply to a term by which one party agrees to indemnify another party for loss suffered by third parties in consequence of the indemnified party's negligence.[290]

3.5.4.2 *Liability arising in contract*

Section 3 of the Act provides that, where a contracting party is dealing on the other party's standard terms of business, that other party cannot by a contractual term exclude or restrict his own liability for breach of the contract, nor purport in pursuance of such a term to render no performance at all or to render a substantially different performance from what was reasonably to be expected under the contract,[291] except in so far as the term satisfies the requirement of reasonableness in section 11. **3.133**

It is difficult to see how section 3 could apply with respect to any possible liability of the arranger to the lenders, as such a liability would not arise from a breach of contract between them but from the arranger's pre-contractual activities, unless any contractual relationship between them related back to such activities. However, as the question must later be discussed concerning the possible liability of the facility agent to the lenders, it is convenient to consider section 3 within the present discussion relating to the Act.[292] There are, for instance, provisions in a syndicated facility agreement (particularly in the agency clause) which have the effect of limiting or excluding the possible liability of the agent for defective performance of its obligations and other provisions which either excuse it from having to perform and observe the obligations that might otherwise be expected of it or which modify those obligations. In that sense, the spirit of section 3 might be engaged. **3.134**

The section only applies if the party relying upon those provisions (that is, the agent) is dealing on its written standard terms of business.[293] At one stage, syndicated facility documentation was individually prepared and negotiated. There were no standard forms. More recently, however, recommended forms of syndicated facility documentation have become very common in the London market, particularly those put forward by the LMA. It has been held that the use of a **3.135**

---

[290] *Thompson v T Lohan (Plant Hire) Ltd* [1987] 1 WLR 649.

[291] See eg *Purnell Secretarial Services Ltd v Lease Management Services Ltd* [1994] Tr LR 337.

[292] S 3 will also be relevant when considering attempts by financiers to escape liability under claims relating to equipment financing transactions, as in the *Purnell* case.

[293] The phrase 'on the other's written standard terms of business' was deliberately not defined in the Act: *British Fermentation Products Ltd v Compair Reavell Ltd* [1999] BLR 352. In *Salvage Association v CAP Financial Services Ltd* [1995] FSR 654 (revd in part on unrelated points by the Court of Appeal on 9 July 1993), at 671 Judge Thayne Forbes QC enumerates the factors to be taken into account when determining whether a party dealt on its standard terms of business. See also *Yuanda (UK) Co Ltd v WW Gear Construction* [2010] EWHC 720 [26] and *Commercial Management (Investments) Limited v Mitchell Design and Construct Limited, Regorco Limited* [2016] EWHC 76 (TCC).

standard form put forward by a trade association or a similar body can be treated as being a party's standard terms of business if that party 'invariably or at least usually' contracts on those terms.[294] However, the usual rounds of amendments of facility documentation based on the LMA recommended form would very likely take the matter outside of section 3.[295] Material adaptation of preferred terms to a particular situation has been held not to be 'dealing' on standard terms.[296] Some courts have also expressed a view that 'written standard form' suggests pre-printed contract forms or terms displayed on a website rather than preferred terms proffered by a party as a starting point for negotiations.[297] Nonetheless it is a matter of fact in each case whether the finance parties dealt on written standard terms.[298] It has been held that there could still be standard terms of business where there had been some negotiation of the provisions of a contract, if the terms remained effectively the same.[299] But the presence or absence of negotiations is not itself conclusive.[300] A particular clause or a severable part of a contract—which may even have been tagged by a party or its advisors as 'non-negotiable' in negotiations relating to other terms—could be treated as falling within the section, with the remainder of the agreement falling outside it.[301]

3.136 Whilst there will often be negotiation of the provisions of a facility agreement dealing with commercial matters, it is unusual for the provisions of the agency clause in a syndicated facility agreement to be negotiated and they are usually accepted without dissent. Accordingly, there must be some risk that the provisions on which the agent relies might be held to be its written standard terms of business if the document is based upon the commonly used recommended forms.

---

[294] *British Fermentation Products Ltd v Compair Reavell Ltd* [1999] 2 All ER (Comm) 389 [46]; *SKNL (UK) Ltd v Toll Global Forwarding* [2012] EWHC 4252 (Comm).

[295] *African Export-Import Bank v Shebah Exploration and Production Co Ltd* [2017] EWCA Civ 845.

[296] *Flamar Interocean Ltd v Denmac Ltd* [1990] 1 Lloyd's Rep 434, 438; *Yuanda (UK) Co Ltd v WW Gear Construction* [2010] EWHC 720 [22], [26], and [29].

[297] *Hadley Design Associates v Westminster* [2003] EWHC 1617 (TCC) [78]; *Yuanda (UK) Co Ltd v WW Gear Construction* [2010] EWHC 720 [21]. Contrast *Commercial Management (Investments) Limited v Mitchell Design and Construct Limited, Regorco Limited* [2016] EWHC 76 (TCC) [21].

[298] *Salvage Association v CAP Financial Services Ltd* [1995] FSR 654, 671; evidence of documentation in respect of other transactions is relevant in this regard: *Yuanda (UK) Co Ltd v WW Gear Construction* [2010] EWHC 720 [29].

[299] Nourse LJ held in *St Albans City and District Council v International Computers Ltd* [1996] 4 All ER 481, 491 that it was a question of fact whether there had been a dealing, ie a contracting, on one of the party's standard terms and that there could still be standard terms even if there had been prior negotiations, so long as the terms remained effectively untouched by the negotiations. See also *African Export-Import Bank v Shebah Exploration and Production Co Ltd* [2017] EWCA Civ 845 where it was held that a model form must be habitually used for it to constitute standard terms.

[300] *St Albans City and District Council v International Computers Ltd* [1996] 4 All ER 481 (CA) 490; *Yuanda (UK) Co Ltd v WW Gear Construction* [2010] EWHC 720 [26].

[301] The 'standard form' requirement was held to be applicable to part of a contract in *Pegler Ltd v Wang (UK) Ltd (No 1)* [2000] BLR 218 [72]–[73]; *Fillite (Runcorn) Ltd v APV Pasilac Ltd* (1995) (CA, 26 January 1995); *Commercial Management (Investments) Limited v Mitchell Design and Construct Limited, Regorco Limited* [2016] EWHC 76 (TCC).

But such an argument—raised by the borrower in respect of a clause which prohibited set-off—was rejected in *African Export-Import Bank v Shebah Exploration & Production Company and ors*.[302] There was no basis for inferring that the lenders habitually put forward the LMA form as the basis for their lending transactions or that they always refused to negotiate its terms or refused to do so in the present case.[303] In fact some changes proposed on the borrower's behalf had been accepted. The Court of Appeal held that:

> [the] requirement that the term is part of the other party's standard terms of business means that it has to be shown that that other party habitually uses those terms of business. It is not enough that he sometimes does and sometimes does not. Nor is it enough to show that a model form has, on the particular occasion, been used; the party relying on the Act has to show that such model form is habitually used by the other party.[304]

There was no requirement that negotiations had to relate to the exclusion terms of the contract (such as, in this case, the no set-off clause) for the Unfair Contract Terms Act not to apply.[305]

However, if in an appropriate case provisions were found to be the agent's standard terms of business then it would fall to be considered whether the relevant provisions satisfy the requirement of reasonableness. **3.137**

3.5.4.3 *The requirement of reasonableness*

Section 11 of the Act provides for the 'reasonableness test', that is, the test for meeting the requirement of reasonableness as referable to various provisions of the Act, such as sections 2(2) and 3, and also as referable to section 3 of the Misrepresentation Act 1967, to which further reference is made later. The party relying upon the contract term or notice has the onus of showing that the requirement of reasonableness has been met.[306] The absence of an explanation for why a particular clause was included may lead the court to conclude that it is not reasonable for the purposes of the Act.[307] **3.138**

With respect to a contract term, section 11(1) provides that the test is whether: **3.139**

> The term shall have been a fair and reasonable one to be included having regard to the circumstances which were, or ought reasonably to have been, known to or in the contemplation of the parties when the contract was made.

---

[302] [2017] EWCA Civ 845.

[303] However, that possibility was left open in a suitable case, ibid [37]. The court also noted that the party asserting that a transaction was on standard business terms had to produce some evidence that this was the case. The lender did not need to disclose the terms of other transactions it had entered into before it would be entitled to obtain summary judgment.

[304] ibid [20].

[305] ibid [36].

[306] S 11(5).

[307] *AXA Sun Life Services plc v Campbell Martin Ltd* [2011] EWCA Civ 133 [75].

3.140 It is the incorporation of the term in the contract that must satisfy the requirement of reasonableness. The relevant time to assess if that requirement has been
met is the time of contracting, so it is not relevant to judge the matter at the time
of a later breach of duty or by reference to the way the term has operated in relation to the specific facts of the case[308] except, perhaps, if those facts should have
been in the parties' contemplation when the contract was made. The relevant circumstances must have been known to or in the contemplation of both of the parties, not just the party seeking to rely upon the clause. The question to be decided
is whether the term as a whole is fair and reasonable. The term cannot be severed
so that a reasonable part is enforced whilst an unreasonable part is struck down.[309]

3.141 Section 11(2) provides certain guidelines, which are set out in Schedule 2 to the
Act, to which regard may be had in assessing the reasonableness of a term. Whilst
the guidelines, strictly speaking, are expressed only to apply to sections 6 and 7 of
the Act,[310] they are generally taken as being relevant in providing guidance as to
the application of the reasonableness test in relation to other provisions of the Act
as well.[311] Not all of the guidelines would be relevant in considering the position
of an arranger and the syndicate members, but the following two might be relevant: (a) the strength of the relative bargaining positions of the parties, taking into
account alternate means by which a claimant's requirements could have been met;
and (b) whether a party knew or should have known of the relevant provision,
taking into account market practice and previous dealings between the parties.[312]

3.142 For a notice that is not part of a contract, the test of reasonableness is contained
in section 11(3), namely:

> That it should be fair and reasonable to allow reliance on [the notice], having regard
> to all the circumstances obtaining when liability arose or (but for the notice) would
> have arisen.[313]

The relevant time in this instance is when the liability arose and, in contrast to
section 11(1), the test is judged with respect to all of the circumstances at the
time rather than by reference to the circumstances which were or should have
been known to the parties, as would be the case under section 11(1). Thus, under

---

[308] See *Stewart Gill Ltd v Horatio Myer & Co Ltd* [1992] QB 600, 608 (Stuart-Smith LJ).

[309] *Stewart Gill Ltd v Horatio Myer & Co Ltd* [1992] QB 600, 607–09; *Lobster Group Ltd v
Heidelberg Graphic Equipment Ltd* [2009] EWHC 1919 (TCC) [131].

[310] And they are not an exhaustive list: see eg the further tests outlined by Potter LJ in *Overseas
Medical Supplies Ltd v Orient Transport Services Ltd* [1999] 2 Lloyd's Rep 273, 276–77. Clarity is a
relevant factor but the fact that the relevant terms are prolix does not necessarily mean that they will
be found to be unreasonable: *Camerata Property Inc v Credit Suisse Securities (Europe) Ltd* [2011]
EWHC 479 (Comm) [170] and [187].

[311] See *Stewart Gill Ltd v Horatio Myer & Co Ltd* [1992] QB 600, 608 (Stuart-Smith LJ); *Avrora
Fine Arts Investment Ltd v Christie, Manson & Woods Ltd* [2012] PNLR 35 [149].

[312] *AXA Sun Life Services plc v Campbell Martin Ltd* [2011] EWCA Civ 133 [59]–[61].

[313] For an application of this section see *Barclays Bank plc v Grant Thornton UK LLP* [2015]
EWHC 320 (Comm) [65]–[91].

section 11(3), the court may take into account the defendant's conduct as a relevant circumstance, whereas under section 11(1), such conduct would only be relevant as a possible example of something that might have been contemplated by the parties at the time of contracting.

Section 11(4) makes provision for contractual terms or notices which seek to re-   **3.143** strict the liability of a person to a specified sum of money, in which case regard should be had to the resources that the person could have expected to be available to him to meet the liability if it arose and how far it was open to him to obtain insurance cover.[314]

The position as to reasonableness will vary from one set of circumstances to an-   **3.144** other, so the decisions in the cases which depend on factual matters must be regarded with caution. However, in general the courts have been reluctant to intervene and hold unreasonable a provision which excludes or restricts the liability of a person in situations involving experienced commercial parties of equal bargaining power and adequate resources. They have regarded such provisions as representing an agreed allocation of risk in which the courts should not interfere. Chadwick LJ said in *Watford Electronics Ltd v Sanderson CFL Ltd*:[315]

> Where experienced businessmen representing substantial companies of equal bargaining power negotiated an agreement, they may be taken to have had regard to the matters known to them. They should, in my view, be taken to be the best judges of the commercial fairness of the agreement which they have made; including the fairness of each of the terms of that agreement.[316]

In the light of statements such as that of Chadwick LJ, it would be unlikely that   **3.145** a court would hold to be unreasonable protective provisions aimed at protecting the arranger from liability towards the syndicate members for negligence arising from a wide duty of care, whether in notices contained in materials sent out by the arranger to the lenders prior to the execution of the facility agreement or in contractual provisions in such an agreement. Such an approach would also be consistent with market practice in the syndicated loan market in which it is generally accepted that the arranger should not be expected to accept responsibility towards the syndicate. This is the conclusion that the court reached on this issue in *Raiffeisen Zentralbank Österreich AG v The Royal Bank of Scotland plc*.[317] The position may be different, however, where it is proved that an arranger accepted

---

[314] The availability of insurance cover would be a relevant factor under s 11(1) as well: Lord Griffiths in *Smith v Eric S Bush* [1990] 1 AC 831, 858. But the actual existence or otherwise of insurance cover is irrelevant: *Flamar Interocean Ltd v Denmac Ltd* [1990] 1 Lloyd's Rep 434.

[315] [2001] EWCA Civ 317, [2001] 1 All ER (Comm) 696 [63].

[316] See also *National Westminster Bank plc v Utrecht-America Finance Co* [2001] EWCA Civ 658, [2001] 3 All ER 733 [57]–[62] (Clarke LJ); *Granville Oil and Chemicals Ltd v Davies Turner & Co Ltd* [2003] EWCA Civ 570, [2003] 2 Lloyd's Rep 356 [31] (Tucker LJ); and *Goodlife Foods Ltd v Hall Fire Protection Ltd* [2018] EWCA Civ 1371.

[317] [2010] EWHC 1392 (Comm).

responsibility for a specific matter. In such a case, the reasonableness of the protection that was sought by the arranger would have to be examined.

3.146   In *Raiffeisen Zentralbank Österreich AG v The Royal Bank of Scotland plc*[318] the claimant bank alleged that it had been induced to enter into a syndicated loan facility by several misrepresentations made by the defendant bank who had arranged the facility. The alleged misrepresentations concerned the effect of certain arrangements with subsidiaries of Enron Corp, a US energy company that became insolvent soon after the loan transaction was entered into. These arrangements were designed to ensure that the syndicated loan in question would not appear on the balance sheet of Enron Corp allowing it to realise a profit for US accounting purposes. The confidentiality agreement and information memorandum distributed by the arranger stated, amongst other things:[319]

> This Information Memorandum (the 'Memorandum') has been prepared from Information supplied by the Company.
>
> The contents of this Memorandum have not been independently verified. No representation, warranty or undertaking (express or implied) is made, and no responsibility is accepted as to the adequacy, accuracy, completeness or reasonableness of this Memorandum or any further information, notice or other document at any time supplied in connection with the Facility.

3.147   The claimant bank argued that certain representations had been impliedly made in the information memorandum. The court held that the disclaimers formed part of the context to be taken into account when considering whether the alleged representations were made, and concluded that the parties contracted on the basis that information provided by the arranger was not to be regarded as a representation of fact on which the arranger intended that the syndicate member should rely or upon which it was entitled to rely. Consequently the disclaimers were not in substance an attempt to exclude or restrict liability so as to fall within the Unfair Contract Terms Act.[320] However, in case his Lordship was wrong on this point, Christopher Clarke J went on to consider whether the disclaimers satisfied the requirement of reasonableness in the Unfair Contract Terms Act and concluded that they did so. Both parties were large commercial concerns, experienced in the syndicated lending market. The transaction was an arm's length transaction entered into after mature deliberation. The disclaimers were not unusual; they were in a form habitually used in the syndicated lending market. The disclaimers were a legitimate means of allocating risk and of avoiding future disputes, years after the

---

[318] ibid.

[319] ibid [65].

[320] See also *Carney v NM Rothschild and Sons Ltd* [2018] EWHC 958 (Comm) for a discussion of the distinction between so-called 'basis clauses' (clauses which delineate the scope or basis of the parties' relationship) and exclusion clauses. See also *First Tower Trustees Ltd v CDS (Superstores International) Ltd* [2018] EWCA Civ 1396 [96] where Leggatt LJ heavily criticised the distinction.

transaction, as to the history of its negotiation and the possible ambit of implied representations. His Lordship concluded that:[321]

> The allocation of risk effected by the standard terms was well established and well understood by bankers operating in a sophisticated market. [The claimant bank] did not have to lend to Enron (in effect) in this way (or at all). The clauses made for certainty; were designed to avoid arguments such as the present and, in effect, relieved from liability (insofar as they did) save in the event of bad faith. In the present context that was not unreasonable.

As each case will depend upon its own facts, it is of interest to note the outcome of some other cases in various different areas in the context of commercial transactions, financing arrangements, and the granting of credit, as follows.[322] In *Walker v Boyle*[323] a vendor of land was held not to be protected in relation to a misstatement in an answer to preliminary enquiries.[324] In another case in respect of such enquiries, the Court of Appeal noted that arguments in favour of upholding a provision as reasonable were particularly strong where it had had a long history, was a well-established feature of such transactions, was endorsed by a professional body, both parties were represented by solicitors, and they had negotiated amendments to other standard provisions.[325] **3.148**

In *Smith v Eric S Bush*[326] a provision under which a surveyor commissioned by a putative mortgagee purported to disclaim liability towards a purchaser, the putative mortgagor, for a negligent survey of a dwelling house (the survey having been commissioned by the mortgagee at the expense of the mortgagor), was held to be unreasonable. Lord Griffiths[327] referred to a number of matters that were relevant, including the relative bargaining positions of the parties, if it would have been feasible, taking into account factors such as cost and time, to obtain alternative advice, the difficulty of the task that was undertaken for which liability was excluded, the practical consequences for the parties, bearing in mind the amounts of money involved, the availability of insurance, and the relative ability of the different parties to bear the loss. But that decision has been heavily distinguished. For example, in *Omega Trust Co Ltd v Wright Son and Pepper*[328] it was held that in a commercial context, as opposed to the domestic context in *Smith v Eric S Bush*, it was reasonable for valuers to exclude liability towards a third party for a **3.149**

---

[321] *Raiffeisen Zentralbank Österreich AG v The Royal Bank of Scotland plc* [2010] EWHC 1392 (Comm) [327].
[322] Although each case depends on its own facts, the courts endeavour to take a consistent approach to industry-wide standard terms: *Rohlig (UK) Ltd v Rock Unique Ltd* [2011] EWCA Civ 18.
[323] [1982] 1 WLR 495.
[324] See also *Cleaver v Schyde* [2011] EWCA Civ 929 and *Investments Ltd First Tower Trustees Ltd v CDS (Superstores International) Ltd* [2018] EWCA Civ 1396.
[325] *Cleaver v Schyde* [2011] EWCA Civ 929.
[326] [1990] 1 AC 831.
[327] At 858–59.
[328] [1997] PNLR 424.

negligent valuation of leasehold properties, especially as the existence of the third party was unknown to them. The third party was a commercial entity which could easily have obtained its own valuation, those involved were of equal bargaining power, and the third party could have approached the valuers directly if it wished them to accept responsibility towards it.

3.150 In *Marex Financial Limited v Creative Finance Limited, Cosmorex Limited*[329] it was held that the exclusion of a duty to exercise reasonable care when exercising a contractual right to terminate a transaction was reasonable as the claimant could have contracted with other market participants, had a relatively strong bargaining position (as was reflected in the pricing it had obtained), was given fair notice of the terms, and similar terms had been common in the market for years. In *Camerata Property Inc v Credit Suisse Securities (Europe) Ltd*[330] a term excluding liability for mere negligence or, more accurately, restricting liability for negligence to situations where it was gross was found to satisfy the requirement of reasonableness. In *St Alban's City and District Council v International Computers Ltd*[331] and in *Salvage Association v Cap Financial Services*[332] provisions in relation to the supply of computer software which limited liability to an aggregate amount were held not to be reasonable.[333] In *J Murphy & Sons Limited v Johnston Precast Limited*[334] the shortening of the limitation period for bringing a claim from six years to 28 days was unreasonable. In *Rohlig (UK) Ltd v Rock Unique Ltd*[335] and *Elvanite Full Circle Ltd v AMEC Earth & Environmental (UK) Ltd*[336] shortened limitation periods of nine months and a year respectively were reasonable. In *Regus (UK) Limited v Epcot Solutions Limited* the Court of Appeal dealt with an argument that an exclusion clause left no remedy and for that reason was unreasonable.[337]

3.151 In *Stewart Gill Ltd v Horatio Myer & Co Ltd*[338] a clause which precluded a purchaser from setting off a claim for damages against the payment of the price for the supply and installation of equipment was held to be unreasonable, within the context of section 13(1)(b) of the Act. A clause prohibiting set-off was also

---

[329] [2013] EWHC 2155 (Comm).
[330] [2011] EWHC 479 (Comm) [168]–[170].
[331] [1996] 4 All ER 481.
[332] [1995] FSR 654.
[333] Contrast *The Mayor and Burgesses of the London Borough of Southwark v IBM UK Limited* [2011] EWHC 549 (TCC).
[334] [2008] EWHC 3024 (TCC).
[335] [2011] EWCA Civ 18.
[336] [2013] EWHC 1191 (TCC).
[337] [2008] EWCA Civ 361. See also *Avrora Fine Arts Investment Ltd v Christie, Manson & Woods Ltd* [2012] PNLR 35 [152]. Cf *Lobster Group Ltd v Heidelberg Graphic Equipment Ltd* [2009] EWHC 1919 (TCC) where an exclusion of liability for direct damage was considered to go so far as to be unreasonable. See also *Kingsway Hall Hotel Ltd v Red Sky IT (Hounslow) Ltd* [2010] EWHC 965 (TCC).
[338] [1992] QB 600.

found to be unreasonable in *AXA Sun Life Services plc v Campbell Martin Ltd*.[339] However, most often, clauses precluding the exercise of a right of set-off have been upheld.[340]

3.5.5 Section 3 of the Misrepresentation Act 1967

Section 3[341] will be relevant in relation to an attempt in a contract, such as a facility agreement, to exclude or restrict any liability of an arranger that may arise in relation to a misrepresentation claim against the arranger relating to that contract.   **3.152**

The section provides as follows: **3.153**

> If a contract contains a term which would exclude or restrict—
>
> (a) any liability to which a party to a contract may be subject by reason of any misrepresentation made by him before the contract was made; or
> (b) any remedy available to another party to the contract by reason of such a misrepresentation,
>
> that term shall be of no effect except in so far as it satisfies the requirement of reasonableness as stated in section 11(1) of the Unfair Contract Terms Act 1977; and it is for those claiming that the term satisfies that requirement to show that it does.

It should be noted that the onus of proof is upon the person, the misrepresentor, who relies upon the relevant term. It is the term as a whole that must satisfy the requirement of reasonableness and not the application of the term to the particular facts.[342] Thus, a term which purports to exclude or restrict liability for any misrepresentation, including a fraudulent misrepresentation, would not be considered to be reasonable.[343]   **3.154**

It has been held, however, that a clause in a contract by which a party in the position of a possible representee confirms either (or both) that it did not receive   **3.155**

---

[339] [2011] EWCA Civ 133. However, (i) a clause providing that a statement as to money owed was binding in the absence of manifest error and (ii) an entire agreement clause were both upheld as reasonable in the circumstances. As regards (i), see also *United Trust Bank Ltd v Dohil* [2011] EWHC 3302 (QB).

[340] For example in *United Trust Bank Ltd v Dohil* [2011] EWHC 3302 (QB), *Rohlig (UK) Ltd v Rock Unique Ltd* [2011] EWCA Civ 18, *Deutsche Bank SA v Khan* [2013] EWHC 482 (Comm), *University of Wales v London College of Business Ltd* [2015] EWHC 1280 (QB), and *African Export-Import Bank v Shebah Exploration & Production Company and ors* [2016] EWHC 311 (Comm) affd on appeal [2017] EWCA Civ 845.

[341] As amended by s 8(1) of the Unfair Contract Terms Act 1977 and the Consumer Rights Act 2015.

[342] *Thomas Witter Ltd v TBP Industries Ltd* [1996] 2 All ER 573, 598 (Jacob J).

[343] ibid 598. However, in other cases, courts have taken the view that such clauses are not intended by the parties to apply to fraudulent misrepresentations and would not automatically contravene the legislation only because they do not expressly carve out fraud: *Government of Zanzibar v British Aerospace (Lancaster House) Ltd* [2000] 1 WLR 2333, 2346–47; *Six Continents Hotels Inc v Event Hotels GmbH* [2006] EWHC 2317 [53].

any representations[344] or rely upon any representations[345] from the putative representator in deciding to proceed with the transaction, will act as a contractual estoppel, which will preclude the putative representee from claiming that it had relied upon any representation in deciding to enter into the contract.[346] The party invoking contractual estoppel need not show detrimental reliance or unconscionability.[347] In effect, the putative representee is itself agreeing or acknowledging that no representation was made to it or that it has not placed reliance upon anything that was said. Such clauses purport to set out the basis on which the parties are contracting, rather than purporting to exclude liability for misrepresentation which has arisen. For that reason, in some cases it was held that section 3 was not engaged at all, as it was not possible to establish the essential elements of a representation having been made and of reliance in bringing a claim based upon misrepresentation.[348] However, in other cases the courts had concluded that such provisions should be viewed as an attempt to exclude or restrict liability for a misrepresentation, rather than as precluding the claim for misrepresentation from arising.[349] Most recently, in *First Tower Trustees Ltd v CDS (Superstores International) Ltd*[350] the Court of Appeal ruled that section 3 applied to a 'non-reliance' clause. Leggatt LJ stated:[351]

> [W]henever a contracting party relies on the principle of contractual estoppel to argue that, by reason of a contract term, the other party to the contract is prevented from asserting a fact which is necessary to establish liability for a pre-contractual misrepresentation, the term falls within section 3 of the Misrepresentation Act 1967. Such a term is therefore of no effect except in so far as it satisfies the requirement of reasonableness as stated in section 11 of UCTA.

---

[344] This being a 'no representations' clause: *Raiffeisen Zentralbank Österreich AG v Royal Bank of Scotland plc* [2010] EWHC 1392 (Comm) [267]; *Springwell Navigation Corp v JP Morgan Chase Bank* [2010] EWCA Civ 1221 [170].

[345] This being a 'non-reliance' clause: *FoodCo UK LLP (t/a Muffin Break) v Henry Boot Developments Ltd* [2010] EWHC 358 (Ch) [170]–[171]; *Thornbridge Ltd v Barclays Bank plc* [2015] EWHC 3430 (QB).

[346] *Springwell Navigation Corp v JP Morgan Chase Bank* [2010] EWCA Civ 1221 [143], [155]–[156], affirming *Peekay Intermark and Harish Pawani v Australia and New Zealand Banking Group Ltd* [2006] EWCA Civ 386 [56]. Contractual estoppel was endorsed by the Privy Council in *Prime Sight Ltd v Lavarello* [2014] 2 WLR 84 (PC) [47]. But contrast the Privy Council's more recent decision in *Chen v Ng* [2017] UKPC 27 [28]–[35].

[347] *Springwell Navigation Corp v JP Morgan Chase Bank* [2010] EWCA Civ 1221 [177]; *First Tower Trustees Ltd v CDS (Superstores International) Ltd* [2018] EWCA Civ 1396 [47].

[348] [2015] EWHC 3430 (QB). See also *Raiffeisen Zentralbank Österreich AG v Royal Bank of Scotland plc* [2010] EWHC 1392 (Comm) [297] and [310]–[317]; and *Brown v InnovatorOne plc* [2012] EWHC 1321 (Comm) [899].

[349] *Thomas Witter Ltd v TBP Industries Ltd* [1996] 2 All ER 573, 596–97; *Cremdean Properties Ltd v Nash* (1977) 244 EG 547 (CA); *Government of Zanzibar v British Aerospace (Lancaster House) Ltd* [2000] 1 WLR 2333, 2347; and *Shaftsbury House (Developments) Limited v Lee* [2010] EWHC 1484 (Ch) [67].

[350] [2018] EWCA Civ 1396. The Court specifically disapproved *Thornbridge Ltd v Barclays Bank plc* [2015] EWHC 3430 (QB) on this point.

[351] ibid [111].

In that case, the non-reliance clause was struck down as it did not satisfy the test of reasonableness. **3.156**

3.6 The Agent

3.6.1 The appointment, role, duties, and powers of the agent

The agent bank, usually called the facility agent, is the coordinator of the facility once **3.157** it has been formalised by the signing of the documentation. Its role begins upon execution of the facility agreement and will continue, unless it resigns and is replaced by another agent, until the conclusion of the transaction.[352] Its role is crucial to the management and effective coordination of the arrangements between the lenders and as between them and the borrower. The facility agent may be assisted in a complicated facility by other entities which perform specific roles and, if security is to be taken, there may be a separate security agent, failing which, the facility agent will also hold the security, in either case as a trustee or an agent under a parallel debt structure[353] on behalf of the lenders.[354] Quite often, the same entity that acted as the arranger will be appointed as the facility agent, but it is important to distinguish between the two roles and to understand that the facility agent takes up its role when it is appointed by the lenders to act as their agent. The appointment is normally contained in the facility agreement. The agent will usually also be a lender, and in this context it is necessary to distinguish the rights and obligations it has in its capacity as agent from those it may have in other capacities.[355] Most of the provisions concerning the agent will be found in a specific clause in the facility agreement, which is usually referred to as the 'agency clause'. For convenience, the facility agent will be referred to in the discussion that follows simply as the 'agent'.

The agent is appointed by the lenders to act as their agent.[356] It is usually **3.158** provided expressly that the agent does not act on behalf of the borrower or

---

[352] The facility agreement should contain provisions dealing with the resignation and replacement of the agent. Such provisions should ensure that the protective provisions in the agreement relating to the agent will continue to protect a retired agent in relation to matters concerning the period whilst it was the agent.

[353] For a description of the parallel debt structure see n 3.

[354] The representative capacity of a facility agent and a security trustee to act and hold security on behalf of the lenders, as well as the right of the agent to bind the lenders, was examined in *British Energy Power & Energy Trading Ltd v Credit Suisse* [2008] EWCA Civ 53. That case concerned a syndicated facility. This is subject, of course, to the terms of the facility agreement or other documentation under which the agent and the trustee are appointed to act and to hold the security on behalf of the syndicate members, which may place restrictions upon their functions and powers.

[355] In *Landesbank Hessen-Thüringen Girozentrale v Bayerische Landesbank (London Branch)* [2014] EWHC 1404 (Comm) a waterfall provision dealing with partial payments under a facility agreement gave priority to a bank in its capacity as agent but not in any other capacity. See also *Torre Asset Funding v RBS* [2013] EWHC 2670 (Ch) [196].

[356] Its appointment is not revocable by individual lenders in respect of themselves: *Redwood Master Fund Ltd v TD Bank Europe Ltd* [2002] EWHC 2703 (Ch). See also Richard Hooley, 'Release Provisions in Intercreditor Agreements' (2012) 3 Journal of Business Law 213 and *Re D&D Wines International Ltd (In Liquidation)* [2016] UKSC 47 as to when an agent's appointment is irrevocable.

any other person. The agent performs various roles in acting as the agent of the lenders, which may be summarised as acting as a representative of the lenders, acting as a coordinator of the lenders and of the facility, and acting in an administrative and mechanical capacity.[357] It acts as the representative of the lenders in dealings with the borrower.[358] In that sense, it is the interface between the lenders and the borrower, and the facility agreement will usually provide that the borrower should deal with the agent rather than directly with the lenders. Information and other materials that have to be transmitted by the borrower to the lenders will be given to the agent to be distributed to the lenders. Similarly, requests that the borrower wishes to make and notices that it wishes to give will be given to the agent, which will then inform the lenders of what has been received from the borrower. Where a notice or some other matter, such as a consent, is to be given to the borrower, it will be given on behalf of the lenders by the agent. With respect to payments that are to be made under the facility, the lenders will send their respective contributions to the agent and then an amount equivalent to the total of such contributions will be transmitted by the agent to the borrower. If the borrower is to make a payment under the facility, such as a payment of interest or principal, it will make the payment in an aggregate amount to the agent, which will then divide up the payment and transmit the relevant proportionate amounts to the lenders.[359] The agent will make the calculations that are required during the facility, such as concerning the respective amounts of each lender's contribution to an advance that is to be made, each lender's entitlement in any payment that the agent receives from the borrower, and in the determination of the amounts of interest and other amounts that are payable and related matters such as concerning interest periods. In a multicurrency facility, the agent will make the currency conversion and other calculations for the administration of the facility. The agent will be given priority in respect of costs and expenses which it incurs in its capacity as agent.[360]

---

[357] See para 3.176 below.

[358] Consequently it will bind the lenders by contracts it enters with the borrower 'acting as agent … for the finance parties': *British Energy Power & Energy Trading Ltd v Credit Suisse* [2008] EWCA Civ 53.

[359] The lenders take a credit risk on the agent in respect of the money held by it. It is unlikely that under the terms of a typical syndicated loan agreement the funds held by the agent for distribution to them would be subject to a constructive trust pursuant to the principles explained in *Re D&D Wines International Ltd (In Liquidation)* [2016] UKSC 47.

[360] However, an agent did not have priority over the lenders in recovering its hedging break costs as 'expenses or costs' as they were incurred in its capacity as a hedging counterparty and not in its capacity as agent: *Landesbank Hessen-Thüringen Girozentrale and ors v Bayerische Landesbank, London Branch and anor* [2014] EWHC 1404 (Comm).

On its face, the agent would appear to be invested with a large and wide amount **3.159** of discretion in acting on behalf of the lenders. There are limitations, however, on the apparent width of the agent's authority, which will be stated in the facility agreement. As previously mentioned, in some circumstances the consent of all of the lenders is required for specified matters. In other situations, the facility agreement will usually permit the majority of the lenders to intervene by making decisions and giving instructions to the agent. The agent will also be given the right to seek instructions from the majority of the lenders and to act as instructed by the majority. The agreement will provide that the agent may require security or an indemnity from the lenders if it is to carry out the instructions of the majority.[361] In the absence of a decision by the majority, the agent will be entitled to act as it thinks fit unless the facility agreement provides to the contrary, as, for instance, in relation to a situation where it prescribes that the consent of all the lenders is required. A good example of the interplay between the capacity of the agent to make decisions on its own and to act as instructed by the majority of the lenders will usually be found in the events of default clause in the facility agreement. The clause will normally provide that if an event of default occurs, the agent may take action of its own volition, such as by demanding repayment or suspending the facility, but that the agent will take such action if it is so instructed by the majority of the lenders.

3.6.2 Areas of risk to the agent

The agent may be at risk if the lenders are unhappy about the agent's perform- **3.160** ance of its tasks. They may wish to claim against the agent for breach of its obligations towards them. The discussion that follows proceeds on the assumption that English law would be the applicable law to determine each of the issues that are involved in a dispute. However, it is always relevant to consider if there might be conflict of laws issues that may arise in a particular case. The reader is referred to Chapter 4 of *McKnight, Paterson, & Zakrzewski on the Law of International Finance*[362] for a discussion of those matters. As a matter of English law, the possible areas of claim against the agent will lie in contract, tort, and for breach of fiduciary duty.

---

[361] The right of the agent to such protection will fall to be considered in much the same way as that of a trustee under a bond issue when it seeks an indemnity or security from the bondholders before taking action on their behalf. The position of such a trustee was examined by the House of Lords in *Concord Trust v Law Debenture Trust Corporation plc* [2005] UKHL 27, [2005] 1 WLR 1591.

[362] Sarah Paterson and Rafal Zakrzewski (eds), *McKnight, Paterson, & Zakrzewski on the Law of International Finance* (2nd edn, OUP 2017).

3.6.2.1 *Fiduciary duty*

3.161 The duties of a fiduciary arise in equity from the relationship between it and its principal. At the heart of the relationship is the trust and confidence that the principal reposes in the fiduciary and which, accordingly, is due by the fiduciary to the principal.[363] It follows that the principal feature of a fiduciary's duties is the obligation of loyalty, from which other equitable obligations will arise. This was explained by Millett LJ in *Bristol & West Building Society v Mothew*[364] as follows:

> The distinguishing obligation of a fiduciary is the obligation of loyalty. The principal is entitled to the single-minded loyalty of his fiduciary. This core liability has several facets. A fiduciary must act in good faith; he must not make a profit out of his trust; he must not place himself in a position where his duty and his interest may conflict; he may not act for his own benefit or the benefit of a third person without the informed consent of his principal. This is not intended to be an exhaustive list, but it is sufficient to indicate the nature of fiduciary obligations.

3.162 His Lordship went on to say[365] that if the fiduciary is acting for two (or more) principals:

> he must act in good faith in the interests of each and must not act with the intention of furthering the interests of one principal to the prejudice of the other.

3.163 As to the duty to act in good faith, see *Re Second East Dulwich etc Building Society*.[366] For the duty not to make an unauthorised profit, see *Bray v Ford*.[367] For the duty to avoid a conflict of interest, see *Keech v Sandford*.[368] For the duty not to act for its own or a third party's benefit, see *Boardman v Phipps*.[369] To that list may be added a further duty, to act with care and skill, but although the duty may arise in consequence of the fiduciary relationship, because of the relationship that arises between them, it is more akin to the duty of care in negligence that arises at common law. Whilst the remedy will be for equitable compensation, it will be assessed in a similar way to damages at common law. Similar rules to those which apply at common law as to causation and remoteness of damage may also apply to such a claim against the fiduciary.[370]

---

[363] See *R v Chester and North Wales Legal Aid Area Office, ex p Floods of Queensferry Ltd* [1998] 1 WLR 1496, 1500 (Millett LJ).

[364] [1998] Ch 1, 18.

[365] [1998] Ch 1, 19.

[366] (1889) 68 LJ Ch 196.

[367] [1896] AC 44. Lord Browne-Wilkinson said in *Henderson v Merrett Syndicates Ltd* [1995] 2 AC 145, 206 that, so far as he was aware, this was a duty common to every fiduciary, subject to any authorisation of the profit.

[368] (1726) Sel Cas Ch 61.

[369] [1967] 2 AC 46.

[370] See *Henderson v Merrett Syndicates Ltd* [1995] 2 AC 145, 205–06 (Lord Browne-Wilkinson) and *Bristol & West Building Society v Mothew* [1998] Ch 1, 16–17 (Millett LJ). However, the rules are not necessarily identical: *AIB Group (UK) plc v Mark Redler & Co Solicitors* [2014] UKSC 58 [136]–[137].

Despite the apparent severity of the position as it was outlined by Millett LJ, the **3.164**
nature and extent of the duties of a fiduciary to its principal will depend upon
the context in which it is acting, particularly the contractual context in a situation
where the fiduciary is acting pursuant to an appointment arising from the contract.[371] The fiduciary duties that are owed by an express trustee will not be the
same as the less extensive duties owed by some other types of fiduciary, such as
an agent.[372] And in the case of the latter, as Sales J noted in *Torre Asset Funding
v RBS*,[373] the law does not stipulate a defined set of obligations which attach to
every agency relationship unless excluded by agreement; on the contrary, where
the parties have entered into a detailed loan agreement, they did not intend for
some potential additional set of vague and unspecific duties to apply in addition
to their expressly ag reed terms. This is because it is possible (especially in a commercial context) for the nature and scope of the duties of a fiduciary to be restrictively defined and modified or even excluded by contract,[374] except with respect to
situations involving dishonesty or lack of good faith on the part of the fiduciary.[375]
For instance, in *Kelly v Cooper*[376] Lord Browne-Wilkinson, who delivered the advice of the Privy Council, said that it was inherent in the nature of the role played
by an estate agent, a stockbroker, and others selling property, shares, or goods on
behalf of their principals that they will probably act for several different principals
at the same time. Conflicts of interest may arise concerning the interests of their
principals, yet they must be free to act for several competing principals as, otherwise, they would be unable to perform their functions. They might, for instance,
hold confidential information concerning one principal that may be relevant to
the interests of another principal, yet they would not be compelled to divulge
such information to the other principal.

Generally speaking, whilst it is usual (in the absence of appropriate contractual **3.165**
limitations and depending on the scope of its discretion) that an agent may be
considered to be in the position of a fiduciary towards its principal,[377] it is also

[371] See *New Zealand Netherlands Society 'Oranje' Inc v Kuys* [1973] 1 WLR 1126, 1129–30 (PC)
(Lord Wilberforce); *Hospital Products Ltd v United States Surgical Corp* (1984) CLR 41, at 97 (High
Ct of Aust) (Mason J); *Henderson v Merrett Syndicates Ltd* [1995] 2 AC 145, 206 (Lord Browne-
Wilkinson); and *Saltri III Ltd v MD Mezzanine SA SICAR* [2012] EWHC 3025 (Comm). In the
Saltri case, it was noted that a person may be in a fiduciary position in respect of a part of his activities and but not other parts.
[372] See *Henderson v Merrett Syndicates Ltd* [1995] 2 AC 145, 206 (Lord Browne-Wilkinson).
[373] [2013] EWHC 2670 (Ch) [147].
[374] ibid, *Saltri III Ltd v MD Mezzanine SA SICAR* [2012] EWHC 3025 (Comm), and *Torre Asset
Funding v RBS* [2013] EWHC 2670 (Ch) [146].
[375] See *Armitage v Nurse* [1998] Ch 241, 251–56 (Millett LJ) and *Spread Trustee Company
Limited v Sarah Ann Hutcheson and ors* [2011] UKPC 13.
[376] [1993] AC 205 (PC). In *Bailey v Barclays Bank plc* [2014] EWHC 2882 (QB) it was noted
by reference to *Kelly v Cooper* that a bank will not usually stand in a fiduciary relationship with its
customers unless there are exceptional circumstances.
[377] See eg the references to an agent as a fiduciary by Lord Browne-Wilkinson in *Henderson v
Merrett Syndicates Ltd* [1995] 2 AC 145, 205–06.

important to note that not every agent will be considered to be in that position. In *Henry v Hammond*[378] Channell J held that a shipping agent who was instructed to sell the cargo of a vessel in distress was not in a fiduciary position. The agent was not obliged to keep the sale moneys separate from its own funds, but was entitled to mix those moneys with its own funds, with the consequence that it was merely a debtor for those moneys to its principal. Lord Upjohn in *Boardman v Phipps*[379] said: 'The facts and circumstances must be carefully examined to see whether in fact a purported agent and even a confidential agent is in a fiduciary relationship to his principal. It does not necessarily follow that he is in such a position (see *Re Coomber, Coomber v Coomber*[380]).'

3.166 It is important to keep the background mentioned above in mind when considering the statement that was made by Ackner LJ, on behalf of himself and Oliver LJ,[381] in *UBAF Ltd v European American Banking Corp*.[382] His Lordship said that as the agent of two syndicated loan facilities had received the funds from the banks which were to be lent to the borrowers and it was holding security from the borrowers as trustee on behalf of the banks, the agent was acting in a fiduciary capacity towards the banks. As such, it had a fiduciary duty to pass on any information that it might have received which related to the facility and such security. In so far as it was acting as the trustee of the security on behalf of the syndicate, and received the relevant information in that capacity, that view might be correct (unless the relevant documentation provided otherwise).[383]

3.167 It is doubtful, however, if the same would be the true position had the agent merely been acting as the agent under the facility agreement, at least if the facts and the documentation were consistent with what has been the practice in the syndicated loan markets for quite a number of years. For many years the almost invariable practice has been that the syndicated facility agreement will provide expressly that the agent does not act in a fiduciary capacity towards the lenders or, indeed, anyone else, and there are a number of other provisions that are intended to overcome any fiduciary duties that might otherwise arise or be implied from the role that the agent plays.[384] Further, there is commonly no obligation

---

[378] [1913] 2 KB 515.
[379] [1967] 2 AC 46, 127.
[380] [1911] 1 Ch 723.
[381] There was no third member of the court.
[382] [1984] QB 713, 728. The facts are noted at para 3.108 above. The decision of the Court of Appeal was given in an interlocutory appeal and, as noted earlier, the appeal was only heard by a panel of two judges, so it may be open to review. However, the point under discussion concerning the fiduciary capacity of the agent was directly relevant to the finding of the court on s 32(1)(b) of the Limitation Act 1980, so it cannot be regarded as merely being obiter dicta.
[383] It is necessary to consider the capacity in which the agent received the information and the terms of the relevant documentation. In *Torre Asset Funding v RBS* [2013] EWHC 2670 (Ch) an agent's obligations to pass on information were quite strictly construed and it is doubtful that the conclusions would have been different if the agent had also held security as trustee for the lenders.
[384] Eg see *Torre Asset Funding v RBS* [2013] EWHC 2670 (Ch) [27].

in such documentation for the agent to hold any funds that it receives from or for the lenders in a separate account pending their disbursement. The funds will usually be paid into the agent's own general accounts and will thus be mixed with any other funds it may have. Accordingly, any payment it makes with respect to what it has received will not be of the precise same funds it has received but of an equivalent amount. On the basis of what was said in *Henry v Hammond* and by Lord Upjohn in *Boardman v Phipps*, this fact, when taken with the express provisions in the facility agreement to which reference has just been made, should mean that no fiduciary relationship will exist as between the agent and the lenders.

3.6.2.2 *Contractual duties*

As the agent is appointed in the facility agreement by the lenders to be their agent **3.168** then quite clearly there is a contractual relationship between the agent and the lenders. The facility agreement contains a number of provisions concerning the functions that the agent undertakes, particularly as to administrative and mechanical matters. The agency clause in the usual form of facility agreement will also set out the duties and responsibilities of the agent. For instance, the agent is expressed to have a qualified duty to pass on certain information and the contents of any notices that it receives from the borrower, and if the agent becomes aware that there has been a default, it must tell the lenders. But as will be further seen,[385] the various duties and functions of the agent are expressed in the facility agreement to be of a rather limited nature, and will be subject to a number of qualifications and limitations that are contained in the agreement.

In addition to the matters dealt with expressly by the agreement, there could also **3.169** be various duties and obligations on the part of the agent that might be implied into the contract. Under section 13 of the Supply of Goods and Services Act 1982, there is an implied contractual duty to exercise reasonable care and skill in the supply of services that is imposed upon a person which, under a contract, is supplying services in the course of a business.[386] It may also be argued (if rather faintly) that something similar to some of the duties that might apply to a fiduciary may also be implied into the contract as between the agent and the lenders, such as the duty on the part of the agent to act in good faith, not to have a conflict of interests, and perhaps to pass on to the lenders any relevant information that may come into its possession.

---

[385] See section 3.6.3 below.

[386] By s 12 of the Act, a contract for the supply of a service means a contract under which a person, the supplier, agrees to carry out a service, whether or not goods are to be transferred or bailed under the contract. Section 16(1) of the Act provides that, subject to the Unfair Contract Terms Act 1977, the implied duty may be negatived. Section 16(2) provides that an express term in a contract will not negative the implied term unless it is inconsistent with it. Since the commencement of the Consumer Rights Act 2015, these provisions of the Supply of Goods and Services Act 1982 only apply to non-consumer contracts.

3.170 However, such arguments have limited prospects of success. Given the nature of the usual agency clause, there is very little scope for the implication of additional terms. This point and the limited nature of the agent's express duties, in the context of LMA recommended form documentation, was highlighted by the leading case of *Torre Asset Funding v RBS*.[387] The agent was only bound to pass on the notices and information within the scope of the relevant provisions of the transaction documentation. The agent certainly did not have to pass on all information regarding the borrower, such as its financial projections and business plan, which came into the agent's possession. There was no scope for implying such a term as it was not necessary and would conflict with the express terms of the agency clause.[388] Additionally, where there had not been any actual communication to the agent of a default, the agent was not under a duty to make an evaluative judgement that there had been such a default and accordingly was not required to inform the other lenders of circumstances that could amount to such an event.[389] In the absence of an obvious default which required no evaluative judgement (eg a payment failure), the agent was entitled to assume that no default had occurred. Similarly, the agent was under no obligation, express or implied, to chase the borrower to provide documentation which it was contractually obliged to provide to the lenders. Consequently, it was for the lenders to complain to the borrower about such non-performance of its information obligations.[390]

3.6.2.3 Tortious duties

3.171 In addition to any contractual duty of care and skill that is owed by the agent to the lenders, the agent may also have a duty of care in tort towards the lenders which may arise at general law from the relationship between them.

3.172 At one time it was considered that it was not possible to have concurrent duties of care in both contract and tort. For instance, Lord Scarman, when delivering the advice of the Privy Council in *Tai Hing Cotton Mill Ltd v Liu Chong Hing Bank Ltd*,[391] expressed the view that in commercial relationships, and particularly in the relationship between a banker and its customer, such a relationship should be governed solely by the terms of the contract, so that on the facts of that case it was not possible for the customer to owe a separate duty of care in tort to the banker. That view, however, was rejected by Lord Goff of Chieveley, who gave the leading speech in the House of Lords in *Henderson v Merrett Syndicates Ltd*.[392]

---

[387] [2013] EWHC 2670 (Ch).

[388] ibid [153]–[155]. See *Marks and Spencer plc v BNP Paribas Securities Services Trust Company (Jersey) Ltd* [2015] UKSC 72 which reaffirmed the principles on which terms may be implied in fact.

[389] ibid [162](ii). The modest level of fee charged by the agent (£15,000 pa) was a factor taken into account on this point.

[390] ibid [179].

[391] [1986] AC 80, 107.

[392] [1995] 2 AC 145, 184–94, which included a reference to *Tai Hing*, at 186.

After conducting an extensive review of the case law, including the judgment of Oliver J in *Midland Bank Trust Co Ltd v Hett Stubbs & Kemp*,[393] Lord Goff arrived at the conclusion, in express agreement with that reached by Oliver J in the *Midland Bank Trust* case, that it was perfectly possible for a contracting party to owe the other party a duty of care in tort concurrently with the duties that might arise under the contract.[394] Lord Goff said that, subject to the effect of an exclusion clause, a party to the contract was entitled to assert whichever cause of action was most advantageous in its legal consequences to him, be it in contract or in tort. Lord Goff summarised his conclusions[395] on the point as follows:

> My own belief is that, in the present context, the common law is not antipathetic to concurrent liability, and that there is no sound basis for a rule which automatically restricts the claimant to either a tortious or a contractual remedy. The result may be untidy; but, given that the tortious duty is imposed by the general law, and the contractual duty is attributable to the will of the parties, I do not find it objectionable that the claimant may be entitled to take advantage of the remedy which is most advantageous to him, subject only to ascertaining whether the tortious duty is so inconsistent with the applicable contract that, in accordance with ordinary principles, the parties must be taken to have agreed that the tortious remedy is to be limited or excluded.

It is arguable whether the starting point should be to determine if a duty of care **3.173** might arise and then to decide if the parties have agreed in their contract to limit or abrogate the duty[396] or whether the two issues should somehow be interwoven.[397] However, it does not automatically follow that a duty of care arises in tort just because an obligation to do something has been agreed in contract.[398] If a duty of care does arise, the intention of the parties to exclude or limit liability in negligence must be clear, and it is for the party asserting that the liability has been excluded or limited to prove the point.[399]

---

[393] [1979] Ch 384.

[394] The concurrent contractual obligation does not have to have been expressly agreed; it may be implied. See *Barclays Bank v Quincecare* [1992] 4 All ER 363 and *Singularis Holdings Ltd (In official liquidation) v Daiwa Capital Markets Europe Ltd* [2018] EWCA Civ 84 where a bank was held to owe co-extensive implied duties in contract and tort to exercise reasonable skill and care when executing instructions, which included refraining from implementing instructions where it had reasonable grounds to suspect that this was an attempt to misappropriate funds.

[395] [1995] 2 AC 145, 193–94.

[396] See *Henderson v Merrett Syndicates Ltd* [1995] 2 AC 145, 194 (Lord Goff) and 206 (Lord Browne-Wilkinson), respectively. See also Colman J in *BP plc v AON Ltd* [2006] EWHC 424 (Comm), [2006] 1 All ER (Comm) 789 [66-point vi].

[397] See the discussion in *Riyad Bank v Ahli United Bank (UK) plc* [2006] EWCA Civ 780, [2006] 2 Lloyd's Rep 292 [21] (Longmore LJ) and [45]–[48] (Neuberger LJ).

[398] *Robinson v PE Jones (Contractors) Ltd* [2011] EWCA Civ 9. In that case, no duty of care in tort was found so the claimant was not successful in bringing a negligence claim. He could not bring a claim for breach of contract as it was time-barred.

[399] See eg *Rutter v Palmer* [1922] 2 KB 87, 92 (Scrutton LJ) and *Gillespie Bros Ltd v Roy Bowles Transport Ltd* [1973] QB 400, 419 (Buckley LJ).

3.174 In deciding whether to pursue its remedies in contract or in tort, a claimant will have in mind that there are certain differences that may be relevant in deciding between the two heads of claim, particularly as to the rules concerning damages and limitation periods. Putting it rather simply, and therefore at the risk of an over-simplification,[400] the principal differences may be summarised as follows. In contract, the requirements as to foreseeability and remoteness are judged as at the date of contracting, whereas in tort they are judged as at the time of breach. In contract, damages are assessed on the basis of putting the claimant in the position it would have been in if the contract had been performed. In tort, it is to put the claimant in the position it would have been in if the tort had not been committed.[401] In contract, the limitation period will run from the date of breach, whereas in tort it will begin to run from the date the damage is suffered.

3.6.3 Protecting the agent

3.175 It is now appropriate to consider the protection that the facility agreement might seek to confer upon the agent, in terms of excluding, limiting, or qualifying the duties and the liabilities that it might otherwise owe to the lenders as a matter of general law. The protective provisions will be found in the agency clause of the facility agreement. Having referred to those provisions, it will then be relevant to consider how effective such steps will be as a matter of law, particularly in light of legislative restrictions upon exclusions or limitations of certain types of liability. At the outset it should be noted that these protections are only likely to protect the agent in relation to action taken by the agent in its capacity as agent, but not in other roles.[402]

3.176 The agency clause usually stresses that the agent's duties are mechanical and administrative in nature. In *Torre Asset Funding v RBS*[403] Sales J stated that '[this] clause mandates a reading of the finance agreements which minimises so far as is possible, consistently with the express language and practical workability of the agreements and the arrangements to which they are intended to give effect, the substantive content of the duties on the Agent'.[404] His Lordship repeatedly resorted to this formulation in restrictively construing the obligations of the agent under an LMA recommended form loan agreement and an intercreditor

---

[400] For instance, the rules as to the assessment of damages in tort for negligence will differ between a claim for breach of a duty in providing information and a claim for breach of a duty in providing advice: see section 3.4.3.3 above and *South Australia Asset Management Corp v York Montague Ltd* [1997] AC 191 and *Aneco Reinsurance Underwriting Ltd v Johnson & Higgins Ltd* [2001] UKHL 51, [2002] 1 Lloyd's Rep 157.

[401] The measure in tort may be preferable in the case of a 'bad bargain', that is, where the claimant entered into what would have been an unprofitable transaction even if it had been duly performed.

[402] *Torre Asset Funding v RBS* [2013] EWHC 2670 (Ch) [196].

[403] [2013] EWHC 2670 (Ch) [163](i), [174], [179], and [192].

[404] ibid [34].

agreement.[405] It was also treated as part of the factual matrix to be taken into account in the process of construction.[406] In particular, it bolstered the rejection of arguments that the agent should be subject to additional duties implied in fact or law or as an incident of the agency relationship.[407]

3.177 As already mentioned, it is usually the case that the agency clause will contain a provision which provides that the agent is not to be considered as acting in a fiduciary capacity towards the lenders or any other person.[408] For reasons of caution (for instance, in case it might be argued that the relevant matters should be implied as part of the contract of agency) the agency clause will probably also contain provisions addressing each of the types of duty that a fiduciary may theoretically have, such as in relation to conflicts of interest, having a personal interest in the facility, and the payment of remuneration to the agent by the borrower. For example, the clause may provide that the agent may engage in other business and transactions involving the borrower and its group, including other lending and advisory business, as well as providing that the agent may also be a lender under the facility, and may vote in its own interests and otherwise derive the benefit of being a lender. There will be provisions which deal with the payment by the borrower to the agent for its own account of fees, as well as provisions by which the borrower is obliged to reimburse the agent for expenditure that the agent may incur. Various rules have been developed as to the construction of such provisions. The relevant provision will be construed restrictively but fairly, according to the natural meaning of the words that have been used. Liability can only be limited or excluded by clear, unequivocal, and unambiguous terms, but it would appear that a strict *contra proferentum* rule will not be applied in the absence of doubt about the meaning of a contractual provision.[409] The agent's protections will take effect in accordance with their terms,[410] which in turn illustrates the approach of the courts in upholding the allocation of risks as shaped by the agreement of the parties as set out in the relevant documentation.[411]

3.178 There is also likely to be a provision which provides that the division or section of the entity which is the agent should be treated as if it were separate from the remainder of that entity, so that information which is held at any time by any other

---

[405] ibid [174], [179], [180], and [192].
[406] ibid [163](i).
[407] ibid [204].
[408] ibid [27].
[409] See *Armitage v Nurse* [1998] Ch 241, 255–56 (Millett LJ); *Bogg v Raper* (1998/99) 1 ITELR 267, 280–85; *Spread Trustee Company Limited v Sarah Ann Hutcheson and ors* [2011] UKPC 13; *Egan v Static Control Components (Europe) Ltd* [2004] EWCA Civ 392; *Transocean Drilling UK Ltd v Providence Resources plc* [2016] EWCA Civ 372; *Taberna Europe CDO II plc v Selskabet (Formerly Roskilde Bank A/S) (In Bankruptcy)* [2016] EWCA Civ 1262 [23]; *Persimmon Homes Ltd v Ove Arup & Partners Ltd* [2017] EWCA Civ 373 [52].
[410] *Torre Asset Funding v RBS* [2013] EWHC 2670 (Ch).
[411] *Saltri III Ltd v MD Mezzanine SA SICAR* [2012] EWHC 3025 (Comm).

part of that entity will not be treated as being known by the agent for the purposes of its functions as the agent under the facility agreement, such as in relation to its obligation to pass on relevant information to the lenders. Such a provision on its own may not give all of the protection that the entity needs, because of the risk that information may seep from one part of the entity to the agency division or section. To be sure that this will not be a problem in practice, the entity should have adequate information barriers (also referred to as 'ethical screens' or 'Chinese walls') in place to ensure that the information will not pass into the hands of those who work in the agency section, although there is always a risk that the barrier so erected may be found to be porous and inadequate.[412]

3.179 The agency clause will also contain various provisions designed to negative any responsibility that it might otherwise be alleged that the agent has, within a duty of care and skill, to look out for and protect the interests of the lenders.[413] This will include a provision stating that the agent has no responsibility for the adequacy or effectiveness of any relevant documentation or of any information that may be provided, that it may rely on what it is told by the borrower or in a certificate provided by the borrower, that it has no obligation to monitor or investigate the borrower's affairs, that it may instruct and rely upon the advice of experts, and a provision by which any liability that might arise for any omission[414] or wrongful act is excluded,[415] save where the same arises in consequence of the agent's deliberate or wilful misconduct or gross negligence. There is also likely to be a separate acknowledgement by the lenders that they made their own investigations before deciding to enter into the facility, will be solely responsible for making their own independent appraisal and investigation of all risks,[416] and that they did not rely on the agent in making their decisions.

3.180 The expression 'wilful misconduct' appears to cover intentional or deliberate wrongdoing as well as 'subjective recklessness'.[417] It has also been suggested that dishonesty is an ingredient of wilful misconduct.[418] Bramwell LJ stated in *Lewis v*

---

[412] As to the adequacy and effectiveness of information barriers see *Prince Jefri Bolkiah v KPMG* [1999] 2 AC 222; *Young v Robson Rhodes* [1999] 3 All ER 524; and *Georgian American Alloys Inc v White and Case LLP* [2014] EWHC 94 (Comm). See also the summary provided in *Australian Securities and Investment Commission v Citigroup Global Markets Australian Pty Ltd* [2007] FCA 963 [308]–[321].

[413] As to the construction of such provisions, see section 3.5.3 above.

[414] In *Torre Asset Funding v RBS* [2013] EWHC 2670 (Ch) the relevant clause only protected the agent from 'any action taken by it', however, this was generously construed to include omissions and would have applied to protect the agent, see [197]–[200].

[415] This is likely to be extended to cover the directors, employees, and agents of the agent and the arranger, and such persons will be given the benefit of the Contracts (Rights of Third Parties) Act 1999 to enforce the provision for their own benefit. See further para 3.122 above.

[416] In *Torre Asset Funding v RBS* [2013] EWHC 2670 (Ch) [179] and [204], this provision was found to emphasise the mechanical and administrative nature of the agent's role and to provide a reason for rejecting attempts to imply additional obligations on the agent.

[417] *Spread Trustee Company Limited v Sarah Ann Hutcheson and ors* [2011] UKPC 13 [60].

[418] ibid [117].

Great Western Railway[419] that ' "[w]ilful misconduct" means misconduct to which the will is a party, something opposed to accident or negligence; the *mis* conduct, not the conduct, must be wilful.' The expression appears to be synonymous with 'wilful default' and 'wilful neglect'.[420]

As the expression 'gross negligence' is often used when qualifying the protection **3.181** afforded under an exemption clause, it is relevant to consider how the courts construe that phrase. It would be a matter of construction of the contract in accordance with established principles,[421] but it is submitted that the following considerations should be relevant.

The concept of gross negligence is not easily understood in English civil law, but **3.182** the case law has recently given some helpful guidance as to how the courts view it. In criminal law, it is one of the constituent elements of a charge of involuntary manslaughter (see the discussion by Lord Mackay of Clashfern LC in *R v Adomako*[422]), but it would be dangerous and may be inappropriate to transfer criminal concepts into the civil law. Millett LJ said in *Armitage v Nourse*[423] that English lawyers had a 'healthy disrespect' for distinguishing negligence from gross negligence. Lynskey J said in *Pentecost v London District Auditor*[424] that there was no distinction between the two. In *Tradigrain SA v Intertek Testing Services (ITS) Canada Ltd*,[425] Moore-Bick LJ observed that:

> The term 'gross negligence', although often found in commercial documents, has never been accepted by English civil law as a concept distinct from civil negligence, witness the assent of several judges to the assertion that gross negligence is 'ordinary negligence with a vituperative epithet' (per Willes J in *Grill v General Iron Screw Collier Co* (1866) LR 1 CP 600, 612 referring to a dictum of Rolfe B in *Wilson v Brett* (1843) 11 M&W 113; see also *Armitage v Nurse* [1998] Ch 241, 254 per Millett LJ).

Nonetheless contract draftsmen persistently use the phrase 'gross negligence' in **3.183** contradistinction to ordinary or mere negligence, thereby forcing the courts to give the terms different meanings. In *Camerata Property Inc v Credit Suisse Securities*

---

[419] (1877) 3 QBD 195, 206.

[420] *In re City Equitable Fire Insurance Company Ltd* [1925] 1 Ch 407, 441.

[421] See *Prenn v Simmonds* [1971] 1 WLR 1381, 1384–86 (Lord Wilberforce) and in *Reardon Smith Line Ltd v Yngvar Hansen-Tangen* [1976] 1 WLR 989, 995–97 (Lord Wilberforce), *Investors Compensation Scheme Ltd v West Bromwich Building Society* [1998] 1 WLR 896, 912–13 (Lord Hoffmann) and in *Bank of Credit and Commerce International SA v Ali* [2002] 1 AC 251 [39] (Lord Hoffmann), and *Sirius International Insurance Co (Publ) v FAI General Insurance Ltd* [2004] UKHL 54, [2004] 1 WLR 3251 [18] and [19] (Lord Steyn).

[422] [1995] 1 AC 171.

[423] [1998] Ch 241, 254.

[424] [1951] 2 All ER 330, 332. See also *Sucden Financial v Fluxo-Cane Overseas Ltd* [2010] EWHC 2133 (Comm) [54] (Blair J); and *Marex Financial Ltd v Fluxo-Cane Overseas Ltd* [2010] EWHC 2690 (Comm) [93] (David Steel J).

[425] [2007] EWCA Civ 154 [23], a case where the court had to apply the concept of gross negligence as a matter of German law and found it to comprise both objective and subjective elements.

(Europe) Ltd[426] Andrew Smith J noted that '[t]he relevant question, however, is not whether generally gross negligence is a familiar concept in English civil law, but the meaning of the expression in these paragraphs'. As both the expression 'gross negligence' and the expression 'negligence' had been used, some distinction was clearly intended between them.

3.184 There are civil cases that have sought to draw a distinction between the concepts of negligence and gross negligence.[427] In cases concerning the liability of a gratuitous bailee, the concept has been likened to 'culpable default', as opposed to some mere want of foresight or mistake of judgement: see Lord Chelmsford in *Giblin v McMullen*.[428] Sitting in the Jersey Court of Appeal, Sir Godfrey Le Quesne QC said in *Midland Bank Trustee (Jersey) Ltd v Federated Pension Services Ltd*,[429] when considering a trustee exemption clause, that the concept of gross negligence did not import a requirement for an intentional disregard of danger or recklessness, but rather meant 'a serious or flagrant degree of negligence'. In Scotland, in the context of professional negligence, the Lord President (Clyde) said in *Hunter v Hanley*[430] that 'the phrase "gross negligence" [indicated] so marked a departure from the normal standard of conduct of a professional man as to infer a lack of that ordinary care which a man of ordinary skill would display'.

3.185 The most useful guidance as to the approach to construing the phrase 'gross negligence' was provided in the decision of Mance J in *Red Sea Tankers Ltd v Papachristidis (The Hellespont Ardent)*.[431] In the course of a review of both American jurisprudence, particularly the position under New York law, and some English cases, Mance J said (in relation to the construction of provisions in a commercial agreement under which an exemption for liability was qualified by reference, inter alia, to acts and the consequences of gross negligence) that:

> the concept of 'gross negligence' [under New York law] appears to me to embrace serious negligence amounting to reckless disregard, without any necessary implication of consciousness of the high degree of risk or the likely consequences of the conduct on the part of the person acting or omitting to act. If the matter is viewed according to purely English principles of construction, I would reach the same conclusion. 'Gross negligence' is clearly intended to represent something more fundamental than failure to exercise skill and/or care constituting negligence. But, as a matter of ordinary language and general impression, the concept of gross negligence seems to me capable of embracing not only conduct undertaken with actual appreciation of the risks involved, but also serious disregard of or indifference to an obvious risk ... the question whether any negligence in the present case was 'gross'

---

[426] [2011] EWHC 479 (Comm) [160].
[427] See *Spread Trustee Company Limited v Sarah Ann Hutcheson and ors* [2011] UKPC 13 [50]–[51], [117], and [135].
[428] (1868) 5 Moo NS 434, 461.
[429] [1996] PLR 179, 206.
[430] [1955] SLT 213, 217.
[431] [1997] 2 Lloyd's Rep 547, 586–88.

appears to me ultimately still very much a matter of degree and judgment[432] ... The conclusion which I reach is that the concept of gross negligence in [the clauses under review in that case] does not involve, necessarily, any subjective mental element of appreciation of risk. It may therefore include, taking the language of the American Restatement,[433] conduct which a reasonable person would perceive to entail a high degree of risk of injury to others coupled with heedlessness or indifference to or disregard of the consequences. The heedlessness, indifference or disregard need not be conscious ... [Although rigid restrictions were not justified in limiting the concept of gross negligence to occasions where there was a high degree of serious risk of injury or there were probable consequences of serious injury with a complete absence of any attempt to avoid or minimise the serious risk of injury] I see no difficulty in accepting that (a) the seriousness or otherwise of any injury that might arise, (b) the degree of likelihood of its arising and (c) the extent to which someone takes any care at all are all potentially material when considering whether particular conduct should be regarded as so aberrant as to attract the epithet of 'gross' negligence ... No single factor must be determinative. All the circumstances must be weighed and balanced when considering whether acts or omissions causing damage resulted from negligence meriting the description 'gross' and forfeiting the contractual immunity prima facie afforded by [the exemption provisions].

In *Camerata Property Inc v Credit Suisse Securities (Europe) Ltd*[434] Andrew Smith J **3.186** observed that the distinction between gross negligence and mere negligence was one of degree and not of kind, and because of this it was not easy to define or to describe. His Lordship adopted the concept described by Mance J in the paragraph above to give meaning to the distinctions that the parties had drawn in their agreement by using both the expressions 'gross negligence' and 'negligence' in the relevant clauses. In *Winnetka Trading Corp v Julius Baer International Ltd*[435] Roth J endorsed that approach and added that 'gross negligence' is not the same as subjective recklessness although it may be close to it. In *Marex Financial Ltd v Creative Finance Ltd*[436] Field J adopted Andrew Smith J's reasoning, adding that 'gross negligence' connoted 'a want of care that is more fundamental than a failure to exercise reasonable care'. In *Torre Asset Funding v RBS*[437] Sales J concluded that a facility agent had not been grossly negligent (so as to lose the protections set out in a facility agreement in accordance with their terms) as there had been— adopting the words of Mance J in the *Red Sea Tankers* case—no 'serious disregard of or indifference to an obvious risk' to others.

---

[432] This last point was made after his Lordship had referred to the speech of Lord Mackay of Clashfern LC in *R v Adomako* [1995] 1 AC 171.
[433] Para 500 of the Second Restatement of Contracts.
[434] [2011] EWHC 479 (Comm) [161].
[435] [2011] EWHC 2030 (Ch) [16].
[436] [2013] EWHC 2155 (Comm) [67].
[437] [2013] EWHC 2670 (Ch) [201]–[203].

3.6.4 The Unfair Contract Terms Act

3.187   Finally, it would be relevant to turn to the Unfair Contract Terms Act 1977 to see if any of the provisions in the agency clause which have the effect of acting as limitations or exclusions of duty or liability might be struck down by the Act and, in particular, by section 2(2) of the Act, which concerns attempts by contract to limit or exclude liability for negligence, or by section 3 of the Act, which concerns attempts to limit or restrict contractual liability. The Act is examined at section 3.5.4 above and the reader is referred to what is said there in relation to sections 2(2) and 3, as well as in relation to the requirement of reasonableness under section 11. It is submitted that, even where the Act was applicable, the protective provisions in the facility agreement would not be struck down by the Act.[438] This is principally because they will be regarded as meeting the requirement of reasonableness, in that they represent an agreed allocation of risk as between legally represented and experienced commercial parties on a basis that is commonly accepted in the London syndicated loan market. In addition, for the technical reasons outlined in the discussion of the Act earlier in this chapter, it is doubtful if the provisions of section 2(2) would apply to attempts to limit or exclude any duty of care and skill that the agent may have arising from a fiduciary relationship between it and the lenders.

---

[438] This assumes that the provisions do not go too far by seeking to protect the agent from the consequences of its deliberate or wilful misconduct or, perhaps, gross negligence.

4

LOAN TRANSFERS

4.1 Introduction

4.01 In colloquial terms, the concept of a 'loan transfer' is broader than might first appear, as it may have to address a number of different underlying factors. A transfer may concern a loan that has already been made or a transfer of a facility under which advances have yet to be made or in which some advances have already been made with further advances that may fall to be made in the future. As will be seen, it is relatively straightforward to contemplate the transfer by an assignment of the lender's rights in a debt that is already owing to it. Under English law, it is also possible for a potential creditor to assign the right to debts that may arise in the future. It is a different matter to attempt a transfer by assignment of the lender's obligation under a facility to make advances to a borrower.

4.02 Whilst the transfer may be intended, if viewed from an economic perspective, to pass on the risks and rewards of the facility from the transferor to the transferee, the mechanism that is used to achieve the transaction may, as a matter of law, amount to something other than a simple transfer by assignment of the transferor's rights or a declaration of a trust of those rights. It may, for instance, be structured as a novation or, entirely differently, it might amount merely to a contractual arrangement between the transferor and the transferee by way of a sub-participation, under which the transferee acquires no direct rights in the facility.

4.03 A facility that is to be transferred may comprise a bilateral facility between a single bank and a borrower, or the transfer might involve the transferor's participation in a syndicated facility. The facility may be secured or unsecured, and there may be one or more guarantees that have been given by parties other than the borrower, which may themselves also be secured. The transfer will need to take account of those factors in addition to the transfer of the underlying debt.

4.04 The transfer may concern a single debt or a pool or portfolio of debts. It may relate to indebtedness arising under loan facilities, commercial debt, or indebtedness where credit has been extended in other situations, such as in relation to the financing of equipment or consumer durables, as well as other types of consumer credit. It may also involve rights under financial instruments, such as bonds and other types of securities. The transfer may be a private transaction between a transferor and transferee, such as between banks, or it may be more public and involve a transfer that is funded by investors in the financial markets, such as through a securitisation.

4.1.1 Reasons for a transfer

4.05 There are a number of possible reasons as to why a bank or other financial institution may wish to dispose of its rights, and perhaps its obligations, in debt facilities and other credit or debt instruments that it has granted or which it may hold. One or more may be relevant in any particular situation.

In the first place, it may wish to control its risk of loss arising from a default or **4.06** a possible default of the debtors. The default may not yet have occurred, but the seller may be unwilling to maintain the risk. In this sense, it wishes to get out whilst the going is good. If default has already occurred or is imminent, the seller may feel that it does not wish to expend the time and effort to continue with its exposure, but would prefer to suffer the loss immediately and expend its energies elsewhere. There are institutions which specialise in purchasing such 'distressed' debt, usually at some substantial discount to the face value of the debt; the size of the discount reflecting the level of the anticipated loss in recovery. The purchaser can make a profit from recovering more than it paid in the first place, perhaps by taking a more hard-headed attitude in bringing enforcement proceedings or by engaging in activities designed to achieve a 'turn-around' in the business and fortunes of the debtor. Thus, debt purchased for 20 pence in the pound, where there is a recovery of 25 or 30 pence in the pound, will result in a substantial profit to the purchaser.

Secondly, the transfer may be used to achieve a more balanced overall portfolio, **4.07** by reducing exposure in one segment of the market and, perhaps, increasing commensurately an exposure in one or more other segments of the market. This was the case in the 1970s and 1980s when banks found that they had uneven exposures to various geographic sectors of sovereign debt. There was an active market in which such debt was traded.

Thirdly, the sale and transfer of a debt will raise funds which can be used to fund **4.08** new business, which may yield a higher return than the seller was able to obtain from the debt (and its associated facility, if there is one) that it has transferred. This may be especially true if account is taken of the burden which the transferor would otherwise sustain if it had to maintain a commitment to provide undrawn funds. The new business may be in a different area or line of business, it may involve a different type of risk, and it may be more profitable than what had gone before.

Fourthly, a bank may have been involved in establishing a facility and have earned **4.09** fees and other returns at the outset. Thereafter, the level of continuing reward may not be as great (and the carrying costs may be too much), so it does not have the same incentive to remain tied in to the facility, at least to the same extent as previously. It will look to transfer its position to one or more financial institutions or into some form of structured finance.

There are, however, problems that may arise in consequence of this type of situ- **4.10** ation. In the first place, the originating bank is reliant upon finding other financial institutions to take over its position or it must be able to effect a transfer of its debt via a securitisation. Both of those avenues of escape became scarce, for example, during the crisis in the financial markets that began in 2007. Secondly, there is the temptation that, in incepting the facility, the transferor bank may only have regard to its own short-term interests, without paying proper attention to the situation of the debtor and its ability to observe its obligations under the facility, leaving any ensuing difficulties to be suffered by the banks or other entities that take over its position. This second problem also became evident as a result of the financial crisis that began in 2007. The crisis was triggered in part by US subprime mortgage lending, much of which had been done on lax and insufficiently rigorous lending policies. As a result, a great deal of it went into default when economic conditions worsened in the US housing market. The debt had been sold and was widely dispersed through various forms of structured finance, so that the consequences of the defaults were felt widely in the financial markets. That was one of the prime causes of the financial crisis that followed.

4.11 Fifthly, the transfer may be designed to free-up regulatory capital by the reduction of the transferor's risk exposures, particularly in enabling a bank to meet its capital adequacy and large exposure requirements for regulatory purposes.

4.12 Sixthly, the transfer may have beneficial consequences in an accounting sense for the seller's balance sheet. Subject to meeting the relevant requirements, it can use the funds it has received on the sale to reflect a cash asset or to repay the liabilities it incurred in funding the debt that it has sold. It can also remove any commitment to lend funds and any associated provisions for moneys advanced that may be reflected in its accounts.

4.1.2 Benefits to the transferee

4.13 It stands to reason that, if a transfer is to proceed, there should also be perceived advantages for the purchaser of the debt or for investors in securities that have been issued by the purchasing vehicle. Some financial institutions which have relatively little presence in a particular sector may see an opportunity, via the debt transfer, to acquire knowledge and contacts with debtors which can be used by them to improve their experience and their involvement in that sector. As already mentioned, a purchaser of debt that has fallen into default (distressed debt) may feel that it can make a profit by acquiring the debt relatively cheaply and recovering, by one means or another, a greater amount than it paid. For debt that is considered to be a good credit risk, the holding of the debt (or of an investment derived from it) should provide a relatively safe and dependable use of funds, as well as a steady income or yield. The acquisition may also provide a quick profit, if the debt or investment is sold on for more than the cost of the acquisition. On the other hand, of course, anticipated profits may turn to dust if the actual or ascribed value of the debt (or the securities that are held) declines or market conditions deteriorate.

4.1.3 Effectiveness of the transfer

There is another important factor that such a purchaser or investor should bear in **4.14** mind. It concerns the effectiveness of the transfer of the underlying debt from the transferor and whether the transfer will be robust enough to survive a challenge, particularly in a subsequent insolvency of the transferor. It is essential that the transfer should stand as an outright and unimpeachable sale, so that it cannot be upset and recast or re-categorised as some form of secured financing which might be susceptible to challenge in the insolvency.

4.1.4 Chapter plan

This chapter will proceed by examining two important preliminary issues that **4.15** need to be considered before the transaction can commence, namely, matters concerned with conflict of laws issues, and matters relating to a banker's duty of confidence concerning its customer's affairs. The chapter will then move on to discuss the methods that are available under English law for a debt to be transferred and the consequences of those methods.

4.2 Conflict of Laws Issues

4.2.1 Introduction

There are a number of possible conflict of laws issues that may arise when considering a loan or credit transfer. This is relevant if there are cross-border elements in the transaction, such as where the transferor and the transferee are in different jurisdictions, or the debtor, the guarantor, or any relevant assets that have stood as security are located in more than one place. It is essential that these issues should be explored at an early stage before a transaction is agreed, as they will have an important bearing in considering what can be achieved by the proposed transaction, how it may be achieved, and the overall consequences of the transaction.

The issues that may arise will concern matters along the following lines: the rela- **4.17** tionship between the transferor and the transferee; the proprietary consequences of the transaction, if any; the effect of the transaction on the debtor; the ensuing relationship between the debtor and the transferee; and the priority that the transferee will enjoy against rival claimants in the debt, both in terms of other transfers generated by the transferor and in consequence of involuntary enforcement proceedings taken against the debtor or the transferor and the insolvency of the debtor or the transferor.[1]

---

[1] The analysis that follows should also apply to a transfer by way of security, in addition to a transfer by sale.

4.18 The discussion that follows will proceed on the assumption that the issues will be resolved by the application of the English principles of conflict of laws as applied by an English court as the forum for determining those issues. Of course, a court in another country might take a different approach, and it is always necessary when considering a transaction with cross-border elements to take advice in each relevant jurisdiction.

4.2.2 Novation v assignment

4.19 The most likely difficulties that may arise will be where the transaction representing the transfer of the underlying debt or portfolio of debts is intended to take effect as an assignment by the transferor to the transferee of the transferor's rights in the debt or debts. What follows will concentrate on that aspect. On the other hand, if the transaction is intended to be effected by a novation of the contractual rights and obligations of the respective parties then the conflict of laws issues will be mainly concerned with a determination of how the novation should be put in place so as to achieve a mutual release of the debtor and the transferor and the establishment of a new contract as between the debtor and the transferee. The novation of the credit facility (and any accompanying guarantee) will be characterised as a contractual matter and will be determined in accordance with the governing law of the contract to be terminated and the governing law that will apply to the new contract. Those respective governing laws will be ascertained by applying the rules under the EC Regulation on the law applicable to contractual obligations (Rome I)[2] (in the case of a contract entered into on or after 17 December 2009) or (in the case of a contract entered into before that date) the Rome Convention on the Law Applicable to Contractual Obligations, which was incorporated into English law by the Contracts (Applicable Law) Act 1990.[3] If, in pursuance of the novation, existing security is to be released and new security taken, it will be necessary to consider the law that will apply to achieve the release and the new security.

4.2.3 Characterisation

4.20 At the outset, it is necessary to characterise the relevant issue or issues that may need to be considered. The English approach to characterisation was described by Mance LJ in *Raiffeisen Zentralbank Österreich AG v Five Star General Trading LLC*.[4] English concepts will be used in determining how an issue should be characterised so that a conflicts rule can be allocated to it, although, as his Lordship pointed out, this should be done with reference to the substance of the issue

---

² EC 593/2008 [2008] OJ L177/6.
³ This is consistent with the *obiter* view expressed on this point by Mance LJ in *Raiffeisen Zentralbank Österreich AG v Five Star General Trading LLC* [2001] EWCA Civ 68 [34].
⁴ ibid [26]–[33].

rather than by applying a purely mechanistic formula that might apply in a purely domestic setting, bearing in mind that the court should strive to identify the most appropriate law to govern the relevant issue. For the purposes of the discussion that follows, it will be assumed that the issues should be characterised as relating to the voluntary assignment of a debt.

4.2.4 Article 14 of Rome I

A useful starting point in an examination of the conflicts rules relating to assign- **4.21** ments is Article 14 of Rome I, which replaces Article 12 of the Rome Convention (which dealt with voluntary assignments) and part of Article 13(1) (which dealt with subrogation). Article 14 covers both voluntary assignments and contractual subrogation,[5] which are dealt with in the same way. Apart from including a partial definition of what is included within the term 'assignment',[6] Article 14 makes no changes of substance to the Rome Convention provisions. The word 'voluntary' in Article 14 is used in the sense of something freely undertaken between the assignor and the assignee, as opposed to an involuntary assignment, such as would occur under a compulsory seizure or transfer of rights or assets (eg by garnishee or attachment proceedings). The first part of Article 14 concerns the relationship between the assignor and the assignee. The second part concerns matters such as the assignability of the underlying debt, the effect of the assignment upon the debtor and if the assignment can be invoked against it, if the debtor will be discharged by making payment to the assignee, and the procedures to make the assignment effective against the debtor.

Article 14 provides as follows: **4.22**

1. The relationship between assignor and assignee under a voluntary assignment or contractual subrogation of a claim against another person (the debtor) shall be governed by the law that applies to the contract between the assignor and assignee under this Regulation.
2. The law governing the assigned or subrogated claim shall determine its assignability, the relationship between the assignee and the debtor, the conditions under which the assignment or subrogation can be invoked against the debtor and whether the debtor's obligations have been discharged.
3. The concept of assignment in this Article includes outright transfers of claims, transfers of claims by way of security and pledges or other security rights over claims.

---

[5] The latter being used in some jurisdictions in place of assignment, which may be more difficult to achieve. Subrogation arising by law is dealt with in art 15.
[6] See art 14(3).

4.2.5 The effect of Article 14

4.23 On its face, Article 14 appears to cover most of the matters that might be relevant in considering the effect of a voluntary assignment. Quite clearly, the contractual relationship as between the assignor and the assignee will come within the scope of Article 14(1) and be governed by the relevant applicable law of the contract between them. Nothing much turns on that issue, as the same rule would apply in consequence of the application of Articles 3 and 4 of Rome I.

4.24 Before the decision of the Court of Appeal in the *Raiffeisen Zentralbank* case, however, there had been doubt as to whether, under English principles as to the conflict of laws, the comprehensive approach that appeared to be contemplated by Article 12 of the Rome Convention (which was in substance the same as Article 14 of Rome I) was applicable to the other matters that arise in an assignment of debts and other contractual rights. It had been suggested that some other rule might not be more appropriate, at least in so far as the proprietary issues relating to the effect of an assignment were concerned. Possible candidates were a rule based upon the *lex situs* of the debt, or, in cases of assignments of a portfolio of debts, the residence of the assignor. The doubts reflected the traditional approach in English domestic law to assignments of debts and other choses in action. The English approach proceeds on the basis that an assignment should be seen primarily as a proprietary transaction rather than as a contractual matter (although it may also have consequences relating to the performance of the debtor's obligations). An assignment involves an alienation of the transferor's property through a transfer of the rights of the assignor in the debt to the assignee. It is a subsidiary question as to the consequential effect of an assignment upon the debtor, which will mainly depend on the debtor receiving notice of the assignment.[7] The English approach gained support from the statement in the *Giuliano-Lagarde Report*[8] that the Rome Convention was concerned only with the law applicable to contractual obligations and not with property rights.

4.25 In the *Raiffeisen Zentralbank* case, Mance LJ (with whom Aldous LJ and Charles J agreed) held that the relevant English conflicts rule in relation to issues concerning the voluntary assignments of debts was that provided by Article 12 of the Rome Convention. His Lordship reached that conclusion on the basis that, in the context of Article 12 as part of the Rome Convention, the effect of an assignment

---

[7] See eg the famous commentary provided by Lord Macnaghten in *William Brandt's Sons & Co v Dunlop Rubber Co Ltd* [1905] AC 454, 462. As to the proprietary effect in English law of the assignment between the assignor and the assignee, even without notice being given to the debtor, see *Gorringe v Irwell India Rubber & Gutta Percha Works* (1886) 34 ChD 128, 132 (Cotton LJ) and 135 (Bowen LJ).

[8] See the *Report on the Rome Convention* by Professors Giuliano and Lagarde at [1980] OJ C282/10. Reference may be made to the *Report* in ascertaining the meaning or effect of the Rome Convention: see s 3(3) of the Contracts (Applicable Law) Act 1990.

was essentially contractual, in that it put the assignee into the position by which the debtor's contractual obligations thereafter fell to be performed in favour of the assignee.[9] It had been argued in the case that a distinction should be drawn between the proprietary matters that were involved in an assignment, which would fall to be considered under the relevant common law conflicts principles, and the ensuing consequences of a successful assignment upon the debtor, which would be considered under Article 12(2) (which was the same in substance as Article 14(2) of Rome I). If there had not been a successful assignment in a proprietary sense as judged under common law principles, then there would be nothing to which Article 12(2) could be relevant. That argument was rejected by Mance LJ. He said:[10]

> Article 12(1) concentrates on its face on the contractual relationship between assignor and assignee. In contrast, there is no hint in article 12(2) of any intention to distinguish between contractual and proprietary aspects of assignment. The wording appears to embrace all aspects of assignment. If the draughtsmen [of the Rome Convention] had conceived that the basic issue, whether and under what conditions an assignee acquires the right to sue the obligor, could involve reference to a quite different law to either of the two mentioned in article 12(1) and (2), one would have expected them to say so, if only to avoid confusion. Further, on [the contrary case as it had been argued], it is unclear why the draughtsmen troubled to refer so explicitly in article 12(2) to the relationship of the parties and the conditions under which the assignment could be invoked against the debtor. It seems self-evident that an assignee could not succeed to any other relationship with the debtor than that established by the contract assigned, and that he could not avoid any conditions prescribed by the contract.

The facts of the *Raiffeisen Zentralbank* case involved a purported equitable assign- **4.26**
ment of claims under a marine insurance policy, of which notice had been given to the French insurers, who were the 'debtors' for the purposes of Article 12.[11] There had also been an attempt to attach the policy and the proceeds of a claim in France following procedures under French law. Those involved in the attachment had challenged the effectiveness of the assignment. The policy was stated to be governed by English law. In pursuance of Article 12(2), Mance LJ applied English law, as the governing law of the policy under which a claim would arise, to determine if the benefit of any claims under the policy had been assigned and, in consequence, if such assignment bound the insurers to pay the assignee. He held that there had been a successful assignment in favour of the assignee.

---

[9] See [2001] EWCA Civ 68 [34]–[57]. His Lordship left undecided the appropriate conflicts rule where the issue concerns the effect of an involuntary assignment, such as where there have been garnishee proceedings: see Mance LJ's discussion of the point at [2001] EWCA Civ 68 [57].

[10] ibid [45].

[11] Although the point was not referred to in the judgment, it was presumably felt that the contract of insurance under which the assigned debt arose was not excluded from the operation of the Rome Convention by virtue of art 1(3) of the Convention, on the basis that the risk insured (collision on the high seas) was situated outside the territories of the EU Member States.

4.2.6 Article 14(2)

4.27 Mance LJ in the *Raiffeisen Zentralbank* case indicated that the reference in Article 12(2) of the Rome Convention to 'the law governing the right' assigned (rephrased slightly in Article 14(2) of Rome I as 'the law governing the assigned … claim') was a reference to the governing law of the contract under which the relevant obligation arose which gave rise to the right.[12] He also said that when Article 12(2) refers (as Article 14(2) of Rome I also does) to the 'conditions' under which an assignment will bind the debtor, it was referring to matters such as the necessity (or otherwise) of giving notice to the debtor.[13] As English law was the governing law of the insurance policy and notice had been given to the insurers of the assignment, sufficient steps had been taken to make the assignment effective against the insurers and to require them to pay the assignee,[14] notwithstanding that the insurers were located in France. The alternative argument that had been put to the court, which was rejected, was that the effectiveness of the assignment should be determined by the application of French law which was the *lex situs* of the policy and of any claims payable under it.

4.28 Article 14(2) of Rome I refers to the 'assignability' of the claim which is the subject of a purported assignment. A clause in the underlying debt contract which was intended to preclude or restrict an assignment would be a matter relevant to the assignability of the debt[15] and so, on the face of Article 14(2), the interpretation and effect of such a clause would be a matter to be determined in accordance with the governing law of that contract.[16] Under that governing law, if the assignment is effective as against the debtor then it follows that the transaction should also be considered, as to the assignability of the debt, as being effective as between the assignor and the assignee. Although it is not free from doubt, if the transaction is intended by the assignor and the assignee to be effective as against the debtor but fails to achieve that result because it is unassignable, as determined in pursuance of Article 14(2), then it would seem to follow that it should also be treated, as between the assignor and the assignee, as having failed to achieve a transfer to the assignee of the assignor's rights against the debtor, at least in the sense of putting the assignee in a direct relationship with the debtor as would be

---

[12] See [2001] EWCA Civ 68 [43]. See also *Macmillan Inc v Bishopsgate Investment Trust plc (No 3)* [1996] 1 WLR 387, 400–01 (Staughton LJ), and *Cofacredit SA v Morris* [2006] EWHC 353 (Ch) [100] (Warren J).

[13] [2001] EWCA Civ 68 [43].

[14] *William Brandt's Sons & Co v Dunlop Rubber Co Ltd* [1905] AC 454.

[15] See further in what follows as to the effect of such provisions under English domestic law.

[16] Under art 9 of the UNCITRAL Convention (see para 4.30), such a clause does not affect the validity of an assignment, in so far as it relates to assignments of receivables arising from the supply or lease of goods or services, construction contracts, contracts for the sale or lease of real property, the sale or use of IP, the payment obligation under credit cards, and the net settlement of netting agreements between two or more parties. This, however, is inconsistent with art 29 of the Convention, which is in very similar terms to art 14(2) of Rome I.

the case under an English form of legal assignment. The consequences as between the assignor and the assignee would then fall to be resolved in accordance with Article 14(1), through the application of the governing law of their transaction.

The stipulation in Article 14(2), that the governing law of the debt should deter- **4.29** mine if the debtor will be discharged, for instance if the debtor pays the assignee, is consistent with Article 12(1) of Rome I. Article 12(1) provides that the governing law of a contract will determine matters concerning its performance and if the obligations under the contract have been extinguished. The same approach would be reached by the application of the common law conflicts principles, under which it has been held that the governing law of a contract will determine if the obligations under it have been discharged.[17] An interesting question arises as to the application of rights of set-off that the debtor may wish to assert against its obligation to pay the assigned debt. It is submitted that if the governing law of the debt would treat the proposed set-off as affecting the substance of the debtor's contractual obligation and would permit the debtor to assert a right of set-off then the debtor should be permitted to do so.[18] However, if the right of set-off is procedural and so arises as a form of procedural defence or counter-claim then the right to assert the set-off would be determined by the laws of the forum rather than the governing law of the debt.

4.2.7 Priorities

It would also appear that matters of priorities as between competing assignees, in **4.30** so far as might concern the debtor (because, for instance, the debtor may be in a dilemma as to who to pay if it has received notice of competing assignments), would also be resolved by applying the governing law of the debt in pursuance of the rule under Article 14(2).[19] As will be seen later, it is probable that the position at common law, ignoring the Rome Convention and Rome I, is that questions of

---

[17] See Lord Hoffmann, giving the advice of the Privy Council, in *Wight v Eckhardt Marine* [2003] UKPC 37, [2004] 1 AC 147 (PC) [13]–[15].

[18] For instance, under English law if the right of set-off that is asserted is that of a transaction or equitable set-off that impugns the entitlement of the creditor under the contract (see the discussion by Buxton LJ in *Smith v Muscat* [2003] EWCA 962, [2003] 1 WLR 2853; see also s 53(1)(a) of the Sale of Goods Act 1979 and ss 19(3)(c) and 19(4)(b) of the Consumer Rights Act 2015), then it would be a substantive right governed by the governing law of the contract. On the other hand, if the set-off that is asserted is a legal set-off then that is a procedural right that would arise if English law was the *lex fori* of the proceedings.

[19] See the discussion by Mance LJ in the *Raiffeisen Zentralbank* case at [2001] EWCA Civ 68 [49]–[52] in which his Lordship appeared to prefer the position that had been reached by the courts in Germany, in preference to that expressed by the Dutch courts, which had held that the question should be resolved by applying the law that governed the relationship between the assignor and the assignee as determined pursuant to art 12(1) of the Rome Convention. See also the *Macmillan* case at [1996] 1 WLR 387, 400–01 (Staughton LJ). As Mance LJ noted, however, it was unnecessary for him to express a final view because English law would have applied as both the governing law of the debt and as the governing law of the contract of assignment in the case before him.

priority between different claimants should be governed by the *lex situs* of a debt. A rule based upon either the governing law of the debt or the *lex situs* of the debt does mean that, in so far as the debtor might be affected, he should be able to ascertain the position by reference to a law that is directly related to him or the contract to which he is a party. By contrast, the UNCITRAL Convention on the Assignment of Receivables in International Trade[20] provides for a basic rule, to which there are exceptions, that priorities should be determined by the law of the place where the assignor is located.[21] That rule is designed to cover the situation where there is a portfolio or a large number of debts that is or are the subject of an assignment and the practical difficulty of treating the issue differently for each of the debts depending upon its individual *lex situs* or governing law.

4.31 Whilst a rule for determining priorities based upon the location of the assignor has an apparent simplicity, it is not free from difficulties. One immediate point is the problem in determining when it will apply. If it is only to apply where there is an assignment of a portfolio or a large number of debts, then the question arises as to when that numerical situation will have arisen; in other words, when will it be considered that the assignment concerns a sufficient number of debts to invoke the rule? It also removes the focus from a situation that is associated with a debtor to one solely connected with the original creditor. If the debtor is faced with a number of competing claims it may find itself in some difficulty if the priority between them is to be determined under a system of law that is unconnected with the debtor or the governing law of the contract under which the debt has arisen. Furthermore, such a rule will create obvious difficulties where there is a competition involving successive assignments and sub-assignments with the respective assignees and sub-assignees located in different jurisdictions.

4.32 It should be noted that Article 27(2) of Rome I contains a reference to priorities between competing assignments. Article 27(2) contemplates that a rule regarding the effectiveness of an assignment or subrogation of a claim against third parties and the priority of the claim over a right of another person might be incorporated into Rome I in the future. The EC Commission is charged by Article 27(2) to investigate the matter and recommend if such a change should be made. A provision in an early draft of Rome I contained a specific rule dealing with priorities, which was not carried through to the final version of Rome I when it was finally adopted. It would have provided that priorities should be determined by the law

---

[20] Adopted by Resolution 56/81 of the General Assembly of the United Nations in its 56th Session in 2001.

[21] Art 22. By art 5, a person is located where it has its place of business or, if it does not have a place of business, the location of its habitual residence. If the assignor or assignee has a place of business in more than one country, it will be located where it exercises its central administration. If the debtor has a place of business in more than one country, the place of business will be that which has the closest relationship to the original contract, that is, the contract under which the subject debt arose.

of the place of the habitual residence of the assignor. An alternative suggestion (favoured by the UK) was that priorities should be determined by the governing law of the underlying claim. At the time of writing, the Commission has, pursuant to its obligation under Article 27(2), proposed a Regulation which would adopt a mixed approach, with the law of the assignor's habitual residence being the general rule but with certain assignments being subject, as an exception, to the law of the assigned claim, and with a choice of law possibility for securitisations.[22]

4.2.8 Disposition other than by way of notified assignment

Notwithstanding what was said in the *Raiffeisen Zentralbank* case, it is unclear **4.33** if Article 14 applies at all where the transaction between the disponor and the disponee is not one contemplated by Article 14(2). Such would be the situation where the transaction was not intended to have any legal effect upon the debtor because there was to be no change in the person to whom the contractual obligation of the debtor is due, as for instance under the English forms of unnotified equitable assignment or declaration of trust.[23] It is submitted that Article 14(2) should have no role in such a situation. Both the *Giuiliano-Lagarde Report* (in relation to Article 14(2)'s predecessor, Article 12(2) of the Rome Convention) and the approach taken by Mance LJ in the *Raiffeisen Zentralbank* case (in relation to Article 12(2) of the Rome Convention) indicate that Article 12(2) of the Rome Convention (and therefore, logically, Article 14(2) of Rome I) is to be viewed in the context of the contractual obligations of the debtor and the effect that an assignment would have on those obligations. If the transaction is not intended to affect the debtor's obligations and will leave the debtor contractually obliged to its original creditor then Article 14(2) should not be relevant at all.

---

[22] *Proposal for a Regulation of the European Parliament and of the Council on the law applicable to the third-party effects of assignments of claims* COM(2018) 96 final. The Proposal follows an external study in 2011 contracted by the Commission (British Institute of International and Comparative Law, *Study on the question of effectiveness of an assignment or subrogation of a claim against third parties and the priority of the assigned or subrogated claim over a right of another person*) and a report in 2016 by the Commission presenting possible approaches to the matter (*Report from the Commission to the European Parliament, the Council and the European Economic and Social Committee on the question of the effectiveness of an assignment or subrogation of a claim against third parties and the priority of the assigned or subrogated claim over the right of another person* COM(2016) 626 final).

[23] An example of a declaration of trust as a method of disposing of a contractual right will be found in the judgment of Lightman J in *Don King Productions Inc v Warren* [2000] Ch 291 (approved by the Court of Appeal at the same citation). His Lordship emphasised that the effect of the declaration of trust in such a situation would be to leave the underlying relationship between the debtor and its original creditor (which would become the trustee) unaffected by the declaration of trust. It is not clear, however, where that would leave the beneficiary if the trustee refused to act on its behalf and the beneficiary wished to invoke the right to enforce the debt against the debtor using the procedure outlined by the Privy Council in *Vandepitte v Preferred Accident Ins Corp of New York* [1933] AC 70. See further the discussion at paras 4.59 and 4.96 and in *Barbados Trust Co Ltd v Bank of Zambia* [2007] EWCA Civ 148. It is arguable that the *Vandepitte* procedure (as that description implies) is merely a matter of procedure, so the issue would fall to be resolved by the *lex fori* rather than by the governing law of the assignment.

4.34 Assuming that Article 14(2) would have no relevance in such a situation, it now falls to be considered whether Article 14(1) has any role to play in finding:

(1) a governing law to determine the obligations of the disponor to the disponee;

(2) the consequential relationship between them (including, for instance, if there are any proprietary consequences of that relationship, which may be a crucial issue if the assignor becomes insolvent and the assignee is faced with a claim that the debt falls into the estate of the insolvent assignor); and

(3) the effect upon the relationship of a restrictive clause in the underlying debt contract which purports to prohibit or restrict assignments.

4.35 In the overall context of Article 14, it appears that the concept of a voluntary assignment, as mentioned in Article 14(1) and as partially defined in Article 14(3), is that contemplated by Article 14(2) and not other forms of transaction which are intended to have an effect as between the disponor and the disponee but to leave the debtor's relationship with its original creditor unaffected. Further, in the overall scheme of Article 14, the issue as to assignability is placed in Article 14(2), which implies that it is not a matter to be considered under Article 14(1) or as a consequence of the mutual obligations of the assignor and the assignee to which that article makes reference.

4.36 In a purely contractual sense, nothing very much will turn on whether the contractual relationship between the assignor and the assignee is determined by reference to Article 14(1) or by the application of the general rules in Rome I, particularly those in Articles 3 and 4.[24] In so far, however, as it might be relevant to determine the proprietary consequences of a purported assignment or a similar dealing, such as might arise under a declaration of trust or a charge, Rome I should not apply, bearing in mind (i) the statement in the *Giuliano-Lagarde Report*, to which reference has already been made, that the Rome Convention was concerned only with the law applicable to contractual obligations and not with property rights, and (ii) the fact that the relevant provisions of Rome I are in substance the same as those of the Rome Convention.

4.2.9 The common law approach and the *lex situs*

4.37 If that view is correct then it is necessary to fall back on the conflicts approach that would be taken at common law, without taking account of Article 14.[25] Jenkins

---

[24] As Mance LJ noted in the *Raiffeisen Zentralbank* case [2001] EWCA Civ 68 [52], art 12(1) of the Rome Convention (the predecessor of art 14(1)) restates the contractual position that would flow from the other provisions of the Rome Convention.

[25] It is submitted that the analysis that follows would apply to both an unnotified equitable assignment and to a declaration of trust. Under English conflicts rules, the law governing matters such as the administration of the trust would depend upon the application of the Hague Convention on the Law Applicable to Trusts and their Recognition of 1985, which applies under English law by virtue of The Recognition of Trusts Act 1987. However, art 4 of the Convention provides that the Convention does not apply to preliminary issues concerning the validity of the establishment of the

LJ in *Re United Railways of the Havana and Regla Warehouses Ltd*²⁶ said that the validity and effect of an assignment of a debt was governed by the *lex situs* of the debt rather than by the proper, or governing, law of the debt. This view was approved by Lord Hoffmann in the Privy Council in *Wight v Eckhardt Marine GmbH*.²⁷ The problem with an approach based upon the *lex situs*, however, lies in determining the location of the situs.²⁸ Unlike the position with physical assets, the concept of a situs (or location) of a debt is rather artificial. The situs of a debt is said to be where the debtor resides, on the basis that the place of residence would be where enforcement action would be taken against the debtor.²⁹

Difficulties will arise if the debtor has more than one place of residence or moves. **4.38** If one of several places of residence of the debtor is also specified in the contract as the place where the debt should be paid, it will be regarded as being the situs of the debt.³⁰ In the absence of such specificity, Lord Hobhouse in *Société Eram Shipping Co Ltd v Hong Kong & Shanghai Banking Corp Ltd*³¹ speculated that in the case where the debtor was an ordinary trading company and the debt was an ordinary commercial debt, the debtor might be sued wherever it had a place of residence and, consequently, there might be more than one situs for the debt. In any event, enforcement action may be taken in places other than where the debtor has a residence such as, for instance, where the debtor has assets (including assets which have been given as security for payment of the debt) or where it has submitted to jurisdiction, as it might do expressly in a loan agreement. All of this goes to demonstrating the artificial nature of a concept of the situs of a debt, as well as the problems that might arise in determining the situs in particular cases. These difficulties were referred to by Mance LJ in the *Raiffeisen Zentralbank* case.³²

---

trust and the transfer of the assets to the trust. Thus, the Convention would not be relevant in considering if a restrictive clause in the contract under which the debt arises might prevent the effective establishment of the trust over the contractual rights affected by the clause.

²⁶ [1960] Ch 52, 84–88. A similar approach was taken in *Re Maudslay Sons & Field, Maudslay v Maudslay* [1900] 1 Ch 602, but the majority of the Court of Appeal rejected this approach in *Republica de Guatemala v Nunez* [1927] 1 KB 669.

²⁷ [2003] UKPC 37 [13]–[15].

²⁸ Interestingly, art 2(g) of the EC Insolvency Regulation (EC 1346/2000 [2000] OJ L160/1) specifies that claims will be treated as situated at the place of the debtor's centre of main interests.

²⁹ See eg *Jabbour (F & K) v Custodian of Israeli Absentee Property* [1954] 1 WLR 139 and *Alloway v Phillips* [1980] 1 WLR 888. With respect to the obligations of a bank under a letter of credit, see *Taurus Petroleum Ltd v State Oil Marketing Co of the Ministry of Oil, Iraq* [2017] UKSC 64 (overruling *Power Curber International Ltd v National Bank of Kuwait SAK* [1981] 1 WLR 1233).

³⁰ *Re Claim by Helbert Wagg & Co Ltd* [1956] Ch 323. This would be the case with respect to the payment obligations of a bank on an account in credit which is maintained for its customer (see *Société Eram Shipping Co Ltd v Hong Kong & Shanghai Banking Corp Ltd* [2003] UKHL 30 [73] (Lord Hobhouse)), and the payment obligations of a bank under a letter of credit issued subject to a term that branches of the bank in different countries were considered to be separate banks (see *Taurus Petroleum Ltd v State Oil Marketing Co of the Ministry of Oil, Iraq* [2017] UKSC 64 [31] (Lord Clarke)).

³¹ [2003] UKHL 30.

³² At [2001] EWCA Civ 68 [36] and [37].

4.39 It is tentatively submitted that under English common law conflicts principles (in cases where Article 14(2) of Rome I did not apply) the *lex situs* of a debt would also determine matters of priority as between rival dispositions of the debt. This follows from *Re Queensland Mercantile and Agency Co*[33] and from *Re Maudslay Sons & Field, Maudslay v Maudslay*.[34] This is said with some hesitancy because it may be that the authority of the first of those cases should be confined to an issue involving the determination of the priority of an involuntary assignment over an earlier voluntary assignment. Furthermore, the same result would have been achieved in *Re Maudslay Sons & Field*, on the facts of the case, if the proper law of the debt had been applied rather than the *lex situs*.[35]

4.40 In relation to the effect of a clause in the contract under which the debt arises, which purports to prohibit or restrict the ability of the creditor to deal with the debt or its rights in relation thereto, it is submitted that English common law conflicts principles would apply the governing law of the debt to determine the effect of such a clause. The interpretation of the clause must be ascertained in accordance with contractual principles, by the application of the governing law of the contract, to be found by the application of Rome I.[36] It is reasonable for the debtor to expect that the consequences of such a clause should also be determined by the governing law of the contract.[37]

4.41 Notwithstanding the views already expressed, in *Dicey, Morris & Collins*[38] it is suggested that the common law, ignoring Rome I, would take an approach similar to that taken under Article 14. Thus, the view is advanced in that work that the effect of an intended assignment as between the assignor and the assignee should be determined by the governing law of their transaction, whilst the question as to the right to alienate a debt would be governed by the governing law of the debt.[39] The examination in that work on this point is based upon an assignment of contractual rights and appears to assume that the assignment is intended to have an effect upon the debtor. Where the transaction between the disponor and disponee is not intended to have that effect, that view might not apply. The Court of Appeal made some general obiter comments on the conflicts rules relating to assignment of debts in *Macmillan Inc v Bishopsgate Investment Trust plc (No 3)*.[40] The comments were made in the context of a battle over competing priorities in shares in a corporation, and none of the comments was addressed to the specific issue of the

---

[33] [1892] 1 Ch 219.
[34] [1900] 1 Ch 602.
[35] See the *Raiffeisen Zentralbank* case at [2001] EWCA Civ 68 [53]–[56] (Mance LJ).
[36] See art 12(1)(a).
[37] Art 12(1)(c) of Rome I provides that the consequences of a total or partial breach of the contract should be determined by the governing law of the contract.
[38] *The Conflict of Laws* (15th edn, London: Sweet & Maxwell 2012).
[39] ibid paras 24-054 and 24-055.
[40] [1996] 1 WLR 387.

right to alienate a debt in a situation where Article 14(2) may not be applicable. Staughton, Auld, and Aldous LJJ generally appeared to favour the approach taken by *Dicey, Morris & Collins* in relation to matters concerning the assignment of debts, but not other intangible rights. Their views as to the assignment of debts, however, were influenced by Article 12 of the Rome Convention (now Article 14 of Rome I).[41] For the reasons stated earlier, it is submitted that those views should not apply to a situation that is outside the scope of Article 14.

4.3 The Banker's Obligation of Confidence

In *Tournier v National Provincial and Union Bank of England*[42] the Court of Appeal held that a banker has a duty to maintain the confidence of information concerning its customer's affairs which becomes known to the banker during the course of the banking relationship between them.[43] This includes information from other sources of which the bank becomes aware in the course of that relationship.[44] In the absence of an express term, the duty arises from an implied term of the contract between the bank and its customer.[45] One of the four exceptions to the duty, where disclosure is permitted within the compass of the implied term of the contract, is disclosure with the customer's consent. Such consent may be given prospectively by a customer in the facility agreement between it and the bank, or it may be given at the time that the bank intends to make the disclosure to a potential purchaser.[46] In passing, it should be noted that another one of the

4.42

---

[41] ibid 400–01 (Staughton LJ), 410 (Auld LJ), and 419 (Aldous LJ).

[42] [1924] 1 KB 461.

[43] See, in particular, Bankes LJ in ibid.

[44] ibid.

[45] Information of a confidential nature which is imparted in circumstances of confidence may also be protected under the more general law as to confidential information (see *Attorney-General v Guardian Newspapers Ltd (No 2)* [1990] 1 AC 109, 281–82 (Lord Goff of Chieveley)). Examples of the difficulties that a bank may find itself in if it breaches the obligation of confidence will be seen in *United Pan-Europe Communications NV v Deutsche Bank AG* [2000] 2 BCLC 461 and in *Jackson v Royal Bank of Scotland plc* [2005] UKHL 3, [2005] 1 WLR 377.

[46] Whilst *Tournier's* case contemplates that the customer's consent may be given impliedly (see eg [1924] 1 KB 461, 484 (Atkin LJ)), *Turner v Royal Bank of Scotland plc* [1999] 2 All ER (Comm) 664 indicates that it may be difficult in practice to establish circumstances from which the consent could be implied. See also *Richmond Pharmacology Ltd v Chester Overseas Ltd* [2014] EWHC 2692 (Ch), where a shareholders' agreement contained a confidentiality clause with no exception for disclosure to potential purchasers of shares, even if done subject to a non-disclosure agreement: the court refused to imply such an exception. Nonetheless, it might be argued that if the facility agreement specifically contemplates a disposal by the bank of its rights then the customer could be taken impliedly to have consented to disclosure of information in connection with such a disposal. In any event, the Loan Market Association's recommended forms of loan agreement contain express provisions permitting the lender to provide information about the loan to potential assignees. In *Irish Bank Resolution Corporation Ltd v Camden Market Holdings Corp* [2017] EWCA Civ 7, the Court of Appeal rejected an argument that there was an implied term restricting the lender's right to disclose, as that would be inconsistent with the express terms of the agreement.

exceptions, disclosure in the bank's own interests, will not permit disclosure for the purposes of a loan transfer. That exception, whilst appearing on its face to be fairly wide, has generally been construed narrowly and covers action which a bank has to take in its own self-defence, such as in legal proceedings. It may also extend to action that a bank takes to protect its commercial reputation.[47]

4.43 In addition to the duty arising under *Tournier's* case, a similar duty may arise under the EU General Data Protection Regulation[48] (which became applicable on 25 May 2018), concerning information that might be held by a bank about its customers and others who are natural persons. For instance, such information must be processed in a manner that ensures its appropriate security.[49] This includes protection (through the use of appropriate technical or organisational security measures) against unauthorised or unlawful processing and against accidental loss, destruction, or damage.

4.44 In summary, in the context of a transaction under which a bank proposes to transfer (using the expression in a broad sense) loans owing to it by its customers, the bank must bear in mind that, in pursuance of its duty of confidentiality, it should not make disclosure to the proposed purchaser or others of any details concerning the identity of its customers and the loans it has made to them without their consent. If such disclosure is not possible then it is unlikely that the transaction could proceed, as the purchaser and others will wish to investigate what is to be bought, which cannot be done without the relevant information.

4.4 The Methods of Transfer under English Law

4.45 There are various possible methods of structuring a transaction under English law so as to achieve a transfer of a debt or a credit facility. The nature and characteristics of the underlying facility and the rights vested in the transferor, as well as its continuing obligations under the facility, will be important matters that should be taken into account in deciding upon the method to be chosen, as well as the relationship that it is desired to achieve between the transferee and the debtor. The methods are as follows:

(1) an assignment of the transferor's rights, either by way of an absolute, or legal, assignment under section 136 of the Law of Property Act 1925 or as an equitable assignment of those rights;

(2) a declaration of trust of the benefit of the transferor's rights;

---

[47] See *Christofi v Barclays Bank plc* [1999] 2 All ER (Comm) 417, 425 (Chadwick LJ).
[48] Regulation (EU) 2016/679 [2016] OJ L119/1.
[49] See art 5(1)(f).

(3) a novation of the transferor's rights and obligations under the underlying facility between it and the borrower; and

(4) a contractual sub-participation granted by the transferor to the transferee.

Each of those methods of structuring a transaction will be outlined in turn. **4.46** Because of the size and complexity of the issues involved, there will then follow an examination of a number of legal issues that might affect an assignment (nearly all of these issues will also be relevant to a declaration of trust).

4.5 Assignment

There are two forms of assignment of debts and other choses in action that are **4.47** recognised by English law. In historical order of development they are an equitable assignment and an absolute (or legal) assignment under section 136 of the Law of Property Act 1925. As between the assignor and the assignee, each of them will achieve a transfer of the assignor's rights, so that, in the assignor's insolvency, the transferred rights will be treated as belonging to the assignee and will thus fall outside the ambit of the insolvent's estate.[50] However, there may still be a practical difficulty, particularly in the case of an unnotified equitable assignment, if the assignor has collected the proceeds and dissipated them in such a way as to defeat an attempt to trace the funds. The principal benefit of an assignment within section 136 is a procedural benefit, as the legal right in the assigned debt is vested in the assignee, so that the assignee can sue in its own name at law to recover the debt and the debtor is obliged to pay the assignee.

The discussion that follows will begin by looking at the particular characteristics **4.48** of each of these methods of assignment. It will then examine a number of issues that are common to both of them. In the background to many of those issues are the basic principles that the debtor should not be put in a worse position in consequence of an assignment than that in which the debtor would have been placed without the assignment, and that an assignee cannot inherit a better position or a wider set of rights than was possessed by the assignor.[51]

---

[50] As to the proprietary effect in English law of the assignment between the assignor and the assignee, even without notice being given to the debtor, see *Gorringe v Irwell India Rubber & Gutta Percha Works* (1886) 34 ChD 128, 132 (Cotton LJ) and 135 (Bowen LJ). This assumes, however, that the assignment is intended to be an outright assignment by way of sale, rather than by way of security. If the assignment is a form of security then other considerations will also apply, particularly concerning the need to register the assignment under s 859A et seq of the Companies Act 2006.

[51] See *Dawson v Great Northern & City Railway Co* [1905] 1 KB 260. However, it may be possible for a party to a contract to assign an accrued right that arises from a breach of contract by the other party, even though the loss or damage that follows from the breach had not manifested itself before the assignor had disposed of the subject matter of the contract, so that the assignor had not personally suffered any loss: see *Offer-Hoar v Larkstore Ltd* [2006] EWCA Civ 1079, [2006] 1 WLR 2926 and *Pegasus Management Holdings SCA v Ernst & Young* [2012] EWHC 738 (Ch). See also ch 2, where there is more discussion of this point.

4.5.1 Absolute or legal assignment

4.49 Section 136 of the Law of Property Act 1925[52] provides that a debt or other legal thing in action may be assigned at law. The section substantially re-enacts the provisions of section 25(6) of the Judicature Act 1873, which introduced the concept of an assignment which would be effective at law, rather than merely in equity. Before that time, it was not possible to have an assignment that would be recognised at law.

4.50 Such an assignment at law will only be effective if the following requirements are met. The assignment must be in writing and signed by the assignor;[53] the assignment must be absolute and not merely conditional nor by way of charge;[54] as the assignment must be of a debt or other legal thing in action, it must be in existence at the time of the assignment, although it need not then be due for payment, and it must be an assignment of the whole debt and not merely a part of it; and written notice of the assignment must be given to the debtor.[55] There is no requirement that the assignment must be for valuable consideration.[56]

4.51 If the requirements of section 136 are met then the effect of the assignment is that, from the time the notice is given, the assignment will be recognised at common law, so that the legal right in the debt will be transferred to the assignee, who will acquire the right to give a good discharge to the debtor and to sue the debtor in the assignee's own name, without having to join the assignor in the suit. The corollary of this is that the debtor will not obtain a good discharge of the debt if it pays the assignor. If the debtor is in doubt, section 136 provides that it can gain protection by interpleading and paying the debt into court. It should be noted that the right of the assignee is expressly made subject by section 136

---

[52] Similar provisions will be found in s 1 of the Policies of Assurance Act 1867 and s 50 of the Marine Insurance Act 1906.

[53] The requirement for the assignor's signature is dispensed with in relation to a financial collateral arrangement by virtue of reg 4(3) of the Financial Collateral Arrangements (No 2) Regs, SI 2003/3226.

[54] As to which see *Tancred v Delagoa Bay & East Africa Ry Co* (1889) 23 QBD 239; *Hughes v Pump House Hotel Co Ltd* [1902] 2 KB 190; and *Bexhill UK Ltd v Razzaq* [2012] EWCA Civ 1376.

[55] Curiously, the section does not specify who should give the notice. Common sense might dictate that the notice should be given by the assignor, being the person to whom the debtor was obliged before the assignment, rather than by the assignee, of whom the debtor would be unaware. Nonetheless, a notice which was given by the assignee's solicitors was held to be an effective notice for the purposes of s 25(6) of the Judicature Act 1873, which was the predecessor of s 136: see *Denney, Gasquet & Metcalfe v Conklin* [1913] 3 KB 177. No special form of notice is necessary, so long as the fact of assignment and the identity of the assignee appear with reasonable certainty: see *Van Lynn Developments Ltd v Pelias Construction Co Ltd* [1969] 1 QB 607.

[56] *Harding v Harding* (1886) 17 QBD 442; *Re Westerton* [1919] 2 Ch 104. However, a lack of proper value received by the assignor may be relevant to a challenge mounted in the context of insolvency proceedings concerning the assignor: see the following sections of the Insolvency Act 1986: ss 238 and 339 (transactions at an undervalue), s 423 (transactions defrauding creditors), ss 239 and 340 (preferences), and s 245 (avoidance of certain floating charges).

to any equities which have priority over the assignee, such as rights of set-off that the debtor may wish to assert and the rights of third parties who assert competing priorities.[57]

It will be apparent that section 136 will not apply, and so it will not be possible **4.52** to have an assignment under that section, if any of the requirements mentioned above are missing. For instance, if the proposed assignment is to be for part only of the debt, if notice is not to be given to the debtor, or if the assignment is to be of a future debt, then a different method of achieving the transfer will have to be found, such as by using the form of an equitable assignment.

4.5.2 Equitable assignment

Historically, equity was willing to recognise assignments of choses in action, **4.53** whether by way of outright transfer or by way of security, thereby supplying proprietary effect to transactions which the common law was unable to comprehend. Indeed, equity even recognised assignments of parts of choses in action and assignments of future property. In effect, equity directed the assignor to act on behalf of the assignee, such as by directing the assignor to sue the debtor and to hold the benefit of the chose, including the proceeds of payment, on trust for the assignee. Despite the passing of the Judicature Act 1873, it remained possible to have an equitable assignment of legal or equitable property and to have an equitable assignment in situations where the requirements of section 25(6) of that Act or of section 136 of the Law of Property Act 1925 may not have been met (eg an assignment of part of a debt, an assignment of future property, or where notice had not been given to the debtor).[58]

An equitable assignment does not require any particular form or procedure.[59] **4.54** Indeed, except in cases where section 53(1)(c) of the Law of Property Act 1925 requires it, an equitable assignment does not even have to be in writing.[60]

---

[57] See *E Pfeiffer Weinkellerei-Weineinkauf GmbH v Arbuthnot Factors Ltd* [1988] 1 WLR 150, 161–63 and *Compaq Computer Ltd v Abercorn Group Ltd* [1991] BCC 484, 497–502 where it was said that the rules of priority as between competing interests, be they legal or equitable interests, will be the same as those that apply as between competing equitable assignments. Those rules, and the rules concerning the debtor's rights of set-off, are discussed further in what follows.

[58] See *William Brandt's Sons & Co v Dunlop Rubber Co Ltd* [1905] AC 454, 461 (Lord Macnaghten).

[59] Lord Macnaghten in *William Brandt's*, at 462. However, there must be a sufficient externally observable indication of an intention to assign: see *Finlan v Eyton Morris Winfield* [2007] EWHC 914 (Ch), [2007] 4 All ER 143 [33]. In *The Argo Fund Ltd v Essar Steel Ltd* [2005] EWHC 600 (Comm), [2005] 2 Lloyd's Rep 203 (affd [2006] EWCA Civ 241), it was held that it was incompatible with such an intention that the parties had structured the transaction as a novation. They could not, if the novation failed, then assert that they really intended an assignment.

[60] A point that was of some significance when a written assignment might have attracted stamp duty. Duty on such transactions was abolished by the Finance Act 2003.

4.55 There remains the question, however, as to whether an equitable assignment must be supported by valuable consideration.[61] In this, there are two of the famous equitable maxims in play. One is that equity recognises as done that which ought to be done. The other is that equity will not assist a volunteer. In his speech in *William Brandt's Sons & Co v Dunlop Rubber Co Ltd*[62] in which he described equitable assignments, Lord Macnaghten did refer to the presence of value in support of an equitable assignment. Nonetheless, value is not always required in equity to support an assignment of either legal or equitable property,[63] as evidenced by the discussion of the Court of Appeal in *Milroy v Lord*,[64] in which the court acknowledged the possibility of a voluntary assignment but said that the court would not perfect an imperfect gift. Thus, it would not enforce an imperfect voluntary assignment by imposing a trust and vice versa. This left for subsequent generations the question as to what steps must have been taken, by the donor in particular, to establish the validity of the gift.[65] A voluntary conditional agreement[66] to assign property will be regarded as an imperfect gift, and so as not binding on the purported assignor where the fulfilment of the condition is within the discretion of that person. There are instances, however, where value will undoubtedly be required. One is where there is an agreement to assign future property.[67] Another concerns the granting of an equitable charge.[68]

4.5.3 Future property

4.56 Future property means property that is not in the hands of the purported assignor at the time it agrees to assign the property. The property may not exist at all (eg next year's apple crop) or, whilst in existence, it may not yet have vested in the hands of the assignor (eg the apple in the shop that the assignor is about

---

[61] The concept of consideration in equity requires real value or detriment (for instance, *Glegg v Bromley* [1912] 3 KB 474) and is different from the simple consideration or agreement by way of deed that is required at law to support a contract.

[62] [1905] AC 454, 462.

[63] However, a lack of proper value received by the assignor may be relevant to a challenge mounted in the context of insolvency proceedings concerning the assignor: see the following sections of the Insolvency Act 1986: ss 238 and 339 (transactions at an undervalue), s 423 (transactions defrauding creditors), ss 239 and 340 (preferences), and s 245 (avoidance of certain floating charges).

[64] (1862) 4 De GF & J 264.

[65] In *Kekewich v Manning* (1851) 1 De GM&G 176, it was held that there had been a binding voluntary settlement of an equitable interest in property as sufficient had been done to effect a transfer of the property so as to bind the settlor. In *Fortescue v Barnett* (1834) 3 My&K 36, it was held that a voluntary deed of assignment of a life policy was binding upon the assignor. Recent cases which have examined the subject include *T Choithram International SA v Pagarani* [2001] 1 WLR 1 (Privy Council); *Pennington v Waine* [2002] EWCA Civ 227, [2002] 1 WLR 2075; *Zeital v Kaye* [2010] EWCA Civ 159; *Shah v Shah* [2010] EWCA Civ 1408; *Curtis v Pulbrook* [2011] EWHC 167 (Ch); *Winkler v Shamoon* [2016] EWHC 217 (Ch); *ND v SD* [2017] EWHC 1507 (Fam); and *Deslauriers v Guardian Asset Management Ltd* [2017] UKPC 34.

[66] Including where there is only past consideration.

[67] See *Tailby v The Official Receiver* (1888) 13 App Cas 523, 543 (Lord Macnaghten).

[68] See *Re Earl of Lucan, Hardinge v Cobden* (1890) 45 ChD 470.

to purchase). Particularly in the case of debts and other contractual rights, future property should be distinguished from presently existing property, such as where there is an accrued right to performance at a future date. Thus, a debt that has been incurred but which is payable at a future date is presently existing property of the creditor.

The common law is unable to recognise, in a proprietary sense, transactions in fu- **4.57** ture property. At best, it may conclude that there was a binding contract to assign the property when it came into the hands of the purported assignee. All it can do in relation to such a contract is to award damages if the contract is breached. Such an award of damages is not of much use if the defendant is insolvent.

In *Holroyd v Marshall*[69] the House of Lords held that equity, however, was able to **4.58** give proprietary recognition to such transactions,[70] so that an equitable interest may vest in the transferee as soon as the asset comes into existence in the hands of the transferor. This was developed further by the House of Lords in *Tailby v The Official Receiver*,[71] where it was held that such recognition will be given so long as the transaction is supported by valuable consideration, there is sufficient identity of the relevant assets so that when they come into existence they were clearly intended to be caught by the agreement, and the intention between the parties is that immediately the assets come into existence in the hands of the putative transferor (and without further condition) the intended proprietary interest should vest in the transferee. Such a transferee could be either an absolute purchaser or someone taking security. In *Re Lind*[72] it was said that the principle will apply notwithstanding an intervening insolvency of the intended transferor which occurs after the date of contracting but before the asset comes into existence.[73]

---

[69] (1862) 10 HLC 191, 11 ER 999.

[70] Except in the case of sale of goods: see *Re Wait* [1927] Ch 606.

[71] (1888) 13 App Cas 523. See, in particular, the speech of Lord Macnaghten where the requirements are clearly set out. His Lordship also dispelled the red herring linking the recognition of assignments of future property to a requirement that the transaction should be one that was capable of being the subject of a decree for specific performance, which had arisen from what had been said by Lord Westbury in *Holroyd v Marshall* (1862) 10 HLC 191, 209 and 211.

[72] [1915] 2 Ch 345. In *Peer International Corp and ors v Termidor Music Publishers Ltd and ors* [2002] EWHC 2675 (Ch) Neuberger J said, at [74]–[82], that he preferred the analysis in *Re Lind* to that of the Court of Appeal in *Collyer v Isaacs* (1881) 19 ChD 342. See further the discussion in *Meagher, Gummow & Lehane's Equity: Doctrines and Remedies* (5th edn, LexisNexis Australia 2015) paras 6-275 to 6-330.

[73] Where, however, the purported assignor subsequently becomes bankrupt and an asset arises in the course of the trustee in bankruptcy running the business, such an asset will vest in the trustee, despite an earlier purported assignment executed before the assignor became bankrupt: *Re Jones, ex p Nichols* (1883) 22 ChD 782. This is consistent with s 306 of the Insolvency Act 1986, by virtue of which property comprised in the bankrupt's estate vests in the trustee. The position may be different in a winding up, as the assets of the insolvent company do not vest in the liquidator unless the court, at the liquidator's request, makes an order vesting the property in the liquidator pursuant to s 145(1) of the Insolvency Act 1986.

4.6 Declaration of Trust

4.59 The decision of the Court of Appeal in *Milroy v Lord*[74] is authority for the basic proposition that it is possible in equity to alienate a right under a contract, such as a debt or other chose in action, by means of an equitable assignment or by a declaration of trust. In *Don King Productions Inc v Warren*[75] it was held that a restrictive clause in a contract which prohibited an assignment by a party of its contractual rights was not applicable to a transaction by way of a declaration of trust.[76] Apart from that point, which depends for its validity on the construction of the relevant restriction, or when, for relationship reasons, the lender wishes to continue being the lender of record to the debtor, it is difficult to envisage circumstances where it would be better to structure a transaction as a declaration of trust rather than an equitable assignment. The issues discussed later in relation to assignments are also of relevance in relation to declarations of trust.

4.7 Novation

4.60 In structural terms, a novation of a loan facility involves an agreement between the old lender and the borrower that they should each be discharged, either in whole or in part, from their rights and obligations towards each other under the existing contract and an agreement between the new lender and the borrower that, to the same extent as the discharged rights and obligations, they will enter into an agreement under a new contract that was of similar effect to the old contract that was terminated by the novation.

4.61 There are a number of points that can be made to illustrate a novation in contrast to an assignment.[77]

4.62 First, a novation requires the agreement, and thus the consent, of all the parties that are involved.[78] In the absence of restrictions on assignment in the contract,[79] an assignment of contractual rights does not require the consent of the debtor.

---

[74] (1862) 4 De GF & J 264.

[75] [2000] Ch 291. See also *Explora Group plc v Hesco Bastion Ltd* [2005] EWCA Civ 646 [104] (Rix LJ); *Barbados Trust Co v Bank of Zambia* [2007] EWCA Civ 148; *Co-Operative Group Ltd v Birse Developments Ltd* [2014] EWHC 530 (TCC) [88]; and *First Abu Dhabi Bank PJSC v BP Oil International Ltd* [2018] EWCA Civ 14 [26].

[76] See further para 4.96.

[77] See *The Argo Fund Ltd v Essar Steel Ltd* [2005] EWHC 600 (Comm), [2005] 2 Lloyd's Rep 203 (Aikens J). The case was the subject of an appeal (reported at [2006] EWCA Civ 241, [2006] 2 Lloyd's Rep 134) which did not touch on this aspect.

[78] Albeit that in a syndicated facility document the borrower's agreement is often contained within the mechanisms provided by the facility agreement, as to which see further later.

[79] And, it might be added, except for those limited categories of contractual rights that may not be assigned, such as under a contract for personal services.

Secondly, a novation effects a termination, in whole or in part, of one contract **4.63** and its replacement, to that extent, by a new one. An assignment effects a transfer of the assignor's contractual rights but the contract remains in place, the assignor remains a party to it, and is obliged to perform its remaining obligations under it.

Thirdly, a novation may involve the transfer of both rights and obligations, **4.64** whereas an assignment can only concern a transfer of rights,[80] although the assigned rights are 'subject to equities', such as the debtor's rights of set-off and the priorities of third parties.

Fourthly, both the termination of the old contract and the creation of a new **4.65** contract under a novation must be supported by consideration, whereas at least absolute assignments under section 136 of the Law of Property Act 1936, and, it might be added, some types of equitable assignment, do not need to be supported by consideration.

Fifthly, whereas a novation can achieve a transfer of all of the transferor's stated **4.66** rights and obligations, an assignment may not achieve a transfer of those rights which are entirely connected with and personal to the old lender, unless the contract indicates an intention that they be assignable. These could include rights under indemnity clauses, rights to levy a charge for increased costs associated with the lender's capital adequacy position, and, perhaps, rights to a gross-up for the imposition of withholding tax on interest payments to the old lender.

Sixthly, if the old lender enjoyed the benefit of guarantees or security, they may **4.67** (if they do not contain appropriate wording to the contrary) expire with the release of the borrower from its obligations to the old lender. In that case, it will be necessary for the new lender to take new guarantees and security for its own benefit.[81] In an assignment,[82] it should be possible to include an assignment of such guarantees and security in so far as they relate to the rights of the old lender against the borrower that are included in the assignment.[83]

---

[80] See Sir Richard Henn Collins MR in *Tolhurst v Associated Portland Cement Manufacturers (1900) Ltd* [1902] 2 KB 660 (affd [1903] AC 414).

[81] However, it is possible when taking the guarantees or security to construct a trust, under which the guarantees or security are given or constituted in favour of a security trustee, which will hold the same for the benefit of the lenders for the time being. This is commonly done in the context of syndicated lending (see eg *British Energy Power & Energy Trading Ltd v Credit Suisse* [2008] EWCA Civ 53). A similar structure is used in relation to bond issues, where there can be a trustee which holds such guarantees or security (as well as the benefit of the issuer's covenant to pay and other covenants) for the bondholders for the time being.

[82] Subject to any restrictions that might apply.

[83] As noted earlier, if there is any risk that new security which is taken with respect to novated debt might be vulnerable (for instance, because of hardening periods under relevant insolvency law or because of the risk of third parties gaining priority in the secured assets) then it may be advantageous to assign the existing debt and the security which secures that debt.

4.7.1 Syndicated facilities

4.68 It is common in syndicated facilities to find a mechanism providing for the syndicate members to be able to transfer their participations in the facility, that is their rights and obligations, by way of a novation through use of transfer certificates in a form scheduled to the facility agreement. Aikens J in *The Argo Fund Ltd v Essar Steel Ltd*[84] looked at the mechanics by which a novation came about in consequence of the use of such a transfer certificate, in view of the fact that the borrower was not physically involved in the process of the novation at the time it took place.[85] His Lordship's analysis may be summarised as follows.

4.69 The novation is achieved through the provisions of the syndicated facility agreement on the basis of there being unilateral contracts, under which there is a standing offer by the borrower to accept the discharge of the old contract and a standing offer by the borrower to accept the agreement with the new lender constituted by the new contract.[86] The standing offer by the borrower to terminate the old contract is made to each member of the syndicate for the time being, which can be accepted by the delivery by the transferring lender of a transfer certificate to the Facility Agent, as specified in the facility agreement. The consideration to support the agreement to terminate is provided by the mutual agreement of the borrower and the old lender to give up their respective rights and obligations. The standing offer by the borrower to enter into a new contract on the terms of the facility agreement is made to those who were eligible to be a transferee. The act of acceptance of that offer by the new lender was not spelt out in the relevant agreement in that case, but his Lordship said it would arise by the new lender's agreement to the transfer on the terms set out in the facility agreement and its agreement to the transferor sending the Transfer Certificate to the Facility Agent. Although there was no provision in the facility agreement for the transfer to be notified to the borrower, it is not a requirement for the conclusion of a contract

---

[84] [2005] EWHC 600 (Comm), [2005] 2 Lloyd's Rep 203. The case was the subject of an appeal, as noted in the footnote to para 4.61.

[85] A preliminary point, which is illustrated by that case, is the necessity of ensuring that the intended transferee falls within the category of persons which the documentation states will be acceptable as a transferee. Aikens J held that the requirement was met on the facts although David Steel J had arrived at a contrary conclusion at an earlier stage in proceedings in the same case, *The Argo Fund Ltd v Essar Steel Ltd* [2004] EWHC 128 (Comm). Except for a brief note that the earlier proceedings had taken place, there is no further reference made by Aikens J to the earlier proceedings or to David Steel J's judgment. The Court of Appeal construed the relevant wording more generously, but otherwise upheld the decision of Aikens J (*Essar Steel Ltd v The Argo Fund Ltd* [2006] EWCA Civ 241, [2006] 2 Lloyd's Rep 134; for related proceedings, see *Argo Capital Investors Fund SPC v Essar Steel Ltd* [2005] EWHC 2587 (Comm)). The Court of Appeal decision on this point has been followed by *Grant v WDW 3 Investments Ltd* [2017] EWHC 2807 (Ch). See also the approach taken by the Court of Appeal in *Barbados Trust Co Ltd v Bank of Zambia* [2007] EWCA Civ 148, [2007] Lloyd's Rep 495, which concerned the description of permitted assignees under a loan agreement.

[86] See *Carlill v Carbolic Smoke Ball Co* [1893] 1 QB 256 and *New Zealand Shipping Co Ltd v AM Satterthwaite & Co Ltd; The Eurymedon* [1975] AC 154.

that the person accepting an offer in the manner specified in the offer must also notify the offeror of that acceptance.

Aiken J's analysis has subsequently been approved by the Court of Appeal, in **4.70** *Habibsons Bank Ltd v Standard Chartered Bank (Hong Kong) Ltd*.[87]

Whilst it was not mentioned in the judgment, a similar analysis would apply **4.71** to the novation that is usually provided for in such facility documentation concerning the respective rights and obligations as exist between the old lender, the other members of the syndicate, the Facility Agent, the Arranger, and the new lender. That is important in relation to matters such as those which arise under the sharing clause, the agency clause, and the provisions relating to the effect of a majority vote (see further, ch 3).

4.8 Sub-participation

Sub-participation arrangements are usually documented as a contract entered **4.72** into between two banks (or similar institutions) in relation to a loan or a similar facility made available by one of the banks to a borrower. The sub-participation may be either a 'funded' sub-participation or a 'risk' sub-participation (in practice, more commonly referred to as a funded participation and a risk participation—the terms 'sub-participation' and 'participation' being used interchangeably). A funded participation arrangement will normally take a form by which the lending bank, the grantor, grants a sub-participation to the other bank, the grantee, concerning the receipt by the grantor of payments of principal and interest under the loan facility. The grantor agrees to pay to the grantee amounts equivalent to the principal payments that it receives from the borrower. The grantor will also agree to pay to the grantee amounts referable, in whole or in part, to interest payments and the like that are received from the borrower.[88] In return the grantee will make a payment to the grantor at the outset of an amount equivalent to the outstanding amount of the facility. In effect, the grantee takes on the risk of failure by the borrower and the reward of future performance by the borrower. From the commercial perspective of the grantor, it has parted with the risks and rewards of the facility, and, if the sub-participation is properly structured,

---

[87] [2010] EWCA Civ 1335 [22] and [23]. See also *Standard Chartered Bank (Hong Kong) Ltd v Independent Power Tanzania Ltd* [2016] EWHC 2908 (Comm) [46]. See, however, *Deutsche Bank AG v Unitech Global Ltd* [2013] EWCA Civ 1372 [32]–[37], where, in the context of a syndicated loan agreement following the Loan Market Association recommended form, the Court of Appeal queried whether the term 'novation' was being used in its strict legal sense, and suggested that, if it was, it was arguable that the change of lenders operated only by way of a partial novation.

[88] It is likely that the grantor will agree to pay over all of the interest it receives as, otherwise, it will have a continuing economic interest in the underlying facility which will cause it accounting and regulatory difficulties.

it should therefore constitute 'significant risk transfer' for the purposes of the EU Capital Requirements Regulation[89] and thereby provide a regulatory capital benefit for the grantor. Indeed, obtaining that benefit is often an important reason for the grantor entering into a sub-participation.

4.73 A less common arrangement[90] is a risk participation. It has a similarity with a guarantee or a credit default derivative contract. It arises where the grantee agrees to make a payment to the grantor of the outstanding principal amount under the facility if and when the borrower defaults. In return, the grantor agrees to pay to the grantee all or some portion of the interest it receives until default, whereafter it will pay over any amounts of principal and interest received from the borrower.

4.74 Unlike an assignment, where the lending bank transfers a proprietary right in the facility, the intention under a properly drawn contract of sub-participation is that the grantor should remain as the beneficial owner of its rights against the borrower. The grantee is merely given a contractual right by the grantor to be paid equivalent amounts by the grantor if and when it receives payments by the borrower. An important consequence of this is that, if the grantor becomes insolvent and goes into liquidation, the grantee merely has an unsecured claim against the grantor and cannot claim any proprietary entitlement in the underlying facility, even with respect to payments made by the borrower after the commencement of the insolvency of the grantor. The grantee has therefore assumed a 'double credit risk'; namely, the risk of default by either (or both) the borrower and the grantor.

4.75 In *Lloyds TSB Bank plc v Clarke (Liquidator of Socimer International Bank Ltd) and Chase Manhattan Bank Luxembourg SA*,[91] which concerned the more usual form of funded sub-participation arrangement and not a risk participation, the Privy Council confirmed that under a sub-participation the grantee will receive no proprietary rights in the facility. Hence, on the facts of the case before it, the sub-participant was found to have no claim in the underlying facility and was just an ordinary unsecured creditor in the grantor's insolvency.[92] Of course, as the arrangement between the grantor and the grantee depends upon the terms of the contract between them, it might always be possible for the contract to depart from the usual form and be fashioned, perhaps unwittingly, as an assignment of the grantor's rights under the facility or it might include a charge over those rights, but that would be unusual.

---

[89] Reg (EU) 575/2013. See arts 243 and 244. Amendments to these provisions will be made with effect from 1 January 2019 (pursuant to Regulation (EU) 2017/2401 [2017] OJ L347/1), as part of the EU's new harmonised legislative framework for securitisations.

[90] Because its regulatory capital treatment will be unlikely to be as favourable to the grantor.

[91] [2002] UKPC 27, [2002] 2 All ER (Comm) 992.

[92] The decision of the Privy Council was referred to by Andrew Smith J in *Adolfo Altman v Australia and New Zealand Banking Group Ltd* [2002] EWHC 2488 (Comm) and by Gloster LJ in *First Abu Dhabi Bank PJSC v BP Oil International Ltd* [2018] EWCA Civ 14 [26].

On a practical level,[93] it will be necessary for the contract to provide for the making   **4.76**
of decisions in relation to the conduct of the facility and the exercise of the lender's
rights, as well as for the carrying out of enforcement action should the borrower default. The grantee would normally wish to be able to determine such matters, but the
grantor may be reluctant to concede the point if it has a continuing exposure to, or
other commercial connection with, the borrower. In any event, the grantor would
wish the grantee to accept the responsibility for any costs and expenses that might
be incurred by the grantor in taking action against the borrower for the benefit of
the grantee. Difficulties may also be encountered where the grantor has other exposures to the borrower in addition to the participated facility. There could then
be a problem in determining if a payment, or its equivalent, had been received by
the grantor which was referable to the participation, particularly if the grantor had
received a benefit through the operation of set-off rights, either before or in consequence of the insolvency of the borrower, or through the realisation of security or a
guarantee that was held by the grantor. If the grantor is to be treated as having received a payment from the borrower, it will then be a question of determining the
extent to which that payment should be allocated towards the participation, as opposed to the other exposures that the grantor has towards the borrower. If there is any
likelihood of those circumstances arising, they should be addressed in the contract
between the grantor and the grantee.

4.9 Common Issues Concerning Assignments

It is now convenient to examine a number of issues that relate to assignments   **4.77**
and are common to whichever form of assignment is undertaken. A great many
of them should also apply in the case of a declaration of trust. As previously mentioned, in the background to many of those issues is the basic principle that the
debtor should not be put in a worse position in consequence of an assignment
than that in which the debtor would have been placed without the assignment,
and that the assignee cannot acquire greater rights against the debtor than were
possessed by the assignor.

4.9.1 Rights v obligations

One difficulty with assignments is that it is only possible for the assignor to assign   **4.78**
its rights. It cannot assign its obligations.[94] Thus, if at the time of the assignment

---

[93] Many of these points will also be relevant in the case of an equitable assignment, particularly
if it is only a partial assignment of the original lender's exposure to the borrower.

[94] See eg Sir Richard Henn Collins MR in *Tolhurst v Associated Portland Cement Manufacturers
(1900) Ltd* [1902] 2 KB 660, 668. For a recent example, see *Deane v Coutts & Co* [2018] EWHC
1657 (Ch) [110] ('there are no circumstances in which the debtor can recover money from the assignee. It accords with the principle that liabilities do not pass with an assignment').

the assignor remains obligated to make further performance under the relevant contract, such as would be the case under a loan agreement if the borrower has the right to request further drawings, the assignor cannot transfer that obligation, at least without the consent of the borrower, in which case there would be a novation of the contractual obligations rather than an assignment of such obligations.[95] This problem may have regulatory and accounting consequences for the transferor, as (in the absence of such consent) it will not have divested itself of its responsibilities and so it cannot say that it has transferred all of the risks and rewards associated with the facility.

4.9.2 Rights that are personal to the assignor

4.79 It is a principle of the law of assignments that the rights of the assignee are subject to equities, which includes the proposition that the debtor/obligor whose obligation has been assigned should not be put in a worse position in consequence of the assignment than it would have been if the assignment had not taken place. One example of this is to the effect that the assignee cannot recover from the debtor or other obligor more than the assignee could have recovered if there had been no assignment. Thus, the assignee cannot recover from the debtor/obligor for loss that would not have been suffered by the assignor if the claim had not been assigned. In *Dawson v Great Northern & City Railway Co*,[96] an assignee was refused recovery of extra loss it had suffered which was referable to the assignee's circumstances and which the assignor would not have suffered. Another example relates to the debtor's rights of set-off which it could have asserted against the assignor and which it is permitted to assert against the amount payable to the assignee.[97] As with most principles in the law, the devil is in the detail.

4.80 From the principle stated above, it follows that, unless clear wording is included to indicate the relevant intention, not all of the rights that are granted to the lender in a facility agreement may be capable of assignment in the sense of conferring the same advantages upon the transferee as were applicable to the transferor. This is because some of the rights may be characterised as being personal to the transferor and its own circumstances and so not capable, through assignment,

---

[95] There may be an advantage in structuring a transaction as an assignment of the assignor's accrued rights to payment and a novation of its obligations as to future performance, particularly if security was given for the original debt. If there is any risk that the new security which is taken with respect to the novated debt might be vulnerable, for instance because of hardening periods under relevant insolvency law or because of the risk of third parties gaining priority in the secured assets, then an assignment of the existing debt with the security for it may be advantageous.

[96] [1905] 1 KB 260.

[97] See *Government of Newfoundland v Newfoundland Railway Co* (1888) 13 App Cas 199, 212–13 (Lord Hobhouse); *Business Computers Ltd v Anglo-African Leasing Ltd* [1977] 1 WLR 578 (Templeman J); *Smith v Muscat* [2003] EWCA Civ 962, [2003] 1 WLR 2853 (Buxton LJ); *S v S* [2010] EWHC 1415 (Fam) (Macur J); and *Bibby Factors Northwest Ltd v HFD Ltd* [2015] EWCA Civ 1908 (Christopher Clarke LJ).

of conferring protection upon the transferee for its personal position (unless the drafting indicates that that is the intention). For instance, the protection that is commonly given to a lender under a change in circumstances or an increased costs clause in a loan facility agreement relates to the consequences of a diminution in the lender's rate of return arising from matters such as an increase in the costs of complying with capital adequacy requirements. A similar problem might arise under an indemnity clause designed to give the lender, as a contracting party under the agreement, protections against the outcome of various adverse matters affecting the lender. In both cases, it would be debatable whether (in the absence of wording to indicate the relevant intention) such clauses would be effective in conferring the protection upon a transferee that was originally intended to be given to the transferor. In practice, many loan agreements do contain wording to indicate the relevant intention. In the Loan Market Association's recommended forms of facility agreement, for example, the drafting makes it clear that transferees do take the benefit of such clauses, but (for the borrower's protection) provides that, where the obligation arises as a result of circumstances existing at the date of the transfer, the transferee is only entitled to receive payment under those clauses to the same extent as the transferor would have been if the transfer had not occurred.

4.9.3 Contractual restrictions upon dealing

The lender may be precluded by the contract from assigning or otherwise dealing **4.81** with its rights if the contract contains a provision to that effect.[98] Most contractual rights are assignable in the absence of some particular restriction upon assignment.[99] Such a restriction may be imposed in the contract under which the relevant right arises. Before examining the effectiveness of such provisions, it is pertinent to consider the various reasons why a debtor may wish to impose them upon its creditor.

First, the debtor may wish to keep available its rights of set-off against its original **4.82** creditor, not just in relation to claims arising out of the same or a closely related transaction to that under which the debt arose, but also in relation to present and future claims of a more general nature. Once a debtor has received notice of an

---

[98] For more detailed treatments of this subject, see Andrew McKnight, 'Contractual Restrictions on a Creditor's Right to Alienate Debts' [2003] JIBL 1 and [2003] JIBLR 43; Roy Goode, 'Contractual Prohibitions Against Assignment' [2009] LMCLQ 300; and Michael G. Bridge, 'The Nature of Assignment and Non-Assignment Clauses' (2016) 132 LQR 47.

[99] However, the benefit of a contract for personal skill and confidence is not assignable without the servant's or employee's consent but such a person can assign his right to be paid: see *Don King Productions Inc v Warren* [2000] Ch 291, 319 (Lightman J); and *Akai Holdings Ltd v RSM Robson Rhodes LLP* [2007] EWHC 1641 (Ch). It is also arguable that certain rights conferred by statute, such as a right to levy fees or duties in return for the supply of a statutory service, may not be assignable in the absence of a statutory permission, especially where the grantee of the rights is performing a quasi-administrative or quasi-official role.

assignment of a debt, the availability to it of set-off in the latter type of general situation becomes limited, essentially, to claims which have accrued due prior to its receipt of a notice of the assignment.[100]

4.83 Secondly, in a winding up of the creditor or the debtor, the debtor may wish to be able to bring into account the debt it owes the creditor against amounts due to it from the creditor for the purposes of rule 14.25 of the Insolvency (England and Wales) Rules 2016,[101] which it can only do if the person beneficially entitled to the debt is the same creditor.[102]

4.84 Thirdly, the debtor will be at risk if, having received a notice of assignment, it overlooks the notice and pays the original creditor rather than the assignee. In such a case, the debtor will not obtain a good discharge for payment of the debt and will remain liable to pay the financier, being left to seek a refund from the creditor, for what that is worth.[103]

4.85 Fourthly, the debtor will be at risk if, having received a notice of the assignment, the debtor pays the assignee and thereafter wishes to claim a refund, for instance due to a total failure of consideration concerning the underlying contract, as it must seek its refund from the original creditor and not the assignee whom it paid, despite the fact that the assignee has the money and the original creditor may by then be insolvent.[104]

4.86 Fifthly, and subject to the question as to whether such provisions can be effective in favour of an assignee, the debtor may be exposed to higher costs if the identity of its creditor changes. This would be due to the effect of certain provisions in loan agreements such as increased costs and tax clauses, although (as seen earlier) it is not uncommon for such agreements to contain provisions designed in part to protect the debtor against such adverse effects if they arise in consequence of a change of its creditor.

4.87 Sixthly, on a more general and commercial basis, the debtor may be concerned to ensure that its creditor remains the same. Indeed, the assignee may be a person

---

[100] See *Business Computers Ltd v Anglo-African Leasing Ltd* [1977] 1 WLR 578; *Bibby Factors Northwest Ltd v HFD Ltd* [2015] EWCA Civ 1908 [32] .

[101] SI 2016/1024.

[102] See *In re City Life Assurance Co Ltd; Stephenson's Case* [1926] Ch 191, 217.

[103] See, in relation to an absolute assignment at law, s 136 of the Law of Property Act 1925. In *William Brandt's Sons & Co v Dunlop Rubber Co Ltd* [1905] AC 454 the House of Lords held that the same consequences would arise under an equitable assignment of a legal chose in action where notice had been given to the debtor. See also the majority of the Court of Appeal in *Three Rivers District Council v Bank of England* [1996] QB 292. With respect to the latter case, it is submitted that the minority view expressed by Staughton LJ, who queried the approach taken on this point by the House of Lords, is much to be preferred to that of Waite and Peter Gibson LJJ who comprised the majority. The importance of giving notice of the assignment to the relevant obligor is illustrated by the Court of Appeal's decision in *Warner Bros Records Inc v Rollgreen Ltd* [1976] QB 430.

[104] *Pan Ocean Shipping Co Ltd v Creditcorp Ltd* [1994] 1 WLR 161.

with whom the debtor would not wish to have a commercial relationship, and it may even at some time have rejected that possibility. The debtor may wish that the creditor should remain in place not just on a superficial or nominal basis but also substantively, because of the working relationship that exists between them. The debtor may feel that the original creditor would be more amenable to requests for consents and assistance when times become hard than would an assignee which has a more limited concern simply to be paid. Even if the assignee only has an equitable interest whilst the original creditor remains nominally as the legal owner of the debt, the assignee is likely to be in the driving seat behind the scenes and thus, realistically, the person dictating the attitude to be taken towards the debtor.

There are counter-arguments in support of the original creditor being able to transfer its rights without the impediments placed upon it by such restrictions. **4.88**

First, it may become unlawful for such a creditor to maintain a loan, which difficulty might be overcome by the creditor transferring its rights to a third party which is not affected by the illegality. **4.89**

Secondly, an original creditor may be exposed to an increase in its regulatory costs of maintaining the loan, or there might be a tax imposition upon the creditor or the debtor which could perhaps be mitigated by a transfer. **4.90**

Thirdly, the original creditor might have extended its credit to the debtor on the basis of the debtor's then existing credit worthiness. That may have subsequently declined, thereby exposing the creditor to a greater degree of risk than it had originally been prepared to accept or which may no longer justify a favourable rate of interest enjoyed by the debtor. **4.91**

Fourthly, if the debtor is in default, the original creditor may wish to crystallise its losses by disposing of the debt. **4.92**

Fifthly, on a more positive note, it may be the case that the original creditor funds its business by selling its debts, thereby generating new finance to make further loans or to provide its working capital. If it did not do so then it would not be able to extend credit to people or entities like the debtor in the first place. **4.93**

Finally, where the transfer is of a whole portfolio of debts, it might be thought to be an unreasonable imposition upon the transferee if it has to check each contract under which a debt arises to see if there might be some restriction which could prevent the debt from being assigned. **4.94**

4.9.3.1 *The effect of a contractual restriction*

Having considered the arguments for and against restrictive provisions, it is now possible to examine their effectiveness as a matter of English law. The starting point is to discern the nature and extent of the restriction, which will depend **4.95** upon its proper construction.[105] The rules for the construction of contracts and their provisions were summarised by Lord Hoffmann in *Investors Compensation Scheme Ltd v West Bromwich Building Society*[106] and have been addressed in a number of cases subsequently.[107] The process of construction will involve a determination of the rights under the contract to which the restriction relates and the extent to which dealings with those rights are intended to be restricted. As to the rights to which the restriction relates, it will generally be assumed that a restriction upon a party's right to deal with and assign its benefit of a contract is intended to cover both the party's underlying rights to demand performance by the other party and the fruits of those rights manifested in the right to be paid.[108] It is possible, however, for the restriction to be aimed at preventing a dealing by a party with its underlying right to future performance whilst leaving it free to assign or otherwise deal with the fruits thereof.[109]

4.96 Subject to an argument based upon public policy, which will be examined below, it will also be a matter of the proper construction of a contract to determine the types of dealings which the restriction is intended to prevent.[110] It has been held

---

[105] See, generally, the approach taken by Lord Browne-Wilkinson in *Linden Gardens Trust Ltd v Lenesta Sludge Disposals Ltd* [1994] AC 85. Note that restrictions on the assignment of rights to be paid amounts under certain business contracts for goods, services, or intangible assets may be invalidated by regulations made under s 1 of the Small Business, Enterprise and Employment Act 2015. Draft regulations were published in July 2018: as drafted, they do not apply if the person to whom the receivable is owed is a large enterprise or a special purpose vehicle, and they are therefore unlikely to have any material impact on syndicated loan facilities. Note also that a proposed EU legislative package (*Proposal for a Directive of the European Parliament and of the Council on credit servicers, credit purchasers and the recovery of collateral* COM(2018) 135 final and *Proposal for a Regulation of the European Parliament and of the Council on amending Regulation (EU) No 575/2013 as regards minimum loss coverage for non-performing exposures* COM(2018) 134 final), released in March 2018, would impose compulsory levels of disclosure and reporting requirements on transfers to non-banks of loans originally made by EU established banks.
[106] [1998] 1 WLR 896, 912–13.
[107] See eg *Sirius International Insurance Co v FAI General Insurance Ltd* [2004] UKHL 54; *Chartbrook Ltd v Persimmon Homes Ltd* [2009] UKHL 38; *AG of Belize v Belize Telecom Ltd* [2009] UKPC 10; *Re Sigma Finance Corp* [2009] UKSC 2; *Rainy Sky v Kookmin Bank* [2011] UKSC 50; *K/S Victoria Street v House of Fraser (Stores Management) Ltd* [2011] EWCA Civ 904; *Lloyds TSB Foundation for Scotland v Lloyds Banking Group plc* [2013] UKSC 3; *Arnold v Britton* [2015] UKSC 36; *BNY Mellon Corporate Trustee Services Ltd v LBG Capital No. 1 plc* [2016] UKSC 29; and *Wood v Capita Insurance Services Ltd* [2017] UKSC 24.
[108] See *Linden Gardens Trust Ltd v Lenesta Sludge Disposals Ltd* [1994] AC 85 (Lord Browne-Wilkinson).
[109] As, for instance, occurred in *R v Chester and North Wales Legal Aid Area Office (No 12), ex p Floods of Queensferry Ltd* [1998] 1 WLR 1496.
[110] A point originally made by Professor Sir Roy Goode in a *Note* at (1979) 42 MLR 553 and subsequently developed by Lord Browne-Wilkinson in the *Linden Gardens* case at [1994] 1 AC 85, 104. See also *Bawejem Ltd v MC Fabrications Ltd* [1999] BCC 157. In addition to the possibility that the restriction might be intended to prevent a legal assignment, an equitable assignment, or both, Sir Roy also suggested that the restriction might, alternatively, be construed as either a mere personal undertaking which was not intended to prevent a dealing with the relevant rights or as being a provision of such importance that a breach would amount to repudiatory conduct which would entitle the innocent party to terminate the contract for repudiatory breach. Lord

that a prohibition upon assignment will generally be taken as being intended to prevent both legal and equitable assignments.[111] It has also been held that it is a matter of construction of the relevant restriction to determine if other types of dealings might fall within its compass, such as by way of a declaration of trust[112] or by the grant of a security interest over the relevant right. An indication of the difficulties that might be presented in going through the process of construction is provided by the outcome of *Don King Productions Inc v Warren*[113] in which it was held that a restriction that prevented a contracting party from assigning, either at law or in equity, the benefit of its rights under a contract would not prevent it from declaring a trust of that benefit. From the perspective of the debtor, if it wishes to ensure that such a view would not be taken in another case, the practical advice must be to make sure that the wording of the relevant restriction clearly covers all of the possible dealings by the creditor that it wishes to prevent.

The public policy argument was initially raised by Professor Sir Roy Goode[114]   **4.97** and was referred to, without deciding the point, by Lord Browne-Wilkinson in *Linden Gardens Trust Ltd v Lenesta Sludge Disposals Ltd*.[115] The point concerns a principle of public policy which is against making property inalienable, as the right of alienation is an incident of ownership.[116] It is submitted, however, that the principle does not have application in this area. From a practical perspective, a debtor does have a legitimate interest in asserting the restriction for the various reasons advanced earlier, which would continue whilst it remains indebted. The legitimacy of the debtor's interest in the restriction (to which the creditor has,

---

Browne-Wilkinson in the *Linden Gardens* case said (at 104) that he thought neither additional interpretation was likely to arise in practice.

[111] The *Floods of Queensferry Ltd* case [1998] 1 WLR 1496. See also *Barbados Trust Co v Bank of Zambia* [2007] EWCA 148 [43] (Waller LJ); and *First Abu Dhabi Bank PJSC v BP Oil International Ltd* [2018] EWCA Civ 14 [24] and [37].

[112] See *Don King Productions Inc v Warren* [2000] Ch 291; *Explora Group plc v Hesco Bastion Ltd* [2005] EWCA Civ 646 [104] (Rix LJ); and *Barbados Trust Co Ltd v Bank of Zambia* [2007] EWCA Civ 148, [2007] 1 Lloyd's Rep 495.

[113] [2000] Ch 291. Professor McKnight criticised that finding in his article at [2003] JIBL 1 and [2003] JIBLR 43. Nonetheless, the view was expressed by Rix and Waller LJJ in *Barbados Trust Co Ltd v Bank of Zambia* [2007] EWCA Civ 148, [2007] 1 Lloyd's Rep 495 that a distinction could be made, on similar lines to that in the *Don King* case, so that a bar upon legal and equitable assignment might not prevent a declaration of trust. Their Lordships also suggested that a beneficiary under a declaration of trust may be able to enforce the debt directly against the debtor (in a case where the trustee was reluctant to act) by employing the procedure laid down in *Vandepitte v Preferred Accident Ins Corp of New York* [1933] AC 70. However, there is inevitably a potential difficulty in reconciling this conclusion with the prohibition on assignment. The prohibition upon assignment presumably reflects an agreement between the original creditor and the debtor that the debtor should not be placed in a position where it might be sued by someone other than the original creditor. If so, it could be argued that they also intended that the debtor should not be at risk of being sued by a third party via the combined mechanism of a declaration of trust by the original creditor of its rights and the use by the beneficiary under that trust of the *Vandepitte* procedure.

[114] In his *Note* at (1979) 42 MLR 553.

[115] [1994] AC 85.

[116] The principle is discussed in *Halsbury's Laws of England* (5th edn) vol 80, paras 869–72.

presumably, freely consented) should be more than a counterweight to the operation of the public policy seeking to protect the creditor's property rights. In any event, it is submitted that the restriction should not be viewed as something separate from the creditor's property, acting as an impediment preventing the creditor from alienating that property. It is not a matter of the creditor receiving an item of property and then agreeing to a restriction upon the alienation of that property. The restriction actually forms an integral part of the definition of that property. In other words, the nature and character of the creditor's property is the benefit or rights, the chose in action, that it has under the contract and the restriction goes to defining and limiting the scope of the chose. Thus, the restriction is not preventing an alienation of property but forms part of the make-up of the property.

4.98 If that analysis is incorrect, it may still be possible to have a partial restriction upon alienation by the creditor. The operation of the rule of public policy does allow for a partial restriction upon alienation provided that the restriction does not prevent the restricted party from enjoying the substantial right to dispose of its property.[117] Thus, a restriction upon entering into a legal assignment of the party's rights should be permissible if it could assign them equitably or dispose of them by way of a declaration of trust.

4.9.3.2 Where the debtor's consent may not be unreasonably withheld

4.99 Sometimes the restrictive provision will be qualified by stating that the creditor may not assign etc its rights without the debtor's consent, such consent not to be unreasonably withheld. A provision along those lines was considered by the Court of Appeal in *Hendry v Chartsearch Ltd*[118] where, in disregard of the clause, there was a purported legal assignment without a request for consent. Evans LJ thought that the assignment might have been effective if, notwithstanding the lack of any request for consent, it would have been unreasonable on the facts for consent to be refused. However, Henry and Millett LJJ held[119] that there could not have been a valid assignment where consent had not been requested at all. Henry LJ said that an assignment could only be valid if either the consent had been granted or, if it had been refused, the court had declared that the consent had been 'unnecessarily' refused.[120] Millett LJ said that the assignment could not proceed unless consent had been given or, following a request, the consent had been unreasonably refused.[121]

---

[117] See eg *Re Rosher, Rosher v Rosher* (1884) 26 ChD 801 in which it was said that a restriction upon alienation to a particular person or class of persons may be permitted.

[118] [1998] CLC 1382.

[119] At [1998] CLC 1382, 1393, and 1393–94, respectively.

[120] [1998] CLC 1382, 1393.

[121] [1998] CLC 1382, 1394.

The approach that was taken by Henry LJ is supported by the outcome of the **4.100** later majority decision of the Court of Appeal in *Barbados Trust Co Ltd v Bank of Zambia*.[122] The relevant clause in that case required that the debtor's consent should be sought before an assignment took place, but it went on to provide that the consent should not be unreasonably withheld and would be deemed to have been given if the borrower failed to respond within a stipulated period after the consent was sought. It was held that the failure to receive the debtor's consent or to wait for the period to elapse before proceeding with the purported assignment meant that the purported assignment was entirely ineffective.[123]

The safest course, when faced with such a provision like that in *Hendry v* **4.101** *Chartsearch*, would be to request consent from the debtor. If consent is refused and it is thought that the refusal is unreasonable (and there is no deeming provision similar to that in the *Barbados Trust* case), an application should be made to the court for a declaration that the refusal was unreasonable, before proceeding with the assignment.

4.9.4 Negative pledges and anti-disposal provisions in third party contracts

For the purpose of the discussion that follows[124], the putative assignor is the ori- **4.102** ginal creditor and the debt that is to be assigned may fall within the subject matter of an agreement between the original creditor and a third party, such as a financier that has provided funding to the original creditor. It may also fall within the

---

[122] [2007] EWCA Civ 148, [2007] 1 Lloyd's Rep 495.
[123] Other recent decisions regarding provisions expressly providing that consent is not to be unreasonably withheld include: *Porton Capital Technology Funds v 3M UK Holdings Ltd* [2011] EWHC 2895 (Comm) [219]–[228] (while not a case on the withholding of consent to an assignment, it draws on the law developed in that context: the question is not whether the refusal of consent was right or justified, but whether it was reasonable in the circumstances); *Commercial First Business Ltd v Atkins* [2012] EWHC 4388 (Ch) [92]–[100] (following *Citibank International plc v Kessler* [1999] Lloyds Rep Bank 123) (where a lender is required to act reasonably in deciding whether to give its consent, its failure to do so will not normally give the borrower a right to damages but will simply make the refusal a nullity: a right to damages would potentially arise, however, if the provision took the form of a covenant by the lender not to withhold consent unreasonably); *Barclays Bank plc v Unicredit Bank AG* [2014] EWCA Civ 302 (where early termination of a financial contract required B's consent, to be determined by B in a commercially reasonable manner, the Court of Appeal held that: given the wording of the clause it was the manner of the determination which had to be commercially reasonable not the outcome (although if the outcome was not reasonable the manner of arriving at it would have to be looked at critically); and it was commercially reasonable for B to have primary regard to its own commercial interests, and it did not have to balance its interests against the other party's interests); *No. 1 West India Quay (Residential) Ltd v East Tower Apartments Ltd* [2018] EWCA Civ 250 (a landlord and tenant case, in which the court held that the question is whether the decision is reasonable, not whether all the reasons behind it are reasonable); and *Crowther v Arbuthnot Latham & Co Ltd* [2018] EWHC 504 (Comm) (holding that the purpose of the requirement on a bank not to withhold consent unreasonably was to preserve the bank's contractual rights, not to enhance them).
[124] This matter is also discussed in ch 2.

covenants given by the original creditor in a security instrument, such as a mortgage or a charge. Pursuant to the agreement or covenant, the original creditor may have agreed with the third party that the original creditor will not dispose of, nor give security over, its assets or, at least, the debt or debts that it wishes to assign or over which it wishes to create security. The compass of such a provision will depend upon its drafting and interpretation. For instance, it is not uncommon to find in a loan agreement that the provision permits disposals of business assets at a fair or market value.

4.103 If the original creditor chooses to ignore the provision when it would be applicable to what the creditor proposes to do and proceeds to assign a debt in breach of it then, obviously, that will amount to a breach of contract on the part of the original creditor. That may, in turn, amount to an event of default under the original creditor's funding arrangements, with the additional risk of triggering cross-default provisions in other agreements. There may also be a claim by the third party against the original creditor in damages for breach of contract. If the third party discovers in time that the original creditor intends to breach its contract, it may be able to obtain an injunction to restrain the threatened breach of the negative stipulation, provided it acts expeditiously and has not condoned the proposed breach, relying upon the principle propounded by Lord Cairns LC in *Doherty v Allman*.[125] It is unusual, however, for a third party to be given advance warning by a person in the position of the original creditor, that the latter intends to breach its contract.

4.104 The aggrieved third party may also wish to visit its anger upon the assignee. It will not have a contractual claim against the assignee. Instead, it will have to ground its claim in the economic tort of inducing or procuring a breach of contract. If it succeeds, it should be able to claim tortious damages which, however, may be difficult to establish in a substantial amount. More importantly, the third party may be able to obtain an injunction against the assignee, to prevent the assignee from relying upon or benefiting from the assignment.[126] To succeed in establishing that the tort has been committed, however, the third party must prove that the assignee acted with sufficient knowledge of the relevant contractual provision[127] and that it intended, in the sense of having a specific subjective intention, to cause the claimant harm.[128] If the assignee was unaware of the restriction then it cannot be responsible for the consequences of the original creditor's wrongful

---

[125] (1878) 3 App Cas 709.

[126] As was contemplated by Browne-Wilkinson J in *Swiss Bank Corpn v Lloyds Bank Ltd* [1979] Ch 548.

[127] ibid. Sir John Donaldson MR in *Merkur Island Shipping Corpn v Laughton* [1983] 2 AC 570, 591, suggested that 'almost certain knowledge' would suffice, which gains some support from the approach that was taken by Lord Hoffmann in *OBG Ltd v Allan* [2007] UKHL 21, [2007] 4 All ER 545 [39]–[44].

[128] *OBG Ltd v Allan* [2007] UKHL 21, [2007] 4 All ER 545.

acts. Furthermore, if the assignee was aware of the relevant contractual stipulation but, before taking the assignment, obtained confirmation from the original creditor that it had obtained the third party's consent to the transaction, it will not have the relevant intention to cause harm to the third party and, once again, it will not be responsible for the consequences.[129]

4.9.5 The debtor's rights of set-off

This issue concerns the effect of an assignment upon rights of set-off that the **4.105** debtor may have wished to assert against the assignor, had the assignment not occurred. Without the assignment, the effect of such a set-off, where available, would be to reduce the amount of the debt that would be payable by the debtor when the debt fell due for payment, to the extent of the set-off. Thus, if the debt was for an amount of £100 and the debtor had a counter-claim back against its creditor for £25, the debtor's liability would be reduced to a sum of £75. Such a right of set-off may relate to a counter-claim that had accrued either before the date of the assignment or at a later date. It is also relevant to note that, in addition to rights of set-off, the debtor may also wish to raise substantive defences and rights of abatement that were available against the title of the original creditor to sue the debtor. Such a right of abatement, for instance, would arise under section 53(1)(a) of the Sale of Goods Act 1979[130] and the debtor could also raise against the assignee, in a claim for the price of the goods, a defence based upon the debtor's rejection of the goods.

In the context of an assignment of the debt, the question that must be addressed **4.106** is the extent to which the debtor can assert those rights against the assignee or whether the assignee takes free of them, leaving the debtor in the position that it must make a separate claim against the assignor for rights for which it might, but for the assignment, have been entitled to claim a right of set-off or abatement.

The underlying position as to the availability to the debtor of rights of set-off **4.107** or abatement that it can assert against an assignee was set out by James LJ in *Roxburghe v Cox*,[131] who said as follows:

> Now an assignee of a chose in action ... takes subject to all rights of set-off and other defences which were available against the assignor.[132]

---

[129] ibid.

[130] Although Hoffmann LJ in *Aectra Refining & Marketing Inc v Exmar NV* [1994] 1 WLR 1643, 1648–49, included a common law abatement of the price of goods or services for breach of warranty as a form of transaction or equitable set-off.

[131] (1881) 17 ChD 520, 526.

[132] See also *Government of Newfoundland v Newfoundland Railway Co* (1888) 13 App Cas 199, 212–13 (Lord Hobhouse).

4.108 In practice, the two particular rights of set-off to which this principle applies are rights of legal set-off and rights of transaction or equitable set-off to which the debtor may be entitled. For this purpose, rights of abatement are treated as if they were rights of transaction set-off. In an historic sense, the principle was originally applied in the context of equitable assignments but it has been held that the principle applies as much to an assignment at law under section 136 of the Law of Property Act 1925 as it does to an equitable assignment. This is because section 136 makes express provision that the assignment is 'subject to equities having priority over the right of the assignee' and such equities include the same rights of set-off as would be available to the debtor in the context of an equitable assignment.[133]

4.109 The debtor may be precluded, however, from asserting rights of set-off against its original creditor by a clause in the contract to that effect,[134] and if the debtor cannot assert the set-off against the original creditor then, similarly, it will be unable to do so against the assignee. The effectiveness of such a clause is dependent upon its interpretation.[135] It may also be subject to the operation of the Unfair Contract Terms Act 1977[136] or the Consumer Rights Act 2015.[137]

4.9.5.1 Legal rights of set-off

4.110 The rights of legal set-off[138] which the debtor can assert against the assignee were summarised by Templeman J in *Business Computers Ltd v Anglo-African Leasing Ltd*.[139] A separate and unconnected debt or other liquidated sum which has

---

[133] *Lawrence v Hayes* [1927] 2 KB 111, 120–21 and *E Pfeiffer Weinkellerei-Weineinkauf GmbH v Arbuthnot Factors Ltd* [1988] 1 WLR 150. See also *Smith v Muscat* [2003] EWCA Civ 962, [2003] 1 WLR 2853 [47] (Buxton LJ).

[134] See *Coca-Cola Financial Corp v Finsat International Ltd* [1998] QB 43; *John Dee Group v WMH (21) Ltd* [1998] BCC 972; *International Lease Finance Corp v Buzz Stansted Ltd* [2004] EWHC 292 (Comm); *AXA Sun Life Services plc v Campbell Martin Ltd* [2011] EWCA Civ 133; *FG Wilson (Engineering) Ltd v John Holt & Co (Liverpool) Ltd* [2013] EWCA Civ 1232; *Deutsche Bank (Suisse) SA v Khan* [2013] EWHC 482 (Comm); *Standard Chartered Bank (Hong Kong) Ltd v Independent Power Tanzania Ltd* [2016] EWHC 2908 (Comm) [57].

[135] See *Connaught Restaurants Ltd v Indoor Leisure Ltd* [1994] 1 WLR 501; *The Teno* [1977] 2 Lloyd's Rep 289; *BOC Group plc v Centeon LLC* [1999] 1 All ER (Comm) 970.

[136] See *Stewart Gill Ltd v Horatio Myer & Co Ltd* [1992] QB 600; *AXA Sun Life Services plc v Campbell Martin Ltd* [2011] EWCA Civ 133; *United Trust Bank Ltd v Dohil* [2011] EWHC 3302 (QB); *Deutsche Bank (Suisse) SA v Khan* [2013] EWHC 482 (Comm); *African Export-Import Bank v Shebah Exploration and Production Co Ltd* [2017] EWCA Civ 845 (where it was held that the Act was not engaged because the use by the lenders of the Loan Market Association recommended form of loan agreement was not sufficient to mean that they had contracted on their 'written standard terms of business'). Not all anti-set-off provisions will fall within the compass of the Act, as demonstrated by *Governor & Co of the Bank of Scotland v Singh* (HHJ Kershaw QC, sitting in the High Court in Manchester, 17 June 2005).

[137] In particular, see para 2 of pt 1 of sch 2 to the Act.

[138] As to a legal right of set-off and the distinction between that and equitable or transaction set-off, see *Stein v Blake* [1996] AC 243, 251 (Lord Hoffmann), *Aectra Refining & Marketing Inc v Exmar NV* [1994] 1 WLR 1643, 1649–53 (Lord Hoffmann), and *Glencore Grain Ltd v Agros Trading Co Ltd* [1999] 2 Lloyd's Rep 410, 415–17 (Clarke LJ).

[139] [1977] 1 WLR 578.

accrued due by the assignor to the debtor before the date on which notice of the assignment is received by the debtor, whether or not it is payable before that date, may be set off by the debtor against the assignee. If such a debt or sum has not accrued due, even though it arises under a contract made before such date, it may not be set off.[140] The latter would be the position, for instance, where rent falls due by a tenant after the date the notice of an assignment was received, even though the lease of the property was entered into before that date.[141] It would also be the case in relation to a cross-claim by the debtor that relates to a wrongful repudiation by its creditor of a separate hire-purchase agreement which was entered into before notice of assignment was received by the debtor but where the repudiation was not accepted until after that date.[142]

4.9.5.2 Equitable transaction set-off

The rights of equitable or transaction set-off between a debtor and creditor (and **4.111** which would therefore apply between a debtor and an assignee) were considered by Rix LJ in *Geldof Metaalconstructie NV v Simon Carves Ltd*,[143] who broadly adopted the test laid down by Lord Denning MR in *Federal Commerce & Navigation Co Ltd v Molena Alpha Inc (The Nanfri)*.[144] In essence, the debtor's cross-claim must be so closely connected with the claimant's demands that it would be manifestly unjust to allow the claimant to enforce payment without taking into account the cross-claim. Usually, the assigned right will be a liquidated sum and the set-off will be in respect of an unliquidated claim for damages, but the right to equitable set-off can also be asserted where both the claims are for unliquidated damages.[145]

4.9.5.3 Successive assignments

The position is complicated if there have been successive assignments of the ori- **4.112** ginal debt owed by the debtor to the original creditor.[146] The debtor should be able to assert rights of set-off that arise as between the debtor and the original creditor, on the basis and to the extent outlined earlier. The debtor should also be able to assert a legal set-off as between the debtor and the ultimate assignee, where notice has been given of that assignment, for the reasons outlined in what follows.

---

[140] See also *Christie v Taunton, Delmard, Lane & Co* [1893] 2 Ch 175; *In re Pinto Leite and Nephews, ex p Visconde des Olivaes* [1929] 1 Ch 221, 233 and 236 (Clauson J); and *Bibby Factors Northwest Limited v HFD Limited* [2015] EWCA Civ 1908 [32] and [55] (Christopher Clarke LJ).

[141] *Watson v Mid Wales Railway Co* (1867) LR 2 CP 593.

[142] The *Business Computers* case itself. By contrast, hire which had fallen due in that case before the notice of assignment of the separate debt was received could be set off.

[143] [2010] EWCA Civ 667. See also *Bibby Factors Northwest Limited v HFD Limited* [2015] EWCA Civ 1908 [34]–[53] (Christopher Clarke LJ).

[144] [1978] 2 QB 927. Rix LJ also relied heavily on the analysis by Potter LJ in *Bim Kemi AB v Blackburn Chemicals Ltd* [2001] EWCA Civ 457.

[145] See the *Bim Kemi* case, [21]–[23] (Potter LJ).

[146] See the discussion on this point in Rory Derham, *Derham on The Law of Set-off* (4th edn, Oxford: OUP 2010) paras 17.60–17.63.

The question then arises as to whether the debtor should be entitled to assert, as against the ultimate assignee, a set-off with respect to a claim of the debtor against an intermediate assignee, particularly a claim to legal set-off. The position would appear to be that if the intermediate assignment was merely equitable and no notice of the assignment was given to the debtor, the ultimate assignee should not be affected by the claim of the debtor against the intermediate assignee, because the ultimate assignee is asserting the rights, and suing in the name, of the original creditor, not those of the intermediate assignee.[147] However, if the intermediate assignment was effective at law under section 136 of the Law of Property Act 1925 or, perhaps, if it was an equitable assignment that was notified to the debtor,[148] the debt would be enforceable by the assignee in its own right and the ultimate assignee would be suing upon an assignment of that right and so would be subject to the equities available against the intermediate assignee.[149] This should be the case whether the assignment to the ultimate assignee was equitable or statutory.

4.9.5.4 Direct counter-claims against the assignee

4.113 Where the assignee, in its own name, sues the debtor then the debtor should also be able to assert any legal right of set-off for a separate liquidated claim that may have accrued due to it by the assignee. This is a simple application of the procedural rights of legal set-off that are available as between the parties to an action at law.

4.9.5.5 Claims that arise against the assignor after the payment of the debt

4.114 Such claims cannot be the subject of a set-off, for the simple reason that they arose after the payment of the debt. Accordingly, the debtor will be at risk if the debtor pays the assignee and thereafter a claim arises against the assignor, even if the claim is closely connected with the transaction that gave rise to the debt. An example would be a claim based upon a total failure of consideration concerning the underlying transaction between the debtor and the assignor. In such a case, the debtor must seek its refund from the original creditor and not the assignee whom it paid, despite the fact that the assignee has the money and the original creditor may by then be insolvent.[150]

---

[147] See *Banco Central SA v Lingoss and Falce Ltd, The Raven* [1980] 2 Lloyd's Rep 266, 273 (Parker J).

[148] By application of the decision of the House of Lords in *William Brandt's Sons & Co v Dunlop Rubber Co Ltd* [1905] AC 454, in which it was held that the equitable assignee could sue in its own name. This has been followed by the Court of Appeal in *Three Rivers District Council v Bank of England* [1996] QB 292; *National Westminster Bank plc v Kapoor* [2011] EWCA Civ 1083; *Bexhill UK Ltd v Razzaq* [2012] EWCA Civ 1376; and *First Abu Dhabi Bank PJSC v BP Oil Exploration Limited* [2018] EWCA Civ 14 [37].

[149] See *Read v Brown* (1888) 22 QBD 128, 132 (Lord Esher MR).

[150] *Pan Ocean Shipping Co Ltd v Creditcorp Ltd* [1994] 1 WLR 161.

4.9.6 Priorities

In English law it is possible for one, two, or several people to claim proprietary **4.115**
interests in the same asset, whether by way of ownership or security, particularly if
the asset is a chose in action such as a debt. Such an extravagance of interests arises
from the recognition that is given to the possible existence of legal and equitable interests in assets,[151] to transactions taking place at law or in equity, and the
willingness of equity to contemplate the possibility of several different equitable
interests existing at the same time in an asset.

A dichotomy of interests may be perfectly acceptable on the facts of the par- **4.116**
ticular case and the claims will then be ranked in the order that those involved
will understand and expect. An example is the case of a single creditor which has
taken security from a borrower. Each of them has an interest in the same asset, but
the secured creditor's interest should prevail to the extent of its legitimate interest.
Another example is where two creditors have taken forms of fixed security over
the same asset.[152] If the second in time has done this with its eyes wide open and
in knowledge of the earlier security, then it will expect to rank behind the first
creditor,[153] at least, in so far as the first creditor has made advances before it learns
of the second security.[154] Nonetheless, they will each have a proprietary interest
in that asset, but the second creditor's interest will be subject to the prior rights
of the first secured creditor. Alternatively, the two secured creditors may agree between themselves as to the ranking of their respective interests, under a priority
agreement which should be determinative of their respective positions.[155]

---

[151] Note, however, that if there is only one person with an interest in an asset, that interest can
only be the full comprehensive legal title, as it is not possible to have a separate legal and equitable
title vested in one person if there is no other person with an interest in the asset: see *Commissioner
of Stamp Duties (Qld) v Livingston* [1965] AC 694, 712 (Viscount Radcliffe); *Re Bond Worth Ltd*
[1980] Ch 228 (Slade J); and *Westdeutsche Landesbank Girozentrale v Islington LBC* [1996] AC 669,
706 (Lord Browne-Wilkinson).

[152] The position will be different if one of the securities is by way of floating charge, as the
granting of a subsequent fixed security is likely to fall within the ordinary course of the chargor's
business and will thus be given priority over the earlier floating charge: *Re Benjamin Cope & Sons
Ltd* [1914] 1 Ch 800. Similarly, a purchaser will usually take free of the floating charge: *Re Florence
Land and Public Works Co, ex p Moor* (1878) 10 ChD 530; *Hamer v London, City & Midland Bank
Ltd* (1918) 87 LJKB 973, even if the floating charge instrument contains provisions restricting the
chargor's right to deal with the charged property: see *Siebe Gorman & Co Ltd v Barclays Bank Ltd*
[1979] 2 Lloyd's Rep 142, 160 (Slade J).

[153] Save in the case where the second security is a purchase money security interest taken to secure an advance to fund the purchase price of the asset. See *Abbey National Building Society v Cann*
[1991] 1 AC 56; and *Re North East Property Buyers Litigation* [2014] UKSC 52.

[154] See s 94 of the Law of Property Act 1925 (which applies with respect to assets other than
registered land). Once the earlier security holder receives notice of the later security, it is in danger of
losing its priority for any further advances it makes. Much the same will apply if the earlier security
holder receives notice of a purchaser's interest and continues to make advances: *Siebe Gorman & Co
Ltd v Barclays Bank Ltd* [1979] 2 Lloyd's Rep 142.

[155] *Cheah Theam Swee v Equiticorp Finance Group Ltd* [1992] AC 472 and see alsos 94(1)(a) of
the Law of Property Act 1925. It is also possible by agreement to regulate the priorities between a
purchase interest and a security interest.

4.117 Unfortunately, situations may arise where there is not such harmony and there will then be a battle for supremacy, or, to give it the correct terminology, there will be a competition for priority between the competing interests. This might arise because of fraud on the part of a party granting an interest in an asset, or through a mistake or administrative oversight. There are rules to resolve the conflict which are of a somewhat piecemeal nature and which tend to depend upon the nature of the particular asset concerned. Nonetheless, the effect of notice looms large in this. It should also be noted that the priority conflict may exist between different types of interest (eg legal v equitable, equitable v equitable, security v security, purchaser v security, and purchaser v purchaser), and the resolution of the conflict may have to cross over between the different interests.

4.9.6.1 *The basic rule*

4.118 The basic rule of priorities as between competing interests in a chose in action, such as a debt, is that, where the equities are equal, the first in time prevails.[156]

4.9.6.2 *The rule in Dearle v Hall*

4.119 That basic rule, however, is subject to the operation of the rule in *Dearle v Hall*,[157] which is to the effect that the holder of the second interest in time[158] may displace the priority of the first interest in time if it meets two conditions. First, that at the time that value was given for the second interest,[159] its holder had no notice of the first interest. Secondly, that notice of the second interest in time was given to the debtor before notice was given to the debtor of the first interest in time.[160] The same approach applies if there is a multiplicity of competing interests, so that the holder of a later interest will prevail over an earlier interest of which it was unaware when it gave value, provided that notice is given to the debtor of the later interest before notice of the earlier interest is given to the debtor.

---

[156] See *E Pfeiffer Weinkellerei-Weineinkauf GmbH v Arbuthnot Factors Ltd* [1988] 1 WLR 150, 161–63 (Phillips J) and *Compaq Computer Ltd v Abercorn Group Ltd* [1991] BCC 484, 497–502 (Mummery J).

[157] *Dearle v Hall, Loveridge v Cooper* (1828) 3 Russ 1, 38 ER 475. A comprehensive exposition of the rule is to be found in *Meagher, Gummow and Lehane's Equity: Doctrines and Remedies* (5th edn, LexisNexis Australia 2015) paras 8-095 to 8-215.

[158] Other than an interest acquired through an involuntary assignment. However, the holder of such an interest may preserve its priority as against subsequent interests by giving notice to the debtor. See *Meagher, Gummow and Lehane*, para 8-175.

[159] The rule does not apply for the benefit of a volunteer who seeks to assert priority over an earlier interest: see *United Bank of Kuwait plc v Sahib* [1997] Ch 107, 119–20 (Chadwick J). However, an earlier volunteer who has given notice to the debtor will gain priority over a subsequent purchaser: *Mutual Life Assurance Soc v Langley* (1886) 32 ChD 460.

[160] As notice must be given to the debtor, it is not possible for the purpose of gaining priority under the rule to give notice before the debt has come into existence (as opposed to giving notice where the debt exists but is payable in the future). Hence, where there is an assignment of future property, it is not effective to give notice to someone who may become a debtor in the future. The notice can only be given once the debt has come into existence. See the discussion on this point in *Meagher, Gummow and Lehane*, at para 8-165, and see also *Re Dallas* [1904] 2 Ch 385.

The rule in *Dearle v Hall* applies to competitions resulting from assignments of **4.120** equitable interests and equitable assignments of legal interests.[161] It has also been held to apply where the competition involves a legal assignment under section 136 of the Law of Property Act 1925,[162] thereby displacing the possible operation of a rule in favour of the bona fide purchaser of the legal estate taking without notice of an earlier equitable interest. This was explained by Phillips J in *E Pfeiffer Weinkellerei-Weineinkauf GmbH v Arbuthnot Factors Ltd*.[163] Section 136 provides that the effectiveness of an assignment under that section is to be 'subject to equities having priority over the right of the assignee'. Section 136 replaced section 25(6) of the Judicature Act 1873 but was intended to re-enact the earlier provision. Section 25(6) had used slightly different wording when it said that an assignment under section 25(6) was 'subject to all equities which would have been entitled to priority over the right of the assignee if this Act had not been passed'. As it was not possible to have assignments at law of choses in action before section 25(6) was enacted, the intention was that, whilst conferring the procedural advantages upon an assignee of being able to sue the debtor at law, the priority rules that applied beforehand should continue and be equally applicable to legal assignments as they were to equitable assignments.

There are two circumstances in which the rule in *Dearle v Hall* may not apply, **4.121** although the position is not entirely clear. The first is where the holder of the postponed interest manages to get in payment of the debt in a situation where it does not have notice, at the time of receipt of the payment, of the other interest that had priority in the debt. In such a case it has been argued that, by getting in the payment, the recipient establishes a legal entitlement in that payment which overreaches the claim of the other party in the debt.[164] Secondly, doubt has been expressed as to whether the rule can apply where the assignor had assigned its beneficial interest under a trust or where such rights as it purportedly acquired were already subject to comprehensive trusts with their own beneficial interests that were inconsistent with the alleged interest of the assignor, so that the assignor really had no beneficial interest that it was capable of assigning.[165]

---

[161] *Marchant v Morton Down & Co* [1901] 2 KB 829; *E Pfeiffer Weinkellerei-Weineinkauf GmbH v Arbuthnot Factors Ltd* [1988] 1 WLR 150, 163 (Phillips J); *Compaq Computer Ltd v Abercorn Group Ltd* [1991] BCC 484, 498–99 (Mummery J).

[162] See *E Pfeiffer Weinkellerei-Weineinkauf GmbH v Arbuthnot Factors Ltd* [1988] 1 WLR 150, 161–63 (Phillips J) and *Compaq Computer Ltd v Abercorn Group Ltd* [1991] BCC 484, 497–502 (Mummery J).

[163] [1988] 1 WLR 150, 161.

[164] This point was discussed but left unresolved by Phillips J in *E Pfeiffer Weinkellerei-Weineinkauf GmbH v Arbuthnot Factors Ltd* [1988] 1 WLR 150, 163 and it was conceded in *Compaq Computer Ltd v Abercorn Group Ltd* [1991] BCC 484 (see at 500).

[165] See *Hill v Peters* [1918] 2 Ch 273, 297 (Eve J); the House of Lords in *BS Lyle Ltd v Rosher* [1959] 1 WLR 8; and the discussion in *Compaq Computer Ltd v Abercorn Group Ltd* [1991] BCC 484, 499–500. The approaches taken in *Hill v Peters* and in *BS Lyle Ltd v Rosher* have been trenchantly criticised in *Meagher, Gummow and Lehane*, at paras 8-180–8-215. It is clear, at least, from *BS Lyle Ltd v Rosher* that the rule in *Dearle v Hall* will apply to successive assignments of the same

4.122 It is essential that the party which is attempting to gain priority in reliance upon the rule in *Dearle v Hall* should not have had notice[166] of the earlier interest over which it is claiming priority under the rule. The relevant time for considering if it had notice is the point at which that party gave value for its interest[167] not, if it were earlier, the date it took its interest.

4.9.6.3 Notice

4.123 Section 199(1)(ii) of the Law of Property Act 1925[168] provides for the circumstances in which a 'purchaser', which includes a person taking a security interest,[169] is affected by notice of 'any other instrument or matter or any fact or thing', although section 199(3) makes it clear that section 199 is not intended to expand upon the circumstances where, before the statute, a purchaser would have been taken to have knowledge. The circumstances provided for by section 199(1)(ii) are as follows.

4.124 First, if the relevant matter is within the purchaser's own knowledge,[170] that is, it has actual notice of the matter. This would probably include reasonably explicit information, even if it has come from a disinterested person.[171]

4.125 Secondly, a purchaser will have notice of any matter imputed to it by virtue of the actual or constructive knowledge of the purchaser's agent, including its legal representative, provided that the agent has come by that knowledge whilst acting in the same transaction.[172] It has been held that this will only apply if the knowledge came to the agent whilst acting on behalf of the principal.[173]

4.126 Thirdly, a purchaser will be affected by constructive notice, which will be relevant in cases where the purchaser has made no enquiries or where the enquiries that were made were insufficient. Because of its importance, it is relevant to examine the doctrine of constructive notice in further detail.

4.9.6.4 Constructive notice

4.127 A purchaser (which, as noted earlier, includes a person taking a security interest) will have constructive notice of those matters that would have come to the

---

interest, where the assignor did have an interest capable of assignment at the time of the first of those assignments, albeit that the assignor had thereby evinced an intention to deprive itself of anything that it could further assign under the subsequent assignment.

[166] Including constructive notice: *Spencer v Clarke* (1878) 9 ChD 137.
[167] *Mutual Life Assurance Society v Langley* (1886) 32 ChD 460.
[168] S 199(1)(i) concerns transactions to which the Land Charges Act 1925 might apply.
[169] See s 205(1)(xxi) of the Law of Property Act 1925.
[170] S 199(1)(ii)(a).
[171] *Lloyd v Banks* (1868) LR 3 Ch App 488.
[172] S 199(1)(ii)(b).
[173] *Société Générale de Paris v Tramways Union Co Ltd* (1884) 14 QBD 424 (affd (1885) LR 11 App Cas 20); *Halifax Mortgage Services Ltd v Stepsky* [1996] Ch 207.

purchaser's knowledge if it had conducted such enquiries and inspections as ought reasonably to have been made.[174] What is reasonable will be judged by the standard of what would usually be done as a matter of prudence in the protection of their interests by men of business in similar circumstances.[175] Nonetheless, Lindley LJ said in *Manchester Trust v Furness*[176] that the doctrine of constructive notice generally does not apply to commercial transactions. It is doubtful, however, if this goes much further than giving a purchaser protection in cases concerning the sale of goods in the ordinary course of business, as it would not be practical to require such a person to undertake extensive investigations, in contrast to what would be undertaken in a conveyancing transaction.[177] As Millett J said in *Macmillan Inc v Bishopsgate Investment Trust (No 3)*:[178]

> It is true that many distinguished judges in the past have warned against the extension of the equitable doctrine of constructive notice to commercial transactions (see *Manchester Trust v Furness* ... per Lindley LJ), but they were obviously referring to the doctrine in its strict conveyancing sense with its many refinements and its insistence on a proper investigation of title in every case. The relevance of constructive notice in its wider meaning cannot depend on whether the transaction is 'commercial': the provision of secured overdraft facilities to a corporate customer is equally 'commercial' whether the security consists of the managing director's house or his private investments. The difference is that in one case there is, and in the other case there is not, a recognised procedure for investigating the mortgagor's title which the creditor ignores at his peril.

In an analogous area of liability for knowing receipt of trust property, the courts **4.128** have sometimes been prepared to admit liability based upon constructive knowledge, rather than actual knowledge.[179] Furthermore, in *Spencer v Clarke*[180] it was held that a purchaser of a life policy by way of equitable assignment, who gave notice to the relevant life company, was affected by constructive notice of an earlier equitable mortgage of the policy because the earlier equitable mortgagee had possession of the policy documents. That should have put the subsequent purchaser on enquiry, which enquiry the purchaser failed to make, relying upon a deceitful excuse proffered by the assignor as to why the documents were unavailable.

---

[174] S 199(1)(ii)(a).

[175] *Bailey v Barnes* [1894] 1 Ch 25, 35; *Abigail v Lapin* [1934] AC 491, 505–06; *Gray v Smith* [2013] EWHC 4136 (Comm) [132]–[140]. See also the approach taken by Millett J at first instance in *Macmillan Inc v Bishopsgate Investment Trust (No 3)* [1995] 1 WLR 978, 1000 and 1014. This particular aspect did not arise in the judgments in the Court of Appeal, which affirmed the result at first instance on other grounds (at [1996] 1 WLR 387).

[176] [1895] 2 QB 539, 545–46. See also *Feuer Leather Corp v Frank Johnstone & Sons* [1981] Comm LR 251 (Neill J) (a sale of goods case); and *Gray v Smith* [2013] EWHC 4136 (Comm) [132]–[140] (Cooke J).

[177] See Ewan McKendrick, *Goode on Commercial Law* (5th edn, Penguin 2016) para 24.45.

[178] [1995] 1 WLR 978, 1000, but see n 175.

[179] See eg *Agip (Africa) Ltd v Jackson* [1990] 1 Ch 265, 291–92 (Millett J); and *Bank of Credit and Commerce International (Overseas) Ltd v Akindele* [2001] Ch 437, 450 and 455 (Nourse LJ).

[180] (1878) LR 9 ChD 137.

4.129 Of particular relevance, in the context of constructive notice, is the question of whether it would be reasonable to expect a person taking an interest in a debt from a company, whether the interest to be taken is to be by way of security or purchase, to search the register of company charges maintained under section 859A et seq of the Companies Act 2006 before the interest is taken, so as to ascertain if any security over the debt was already registered against the person from whom the interest was to be taken.[181] It would appear from the passage in *Macmillan Inc v Bishopsgate Investment Trust (No 3)* just quoted that Millett J would expect a person taking security to make the usual enquiries, such as by conducting searches which, it is submitted, should include a search of the register of charges where the person giving the security is a company. By similar reasoning, where the seller of a debt is a company and the purchaser is a financial institution, it would be reasonable to expect the purchaser to make such a search.

4.9.6.5 Further advances

4.130 Where the interest which has priority[182] is a security interest, the holder of that security is in danger of losing its priority for any advances that it makes after it receives notice of a subsequent security or purchase interest. Under section 94 of the Law of Property Act 1925, which applies with respect to assets other than registered land,[183] a prior mortgagee[184] which makes advances after it receives notice[185] of a subsequent mortgage or charge will lose priority under its security for those advances unless the second security holder agreed that the priority would be preserved or the prior security holder was obliged by the terms of its security instrument to make the advances. Whilst the receipt of notice will not affect its priority for advances made before the notice was received, the prior security holder will be in danger of effectively losing that priority if it is lending upon a revolving account, with advances made by withdrawals from the account and repayments being credited to the account, by virtue of the operation of the rule in *Clayton's* case.[186] This can be overcome by ruling off the account and opening a new account from which further advances are made and into which repayments

---

[181] Ss 859A–859Q of the Companies Act 2006 provide for registration of charges by a company on its property, and make a charge on a company's property ineffective in administration or winding up unless it is so registered. See n 152 as to the effect of an earlier floating charge.

[182] Either under the first in time rule or under the rule in *Dearle v Hall*, n 157.

[183] To which there are separate provisions that apply under s 49 of the Land Registration Act 2002.

[184] Which expression includes a chargee, by virtue of s 205.

[185] It is submitted that such notice would have to be actual notice and that constructive notice, such as by virtue of the registration of the second security under s 859A of the Companies Act 2006, would be insufficient notice for the purposes of s 94. It would not be reasonable to expect the prior security holder to conduct a search before each occasion on which it makes a further advance. It might, however, be reasonable to expect it to search before making its first advance, if there was a gap in time between the date it took its security and the date it made the advance.

[186] *Devaynes v Noble, Clayton's Case* (1816) LJ Ch 256, 35 ER 767. This was the position under the general law before s 94 was introduced: *Deeley v Lloyds Bank Ltd* [1912] AC 756.

are credited, thereby preserving the protected position for advances that were outstanding when the notice was received.

Section 94 does not apply where the subsequent interest is a purchase interest rather than a security interest, but much the same consequences will follow. In *Siebe Gorman & Co Ltd v Barclays Bank Ltd*[187] Slade J held that a prior security holder, whose fixed security encompassed certain specific debts[188] due to the chargor and which continued in its discretion to make advances after receiving notice of a purchaser's interest in those debts which the purchaser had acquired by assignment, should have its security for those further advances postponed behind the interest of the purchaser of those debts. His Lordship held that it would be inequitable to allow the security holder to assert its priority for advances it made with notice of the purchaser's interest, to the detriment of the purchaser, when it had not been obliged to make those advances. It follows that if the security holder had been under a committed obligation to make the further advances, it would have been able to assert its priority for those further advances. **4.131**

4.9.7 The risk of re-characterisation

Re-characterisation is the process by which a transaction that has the appearance of, or is labelled as being, one type of transaction is held by the courts to be another type of transaction. Different considerations and consequences may apply in such a case to those that would have been relevant to the transaction in its originally intended form. In the context of financing transactions,[189] this issue may arise where finance has been provided to a person on the strength of a supposed acquisition by the provider of the finance of an outright proprietary interest in assets that were previously owned by that person or which are in that person's use. In relation to the purchase, through an assignment, of debts that are or may become owing to the seller,[190] the argument may be advanced that the transaction, when taken as a whole, really represents an extension of finance to the seller on the strength of security that it has given over the debts, rather than through an outright purchase of the debts. In other words, that a proprietary transaction that has the superficial appearance of a sale is more truly a transaction under which credit was extended to the transferor in return for the transferor creating a proprietary interest in the debts in favour of the supplier of the credit, such interest being by way of security rather than an outright sale. **4.132**

---

[187] [1979] 2 Lloyd's Rep 142.

[188] In fact, they were rights in negotiable instruments.

[189] The issue may arise in other areas, such as in the fields of landlord and tenant (see *Street v Mountford* [1985] AC 809 and *Bruton v London & Quadrant Housing Trust* [2000] 1 AC 406) and taxation (see *Furniss v Dawson* [1984] AC 474).

[190] The point has also been raised, in the context of financing transactions, in relation to requirements under the Bills of Sale Act (1878) Amendment Act 1882 and legislation that is now repealed, such as the Moneylenders Acts 1900–1927 and the Hire Purchase Acts 1938–1965.

4.133 The argument is most likely to arise in the context of a liquidation or administration of the transferor, because it is unlikely that the assignment would have been registered as a 'charge' under section 859A of the Companies Act 2006.[191] If it really was a charge, failure to deliver the relevant statement of particulars to the Companies Registry within the prescribed period has the result that the security is avoided[192] as against the relevant insolvency practitioner or another secured creditor.[193] A further risk that could then follow is that the nature of the security would be characterised as a floating charge[194] with the disadvantages that are suffered by such a security.[195]

4.134 It is also possible that other persons might raise an argument as to the true nature of the transaction. For instance, the point has been raised in relation to a negative pledge provision in a security document which prevented a company from creating other security over its assets. The question then turned upon whether a subsequent proprietary transaction, which the parties intended to be by way of sale, had been entered into in breach of that provision, which would have been the case if it were to be re-characterised as a form of security.[196]

4.9.7.1 The bases for challenge

4.135 There are two bases in English law for challenging the nature of a transaction.[197] The first is that the outward form of the transaction is a sham, deliberately

---

[191] Replacing s 860 of the Companies Act 2006 with effect from 6 April 2013.

[192] Under s 859H(3) of the Companies Act 2006. Under s 859H(4), the amount secured by the security becomes immediately payable, which is not of very much practical use if the chargor is insolvent.

[193] The liquidator or administrator would be acting in a representative capacity on behalf of the chargor and its unsecured creditors: *Smith (Administrator of Cosslett (Contractors) Ltd) v Bridgend CBC* [2002] 1 AC 336. A third party with competing security, if registered, may also rely on s 859H(3) of the Companies Act 2006 to claim that the unregistered security is void against the third party: see *Victoria Housing Estates Ltd v Ashpurton Estates Ltd* [1983] Ch 110 (Lord Brightman (sitting in the Court of Appeal)). In *Orion Finance Ltd v Crown Financial Management Ltd* [1996] BCC 621, the Court of Appeal held that the debtor whose debt had been assigned, with notice, could also take the point that the security was void against it where the assignor was in liquidation or administration, so as to avoid the double jeopardy of being liable to the insolvent assignor and being also subject to the risk of a demand by the assignee.

[194] In accordance with the approach taken by the Privy Council in Agnew v Commissioner of Inland Revenue ('Brumark') [2001] UKPC 28, [2001] 2 AC 710 and by the House of Lords in *National Westminster Bank plc v Spectrum Plus Ltd* [2005] UKHL 41, [2005] 2 AC 680.

[195] Eg that it has to defer to the claims of the preferential creditors of the chargor under ss 40 and 175(2)(b) and sch B1, para 65(2), of the Insolvency Act 1986 and s 754 of the Companies Act 2006 and to the expenses of the insolvency pursuant to s 176ZA of the Insolvency Act 1986, and that there will be depredations from recoveries in the hands of an insolvency practitioner on enforcement, to be placed into a fund for the unsecured creditors of the chargor pursuant to s 176A of the Insolvency Act 1986. It is also possible that third party purchasers with a rival claim in the assets may claim that they have priority over the security if they have taken their interests in consequence of disposals by the chargor in the ordinary course of business.

[196] *Welsh Development Agency v Export Finance Co Limited* [1991] BCLC 936 and [1992] BCLC 148.

[197] See the review provided by Millett LJ in *Orion Finance Ltd v Crown Financial Management Ltd* [1996] BCC 621, 625–27. The facts in that case did not involve an assignment of debts or

designed to cloak its true nature.[198] Challenges on this basis are now rare in the field of financing transactions, as they are tantamount to an allegation of a deliberate attempt to mislead.[199] Secondly, and more probably, the challenge may be mounted on the basis that, despite the descriptive form used by the parties and their expressed intention, when the true legal effect of the transaction as documented is examined, what the parties actually achieved was really a form of security in support of the provision of finance. There is often a fine dividing line in coming to a conclusion on this subject. The discussion that follows will concentrate on this second basis for challenging a transaction.

4.9.7.2 *The equity of redemption*

If the transaction is one by way of security for finance that has been provided **4.136** then the person granting the security will have an equity of redemption, that is, the right to regain the unencumbered title in the asset once the secured obligation has been discharged. If the transaction is by way of outright sale, the seller does not retain any interest in the asset it has sold.[200] Unfortunately, the quest does not simply end at this point, as the difficulty is in determining if there is an

---

receivables in the usual types of debt financing transactions. Instead, the case involved a situation where the rental stream payable to the assignor under an equipment lease had been assigned with reference to the obligations of the assignor under an associated hire-purchase agreement, under which the assignor had financed its acquisition of the equipment. It was argued that the assignment was the consideration provided in satisfaction of the obligations of the assignor under the hire-purchase agreement. The Court of Appeal held, however, that the assignor retained an interest in the assigned rental stream and that the assignment was by way of security for the assignor's obligations under the hire-purchase agreement. Such security was in the nature of a form of non-recourse security (as to the efficacy of such a form of non-recourse security, see the decision of the House of Lords in *Mathew v Blackmore* (1857) 1 H&N 762, which was followed in *De Vigier v IRC* [1964] 1 WLR 1073).

[198] See eg *North Central Wagon Finance Co Ltd v Brailsford* [1962] 1 WLR 1288.

[199] In *Kensington International Ltd v Republic of the Congo* [2005] EWHC 2684 (Comm) Cooke J explored the basis for the court to look through a sham, and thereby to pierce a corporate veil, in a case involving an allegation that a series of transactions were a sham or a façade to conceal the true nature of the real underlying ownership of assets. Note, however, that the Supreme Court, in refusing to extend the circumstances in which the veil could be pierced, doubted whether *Kensington* was rightly decided: *VTB Capital plc v Nutritek International Corp* [2013] UKSC 5 [127] (Lord Neuberger).

[200] *Re George Inglefield Ltd* [1933] 1 Ch 1, 28 (Romer LJ). See also *Re Bank of Credit & Commerce International SA (No 8)* [1998] AC 214 (Lord Hoffmann). Romer LJ was attempting to explain the difference between a transaction by way of sale as opposed to one by way of security. He said that a sale conferred an outright title on the purchaser, whereas under a security the obligor had the right to redeem the property. In addition, if the transaction was a sale, the purchaser would be entitled to any profit on re-sale and would suffer the loss if the re-sale was for less than the original price. If the transaction was by way of security, the profit would have to be handed over to the chargor/mortgagor, but if there was an insufficiency, the chargor/mortgagor would have to make up the loss. As Millett LJ pointed out in *Orion Finance Ltd v Crown Financial Management Ltd* [1996] BCC 621, 625, the additional tests put forward by Romer LJ are not determinative, as it is possible in a sale for the parties to agree how any future profit should be allocated between them, and it is also possible for a secured transaction to be without recourse to the borrower: see *Mathew v Blackmore* (1857) 1 H&N 762 and *De Vigier v IRC* [1964] 1 WLR 1073.

equity of redemption. The essential question is to discern whether the interest that was conferred upon the transferee is defeasible upon satisfaction of the relevant liability. If so, then, in consequence, the transferor is taken to have retained a proprietary interest in the asset, which is protected by its equity of redemption. The right to the unencumbered title in the asset will revert to it when the liability has been satisfied.[201] It also follows that the transferee will not have acquired an outright interest when it entered into the transaction, but merely an interest by way of security.

4.9.7.3 *The commercial characteristics of the transaction*

4.137 The question as to the true nature of a transaction has arisen in a number of cases concerning the purported purchase of portfolios of debts or receivables (such as block discounting transactions), where the debtors had not been notified of the purchase and had continued to treat the seller as their creditor. In those transactions, the seller had often been given a right to re-purchase the debts it had sold and it had undertaken a recourse obligation by way of guaranteeing the payment by the debtors of their debts. In some cases the seller had continued to collect payment from the debtors without having to account for the collections to the purchaser or to hold them on trust pending payment over to the seller. The reason why the seller had been allowed to collect the payments from the debtors, effectively for itself, was because the seller had undertaken its own payment obligation to the purchaser, under which the seller undertook to pay to the purchaser the amount it expected to receive by way of repayment of the financing, irrespective of what, if anything, was collected from the debtors. In other situations, the seller had only been required to account to the seller for a proportion of the collections, equivalent to the finance that had been provided, with the seller retaining any excess that was recovered by it from the debtors. Alternatively, where it was contemplated that payment by the debtor would be collected and so received by the purchaser (eg where notice of the assignment had been given to the debtors), the purchaser had undertaken to pay over to the seller the balance remaining once the purchaser had deducted sufficient to be reimbursed for its charges and the finance it had provided.

4.138 When such transactions are considered from a purely commercial or economic perspective, the overall impression is that they were really no more than a form of secured financing. It appeared that the purchaser was really looking to the seller for the recoupment of the finance provided by the purchaser to the seller, that the seller retained an interest in the debts it had assigned by way of its right to repurchase the debts (and its right to retain or to be paid any balance over the finance it had received), and that the purchaser was only interested in the underlying

---

[201] See *Re Bond Worth Ltd* [1980] Ch 228, 248–56 (Slade J) and *Orion Finance Ltd v Crown Financial Management Ltd* [1996] BCC 621, 625–27 (Millett LJ).

portfolio of debts as a security backstop. The seller would only intervene for its own account if it decided to enforce its security. Those factors might be taken to indicate that the seller had retained a real connection with the debts it had purported to sell and that it continued to bear the risks and rewards attached to the assets. Seen in that light, it might be difficult to escape the conclusion that such transactions should really be seen as a form of secured lending.

4.9.7.4 *The traditional approach of the courts*

Generally speaking, however, the traditional attitude taken by the English courts **4.139** in the context of such purported debt or receivables purchase transactions has been against re-characterising them as forms of secured finance. The courts have taken a fairly lenient attitude, in honouring the intention of the parties as expressed in the documentation and giving precedence to legal form over the economic and commercial substance of a transaction. This can particularly be seen from decisions such as those of the Court of Appeal in *Re George Inglefield*[202] and of the House of Lords in *Lloyds & Scottish Finance Ltd v Cyril Lord Carpet Sales Ltd*.[203] It may also be seen, in the context of an apparent sale of chattels, but in reality a financing based on receivables, in the decision of the Court of Appeal in *Welsh Development Agency v Export Finance Co Ltd*.[204] The following propositions can be drawn from such cases.

First, that the intention of the parties, as expressed in the documentation, is im- **4.140** portant in determining the true nature of the transaction. If the parties expressed their intention that the transaction should be by way of sale rather than by way of loan, then the courts will be loath to intervene. Instead, the courts will be prepared to uphold the transaction in the form as so expressed, save in exceptional circumstances.[205]

Secondly, the mere fact that the transaction concerned the provision of finance **4.141** should not be determinative, as the real question is whether the finance has been extended by way of loan rather than by some other means.[206] Nor is it relevant that the financier had obtained a proprietary interest, as a form of quasi-security, for its protection.[207]

---

[202] [1933] Ch 1.
[203] [1992] BCLC 609 (despite the date of the report, the case was decided in 1979).
[204] [1992] BCLC 148.
[205] The high water mark of such an approach is reflected in the judgments of the Court of Appeal in *Welsh Development Agency v Export Finance Co Ltd* [1992] BCLC 148, but it is also reflected in earlier cases, such as in the opinion of Lord Herschell LC in *McEntire v Crossley Bros Ltd* [1895] AC 457, 463–66 and in the opinion of Lord Wilberforce in *Lloyds & Scottish Finance Ltd v Cyril Lord Carpet Sales Ltd* [1992] BCLC 609, 614–19.
[206] See *Re George Inglefield Ltd* [1933] Ch 1, 27 (Romer LJ) and *Chow Yoong Hong v Choong Fah Rubber Manufactory* [1962] AC 209, 216–17 (Lord Devlin).
[207] See *McEntire v Crossley Bros Ltd* [1895] AC 457, 465–66 (Lord Herschell LC) (which was a case concerning equipment financing).

4.142 Thirdly, the fact that the purchaser had a right of recourse against the seller, should a debtor default in making payment, is not determinative of the position, even if it meant that the seller continued to bear the economic risk associated with the assets that it had sold.[208]

4.143 Fourthly, the seller might legitimately have an option to repurchase the debts it had sold. That is not to be taken to represent an equity of redemption, such as would arise if security had been created.[209]

4.144 Fifthly, the seller might continue to collect the debts and it was not necessary that it should hold the proceeds of collection separately from its other moneys, nor account for and pay over to the purchaser what it had received from the debtors. Instead, it would be acceptable that the seller should make payments from its own resources to the seller of amounts that were sufficient to recoup to the seller the amount of finance that it had extended.[210]

4.145 Sixthly, the parties might stray in the practical operation of their transaction from the strict requirements as laid down in the documentation without imperilling its nature as a sale.[211]

4.146 Seventhly, the language used in a debt purchase transaction may bear similarities with the language used in a loan, such as by using words like 'repayment' and 'facility'. This would not mean that the transaction should be construed as a loan rather than a sale.[212]

4.147 Eighthly, in *Lloyds & Scottish Finance Ltd v Cyril Lord Carpet Sales Ltd*[213] the House of Lords thought that it was material that, in a debt purchase transaction, the purchaser would calculate the consideration for the purchase of a debt by deducting a discount from the face value of the debt, determined at the time of purchase. The discount would be charged without taking into account any factor relating to the time it took for that debt to be paid or the average time that it took for the purchased portfolio of debts to be paid. This was because a factor of the latter type would more closely resemble a calculation of interest on the outstanding amount of loan finance, rather than for a purchase of an asset,

---

[208] See *Re George Inglefield Ltd* [1933] Ch 1; *Olds Discount Co Ltd v John Playfair Ltd* [1938] 3 All ER 275; and *Lloyds & Scottish Finance Ltd v Cyril Lord Carpet Sales Ltd* [1992] BCLC 609.

[209] See *Manchester, Sheffield & Lincolnshire Ry Co v North Central Wagon Co* (1888) 13 App Cas 554, 567–68 (Lord Macnaghten).

[210] *Re George Inglefield Ltd* [1933] Ch 1; *Olds Discount Co Ltd v Cohen* [1938] 3 All ER 281n; *Olds Discount Co Ltd v John Playfair Ltd* [1938] 3 All ER 275; and *Lloyds & Scottish Finance Ltd v Cyril Lord Carpet Sales Ltd* [1992] BCLC 609.

[211] *Olds Discount Co Ltd v Cohen* [[1938] 3 All ER 281n; *Olds Discount Co Ltd v John Playfair Ltd* [1938] 3 All ER 275; and *Lloyds & Scottish Finance Ltd v Cyril Lord Carpet Sales Ltd* [1992] BCLC 609.

[212] ibid.

[213] [1992] BCLC 609.

to which a discount was more appropriate. Nonetheless, the Court of Appeal in *Welsh Development Agency v Export Finance Co Ltd*[214] came to the conclusion that such a distinction was not material and that there could still be a valid purchase of assets where the purchase price reflected a variable interest calculation which depended on the daily balance of the outstanding amount of finance that had been provided and not recouped.

4.9.7.5 A change in judicial approach

There may now, however, be a change in judicial attitudes as to the approach that **4.148** will be taken in the future in characterising transactions, particularly as to the weight that is to be given to the expressed intention of the parties. Lord Millett, in giving the advice of the Privy Council in *Agnew v Inland Revenue Commissioner*[215] ('*Brumark*') in relation to determining if a charge was fixed or floating, said that the parties' expressed intention was not determinative of the character of the transaction. Their intention was relevant as a matter of construction of the contract, so as to determine what rights and obligations they had wished to confer under the contract. However, the characterisation of the consequences of the transaction was a matter of law.[216] That approach was approved by the House of Lords in *Smith (Administrator of Cosslett (Contractors) Ltd) v Bridgend CBC*,[217] which was a case involving the question of whether the transaction was in the nature of security or something else and, if it was by way of security, if it was a fixed or a floating charge. Lord Millett's approach in *Brumark* was again approved by the House of Lords in *National Westminster Bank plc v Spectrum Plus Ltd*.[218] The approach taken by Lord Millett in *Brumark* has echoes of what was said by Hoffmann J (as he then was) in *Re Brightlife Ltd*[219] and the approach taken in land law cases concerning the difference between a lease of land and a licence to occupy the land.[220]

---

[214] [1992] BCLC 148.

[215] Agnew v Commissioner of Inland Revenue ('Brumark') [2001] UKPC 28, [2001] 2 AC 710.

[216] The approach that his Lordship took in the *Brumark* case should be compared with the approach that he had taken earlier in the Court of Appeal in *Orion Finance Ltd v Crown Financial Management Ltd* [1996] BCC 621, 625–27. In the *Orion Finance* case, he said that the court should consider the transaction as represented by the documents and, unless taken as a whole they compelled a different conclusion, the categorisation of the transaction should be done in conformity with the intention of the parties as expressed in the documentation.

[217] [2001] UKHL 58, [2002] AC 336. See, in particular, [40]–[42] (Lord Hoffmann) and [53] (Lord Scott).

[218] [2005] UKHL 41, [2005] 2 AC 680. See eg [141] (Lord Walker). It is interesting to note that Lord Walker put this as a matter of public policy rather than simply a matter of the consequence of a transaction as between the parties to it. This contrasts with the approach taken in earlier cases, where the courts discounted the policy argument in favour of the freedom of the parties to so arrange their transactions that they could escape the net of the relevant legislation. See eg *Re George Inglefield Ltd* [1933] Ch 1, 22–23 (Lord Hanworth MR) and 26–27 (Romer LJ), respectively.

[219] [1987] Ch 200, 209.

[220] See eg *Street v Mountford* [1985] AC 809, 819 and 826 (Lord Templeman); and *Bruton v London & Quadrant Housing Trust* [2000] 1 AC 406, 411–12 (Lord Hoffmann).

4.149 It remains to be seen just how far this new line of judicial approach will, in the future, affect transactions purporting to be by way of an assignment of debts. Given the authority provided by the decision of the House of Lords in *Lloyds & Scottish Finance Ltd v Cyril Lord Carpet Sales Ltd*[221] in relation to the efficacy of debt purchase transactions by way of invoice discounting, it is unlikely that the lower courts would be willing, or indeed able, to upset transactions which followed the pattern of the transaction in that case. In light of the approach taken by the Court of Appeal in *Welsh Development Agency v Export Finance Co Ltd*,[222] it is unlikely that any court under the Supreme Court would upset a purported debt purchase transaction, except in a very unusual case.[223] It would need a re-assessment of the position by the Supreme Court.[224]

4.150 Assuming that such a review were to take place and that the Supreme Court decided to depart from the liberal view taken in the House of Lords' earlier decision, it is submitted that the likely approach that the courts would then take would be to look at an accumulation of factors in deciding if a transaction was a genuine sale or a form of secured financing. They would not place much reliance upon the label that was given to a transaction by the parties, nor upon the expressed intention of the parties. However, a right of recourse against the seller, an element of the purchase price being deferred, or the seller retaining an option for repurchase of the debts (particularly at a market or other realistic value) should not necessarily mean that a transaction would be vulnerable to an attack, as those elements can often be found in a genuine sale transaction.[225] The most vulnerable transactions would be those where the seller continued to collect in the debts effectively for its own account, without having to separate out the proceeds and hold them on trust, pending payment over to the assignee,[226] particularly if the assignor was making payments to the financier of pre-ordained amounts irrespective of the actual amounts received from the debtors.

---

[221] [1992] BCLC 609.

[222] [1992] BCLC 148.

[223] As occurred in the unusual circumstances of *Orion Finance Ltd v Crown Financial Management Ltd* [1996] BCC 621.

[224] As the Court of Appeal is bound by its own previous decisions subject only to limited exceptions (see eg *Willers v Joyce* [2016] UKSC 44 [8] (Lord Neuberger)), the *Welsh Development Agency* case could only be overruled by a decision of the Supreme Court. Of course, in other jurisdictions which follow broadly the English system, such constraints may not be relevant and the courts there might decide to make their own determinations, rather than waiting for a re-consideration by the Supreme Court.

[225] As was pointed out by Millett LJ in *Orion Finance Ltd v Crown Financial Management Ltd* [1996] BCC 621.

[226] See eg the approach taken by Jonathan Parker J in *Re ILG Travel Ltd* [1996] BCC 21, 44–45.

INDEX